Moral Philosophy from Montaigne to Kant

Moral Philosophy from Montaigne to Kant

An Anthology

VOLUME II

Edited and with introductions by

J. B. SCHNEEWIND

The Johns Hopkins University

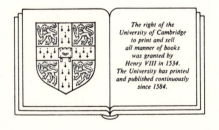

The right of the
University of Cambridge
to print and sell
all manner of books
was granted by
Henry VIII in 1534.
The University has printed
and published continuously
since 1584.

CAMBRIDGE UNIVERSITY PRESS

Cambridge

New York   Port Chester   Melbourne   Sydney

Published by the Press Syndicate of the University of Cambridge
The Pitt Building, Trumpington Street, Cambridge CB2 1RP
40 West 20th Street, New York, NY 10011, USA
10 Stamford Road, Oakleigh, Melbourne 3166, Australia

© Cambridge University Press 1990

First published 1990

Printed in the United States of America

Library of Congress Cataloging-in-Publication Data
Moral philosophy from Montaigne to Kant: an anthology / edited and
with introductions by J.B. Schneewind.
p. cm.
Includes bibliographical references.
ISBN 0-521-35361-0 (v. 1) – ISBN 0-521-35875-2 (pbk.:
v. 1) – ISBN 0-521-35362-9 (v. 2)
(U.S.). – ISBN 0-521-35876-0 (pbk.: v.2)
1. Ethics, Modern.   I. Schneewind, J. B. (Jerome B.), 1930–
BJ301.M67   1990
170 – dc20   89-48061
CIP

British Library Cataloging in Publication applied for

ISBN 0-521-35362-9 hardback
ISBN 0-521-35876-0 paperback

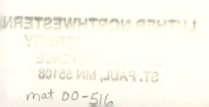

Contents

PART III. EPICUREANS AND EGOISTS

PART IV. AUTONOMY AND RESPONSIBILITY

Immanuel Kant 651

Part III. Epicureans and Egoists

Pierre Gassendi

Introduction

To most contemporary philosophers Pierre Gassendi is known, if at all, as the author of the "Fifth Set of Objections" to Descartes's *Meditations*. In his own time he was considered a major intellectual figure: philosopher, scientist, historian, and moralist, a leader around whom the opposition to Descartes gathered. Gassendi was born in 1592 in a little town in the south of France. He took a doctorate in theology at Aix in 1614 and was ordained two years earlier. Instead of becoming a parish priest, however, he obtained a chair at the local university and taught philosophy there until 1622. His dissatisfaction with the Aristotelian views he was forced to teach eventually led him to write his first major book, *Dissertations in the Form of Paradoxes Against the Aristotelians,* of which part was published in 1624. Gassendi then added scientific work to his philosophical inquiries, publishing a number of essays on astronomy as well as some polemical writings in philosophy. He also worked on a study of the philosophy of Epicurus, which he had become determined to discuss and defend as a whole. Some of his Epicurean views were published in 1647 as *Eight Books on the Life and Character of Epicurus.* In 1649 appeared the *Commentary on the Tenth Book of Diogenes Laertius,* a massive discussion of Diogenes Laertius's summary of Epicurus's doctrines. All this was preliminary to Gassendi's crowning work, the *Syntagma philosophicum* (*Philosophical Synopsis*), which was still unfinished when he died in 1655. It was completed from his drafts and notes by his friends and was published in his *Complete Works* in 1658.

Gassendi published only in Latin; his major works were extremely long and not exactly lively; his scientific achievements were minor; and unlike later thinkers who accepted atomism as a scientific hypothesis, he did not use mathematics to develop his view in a fruitful way. He played an important part in winning acceptance of atomism and was a significant advocate of empiricism before Locke, possibly influencing him. The later elaboration of views similar to his made his own cumbersome and often hesitant formulations unhelpful, and by the eighteenth century Gassendi no longer seemed a philosopher worth discussing. Yet he cannot be ignored if we wish to understand the development of thought in the seventeenth century.

The *Syntagma philosophicum* contains Gassendi's Epicurean systematization of the domain of human knowledge: logic, natural science generally, and morals. It provides canons for reasoning intended to mitigate skepticism, systematizes all knowledge on the basis of an empiricist atomism, and propounds an ethics of self-interested pleasure seeking as a guide to life. Why was Gassendi so attracted to the Epicurean outlook? He was, after all, a Catholic priest and in all probability a serious believer, and

Epicurus's views are hardly Christian. Epicurus did believe that there are gods, but he thought that they are indifferent to our affairs and do not intervene in them. The world as we live in it arose from a chance erratic motion among the atoms that compose it. Life is thus a pattern of moving atoms, and when the atoms that compose us cease to move in that pattern, we are no more. Hence death is not to be feared. It is nothing but the dark after the candle goes out. Pleasure is the only thing we seek, and the only good there is. Why would a good Christian take up such views?

Gassendi was one of a group of advanced thinkers known as "libertines." Although this term carried implications of sexual license and loose living entirely inappropriate to Gassendi and his friends, at the time it referred primarily to those who wished to free themselves from conventional thinking, particularly conventional Christian thinking. Gassendi was strongly inclined toward philosophical skepticism, and this, combined with his interest in the new science and his dislike of the schools' Aristotelianism, made him acceptable to others seeking a new way of understanding the world and themselves. Epicurus, furthermore, was no Aristotelian. He did not appeal to final causes or combinations of form and matter to explain the world. Instead, he believed matter in motion could explain everything. To Gassendi, who corresponded on warm terms with the elderly Galileo, this theory must have been welcome. If one could treat atomism as a hypothesis rather than as a certainty and if one could consider experience as showing us only how things appear and then investigate the appearances, then science might proceed even if Pyrrhonian skepticism seemed unanswerable.

The problem, therefore, was to reconcile Epicureanism with Christian doctrine. In ethics the matter was particularly pressing. Epicurus had been said even by some Romans to advocate a pig's philosophy; Christian thinkers had criticized him for centuries; and his name had become a popular byword for anyone who lived selfishly and for bodily pleasure alone. Gassendi set out to rectify this image, making part of his strategy a scholarly one. On page after page he proclaimed (quite accurately) that Epicurus did not recommend beastly pleasures, did not live loosely, and was not a monster of impiety. A second part of Gassendi's strategy was to confine himself to secular matters, not to appeal to revelation, and to claim that in such matters Epicurus's views could be a reliable guide to life. But he added that Epicureanism teaches us to practice all the virtues and so would be compatible with those that religion requires of us. Finally, Gassendi simply dropped certain Epicurean views. We are immortal, he announced – though not the part of us that desires and feels and is dependent on the body. God does look after the world, and he has made pleasurable everything he wants us to do, so that he can achieve his ends through natural means. There will no doubt be a Last Judgment, but we are not to fear death. Modified Epicureanism turned out to be compatible with Christianity – of a sort.

Gassendi's presentation of an Epicurean ethics in the third division of the *Syntagma philosophicum* is in three books: *Of Happiness; Of Virtue;* and *Of Freedom, Fortune, Fate, and Divination.* They repeat the vindication of Epicurus that Gassendi had given in his two earlier works on the subject and also discuss a number of other issues. Gassendi assumed that all pleasures and pains are comparable, so that we can figure out how to attain the greatest preponderance of the one over the other. He tried to explain the value we place on "honesty" – he used the term in the broad Latin sense to mean a constant regard for principle – which we seem to think is independent of any pleasure the agent will get from being honest. Gassendi offered an Epicurean account of justice, adding to it a concern for individual rights that is not in his classical sources.

And he ended with an effort to show how the maxim of doing to others as you would have done to yourself fits in with his doctrine.

In teaching that a life of self-interested, moderate enjoyment is perfectly acceptable, Gassendi made plain his belief that we can think about moral matters without concerning ourselves with religion. He suggested that laypersons can answer moral questions as well as, or better than, clergy. Because he did not draw from his egoistic psychology the authoritarian implications that Hobbes drew, Gassendi presented an Epicureanism that might lead to politically acceptable conclusions. In all this he brought into the modern conversation about morality several questions that later writers would answer with more care.

The following selections are from an abridgment of the *Syntagma philosophicum* made by Gassendi's faithful disciple François Bernier, who between 1674 and 1678 summarized the work in French in several volumes. Bernier's final volume, on the ethics, was translated into English and published in 1699. The translator's name is not given. I have altered the capitalization and some spelling and punctuation.

Three Discourses of Happiness, Virtue, and Liberty

OF MORAL PHILOSOPHY IN GENERAL

Mankind having a natural inclination to be happy, the main bent and design of all his actions and endeavors tend chiefly that way. It is therefore an undeniable truth that happiness, or a life free from pain and misery, are such things as influence and direct all our actions and purposes to the obtaining of them. And though several persons who want neither the necessities nor conveniences of life, possessing great riches, promoted to dignities and honors, blessed with a beautiful and hopeful offspring, in a word who want nothing that may seem requisite to their present happiness; though, I say, we find many who have all these advantages, yet they lead an anxious and uneasy life, disquieted with cares, troubles, and perpetual disturbances. From whence the wiser sort of mankind have concluded that the source of this evil proceeds from ignorance of the cause wherein our true happiness consists, and of the last end which everyone should propose to himself in all his actions, which being neglected we are led blindfold by our passions, and forsake honesty, virtue, and good manners, without which it is impossible to live happily. For this reason they have undertaken to instruct us wherein true happiness consists; and to propose such useful precepts for the due regulation of our passions, whereby our minds may be less liable to be disturbed. This collection of precepts, reflections and reasonings they name "the art of living" or "the art of leading an happy life." And which they commonly call "Moral Philosophy," because it comprehends such doctrines as relate to the manners[1] of men; that is to say, the accustomed and habitual actions of life.

From whence we may understand that this part of philosophy is not only speculative and rests in the bare contemplation of its object, but proceeds to action, and that [it] is, as we usually say, active and practical; for it directs and governs our manners, rendering them regular and agreeable with the rules of justice and honesty. So that in this respect, it may be said to be the science, or if this term be scrupled at, the art of doing well. . . .

. . . Democritus, Epicurus,[2] and divers others of no small eminence have had so high an esteem for moral philosophy that they have judged the natural [philosophy] to be no further regarded, than only as it was found useful in freeing us from certain errors and mistakes in our understanding which might disturb the repose and tranquillity of our life and wherein it might be serviceable to moral philosophy, or to the better obtaining of that knowledge which teaches us to live happily and comfortably.[3] . . .

The First Book, Concerning Happiness

Chapter I: What Happiness Is

Though felicity or happiness be properly the enjoyment of the sovereign or chief good and therefore the most blessed estate that can be desired, yet because this estate of enjoyment comprehends this sovereign good, it is for that reason called by this name. It is also termed the chief or ultimate happiness, the end of all ends, or The End, for its excellency, because all other things are sought for its sake. And lastly, that it is desired alone for its own sake. . . . But here we may make two considerable remarks.

The first is that we don't concern ourselves here with that happiness mentioned by the sacred penmen when they tell us how happy that man is who being assisted with the divine influences betakes himself entirely to the service of God, and being filled with faith and hope, and inflamed with charity, spends his life in peace and tranquillity. . . .

The second is that by this natural felicity that we here treat of is not to be understood such a state of life as we can't imagine a better, a more pleasant and desirable; in the which we cannot comprehend any evil nor think of any good thing which we shall not possess, nor of anything that we have a desire to do but we shall be able to accomplish it, and that it shall remain fixed and unchangeable. But we understand such a certain state of life in which we may be as happy as is possible, in which there are abundance of good things and very few of any sort evil, and in which consequently we may lead as easy, quiet, and undisturbed a life as the condition of the country, the society we converse with, the constitution of our bodies, the manner of our life, our age and other circumstances will permit. For to propose to ourselves more than this, or to affect during the course of our natural life the highest felicity is not to acknowledge but rather forget ourselves to be men, that is to say, weak and feeble animals who by the laws of nature are subject to an infinite number of mischiefs and evils. . . .

As to Epicurus we shall speak more at large, that he makes happiness to consist in the ease of the body and the tranquillity of mind. . . . Therefore designing to treat afterwards of happiness, he earnestly exhorts to consider thoroughly of the things that conduce to it. And because amongst those things the chief is that the mind may be disengaged from certain mistakes which cause continual disturbances and vain fears, he mentions several particulars, which he believes to be of that importance, that when well examined will settle the mind and procure to it a real and solid happiness.

The first particular is the knowledge and fear of God. . . . though Epicurus delivers some notions that are very just and reasonable, yet he hath others that are not to be entertained by pious men . . . when he denies Providence . . . and when he thinks that it is not consisting with the highest felicity, as if God had no particular care of men;[4] that the just are to expect nothing from his goodness and the wicked are not to dread his justice, are such opinions that our reason and religion will not permit us to entertain.

The second particular relates to death. For as Aristotle observes, death is looked upon as the most dreadful evil because none is exempted, [it] being unavoidable. Therefore Epicurus judges that we ought to accustom ourselves to think upon it, that we might learn by that means as much as is possible to free ourselves from such fears of death as might disturb our tranquillity and consequently the happiness of our life.[5] And for that reason he endeavors to persuade us that it is so far from being the most dreadful of evils that in itself it is no evil at all. . . .

Epicurus hath very good reason to say that in death there is nothing to be feared that may injure the sight, the hearing, the smell, the taste, or the sense of feeling; for all these senses cannot be without the body and then the body ceases to be or is dissolved. But that which we are not to allow is what he affirms elsewhere, that death is also the privation or extinction of the spirit or understanding.[6] . . . Therefore that we may not be hindered by this impiety . . . let us proceed to give a check to the extraordinary apprehensions of death and to those fears that frequently disturb all the peace and quiet of our lives.[7] . . .

Chapter II: What Sort of Pleasure It Is That Epicurus Recommends as the End of a Happy Life

'Tis strange that the word "pleasure" should have blasted the reputation of Epicurus . . . for it is certain that this word comprehends the honest pleasures as well as the loose and debauched. I say it is certain; for Plato, Aristotle, and all other ancient philosophers as well as their disciples speak in express words that amongst the pleasures some are innocent, others impure; some are of the mind, others are of the body; some true, others false. . . . I mention this only because some imagine that this word "pleasure" cannot nor ought not to be taken but in an ill sense. Therefore when Epicurus says that pleasure is the chief end, they fancy that he cannot and ought not to be understood but of sordid and forbidden pleasures. . .

But let us examine this business from the bottom, and first let us begin with the accusation which they bring against him. And as amongst those who allow other pleasures than of the body there are some that will have what he says to be understood only of bodily pleasures, let us weigh his own words as they are found in Laertius.[8] . . . "The end of a happy life," says he, "is nothing else but the health of the body and the tranquillity of the soul. Because all our actions aim and tend to this end, that we may be free from pain and trouble." And because this end he styles by the name of pleasure, some took occasion from thence to scandalize him, saying that hereby he understood the mean and sordid pleasures of the body. Therefore he makes his own apology and clears himself from this calumny by declaring plainly what kind of pleasure he means and what not. For after having made it his main business to recommend a sober life, which is satisfied with plain food and easy to be got, you shall hear what he says next.

When we say that pleasure is the main end, we mean neither the pleasure of debauchery, nor the other sensual delights which terminate in the very moment of enjoyment and by which the senses are only gratified and pleased. . . . But we understand this, to feel no pain in the body and to have no trouble in the soul. For 'tis not the pleasure of continual eating and drinking, nor the pleasure of love . . . that make a pleasant life; but a sound judgment assisted by sobriety and consequently by a serenity and tranquillity of mind which thoroughly inquires into the causes why we ought to embrace or avoid anything and that drives away all mistaken opinion or false notions of things which might raise much perplexity in the soul.[9] . . .

But this ingenuous and plain declaration is sufficient to justify him from the slanderous accusations of his enemies. . . .

What shall we say then to those who charge him with a contrary opinion? Nothing else but . . . that the Stoics who very much hated him . . . have not only misunderstood his opinion, but they have also forged and published in his name scandalous books, whereof they themselves were the authors, that they might the more easily gain credit to their malicious insinuations, and fasten upon him their calumnies without suspicion. Now one of the causes of their hatred against him was that Zeno, their principal leader, was naturally melancholy, austere, rude and severe, and his disciples following their guide affected the same air, and a severe mien. This has caused the virtue of the Stoics or their wisdom to be represented as some very austere and reserved thing; and in regard that caused them to be admired and respected by the common people, and that we suffer ourselves willingly to be carried away to vainglory and to be puffed up with pride if we don't take heed to prevent it, they fancied themselves to be the only possessors of wisdom. And therefore they boasted that he alone was the wise man whose soul was strengthened and fortified with the virtue of the Stoics, that he alone was fit to be a king, a captain. . . . And that such a one never repents, is not touched with remorse, cannot receive affronts, is ignorant of nothing, never doubts of anything, is free from passion, is always at liberty, full of joy and content like God himself. . . . But Epicurus on the contrary was of a sweeter and more candid temper, and as he acted with sincerity and plain-dealing he could not endure this vanity and ostentation. So that when he considered besides the weaknesses of our human nature and what it was capable of undergoing and what not, he quickly understood that all those great boastings which made such noise in the schools of the Stoics were but vain fictions when the glory and the pride of their words were removed.

Therefore he proposed to himself a virtue that he knew our human nature capable of. And because he observed that men in all their proceedings were naturally carried to some pleasure, and after he had well inquired into all the several kinds of pleasure, there was none more universal, more firm, more constant and more desirable than that which consists in the health of the body and the tranquillity of the mind. He therefore declared that to be the chief end of all delights, and that virtue alone was the best means to obtain it, and consequently that a wise or a virtuous man did by his sobriety and chastity – that is to say, by the virtue of temperance – preserve the health of his body, as far as his natural constitution would permit; and that being assisted by moral virtues, by which he appeases the passions of lust, gluttony, covetousness and ambition he endeavors chiefly to preserve likewise as much as he is able the tranquillity of his thoughts. . . .

Now Zeno and the Stoics, understanding this simplicity of manners and doctrine and seeing that many men of parts were undeceived and made no account of their great and glorious words and promises, conceived so great a prejudice against him that they sought always how to defame him, taking occasion from the word "pleasure," and affirming that he thereby understood sensual and debauched pleasure and excess.

We are not therefore too easily to assent to what they say, nor too readily give credit to the report of others, who being imposed upon by their mistakes have exclaimed against him. . . .

. . . we have plainly made it appear that the pleasure meant by Epicurus is not that soft, sensual and debauched pleasure . . . but that which he intends is quite contrary, pure and undefiled, viz., an indolency[10] of the body and the tranquillity of the mind, but chiefly the latter. So that this kind of pleasure cannot hinder any from seeking after virtue, seeing that it is in this only that felicity or happiness of life consists; and that Epicurus proposes no more than the Stoics themselves do who affirm that virtue is sufficient to procure a pleasant and a happy life.

And truly this maxim alone does sufficiently evince that what shift or excuse soever they may seem to frame, yet they suppose virtue designed for no other end but to live well and happily. So that a happy life is desirable for itself, but virtue is not so much desirable for itself as for an happy life.

Chapter III: Wherein a Happy Life Consists

What we have already discoursed of tends to little else than to make a plain discovery of Epicurus's opinion. But now we must come closer to the matter and strictly examine whether he had sufficient ground to say that pleasure is the main end.

Here we must weigh two of his chief maxims, first, that all pleasure is of itself and of its own nature a real good; and on the contrary that all grief and pain is an evil. The second is that notwithstanding sometimes we must prefer some sort of pains before some sort of pleasures.[11]

Whether all pleasure be good of itself?

In respect of the first maxim, it is not without ground that Epicurus asserts that all pleasure is of itself good, . . . for all creatures are of themselves so inclinable to pleasure and delight that it is the first and chief thing that they naturally covet; nor do they willingly reject any pleasure that is offered them, unless it chance to be accompanied by some evil that may after procure a pain and so cause us to repent of its first acceptance. And truly as it is the nature of good to invite and persuade the appetite to love and embrace it, so we can give no reason why all pleasure should not be of itself lovely and to be desired, seeing there is none but in itself is pleasing and desirable, and which does of itself incline our appetites. So that if we refuse any, we refuse them not as pleasures, but because of some inconveniences that are annexed. . . .

Now to illustrate this more plainly by an example, there is no person but will allow honey to be naturally sweet. Yet if poison happens to be mixed with it, whereby the poison doth also become sweet, we shall then have a real aversion for the sweetness of the honey. But this is by accident, for the honey is naturally sweet and pleasing to our taste. . . . Now adjust any pleasure whatsoever to this example, and you will easily perceive it to be never otherwise. For we shall always eschew the evil but not the pleasure itself. . . .

. . . Is it not manifest that all pain in general is of itself evil and hurtful and by consequence every animal hath naturally an aversion against it? So that if at any time it is called good it is only by accident, in regard it hath some good thing that is joined to it which obliges us to love and desire it. But if you remove from pain all hopes or expectation of obtaining any good thing, either honest or profitable or pleasant, there is no man so foolish as to wish for it or seek after it. As this is undeniable so it is apparent that if all pain be of itself evil . . . all pleasure being contrary to pain is of itself good and an evil by accident.

Whether at any time pain ought to be preferred before pleasure

. . . if any pleasure offer itself which might hinder us from obtaining a greater, or which will be attended by a pain that may cause us to repent the suffering ourselves to be drawn to it, or if a pain offer itself which may turn away a greater, or which may be followed by a pleasure very great, there is no reason can persuade us against the shunning such a pleasure and embracing such a pain. . . . Any wise man will decline pleasure and embrace pain if he sees that repentance will follow [the pleasure] or that by admitting a little pain he may avoid a greater.

Of the first good that nature has in its view

. . . let us examine if this pleasure understood in a general sense be really . . . the first and chief good that Nature goes in quest of, for it remains a great question among the philosophers. And it seems [that] as in the order of good things that are desirable, there is one thing that is the ultimate and chief, so ought there to be one thing first, which may be the beginning of all our desires. Some, says Cicero, "conceive pleasure or delight to be the first good, others an exemption or a freedom from pain; for as soon as any creature is born it naturally desires and labors after an indolence or freedom from pain."[12] Others place the first good things of nature amongst those which they call our being, life, perfection, the preservation of all our members entire and in health, our senses, strength, beauty, and such like.

Now among these opinions the first and second are included in that of Epicurus, for he places our exemption from pain among those things we call pleasures. The third opinion, being that of the Stoics, is less probable. For though we may say that every creature desires to have its being, life, health, perfection and preservation of its several parts, etc., nevertheless we must observe that all these things are desired because it is pleasant to enjoy them. And therefore if these things are desirable for being pleasant, doubtless pleasure is the first good thing or holds the chief place among those things that are desired.

This plainly discovers to us two things. First, that though we commonly reckon three sorts of good things, viz., the honest, the profitable, and the pleasant, the pleasant or pleasurable, which is nothing else but pleasure itself, is so intermixed with the rest that it doesn't seem to be a distinct species of itself but part of the common stock which renders the others good and desirable; as if that which is honest and useful were only to be desired because it is pleasing and agreeable. Secondly, that pleasure being common unto all sensible creatures and so fixed and settled in our very first desires, that we have not a liberty of refusing it, seems verily that this should be the first good that we wish for or desire. . . .

From hence therefore we may infer that "good" and "pleasant" are but different names for the same thing, and that good is good, and described to be what all creatures desire, only because it is grateful and pleasing; and by consequence that that good which is pleasing is desired for the pleasure it affords.

That things profitable and useful are sought after for the sake of pleasure

Now there is no difficulty to prove that things profitable and useful relate to what is grateful or to the pleasure which we receive from them. For it is manifest that things useful are not desired merely because they are useful but for something else, which is either pleasure itself or what relates to pleasure. . . .

That those good things which we call honest have the nearest relation to pleasure

This seems a little more difficult to be made out. *Bonum honestum*, or honest good, seems to carry its own intrinsic worth and to be desired only for itself. . . . The word "honest" among the Latins is said to be so from the honor that action deserves . . . for if you please you may interpret it not only "honest" but also "beautiful," "honorable," and "praiseworthy," etc. And you will find that it is not so in respect of itself but in respect of men who allow it to be so, and consequently it appears to them beautiful and honorable and of whom it is and ought to be praised. . . . Epicurus will agree . . . that honest men don't propose to themselves any profit or advantage, such as money and the like low mean things; but they propose to themselves some other benefits, as praise, glory, honor, renown, etc. . . .

But in conclusion, to speak one word to the purpose in reference to that honesty which relates to pleasure, we must observe that this relation hinders not but that honesty in one sense may be said to be desired for itself or for its own sake, because it is desired . . . all profit being laid aside. . . . For some may desire honor, learning and virtue, not because they may thereby advance gain or increase wealth, but for the renown and satisfaction that will arise from the enjoyment of a clear and enlightened understanding . . . and all this nevertheless because it is pleasant to be honored, learned and virtuous and to enjoy a soul calm and serene.

Chapter IV: What Advantage Moral Virtue Procures

. . . it is not without great reason that we compare virtue to a plant whose root is bitter but the fruit very sweet . . . nor is that story without ground, where pleasure and virtue are supposed to meet in a double way and each of them to use the strongest motives to incline Hercules[13] to follow them in their different paths. For that confirms the truth of the rules that are before alleged, when we took notice that we ought to shun that pleasure which is attended with a greater mischief, as we ought to embrace those labors and toils which will procure us greater advantages and delights. I know very well how they have represented Hercules rejecting pleasure, that is to say an easy and effeminate life, to pursue virtue, which is a life full of labor and difficulty. Nevertheless Maximus of Tyre says very well that "when he was under the greatest labors, he felt or had a prospect of wonderful pleasures. You see," says he, "in Hercules extraordinary labors, but you see not the incredible pleasures that either attend or succeed them." Whosoever takes away pleasure from virtue takes from it all strength and efficacy; for were it not for pleasure men would never undertake any great matter . . . we are apt to give divers names to the cause that first moves us to undertake . . . great things; as for instance that which put Achilles upon dying voluntarily for Patrocles[14] we call friendship; that which inclined Agamemnon[15] to enter into and carry on a war with so much care and fatigue was the care of preserving his kingdom. . . . All these several terms are but other names for pleasure. . . .

. . . the philosophers themselves who have declared open war with pleasure[16] . . . don't differ so much from Epicurus in the thing, as in the name. . . . And truly these are their own expressions, so often celebrated among them, "that virtue is sufficient of itself to make us happy." Or as Cicero says, that to live happily, we need only be virtuous. Now if we rightly understand this maxim we must necessarily perceive thereby that virtue itself is not the chief good but a means that contributes in such a manner to obtain it, that it is alone sufficient for that purpose. . . .

. . . notwithstanding some do so much talk and glory of acting by principles out of love to virtue, yet upon a strict inquiry we shall find that pleasure is their chief motive. For they that expose themselves to hazards and dangers for the sake of a friend or for the deliverance of their country, and that defy even death itself, which they know to be unavoidable, do all this in expectation of some pleasure or satisfaction which they shall enjoy after death. But still it is present pleasure which excites and animates them when they think that the actions which they are going about shall procure liberty to their relations, friends or countrymen, or perpetuate their memory and make their generations famous in after ages. It is, I say, the thoughts of being rendered famous to posterity that thus animates and transports them.

Chapter V: Of Life and Active Felicity

. . . there are two kinds of life, and likewise two kinds of felicities, the one in contemplation, the other in action. Wise men have still preferred a contemplative before an active life. However this does not hinder those whom either their birth, genius or necessity of affairs have engaged in business from enjoying tranquillity of mind. For whosoever undertakes this does not go blindfold to work, but after he hath for some time seriously considered and taken a due prospect of the state of human affairs, not as from the midst of the crowd but as from a higher station, and understands that in the active course of life there may happen many accidents that all the wisdom of man cannot foresee; . . . such a one is always upon his guard, ready to take advice upon all sudden emergencies. He knows that he can command what is in himself but cannot govern what depends not on his free will. He acts according to his power and does what becomes the duty of an honest man; and afterwards, whatever happens, he thinks he ought to be content and satisfied. . . .

But after all that can be said in commendation of an active felicity, Aristotle had reason to prefer a speculative. For contemplation exerts the most excellent and divine part of our selves, and besides this sort of action is the most noble, innocent and lasting, and the most easily set on work. . . .

BOOK II

Chapter I: Of Virtue in General

Now to speak something concerning the mutual relation of moral virtues, it is to be collected from two particulars. First, that they are all united with prudence, as all the members with the body, the streams of water with the fountain from whence they run. Secondly, that prudence and all the rest are inseparable from a pleasant life, for life cannot be pleasant without virtue, and wherever virtue resides there life must needs be pleasant. From hence it appears that the consequence of this mutual conjunction of the virtues is grounded upon this maxim, "that things that are united in any third thing are united among themselves." Now 'tis not needful to speak of the second particular, for we shall understand this matter sufficiently hereafter when we consider the saying of Epicurus, "that virtue is not desirable for its own sake but for the sake of pleasure."

Chapter VIII: Of Justice, Equity, and the Laws

There remains yet the fourth virtue[17] for us to discourse of, namely, justice, which consists in rendering to everyone that which belongs to him. Therefore 'tis of a very large extent and esteemed as the source and root of all other duties. . . . Justice is a kind of goodness, or an inclination full of sincerity and desire of doing right in all the world. For that reason there is nothing men respect, reverence and love more than justice. For this cause men have always given to it the name of a most precious possession, and in all times it is acknowledged to be the ligament of societies, as Cicero calls it, that is to say, that tie without which society cannot possibly subsist. . . .

But this virtue is sometimes taken more generally, sometimes more strictly. For there be many that look upon it as the complexion of all the other virtues, because there is no virtue but justice prescribes its functions and offices. As for instance, in the practice of fortitude, when we are in a fight, it orders us to keep our rank and forbids us to run away or throw away our weapons. In the practice of temperance it prohibits adultery; in that of gentleness it commands us to strike nobody nor so much as speak evil of them; and so of the rest.

But not to insist too long upon this, it is not to be questioned but that the two chief offices or general duties of justice consist in hurting or doing wrong to nobody and in giving or rendering to everyone that which he may lawfully claim. . . . This hath given occasion to the lawyers[18] to define justice [as] "a constant and perpetual will or resolution to give or restore to everyone his right," that is to say, what justly belongs to him. This definition causes us to make two observations. First, that 'tis not without reason that it is named a will or resolution. . . . For to deserve commendation for this virtue, 'tis not sufficient to perform some just acts, seeing that he who may do them without knowledge, or for fear or for a friend's sake or for gain . . . cannot therefore be just nor be said to do justly, because the end ceasing, he would act otherwise. But to be just he must proceed willingly of his own accord for the sake of justice. . . .

Secondly, that 'tis also not without reason that they add "to render everyone his right," because these words comprehend the function and the proper act of justice. . . .

As this part of the definition . . . obliges us to understand and seek more at large what this right is and from whence derives its original, let us consider first that this word being taken in several senses, its primitive signification is that right is a faculty to do something, to have something, to enjoy and to do oneself right in something. . . . 'Tis also from hence that the law by a metaphor is called "right," because it declares and prescribes what belongs to everyone as his right, what authority, power and command everyone hath over anything. . . .

. . . Right seems by consequence to be originally more ancient than justice. For as justice is the same thing with that affection or habitual desire or inclination which we have to wrong nobody and that everyone may enjoy their right as we enjoy ours, 'tis certain that this justice supposes that there is in other men a right not depending on it and which nevertheless would be, though itself were not in being. . . . But because Epicurus, whom both many of the ancient and modern authors have followed, hath derived the very beginning of right and whatever is agreeable with equity from utility or profit, let us listen to what he says[19] . . .

As justice is a virtue by which we render unto everyone that which is his due and by which we take heed not to wrong anybody, 'tis certain that in this respect it relates to and respects other men, and that it is convenient for man as he is a member and lives in society, it being the common tie, without which 'tis impossible a society should subsist.

It hath this also in common with other virtues, viz., prudence, temperance, and fortitude, that 'tis not to be separated from pleasure, not only because it injures nobody but also because it settles the mind at rest. . . .

As justice hath been contrived and appointed for the public good, it must needs follow that the right and equity which it chiefly respects is good for each individual person that constitutes a society. And because everyone desires naturally that which is good for himself, it must needs be that what is right or just is according to nature and by consequence must be styled natural.

Now 'tis not without reason that I mention this, because it sometimes happens that in the government of societies some things are ordered as right and just which nevertheless are not good, nor the true interest of a society; and consequently not being natural, but against nature, ought not to be reputed just, but only nominally so, or by mistake.[20] . . . Therefore to speak properly, right or natural equity is nothing else but what is marked out by utility or profit which by common agreement hath been appointed that men might not injure one another nor receive any wrong, but live in security, which is a real good and therefore naturally desired of everyone.

I suppose therefore that which is profitable and that which is good to be but one and the same thing. And therefore to the making up of what is just and right, two things are prerequisite. The first, that it be useful or that it hath usefulness on its side. The second, that it be prescribed and ordained by the common consent of the society. For there is nothing perfectly just but what the society by common agreement or approbation hath thought fit to be observed.[21]

. . . the laws according to Epicurus's judgment being established for the public benefit of mankind, that everyone might enjoy his right, might live peaceably and securely; and seeing there is nothing more agreeable to Nature than this, I think none has reason to upbraid him that he separated from Nature the laws and right, seeing that he had rather joined them inseparably together by the tie of common interest, which is the firmest bond according to the rules of Nature. Nor does there seem any reason to blame him because he hath rather derived the laws and right from profit than from Nature, seeing he could never have derived them from profit but at the same time he must needs derive them from Nature. Nay, let us go further. What cause have we to reprove him, seeing there is no person but will allow that both the primitive and modern legislators had always this thing of profit or public advantage still in their eye, and that no laws can be just and useful but what tend to the public benefit and advantage? . . .

. . . though from what has been said we may conclude that to speak properly there is no law of nations and subsequently no right of nations, because there never hath been any covenant or agreement between all nations, nevertheless we may say that this common precept, "Thou shalt not do to another what thou wilt not that another should do to thee," ought to be esteemed as the first natural law, or according to nature; not only because there is nothing more natural or more according to nature than society, and society being not able to subsist without this precept it ought also to be esteemed natural; but also because God seems to have imprinted it in the hearts of all men, and that this law contains in such a full manner all the other laws of society that no man can invade the right of another but he must violate this law. Therefore this law alone ought to be looked upon as the rule of all our actions that concern our neighbor.

And truly as everyone desires that his right may be religiously preserved to him, so that no man may attempt upon it, he need but think the same thing of others and to put himself in their place and condition to understand what he ought or what he ought not to do.

Therefore as there is nothing nearer at hand and more ready nor more infallible than our own conscience, everyone may consult himself and he alone may be his own proper and true casuist. . . .

Editor's Notes

1. Gassendi used the Latin *mores*, meaning "customs" or "usages," the etymological root of "moral," to point to its true meaning.
2. Democritus (c. 460–370 B.C.E.) is associated with Epicurus (341–270 B.C.E.) because both adhered to an atomistic and materialistic theory of the ultimate constituents of reality. What little we know of Democritus's ethical views suggests that he advocated a position similar to that of Epicurus. In particular he denied any important role to religious sanctions.

   Even in his systematic account of Epicurean ethics, Gassendi drew heavily on the Greek writer Diogenes Laertius (third century C.E.), who inserted into his account of the life and thought of Epicurus the longest writings by him to have survived. They include his "Letter to Menoeceus," the chief statement of his ethical views.

   Diogenes Laertius's *Lives of the Eminent Philosophers* is available in English translation by R. D. Hicks, in the Loeb Classical Library, London and New York, 1925. Book X, the life of Epicurus, is in the second volume. Further references to Epicurus will be to this edition, abbreviated DL.

   For more material on Epicureanism, see A. A. Long and D. N. Sedley, *The*

Hellenistic Philosophers, vol. 1 (Cambridge, England: Cambridge University Press, 1987), pp. 102–39.

3. DL X.85–86, p. 615.
4. DL X.76–77, p. 607; 97–98, p. 625; 123, p. 649.
5. DL X.124–5, p. 651; 139, p. 665.
6. Gassendi distinguished two aspects of the soul. One, which animals also share, operates only through the images of things. The other, not shared with animals, enables us to think without images, although the materials for our thought come from images. It is through this second aspect of the soul that we are immortal.
7. Gassendi goes on to provide a number of commonplace reflections designed to decrease the fear of death.
8. That is, Diogenes Laertius. The following quotation is fairly close to the text: DL X.128, pp. 653–5.
9. DL X.131–2, p. 657.
10. Absence of pain.
11. DL X.129–30, p. 655.
12. Cicero, *De finibus* (*Of ends*), trans. H. Rackham, Loeb Classical Library, 1971, I.29.30, p. 33.
13. The story of "the choice of Hercules," between the life of pleasure and the life of virtue, goes back to Xenophon, *Socratic Memorabilia,* II.1.21–34. It was discussed by many of the ancients, one of whom Gassendi cited, and provided a theme for much art and literature well into the eighteenth century.
14. In the *Iliad,* the favorite companion of Achilles.
15. Leader of the Greeks in the Trojan War.
16. The Stoics.
17. Gassendi discussed prudence, fortitude, and temperance at length, arguing that these virtues are desirable only because they lead to pleasure.
18. The codifiers of Roman law and the lawyers who worked from the materials they provided.
19. The following is a considerable expansion of material in DL X.150–3, pp. 675–7.
20. DL X.152, pp. 675–7.
21. In DL X.151, p. 675, Epicurus spoke of the social compact and asserted that justice exists only because of such a compact or agreement among men.

Further Reading

The only readily accessible work by Gassendi is his criticism of Descartes, the "Fifth Set of Objections," available in John Cottingham et al., trans., *The Philosophical Writings of Descartes* (Cambridge, England: Cambridge University Press, 1984), vol. 2, pp. 179–240, and elsewhere. Craig Brush translated some of Gassendi's writings, but nothing concerning ethics, in *Selected Works of Pierre Gassendi* (New York: Johnson Reprint, 1972). There is no modern edition of the parts of Gassendi's work that concern ethics, nor have they been translated into English.

Studies of Gassendi have generally concerned his atomism, his work in science and its history, and his philosophy's epistemological aspects. Howard Jones, *Pierre Gassendi 1592–1655* (Nieuwkoop, Netherlands: B. deGraaf, 1981), gives a useful biography of its subject, followed by helpful accounts of the development of Gassendi's thought and an overview of his major works insofar as they discuss logic and physics, but Jones says nothing about Gassendi's ethics. The excellent study by Lynn Sumida Joy, *Gassendi the Atomist* (Cambridge, England: Cambridge University Press, 1987), gives the reader a good idea of a number of Gassendi's ideas and activities and of his general historical approach to philosophy. Richard Popkin discussed Gassendi at several places in his *History of Scepticism*, 2nd ed. (Berkeley and Los Angeles: University of California Press, 1979); see especially pp. 99–109 and 141–6.

Gassendi's view of morality is discussed in J. S. Spink, *French Free Thought from Gassendi to Voltaire* (London: Athlone, 1960). There are two good articles on Gassendi by Lisa T. Sarasohn: "The Ethical and Political Thought of Pierre Gassendi," *Journal of the History of Philosophy* 20 (1982): 239–60; and "Motion and Morality: Pierre Gassendi, Thomas Hobbes, and the Mechanical World-View," *Journal of the History of Ideas* 46 (1985): 363–70.

Pierre Nicole

Introduction

Pierre Nicole (1625–95) was a French essayist, religious controversialist, and educator. His whole adult life was bound up with a French religious group known as the Jansenists and with the passionate theological controversies in which its members engaged. Although he spent much of his time teaching in and organizing Jansenist schools for the children of pious members of the aristocracy, it was his marked talents as a scholar and a polemical writer that made him indispensable to the movement. Nicole helped the great mathematician and religious thinker Blaise Pascal prepare the *Provincial Letters* (1656–7), a series of attacks on Jesuit casuistry that did more to destroy the credibility of that form of moral counseling than did any other single piece of work. With the Jansenist apologist Antoine Arnauld, Nicole composed the *Port-Royal Logic* (1662), a textbook used for generations. He also helped Arnauld prepare many defenses of Jansenism and himself against attacks by Jesuits and other defenders of orthodoxy. And from 1675 on, Nicole published ever-growing editions of his *Moral Essays*, a series of writings exhortative, analytical, or polemical by turn, some long, some short, dealing with innumerable aspects of people's relations with God and with one another.

The religious movement that so engrossed Nicole was named after Cornelis Jansen, the bishop of Ypres (1585–1638) who expounded his views on grace and salvation in a lengthy book entitled *Augustinus,* published in 1640 after his early death from the plague. The book presents extreme versions of Saint Augustine's doctrines of grace and predestination. (See the section "Saint Augustine and Saint Thomas" in the Introduction to this anthology.) Although the Augustinian belief that no one can do anything to merit salvation and that therefore grace must come from God before one deserves it was common in Protestant groups, it was opposed by the Catholic Church. Indeed, in 1653 four of five propositions said to characterize Jansenism were declared heretical, and the fifth was declared false.

This controversy extended beyond abstract theological matters. On the basis of their views, Jansen and his followers attacked the less rigorous views held by the Jesuits. Pascal's critique of casuistry was only the most famous of many devastating assaults on the beliefs of that order, which was then the dominant teaching order in France. The Jesuits considered Jansenism to be not only false but also harmful to efforts to convert unbelievers and discouraging to those attempting to improve their lives. Because the Jesuits were actively involved in politics, they had many friends and at least as many enemies. Jansen himself had been deeply involved in controversies with the Jesuits, and his views had been shaped by these battles. His legacy remained a central issue in complex struggles for power in the French church and around the French throne that lasted well into the eighteenth century. Pascal and Arnauld were thus Jansenism's intellectual leaders, and Nicole was their closest collaborator.

This was hardly the kind of situation that breeds abstract philosophical analysis – and Nicole did not write his essays as a philosopher. Yet while attempting to defend Jansenism, often by softening its positions and then asserting that it was itself the orthodoxy that its opponents claimed to be defending, he produced some extremely interesting ideas, not the least interesting of which are those spelled out in the essay excerpted here.

Nicole had read Hobbes and had seen how very Augustinian Hobbes's view of human motivation is. Hobbes, he might have thought, regarded Augustine's vision of fallen man as a simple description of what everyone would be like if there were no political authority able to make men repress their vicious desires. But Hobbes had no vision of what a man might be if he were given grace. Well, if in fact most men are not given grace, as Jansenius claimed, will we not be forced to accept Hobbes's political conclusions? But these were unacceptable to Nicole, because they placed the church and its teachings wholly under the control of the person who happens to be the sovereign. And not only was this contrary to Catholic teaching, but it also put the Jansenists at great risk in France, as the favor of the throne was anything but certain.

What Nicole argued, therefore, is that Hobbes failed to see everything that followed from his thesis of the dominance of self-love in our psychology. He did not see that – because of a providence that is benevolent, no matter how few souls are actually saved – self-love mimics the work of grace-given charity so perfectly that we are never in a position to say from which motive an action springs, not even an action of our own. But if selfishness is nearly the same as Christian love, in regard to observable behavior, then forms of government less authoritarian than Hobbes would allow can be sufficient to guarantee public order and civic decency.

In presenting his case, Nicole relied – he was one of the first to do so – on the unintended consequences of actions. My intention may be to become rich and powerful, no matter what the cost to others. But to do so, I realize, I must accommodate myself to others in innumerable ways. Unintentionally, then, while pursuing my selfish ends, I contribute to others' well-being. The idea was used by many later theorists.

The following excerpts are from one of the *Moral Essays*, "De la charité et de l'amour-propre," translated especially for this volume by Elborg Forster from the text in C. Jourdain, ed., *Oeuvres philosophiques et morales de Nicole*, Paris, 1845.

Of Charity and Self-Love

CHAPTER I

Charity and self-love similar in their effects. What we must understand by the word self-love. *That it is hatred for the self-love of others that obliges it to disguise itself.*

Nothing is more different from charity, which relates everything to God, than self-love, which relates everything to itself; yet nothing is so similar to the effects of charity as those of self-love, which follows the same paths so closely that there is virtually no better means to ascertain where charity should lead us than to uncover the paths taken by an enlightened self-love that knows how to recognize its true interests and pursues the goals it has set for itself by reason.

This conformity of effects springing from such different principles will not seem strange to anyone who has properly understood the nature of self-love. But if we are to know it, we must first examine self-love as to its essence and its original tendencies, so that we can subsequently see how it disguises itself in order to avoid attracting the world's attention.

The word *self-love* is not sufficient to make us understand its nature, for one can love itself in many different ways. We must add other characteristics in order to form a true idea of it. These are that corrupt man not only loves himself but loves himself beyond measure, loves only himself, and relates everything to himself. He wants every kind of property, honor, and pleasure, and he wants them only for himself. Placing himself at the center of everything, he would like to rule over everything and wishes that all creatures were occupied with nothing but pleasing him, praising him, and admiring him. This tyrannical disposition, being firmly implanted deep in the hearts of all men, makes them violent, unjust, cruel, ambitious, obsequious, envious, insolent, and quarrelsome. In a word, it carries within it the seeds of all man's crimes and profligacies, from the slightest to the most heinous. This is the monster we carry in our bosom; it lives and reigns absolutely within us, unless God has destroyed its reign by filling our hearts with a different kind of love. It is the principle of all actions that are untouched by anything but corrupt nature; and we, far from being horrified by it, love and hate all things outside ourselves only according to whether they conform to or contradict these inclinations.

Yet if we love this principle in ourselves, we are not about to treat it in the same way when we perceive it in others. In that case, on the contrary, it appears to us in its natural shape, and indeed the more we love ourselves the more we hate it, because the self-love of others thwarts all the desires of our own. We would like all others to love us, to admire us, to submit to us, to be occupied only with trying to please us. And yet they not only have no desire to do so; they even find us ridiculous for thinking that this is our due and are ready to do their utmost, not only to prevent us from succeeding in our desires, but indeed to subject us to theirs and demand the same submission from us. This is why we see all men at loggerheads with one another; and if the person[1] who said that men are born in a state of war and that every man is by nature the enemy of all others had said this only to show the disposition of men's hearts toward one another, without claiming that this was legitimate and just, what he said would correspond to truth and experience as much as his actual contention is contrary to reason and justice.

CHAPTER II

How self-love has been able to unite men in one society. Description of these societies formed through self-love.

One does not immediately understand how it has been possible to form

societies, republics, and kingdoms out of this mass of people so full of passions
that do not allow unity and only strive to destroy one another; but the very
self-love that is the cause of that war will also find the means to make people
live in peace. It loves to dominate; it loves to subjugate everyone; but even
more it loves life and possessions; and more than domination it loves the
comforts of life; furthermore, it sees clearly that the rest of the world, far from
being willing to let itself be dominated, is ready to take away from every
individual's self-love what it loves most. Everyone thus realizes that he is
unable to attain by force the goals suggested by his ambition and indeed has
reason to fear that the violence of others will cause him to lose his most
essential possessions. It is therefore necessary, first and foremost, to concentrate on one's own preservation, and the only means to achieve that is to unite
with other men in order to fight off those who would attempt to rob [people]
of life or property. And in order to consolidate this union, laws are made and
punishments are ordered for those who break them. In this manner torture
wheels and gibbets set up by the community serve to repress the schemes and
the tyrannical designs of each individual's self-love.

The fear of death is thus the first tie that binds together civil society and the
first check on self-love; this is what forces men, whatever they may say, to
obey the law and makes them forget those grand schemes of domination to
the point that in most people they almost cease to arise, as it is obvious that
they cannot possibly succeed.

Open violence being thus out of the question, men have no choice but to
search for other means and to use artifice instead of force; and all they can do
is to attempt to satisfy the self-love of those whom they need, instead of
tyrannizing it.

Some try to serve [self-love's] interests; others use flattery to win it over.
One gives in order to be given. This is the mainspring and foundation of all
business transacted among men, which is now taking a thousand forms; for
trade is not only a matter of merchandise given for other merchandise or for
money but also one of labor, services, attentions, and civilities; all of this is
exchanged either for things of the same nature or for more concrete goods, as,
for instance, when one obtains actual advantages through mere friendly
words.

By means of this trade, then, all of life's needs are somehow met without
involving charity. Hence there is no reason that in states that have no place for
charity because the true religion is banished from them one would not live as
peacefully, safely, and comfortably as if one were in a republic of saints.

Not that this tyrannical inclination, which makes them wish to dominate
others by force, is not always alive in men's hearts; but realizing that they are
powerless to satisfy this desire, they are compelled to dissimulate it until,
having won over other men through acts of kindness, they have become
strong enough to subject yet others by force. Everyone therefore immediately
aims to occupy the highest positions of the society to which he belongs; and if
he cannot reach them, he tries for the next-lower ones. In a word, everyone

rises as high as he can and humbles himself only under constraint. Whatever one's estate or condition, one always tries to acquire some kind of preeminence, authority, supervisory capacity, consideration, and jurisdiction and to extend one's power as far as possible. . . .

Nothing is more apt to represent this spiritual world shaped by concupiscence than the material world shaped by nature, that is, the assembly of bodies that make up the universe; for there too one sees that every part of matter naturally tends to move, to expand, and to break out of its place but that, being pressed upon by other bodies, it is reduced to a kind of prison, from which it will escape as soon as it has become stronger than the surrounding matter. This is the very image of the constraint imposed on the self-love of every individual by that of others, which does not allow him to take up as much room as he would like to have. . . .

Chapter III

That the most widespread impulse to arise from self-love is the desire to be loved.

In its quest for domination, two things self-love craves particularly are that we be considered great and powerful by others and that we provoke in their hearts feelings of respect and humility in keeping with these notions; but although these are the impressions most pleasing to self-love, they are not the only ones on which it feeds. It loves all feelings that are favorable to it, such as admiration, respect, trust, and, above all, love. There are many people who make little effort to do what it takes to be loved, but there is no one who is not happy to be loved and who does not take pleasure in seeing the inclination of others' hearts toward himself, which is what we call love. Whenever it appears that someone does not make an effort to attract this kind of love, it is because he likes even more to use his grandeur to impart feelings of fear and lowliness or else because, trying too passionately to please some people, he takes less care to please others.

Yet this does not mean that even those who, carried away by stronger passions, behave in a manner unlikely to arouse love, do not wish to be loved, and do not feel ill at ease when they perceive in the minds of others stirrings of hatred and aversion. There are even many people in whom the inclination to make themselves loved is stronger than the desire to dominate, and who fear the hatred and aversion of men and the judgments that produce them more than they love to be rich and powerful and great. And finally, whereas few are powerful, and indeed not many can even aspire to power, making oneself loved is within everyone's reach.

If the desire to be loved is thus not the strongest passion to be born from self-love, it is at least the most common. Considerations of self-interest, ambition, and pleasure often attenuate its effects, but they never stifle it altogether; it always remains alive in the depths of our hearts, and as soon as it is given free rein it will not fail to act and to prompt us to do our utmost to attract the love of our fellow men, just as it causes us to avoid those things that we imagine will bring us their aversion. It is true that one can make mistakes in ascertaining the things that will attract love or hate and that in this matter some people have much better judgment than others do. But regardless of whether or not one is mistaken, the same passion is always at work and makes us avoid or seek certain things. Indeed, to some degree there is a discernment common to all men; that is, up to some point everyone knows that certain actions provoke hatred and others love.

CHAPTER IV

That self-love imitates charity in several respects, particularly in hiding itself. Wherein consists human honnêteté.[2]

There is no need to go further in the description of the ways of self-love to make it clear how closely it imitates charity. Suffice it to say that self-love, which prevents us from breaking the law through fear of punishment, thereby removes from us the external appearance of all crime, making us look outwardly like those who avoid crime out of charity; that just as charity ministers to the needs of others according to the commands of God, who wants us to acknowledge his kindness by serving our fellow man, so self-love ministers to them according to the commands of its own interest; and finally that there is virtually no deed inspired by charity for the sake of pleasing God that self-love could not prompt us to perform for the sake of pleasing men.

Self-love thus tends by means of these three endeavors to ape charity; yet it must be granted that the last of these comes closest and that it is much more widespread than the two others are, for there are many occasions in which neither fear nor self-interest is involved, and it is often quite easy to distinguish what is being done out of fear of other men or out of vulgar self-interest from what is done out of charitable impulse; but this is not the case when it comes to the pursuit of men's love and esteem. This inclination is so cunning and so subtle, and at the same time so pervasive, that there is no action into which it cannot creep; and it knows so well how to assume the appearances of charity that it is almost impossible to know clearly what distinguishes the two; for by pursuing the same course and producing the same effects it obliterates with marvelous canniness all traces and all marks of the self-love that has given rise to it, knowing full well that it would not obtain any of the things it desires if they were noticed. The reason is that nothing attracts as much aversion as self-love does and that it could not possibly show itself without arousing it. We ourselves feel aversion for the self-love of others. We will not tolerate it whenever we uncover it, and this makes it easy for us to judge that others will not be more favorably disposed toward our own self-love when they uncover it.

This is what prompts those who are sensitive to the hatred of others and do not like to expose themselves to it to try their very best to hide their self-love from the sight of others, to disguise it, never to show it in its natural form, and to imitate the conduct of those who would be entirely free from it, that is, people who, inspired by the spirit of charity, would act only out of charity.

It is this suppression of self-love that in fact creates human *honnêteté*, which consists of just that; this is also what caused a great mind of our century[3] to say that Christian virtue destroys and annihilates self-love and that human *honnêteté* hides and suppresses it.

This *honnêteté*, then, which the pagan sages idolized, is actually just a more intelligent and more adroit self-love than that of the world at large. Steering clear of what might harm its designs, it pursues its aims, which is the esteem and the love of men, by following a more direct and reasonable route. It is easy to make everyone see this by showing how self-love imitates the principal actions of charity.

CHAPTER V

How self-love imitates humility.

It is not difficult to understand in which manner charity makes us humble; for by making us love justice, which is God himself, it makes us hate injustice, which offends him. Now of course it is a most obvious injustice that, being as full of faults and guilty of as many sins as we are, we yet want to be honored by men and that we claim to deserve their praise, either because of our human – and hence vain and frivolous – qualities or because of talents we have received from God, which do not belong to us at all. Not only is it not just that the sinner be honored, it is also just that he be brought low and humbled. Thus it is ordained by the eternal law, and charity not only accepts this law but loves it and, because of this love, joyfully embraces every humiliation and every abasement; it makes us hate everything that smacks of pride and vanity, and just as it condemns these impulses when they arise in our hearts, so it prevents them from showing outwardly in our words and deeds, thus reducing them to a decent modesty.

But there is nothing in this that self-love does not imitate perfectly; for seeing every man's heart turned entirely toward himself, and naturally hostile to the elevation of others, it is very careful not to incur their annoyance or spite.

Anyone who praises himself and displays to the world what he believes to be his good points thereby hopes to attach others to himself; this almost amounts to asking them outright to give him praise and look upon him with esteem and love. But in truth, few demands seem as improper and as trouble-some to men's self-love as this one. It reacts with irritation and is most unlikely to respond with anything other than mockery and contempt. Those who are cunning enough to know the ways of self-love therefore avoid making such demands; that is, they usually steer clear of anything that smacks of vanity, anything liable to attract attention and display their advantages, try-ing, on the contrary, to appear indifferent to them and unaware that they possess them. This, then, is the kind of modesty that *honnêteté* can provide.

Honnêteté not only causes us to avoid indulging in base and coarse vanity and openly praising ourselves; it also, knowing that the self-love of others is admirably cunning in uncovering the detours we might take to show off the thing we would like the world to know, relinquishes these little artifices and earnestly endeavors to avoid them. Indeed, *honnêteté* would rather have us speak of ourselves plainly and openly than make us use these paltry tricks, for it is always in fear of being caught in them and knows that if they are found out the world will take even greater pleasure in holding them up to ridicule. Therefore nothing is simpler or more humble than its speech. It does not dramatize itself or show off in any manner and makes it a rule that we must never speak of ourselves or do so with more coldness and indifference than we show in speaking of others. . . .

But beyond the fear of *honnêteté* that it might bring upon itself the natural aversion all men have for the vanity of others, there may also be in its conduct a subtler and more delicate conception of the pride that is born with man and never forsakes him. Those people whom we see so obsessed with the few occasions on which they have distinguished themselves that they continually harp on them, as Cicero used to do with his consulate, show by doing so that virtue is not natural to them and that great efforts were required to hoist up their souls to the state where they are so happy to show themselves. Yet it is much grander not to mention one's greatest accomplishments, thereby making it seem that we have forgotten about them and that they arise so naturally from the disposition of our soul that it is not even aware of them. This degree of virtue is surely much more heroic, and human *honnêteté* at its highest point may, without explicitly trying to do so, convey the same idea, or else it may imitate it with skill and calculation because it is not perfect, fashioned by reason rather than by nature.

Chapter VI

Both honnêteté *and charity make us eschew affectation, above all with respect to things that do not befit our condition.*

Who could fail to love the *honnête homme* whom a great man of our century has painted so beautifully:

Society, he says, does not consider us knowledgeable about verses unless we have hung out a poet's shingle, nor clever in mathematics unless we display that of the mathematician. But the true *honnêtes gens* do not like shingles and make little distinction between the craft of the poet and that of the embroiderer. They are not called poets or geometers, but they can judge all of these. One cannot guess what they are. They will speak of the things that were being discussed when they entered the room. One does not notice in them one quality more than another, unless they are called upon to use it; but then one does realize it, for it is also part of this characterization that one does not say of them that they speak well if language is not being discussed and that one does say so when it is being discussed. It is therefore false praise if one says of a man as he enters the room that he knows all about poetry, and it is a bad sign if one calls upon him only when verses are to be judged. Man is full of needs. He loves only those who can satisfy them. "He is a good mathematician," it will be said. "Yes, but I don't need mathematics." "He is a man who knows about war"; "yes, but I don't want to go to war against anyone." What we need, therefore, is an *honnête homme* who can meet all of our needs.[4]

It is impossible not to love a man of this kind, but why do we love him? It is because he seems made for others and not for himself. He does not upset our self-love by a tiresome affectation. He does not mean to force us to praise him by showing off qualities in him that we do not want to see. If he does show us his good points, it is for our benefit, not for his. In this manner *honnêteté*, by making us aware of these judgments and of the favorable impressions left by such conduct in the minds of others, will endeavor to deserve them by adopting it.

Now if *honnêteté* generally eschews all forms of affectation, it is even more careful to shun what tends to attract attention by qualities or manners that do not befit our condition or our profession, knowing that the self-love of other men, which is always offended by it, will not fail to turn it into ridicule and will be proud indeed if, having reason on its side, it can use it to curb a misplaced vanity. . . .

There is no need to prove that charity is even farther from affectation than is simple *honnêteté;* for because charity loves others and does not love itself, it need only follow its natural impulses to act with perfect *honnêteté*. And it does so all the better because it is more sincere and because there is nothing within it to contradict its actions, whereas *honnêteté*, being impelled by self-love, is not usually as unmixed. If it represses self-love in one place, it may well crop up in another and thus leave those who watch it very carefully somewhat disgusted with themselves. But because this happens involuntarily, self-love is ashamed when it becomes aware of it or, rather, when it senses that others become aware of it.

CHAPTER VII

That self-love gives the same answer as charity does to most questions we can ask of it.

Prompted by reason to seek the esteem and affection of men, self-love so perfectly imitates charity that if we consult it on how to conduct our outward actions, it will give us the same advice as charity will and launch us on the same course.

For if we ask charity what attitude we should adopt, for instance, toward our own faults, it will tell us that we must be extremely wary concerning our understanding of even those we do not believe we have and that we need a general awareness of our blindness on this point so that we will be ready to give more credence to the views of others than to our own; but that concerning the faults of which we are certain, it would be utterly wrong to try to deny and destroy, as it were, the understanding of God himself by attempting to justify what it condemns and that therefore the least we can do to avoid such criminal pride is to admit our faults sincerely and to acknowledge them humbly before God and man.

Now if we ask the same question of self-love, we will see that although it does not speak the same language deep in its heart, it nonetheless gives the same answer. Although it is painful, it will say, to acknowledge one's faults and even though one would wish to efface them from the memory of others as well as one's own, it is nonetheless clear that it is impossible to hide them. The harder one tries to conceal them from others, the more ingenious they will be in uncovering them and the more malicious in pointing them out. The very desire to hide them will be considered the greatest of our faults, and trying to conceal or to justify them will bring us nothing but the world's aversion and contempt. One must therefore by necessity take a completely different route. . . .

It is on such considerations that *honnêteté* models its conduct, and it is this that prompts a man to state openly that he sincerely seeks to acknowledge all of his faults and does not object to others' noticing them. In this manner the *honnête homme* acquires the reputation of an amiable impartiality that enables him to judge himself without blindness and passion, of being someone who knows how to do justice to himself and with whom one can agree without having to provide outward testimony of approval for something of which one does not approve.

From this it is easy to judge that charity and self-love must be exactly alike in their manner of receiving blame and reprimands and that very different considerations and motives must be at the root of the same outward conduct. We know very well what charity will lead us to do; for because it looks on these reprimands as a great benefit and as a useful means of delivering us from our faults, it receives them not only with joy but truly with eagerness. It welcomes the very bitterness that comes with them, as it procures us the blessing of humility and weakens our self-love, which charity considers its greatest foe. Far from treating those who procure us this blessing with loathing and acrimony, charity will therefore make every effort to show them gratitude, to allay their fear that they have offended us, to encourage them to do us this favor often, and to relieve them of all fears that might render them reluctant and create a lingering sense of embarrassment and constraint.

Deep down, to be sure, self-love is always very far from this attitude. It certainly does not want others to notice our faults, and even less to be reprimanded for them. But for all that, it acts outwardly as charity does; for as soon as it learns from the reprimands we receive that we make a bad impression on others, reason leads it to conclude that it must make an effort to mitigate that impression, or at least not to strengthen it. By watching the attitude of others in order to find out how this can be achieved, self-love easily realizes that nothing annoys people more than the pride of those who cannot tolerate being reprimanded for any of their faults, revolt against the truth however clear it may be, and would want the rest of the world to close its eyes to their faults or to repress all but its favorable feelings about them. . . .

It is obvious that such conduct directly fosters the aim of self-love, which is to win the esteem and friendship of men. That is why human *honnêteté* never fails to adopt it and, indeed, often adheres to it more closely than true piety does when it is not perfect; for because charity is often less effectual than self-love is, it can happen that pious persons appear more sensitive and touchier than worldly people do when reprimanded for faults that others find in their conduct or in their works, the reason being that charity has little part in such matters and that pious people lack the enlightened self-love that shapes outward actions in its absence.

CHAPTER VIII

That self-love adopts the same conduct as charity does regarding unjust suspicion and enemies.

The conduct that charity causes righteous people to pursue when they are subject to false suspicions and unreasonable impressions is not to engage in reproaches or to express displeasure and acrimony but, rather, to justify themselves modestly by indicating that, being human, they are not surprised that they have been suspected of human faults. In a word, instead of complaining about these suspicions, honorable people do their best to remedy them, because unjust suspicions must be regarded as dangerous ills for those who have conceived them and because the means of delivering such people is not to reproach them before they are persuaded that they are wrong but gently to show them the falseness of their suspicions and thereby oblige them to condemn them of their own accord.

If on such occasions we follow the first impulses of our self-love, we will, to be sure, be very far from such moderation, for it will bring nothing but outbursts of resentment and anger. But if we consult reason, determined as we are to follow it in order to reach our stated goal, which is to efface these harmful suspicions and to restore our reputation in the minds of those who have conceived them, we must take the same route; for anything that smacks of outbursts and passion can only strengthen the bad notions that others have conceived against us; and whereas this suspicion often affects only people's minds, outbursts and passion will bring acrimony to the will itself and prompt it to second the impressions of the mind. Foreseeing this bad effect, self-love therefore has no choice but to imitate as best it can the gentle and moderate conduct prescribed by charity.

But who could ever believe that self-love, even if it is intended to discredit its enemies, to render them hateful, and to make everyone condemn them for baseness and injustice, could find no better means to succeed than to follow in the footsteps of charity? Yet this is very often the case. For usually there is no better way to expose base and dishonorable proceedings used against us than to meet them with moderation and *honnêteté*. In doing so, one exposes the difference between these opposite forms of conduct and sheds a brighter light on both of them. *Honnêteté* will appear more beautiful, on the one hand; and the lack of it, more disgraceful, on the other. And in this manner self-love obtains exactly what it seeks, which is a means to elevate ourselves and to abase those who have troubled us. . . .

CHAPTER IX

That self-love adopts the same attitude as charity does toward the good and bad qualities of others.

It is not difficult to judge from all that has been said so far, that the attitude of *honnêteté* toward the good and bad qualities of others cannot be different from that of self-love. It is easy to see where charity leads us with respect to the good it notices in others. Rejoicing about it inwardly, it will display that joy outwardly in every manner it can find and, far from tending to obscure it, will do its very best to find and give it all its due. The good that is in others is its own because of the love it has for them, and it will dwell on it even more happily than on its own, because in doing so it does not have to fear complacency and vanity.

Self-love, on the contrary, far from having such kindness and such tender feelings for others, is by nature malicious, jealous, envious, full of venom and bile; what elevates others incommodes and chagrins it, and one would never see it sincerely pleased with praise given to others, unless it could extract some advantage from it or use it as a stepping-stone to elevate itself; nonetheless anyone who considers the impression he would make on the minds of others by openly showing these impulses will immediately conclude that he must hide them. It is obvious that to show them would cause him to be considered a public enemy, to become the object of everyone's hatred and loathing, and that he would be hateful not only to those against whom he had directed his malice but even to those whom he had spared, for no one could be assured of receiving justice from someone who had exhibited this evil disposition, and everyone would be justifiably fearful of becoming the next object of his jealousy. *Honnêteté* therefore makes us adopt precisely the opposite stance, prompting us to display to the world a show of extreme impartiality, to praise willingly what deserves to be praised, to give every possible due to all the good qualities of others, and not to deny even our enemies the marks of esteem they deserve; and in this manner one can succeed in making oneself loved, acquiring friends, mollifying one's enemies, and being on terms with all and sundry.

It is from these same considerations that self-love exhibits extreme indulgence for the faults of others. . . .

CHAPTER X

Resemblance between charity and self-love with respect to other virtues.

One only has to go through the other virtues to discover several additional resemblances between charity and self-love; for if charity patiently endures offenses, thereby hoping to soften the acrimony of those who insult us, if it makes us suffer with joy all kinds of bad treatment in order to satisfy God's justice, and if it convinces us that we deserve even harsher treatment, self-love also has a patience born of self-interest and vanity that outwardly produces the same effects. It prevents us from wanting to appear proud and presumptuous, teaches us that it is always best not to render people more acrimonious than they already are, and, for these reasons, makes us resolve not to acknowledge the offenses we receive.

If charity is beneficent from a sincere desire to serve others, self-love too wants us to act in this manner in order to win them over and to profit from the impulses that kindness arouses in them.

If charity tries to be secretive about doing good to others so as not to attribute anything to itself, self-love does the same thing in order to render those whom it obliges even more indebted, for one feels all the more obliged if those who have done us good have not drawn attention to their acts.

If charity extends its kindness to those from whom it has nothing to expect, and indeed to its very enemies because it looks only to their advantage and not to its own interest, self-love acts likewise, knowing that the more its kindnesses appear disinterested and free of all self-seeking, the more they will attract the attention of the world, as they afford everyone the hope of receiving similar kindnesses.

If charity is grateful to everyone because its gratitude to God extends to all the instruments he uses to bestow his gifts upon us, self-love prompts us to feign gratitude so as not to displease the self-love of others, which takes offense when we fail to show it.

Finally, if charity makes us loyal to everyone from a sincere love of righteousness, self-love makes us practice the same loyalty in order to attract men's confidence.

Charity, as the apostle says,[5] is not ambitious, for those who are filled with it have little use for the human honors and the temporal grandeurs that ambition seeks; indeed, they fear them more than they seek them and are always content in the place where God has placed them. The same cannot be said of *honnêteté* and to judge it by its essence, it is not only not free from ambition, it is altogether nothing but a subtle and delicate ambition. Nonetheless, here too, *honnêteté* outwardly imitates the conduct of charity; for it knows so well how to hide its ambitious desires, fearful that they might be thwarted by the always-watchful self-love of others, that one might believe that it has no ends of its own, thinks only of others, and is oblivious of itself. If it plans to rise in the world, it does so without eagerness and without baseness, creating the impression that good fortune has come to it of its own accord and that there was no need for initiatives or self-promotion designed to attract it.

In some people, self-love goes even further, actually removing them from great fortune and great positions, even though they could have risen to them. The repose of a restful and tranquil life in which one enjoys the company of many illustrious friends – and one does render services to people of quality and merit if, unprompted by self-interest and without being dependent, one settles for being known in society as a civil, obliging, disinterested person and a good friend – such a life, I say, has charms that may make a man prefer it to all the grandeurs of the world by dint of a wise and enlightened self-love that knows how to compare the disadvantages of the various estates. . . .

It is easy to see as well that because charity removes us from sensuous pleasures because it is in command of the soul and does not permit it to attach itself to anything but God alone, *honnêteté* must act in the same manner, because subservience to the pleasures of the body always has about it something base and contemptible that cheapens and disfigures the idea of ourselves that our self-love would like to impress upon the mind of others.

There is even good reason not to trust those who are dominated by their pleasures and to expect every kind of baseness and injustice from them; for what assurance do we have that their passion will not gain the upper hand when it comes into conflict with their duty toward men, seeing that it so often gains the upper hand over what they owe to God?

Honnêteté, which above all wants to preserve its reputation for inviolable loyalty and unassailable firmness, therefore makes it a point to appear exempt from this passion for pleasure, which is the cause of such justifiable distrust.

But I do not wish to pursue this conformity between charity and self-love to the point of tedious detail and will therefore merely add to what I have said that self-love can indeed imitate all the actions of charity, sometimes even creeping into those in which one would hardly expect it to be involved, namely, those designed to mortify and destroy it.

Self-love sometimes can make members of religious communities fast, or at least alleviate some of the pain of their fasting. Sackcloth, hair shirts, and scourging are sometimes put to its use, and there is almost no act of humiliation that it is not capable of performing. And although there is less room for it in solitude, silence, and secret austerities than anywhere else, there are nonetheless certain hidden conduits, certain subterranean channels by which it might find its way even into these. Indeed, it is even capable of making us suffer death joyfully. . . .

Yet there is a difference between virtuous actions that are hard, painful, and humiliating and those that are all ostentation without being painful, and it lies in the fact that if self-love inspires people to humility, patience, and suffering, it has fallen into a kind of extravagance and derangement; for it is quite obvious, for instance, that the way to attain the natural ends that self-love pursues is not to hide away in solitude where one does not converse with anyone or hears only about one's sins and faults. It is therefore rather unlikely that there will be people who embrace and persist in these ways of living that are so contrary to their natural inclinations for motives other than their salvation, but this is not true for most of the virtuous deeds one can carry out in the sight of the world. Self-love can only further its aims by performing them. It cannot forgo them without straying from its end and therefore would have to be carried away by some unreasonable passion against its own interest to take any different course.

CHAPTER XI

Enlightened self-love could correct all the outward faults of the world and make for a very well regulated society. That it would be useful to keep this in mind when educating the powerful.

One can conclude from everything that has been said that what would be needed to reform the world entirely, that is, to banish from it all the vices and all the most glaring disorders and to make humans happy even in this life, would be nothing more than to instill in all of them, in the absence of charity, an enlightened self-love that would know how to discern its true interests and pursue them in the ways pointed out by right reason. However corrupt this society might be inwardly and in the eyes of God, outwardly nothing would be more orderly, courteous, just, peaceful, honorable, and generous; moreover, it would be an excellent thing that, everything being inspired and driven only by self-love, self-love would not show itself and that, society being entirely without charity, what one would see everywhere would be only the forms and the outward marks of charity. It might not be useless for those who are charged with the education of the powerful to keep this firmly in mind so that, if they should be unable to inspire in them the sense of charity they would like to develop, they will try at least to shape their self-love and to teach them that most of the routes they take to satisfy it are quite wrong, inappropriate, and contrary to their true interests and that they could very easily take different routes that would lead them without effort to honor and glory and afford them the affection, esteem, and admiration of the world. By such means they would not succeed, to be sure, in rendering their pupils useful to themselves, but at least they would render them useful to others and also help them enter a path closer, at any rate, to the road to heaven than that on which they are engaged, as they would have to do little more than change their ends and their intentions to become as pleasing to God for their truly Christian virtue as they would be to men for the luster of the human *honnêteté* that would have been imparted to them.

CHAPTER XII

That it is very difficult to discern in ourselves whether we act from charity or from self-love. Three reasons for this difficulty.

It would not matter much that these two entirely different principles, one of which bears the fruits of life and the other the fruits of death, meld together in outward actions, if at least it were easy for each individual to discern which one makes him act, so that he would be in a position to judge his own actions and the state of his soul. Moreover, it is strange that this melding and this confusion often begin in our very hearts, so that we are unable to distinguish whether we are acting from charity or from self-love, whether it is God or ourselves that we seek, whether it is for heaven or for hell that we work.[6] This obscurity has various causes, and I shall expose the three principal ones.

The first is that the attention given to men's judgment and to turning their hearts toward us, which is the very measure, mainspring, and object of human *honnêteté,* is not always accompanied by precise and explicit reflections and that the impulses it produces in us are often not yet perceptible. The mind sometimes needs only a quick glance and certain passing thoughts to steer it almost surreptitiously toward the judgment that others will form of us; as for the heart, it will need only certain hidden inclinations to turn it gently into this direction; which is to say that one does not expressly reflect on either this inclination or the thought that produces it, even though this is what sets our outward actions in motion and is the principle that informs them.

The second cause is that in many cases, even when one is in fact stirred by the fear of displeasing men or by the desire to please them, one has absolutely no awareness or distinct understanding of either one or the other motivation, the reason being that one often acts without distinct knowledge and from mere habit, which is guided only by a confused understanding. By dint of constantly regarding certain actions as capable of bringing us public infamy and the aversion of good people, we form in our mind a confused notion representing them to us as hateful, although the mind fails to unravel why it should be so, and this notion is sufficient to arouse in the heart an impulse of aversion and avoidance. Yet these confused notions and the impulses to which they give rise are so close to the true considerations of charity, which make us hate evil actions because of the injustice they contain, that there is almost no one but God who is able to discriminate between them.

The third cause, finally, is that even when we have charity in our hearts and even when it directs us toward goals that are in keeping with it, it may nevertheless happen that because cupidity often walks the same paths and toward the same goals, albeit from different motives, we find our hearts and minds subjected to a mixture of these two kinds of considerations and impulses, without being able to find out with certainty which of them has gained the upper hand and is the true principle of our actions. We seek God and the world by the same action; the heart is happy to please both, not knowing whether it is God that it means by God,[7] for this is a judgment that can be made only by delving into a certain depth within the heart that is known clearly to no one but God alone.

CHAPTER XIII

That our ignorance as to whether we act from charity or from self-love is useful to us in several respects.

This, then, is the ordinary condition of humans in this life, even if they are God's own. Self-love acts more crudely in some than in others, but it lives and acts in all of them to some degree; and they can rarely be assured that any specific action will be entirely free of all self-seeking. But even though this situation is a great cause of sorrow and fear to them, it can also afford them great comfort if they think about why God permits them to remain in it and does not elevate them to a higher degree of virtue.

It is obvious, first of all, that God's design to hide the heavenly kingdom that he came to establish in this world demands that the righteous be outwardly indistinguishable from the wicked and that they not be set apart by clear and perceptible signs; for if the faithful whom he inspires and in whom he dwells as in a temple were a certain species of humanity separated from all others, and like a nation set apart that the world could recognize by actions never to be found in others, they all would become public, continual, and lasting miracles, which would destroy the practice of the faith through which God intends to save humankind. The wicked who would find themselves incapable of following their example would thereby clearly understand that nature can never attain the state of the righteous. It is therefore necessary that there be purely human actions that so closely resemble supernatural and divine ones that the difference between them is imperceptible. And because the righteous do not commit crimes and hence cannot be confused with the wicked, it is necessary that the wicked be in a position to imitate the virtuous actions of the righteous and indeed perform some that outwardly resemble the former so closely that no one can detect the difference between them.

But it is not only by an effect of God's justice that he has hidden the treasures of grace that he has placed into the righteous from the sight of the wicked; it is also through his mercy toward the righteous themselves. It is useful to them not to know themselves and not to see the righteousness that is in them. This sight would be capable of causing them to backslide, for man is so weak even in his strength that he would be unable to carry this great weight; and owing to a strange reversal that springs from the corruption of his heart, it is more dangerous to him to know his virtues than his faults, even though his happiness consists in possessing the virtues and his suffering, in being full of faults. The knowledge that he is humble makes him proud, and the knowledge that he is proud makes him humble. He is strong when he realizes that he is weak, and he is weak when he believes that he is strong. In the same manner, the obscurity that prevents him from discerning clearly whether he acts from charity or from self-love, far from harming him, is salutary, for it does not take away his virtues but only prevents him from losing them by keeping him always in a state of humility and fear and by causing him to distrust all of his works and to rely on God's mercy alone.

This is the great utility of the outward resemblance between actions prompted by self-love and those prompted by charity. Yet several of its other aspects are of considerable value as well.

It often happens that charity is weak in certain souls, and in this state of weakness it would be easily extinguished by violent temptations if God did not permit these to be weakened and counterbalanced, as it were, by certain human motives that curb their impetus and allow the soul to follow its instinctive craving for grace. The fear of men's judgments is one of these motives, and few others make a more powerful impression on the mind. By itself, to be sure, this fear is not sufficient to overcome temptations in a Christian manner, considering that it springs from vanity alone; but it does suspend the temptations, and if by chance the soul has as much as one spark of true charity, it will thereby be enabled to follow its commands. It is for this reason that the saintly legislators of religious orders have not disdained such human means and have sanctioned certain transgressions with punishments that cause embarrassment before men, intending that the fear of human embarrassment should render the members of the community more careful to avoid them. This was not, of course, meant to be the only means; the intention was to provide it as a defense against negligence in the expectation that this human fear would serve as a weapon and a tool to charity in the effort to resist the inclinations of nature.

It is therefore not useless for men, considering their state of weakness, to be kept away from vice not only by charity but also by the kind of self-love that is called *honnêteté,* so that whenever charity languishes, this *honnêteté* can sustain the spirit and prevent it from falling into dangerous excesses. . . .

And is it not also a considerable advantage for the righteous to be able to hide from others by means of the obscurity that prevents the world from distinguishing true piety from self-love and allows certain actions of charity to pass in the opinion of the world as prompted by simple *honnêteté?* Would it not be most dangerous and troublesome for them if all their good deeds were noticed and if they were immediately rewarded by the praise they would attract? If this were the case, they would be obliged to withdraw altogether from human intercourse, whereas under the cover of this obscurity they have a little more liberty for dealing with the world and following the impulses of their charity, secure in the thought that they will be taken for mere civility. Thus it can be said that just as *honnêteté* is delighted to be taken for charity and does its utmost to borrow its form and its qualities, so charity in turn is happy to pass for *honnêteté;* and even though it does not directly contribute to that impression, it also makes no effort to undo it, both because it is not absolutely certain that it is not partially true and because it is to its advantage that others believe it to be so.

Lastly, is it not a powerful incentive to practice the virtues to tell ourselves that it would be a wretched thing to stray from the path to which both charity and self-interest have directed us and in doing so make ourselves hateful to both God and man? Is it not cause for praising God that he has wanted most of the profligate acts that he prohibits to be contrary to human righteousness even in this life and that we will avoid them for reasons of purely human self-interest? And finally, does it not afford us a better understanding of the strange corruption of nature and the violence of our passions to see that they make us forget not only what we owe to God but also what we owe to ourselves and that they make us wretched in both this world and the next? For if there is less glory and less merit in serving God when doing so serves our self-interest, surely there is greater profligacy and disorder in not serving him if by doing so we also deprive ourselves of what our very interest prompts us to desire and pursue for our own advantage.

Editor's Notes

1. Hobbes.
2. The French term *honnêteté* has no exact English equivalent. As a rendition of the Latin *honestas,* it may be taken to mean "decent," as when we say that someone is a thoroughly decent person. In the latter half of the seventeenth century, the ideal of the *honnête homme* came to be important in court and aristocratic circles in France. Such a person was polite, observing the proprieties and pleasing others in his own search for an enjoyable life. Thus the term can mean, as Nicole intended it to mean, a merely superficial or behavioral decency without genuine inner worth. The meaning of this term was much discussed among French writers of the time, and the translator here has appropriately left the term untranslated.
3. Nicole did not report the remark exactly as it is attributed to Pascal. See Blaise Pascal, *Pensées,* trans. A. J. Krailsheimer (London: Penguin, 1966), p. 356: "Christian piety annihilates the human self, and human civility conceals and suppresses it." This is number 1006 in the Lafuma numbering.
4. Pascal, *Pensées;* Nicole quoted together two sections which in modern editions are given separately, Lafuma number 587 and number 605, which begins with "Man is full of needs." See Krailsheimer, trans., *Pensées,* pp. 227, 232.
5. Saint Paul, 1 Cor. 13, the famous "hymn" to charity or Christian love, which should be read in conjunction with the whole of Nicole's essay and particularly with this chapter.
6. Nicole here took a stand against those Protestant sects that held that one could have full assurance about one's own salvation and that one could form a church composed only of the elect.
7. That is, not knowing whether it seeks God or an image of God made to suit earthly interests.

Further Reading

There is nothing in English discussing Nicole specifically in relation to the traditions or problems of moral philosophy. E. D. James, *Pierre Nicole: Jansenist and Humanist* (The Hague: Nijhoff, 1972), is a general study. Nigel Abercrombie, *Origins of Jansenism* (Oxford: Clarendon Press, 1936), is the best introduction to the thought of the religious party for which Nicole wrote much of his work. There are two interesting chapters on Jansenism in Paul Benichou, *Man and Ethics,* trans. E. Hughes (New York: Doubleday, 1971). The treatment of Nicole's political views in Nannerl O. Keohane, *Philosophy and the State in France* (Princeton, N.J.: Princeton University Press, 1980), is most useful, as is the book generally for those interested in the context of French moral thought. A. W. S. Baird, *Studies in Pascal's Ethics* (The Hague: Nijhoff, 1975), is informative regarding the thought of the great figure in whose shadow Nicole worked. The *Port Royal Logic,* which Nicole wrote with Antoine Arnauld, has been translated by James Dickoff and Patricia James as *The Art of Thinking* (Indianapolis: Bobbs-Merrill, 1964). J. S. Spink, *French Free-Thought from Gassendi to Voltaire* (London: Athlone, 1960), reviews the various skeptical, Epicurean, Stoic, and antireligious movements of thought in France of which Nicole would have been well aware.

Bernard Mandeville

Introduction

Born in Rotterdam in 1670, Bernard de Mandeville (he dropped the "de" in later life) studied philosophy at Leyden and then turned to medicine, which he practiced for some years. Travels took him to England. He liked that country, stayed, learned the language, married, and made his reputation there. Although his books were extremely successful and his fame considerable, little is known about the details of his life, but he seems to have had some connections with the nobility and to have been good company. He died in 1733.

Mandeville is best known for one work, *The Fable of the Bees*. The book began as a poem called "The Grumbling Hive: or, Knaves Turned Honest," which was first peddled in the streets in 1705 as a little pamphlet. The poem tells of a prosperous beehive, with a government neither tyrannical nor democratic, with developed sciences, industries, armies, and arts.

> Vast numbers thronged the fruitful hive,
> Yet those vast numbers made them thrive;
> Millions endeavoring to supply
> Each other's lust and vanity . . .

Some of the bees were openly crooked – the forgers, pimps, thieves, and quacks – but there were cheats secretly at work in every trade, calling, and profession.

> Justice herself, famed for fair dealing
> By blindness had not lost her feeling,
> Her left hand, which the scales should hold,
> Had often dropped them, bribed with gold . . .

Although everyone was similarly trying to make as much money and have as much enjoyment as possible, the result was that everyone was busy, productive, and more or less contented:

> Thus every part was full of vice,
> Yet the whole mass a paradise . . .

Mandeville went on to show what happened to the hive when Jove suddenly got tired of hearing the endless grumbling among the bees about the wickedness of avarice, luxuriousness, sexual indulgence, and gambling. For punishment he made all of them honest, and disaster struck. They all gave up their vices. There was no more demand for luxury goods, fancy food, or alcoholic drinks. The merchants who imported or sold these and the workers who made them sank into poverty. There was nothing for the

388

lawyers, the courts, and the jails to do, and so they closed down, putting many more out of work. Physicians admitted their inability to cure, and the manufacturers of quack medicines gave up. Throughout the hive, the standard of living sank. No one could pay taxes, and so there was hardly any army to defend against foreigners. When they invaded, what army there was fought valiantly, driving out the enemy, but at great cost to life. The few remaining bees went off to live in a hollow tree.

Mandeville drew the moral of his fable quite clearly:

> Then leave complaints: fools only strive
> To make a great an honest hive
> To enjoy the world's conveniences,
> Be famed in war yet live in ease
> Without great vices, is a vain
> Utopia seated in the brain . . .
> Bare virtue can't make nations live
> In splendor; they that would revive
> A golden age must be as free
> For acorns as for honesty.

In 1714 Mandeville reissued the poem, accompanied by a commentary in prose and a substantial number of footnotes, calling it all *The Fable of the Bees: or, Private Vices, Public Benefits*. More editions, further expanded, followed. *The Fable*'s popularity led a grand jury to denounce it as a public nuisance in 1723 – and in later editions Mandeville included his defense as well as other material. The edition of 1725, the last for which Mandeville made significant changes, was a substantial two-volume treatise, introduced by the original poem. What began as a mild joke became a work that was translated into French and German and that eventually stimulated a great deal of serious and illuminating discussion of morality, economics, and the sociology of historical change.

Mandeville's work began to be noticed widely when the edition of 1723 was published, winning thereafter considerable international renown. But the response was overwhelmingly hostile. Mandeville was read as a cynical reincarnation of Hobbes, discarding faith in God and undermining our confidence in our fellow humans. He was understood as praising vice and condemning virtue, as obviously a paradoxer, a frivolous vain posturer, anything but a serious thinker. Readers living in a society in which the importance of doing good was increasingly being preached found it difficult to know what to make of him. Was he saying that what Christianity stigmatized as vices really were not vices? Because good results came from them at least as much as from the traditional virtues and because good results were the test of virtue, could we withhold approval from the traditional vices? Or was Mandeville a more austere Christian than most, seeing depravity and corruption caused by original sin where most people averted their eyes from it and holding firm to the Christian insistence that virtue comes only from unadulterated love of others? His contemporaries also raised the issue of the accuracy of his views. Must there not be something wrong with a portrayal of social processes that led to his paradoxical results? Was his depiction of human selfishness and corruption correct? Replies to Mandeville filled the press with optimistic portrayals of human beings as kindly, sympathetic, generous, in a word benevolent – everything that he had doubted we are. Refuting Mandeville – and the Hobbes who, though unnamed, lurked behind him – became a small industry.

And yet Mandeville's views would not disappear. Despite his flippant phraseology, he was seriously proposing a model of social order that made God superfluous and that attributed the constitution of society to human ingenuity, capitalizing on human traits undeniably present in everyone or nearly everyone. He did not have to place political reliance on generous attributes that in a tough, rapidly changing commercial society it would be difficult to suppose dominant in everyone's behavior. At the heart of this model was the thought that out of actions performed by people, each of whom intends only his or her own crassest private benefit, there can flow results that benefit everyone in the society, and that the unintended consequences of intentional actions can diverge markedly and in highly significant ways from the intended consequences. Society may benefit more from our selfish behavior than people have been willing to admit.

The first selections here come from *The Fable of the Bees*. I have used the fourth edition, published in 1725, modernizing the text somewhat. Next are a few pages from the *Enquiry into the Origin of Honour*, of 1732 (again with minor changes in orthography), in which Mandeville indicated a little about the standpoint from which he was able to condemn our selfish motives as vices.

The Fable of the Bees

THE PREFACE

Laws and government are to the political bodies of civil societies what the vital spirits and life itself are to the natural bodies of animated creatures; and as those that study the anatomy of dead carcasses may see that the chief organs and nicest springs more immediately required to continue the motion of our machine are not hard bones, strong muscles and nerves, nor the smooth white skin that so beautifully covers them, but small trifling films and little pipes that are either overlooked, or else seem inconsiderable to vulgar eyes; so they that examine into the nature of man, abstract from art and education, may observe that what renders him a sociable animal consists not in his desire of company, good nature, pity, affability, and other graces of a fair outside; but that his vilest and most hateful qualities are the most necessary accomplishments to fit him for the largest, and, according to the world, the happiest and most flourishing societies. . . .

THE INTRODUCTION

One of the greatest reasons why so few people understand themselves is that most writers are always teaching men what they should be, and hardly ever trouble their heads with telling them what they really are. As for my part, without any compliment to the courteous reader or myself I believe man (besides skin, flesh, bones, etc. that are obvious to the eye) to be a compound of various passions, that all of them, as they are provoked and come uppermost, govern him by terms whether he will or no. To show that these qualifications, which we all pretend to be ashamed of, are the great support of a flourishing society, has been the subject of the foregoing poem.[1] But there being some passages in it seemingly paradoxical, I have in the Preface promised some explanatory remarks on it; which to render more useful, I have thought fit to enquire how man, no better qualified, might yet by his own imperfections be taught to distinguish between virtue and vice. And here I must desire the reader once for all to take notice that when I say men, I mean neither Jews nor Christians; but mere man, in the state of nature and ignorance of the true deity.

AN ENQUIRY INTO THE ORIGIN OF MORAL VIRTUE

All untaught animals are only solicitous of pleasing themselves, and naturally follow the bent of their own inclinations without considering the good or harm that from their being pleased will accrue to others. This is the reason that in the wild state of nature those creatures are fittest to live peaceably together in great numbers that discover the least of understanding and have the fewest appetites to gratify; and consequently no species of animals is, without the curb of government, less capable of agreeing long together in multitudes than that of man; yet such are his qualities, whether good or bad I shall not determine, that no creature besides himself can ever be made sociable. But being an extraordinarily selfish and headstrong as well as cunning animal, however he may be subdued by superior strength, it is impossible by force alone to make him tractable, and receive the improvements he is capable of.

The chief thing, therefore, which lawgivers and other wise men, that have laboured for the establishment of society, have endeavoured has been to make the people they were to govern believe that it was more beneficial for everybody to conquer than indulge his appetites, and much better to mind the public than what seemed his private interest. As this has always been a very difficult task, so no wit or eloquence has been left untried to compass it; and the moralists and philosophers of all ages employed their utmost skill to prove the truth of so useful an assertion. But whether mankind would have ever believed it or not, it is not likely that anybody could have persuaded them to disapprove of their natural inclinations, or prefer the good of others to their own, if at the same time he had not shewed them an equivalent to be enjoyed as a reward for the violence which by so doing they of necessity must commit upon themselves. Those that have undertaken to civilize mankind were not ignorant of this; but being unable to give so many real rewards as would satisfy all persons for every individual action, they were forced to contrive an imaginary one that as a general equivalent for the trouble of self-denial should serve on all occasions, and without costing anything either to themselves or others be yet a most acceptable recompence to the receivers.

They thoroughly examined all the strength and frailties of our nature, and observing that none were either so savage as not to be charmed with praise, or so despicable as patiently to bear contempt, justly concluded that flattery must be the most powerful argument that could be used to human creatures. Making use of this bewitching engine, they extolled the excellency of our nature above other animals, and setting forth with unbounded praises the wonders of our sagacity and vastness of understanding bestowed a thousand encomiums on the rationality of our souls, by the help of which we were capable of performing the most noble achievement. Having by this artful way of flattery insinuated themselves into the hearts of men, they began to instruct them in the notions of honour and shame; representing the one as the worst of all evils, and the other as the highest good to which mortals could aspire: Which being done, they laid before them how unbecoming it was the dignity of such sublime creatures to be solicitous about gratifying those appetites, which they had in common with brutes, and at the same time unmindful of those higher qualities that gave them the pre-eminence over all visible beings. They indeed confessed that those impulses of nature were very pressing; that it was troublesome to resist, and very difficult wholly to subdue them. But this they only used as an argument to demonstrate how glorious the conquest of them was on the one hand, and how scandalous on the other not to attempt it.

To introduce moreover an emulation amongst men, they divided the whole species into two classes, vastly differing from one another. The one consisted of abject, low-minded people, that always hunting after immediate enjoyment, were wholly incapable of self-denial, and without regard to the good of others, had no higher aim than their private advantage; such as being enslaved by voluptuousness, yielded without resistance to every gross desire, and made no use of their rational faculties but to heighten their sensual pleasure. These vile grovelling wretches, they said, were the dross of their kind, and having only the shape of men, differed from brutes in nothing but their outward figure. But the other class was made up of lofty high-spirited creatures, that free from sordid selfishness, esteemed the improvement of the mind to be their fairest possessions; and setting a true value upon themselves, took no delight but in embellishing that part in which their excellency consisted; such as despising whatever they had in common with irrational creatures, opposed by the help of reason their most violent inclinations; and making a continual war with themselves, to promote the peace of others aimed at no less than the public welfare and the conquest of their own passions. . . . These they called the true representatives of their sublime species, exceeding in worth the first class by more degrees than that itself was superior to the beasts of the field.

As in all animals that are not too imperfect to discover pride we find that the finest and such as are the most beautiful and valuable of their kind have generally the greatest share of it, so in man, the most perfect of animals, it is so inseparable from his very essence (how cunningly soever some may learn to hide or disguise it) that without it the compound he is made of would want one of the chiefest ingredients: Which, if we consider, it is hardly to be doubted but lessons and remonstrances, so skillfully adapted to the good opinion man has of himself as those I have mentioned must, if scattered amongst a multitude, not only gain the assent of most of them as to the speculative part, but likewise induce several, especially the fiercest, most resolute, and best among them, to endure a thousand inconveniences and undergo as many hardships, that they may have the pleasure of counting themselves men of the second class and consequently appropriating to themselves all the excellencies they have heard of it.

From what has been said we ought to expect in the first place that the heroes who took such extraordinary pains to master some of their natural appetites and preferred the good of others to any visible interest of their own would not recede an inch from the fine notions they had received concerning the dignity of rational creatures; and having ever the authority of the government on their side, with all imaginable vigour assert the esteem that was due to those of the second class, as well as their superiority over the rest of their kind. In the second, that those who wanted a sufficient stock of either pride or resolution to buoy them up in mortifying of what was dearest to them, [and who] followed the sensual dictates of nature, would yet be ashamed of confessing themselves to be those despicable wretches that belonged to the inferior class and were generally reckoned to be so little removed from brutes; and that therefore in their own defence they would say as others did, and hiding their own imperfections as well as they could, cry up self-denial and public-spiritedness as much as any. For it is highly probable, that some of them, convinced by the real proofs of fortitude and self-conquest they had seen, would admire in others what they found wanting in themselves; others be afraid of the resolution and prowess of those of the second class; and that all of them were kept in awe by the power of their rulers, wherefore it is reasonable to think that none of them (whatever they thought in themselves) would dare openly contradict what by everybody else was thought criminal to doubt of.

This was (or at least might have been) the manner after which savage man was broke; from whence it is evident that the first rudiments of morality broached by skilful politicians to render men useful to each other as well as tractable were chiefly contrived that the ambitious might reap the more benefit from, and govern, vast numbers of them with the greater ease and security. This foundation of politics being once laid, it is impossible that man should long remain uncivilized. For even those who strove to gratify their appetites, being continually crossed by others of the same stamp, could not but observe that whenever they checked their inclinations or but followed them with more circumspection, they avoided a world of troubles and often escaped many of the calamities that generally attended the too eager pursuit after pleasure.

First, they received, as well as others, the benefit of those actions that were done for the good of the whole society, and consequently could not forbear wishing well to those of the superior class that performed them. Secondly, the more intent they were in seeking their own advantage, without regard to others, the more they were hourly convinced, that none stood so much in their way as those that were most like themselves.

It being the interest then of the very worst of them, more than any, to preach up public-spiritedness, that they might reap the fruits of the labour and self-denial of others, and at the same time indulge their own appetites with less disturbance, they agreed with the rest to call everything, which, without regard to the public, man should commit to gratify any of his appetites, Vice; if in that action there could be observed the least prospect, that it might either be injurious to any of the society, or ever render himself less serviceable to others: And to give the name of Virtue to every performance by which man, contrary to the impulse of nature, should endeavour the benefit of others or the conquest of his own passions out of a rational ambition of being good.

It shall be objected, that no society was ever any ways civilized before the major part had agreed upon some worship or other of an over-ruling power, and consequently that the notions of good and evil, and the distinction between Virtue and Vice, were never the contrivance of politicians, but the pure effect of religion. Before I answer this objection, I must repeat what I have said already, that in this *Enquiry into the Origin of Moral Virtue,* I speak neither of *Jews* or *Christians,* but man in his state of nature and ignorance of the true deity; and then I affirm, that the idolatrous superstitions of all other nations, and the pitiful notions they had of the supreme being, were incapable of exciting man to virtue, and good for nothing but to awe and amuse a rude and unthinking multitude. It is evident from history that in all considerable societies, how stupid or ridiculous soever people's received notions have been as to the deities they worshipped, human nature has ever exerted itself in all its branches, and that there is no earthly wisdom or moral virtue, but at one time or other men have excelled in it in all monarchies and commonwealths that for riches and power have been any ways remarkable.

The Egyptians, not satisfied with having deified all the ugly monsters they could think on, were so silly as to adore the onions of their own sowing; yet at the same time their country was the most famous nursery of arts and sciences in the world, and themselves more eminently skilled in the deepest mysteries of nature than any nation has been since.

No states or kingdoms under heaven have yielded more or greater patterns in all sorts of moral virtues than the Greek and Roman empires, more especially the latter; and yet how loose, absurd and ridiculous were their sentiments as to sacred matters? For without reflecting on the extravagant number of their deities, if we only consider the infamous stories they fathered upon them, it is not to be denied but that their religion, far from teaching men the conquest of their passions and the way to virtue seemed rather contrived to justify their appetites and encourage their vices. But if we would know what made them excel in fortitude, courage and magnanimity, we must cast our eyes on the pomp of their triumphs, the magnificence of their monuments and arches; their trophies, statues, and inscriptions; the variety of their military crowns, their honours decreed to the dead, public encomiums on the living, and other imaginary rewards they bestowed on men of merit; and we shall find that what carried so many of them to the utmost pitch of self-denial was nothing but their policy in making use of the most effectual means that human pride could be flattered with.

It is visible then that it was not any heathen religion or other idolatrous superstition that first put man upon crossing his appetites and subduing his dearest inclinations, but the skilful management of wary politicians; and the nearer we search into human nature, the more we shall be convinced that the moral virtues are the political offspring which flattery begot upon pride.

There is no man of what capacity of penetration soever that is wholly proof against the witchcraft of flattery, if artfully performed and suited to his abilities. Children and fools will swallow personal praise, but those that are more cunning must be managed with greater circumspection; and the more general the flattery is, the less it is suspected by those it is levelled at. What you say in commendation of a whole town is received with pleasure by all the inhabitants. Speak in commendation of letters in general, and every man of learning will think himself in particular obliged to you. You may safely praise the employment a man is of, or the country he was born in; because you give him an opportunity of screening the joy he feels upon his own account under the esteem which he pretends to have for others.

It is common among cunning men that understand the power which flattery has upon pride, when they are afraid that shall be imposed upon, to enlarge though much against their conscience upon the honour, fair dealing and integrity of the family, country, or sometimes the profession of him they suspect; because they know that men often will change their resolution and act against their inclination, that they may have the pleasure of continuing to appear in the opinion of some what they are conscious not to be in reality. Thus sagacious moralists draw men like angels, in hopes that the pride at least of some will put them upon copying after the beautiful originals which they are represented to be. . . .

But here I shall be told that besides the noisy toils of war and public bustle of the ambitious, there are noble and generous actions that are performed in silence; that virtue being its own reward, those who are really good have a satisfaction in their consciousness of being so, which is all the recompense they expect from the most worthy performances; that among the heathens there have been men who, when they did good to others, were so far from coveting thanks and applause that they took all imaginable care to be for ever concealed from those on whom they bestowed their benefits, and consequently that pride has no hand in spurring man on to the highest pitch of self-denial.

In answer to this I say that it is impossible to judge of a man's performance, unless we are thoroughly acquainted with the principle and motive from which he acts. Pity, though it is the most gentle and the least mischievous of all our passions, is yet as much a frailty of our nature as anger, pride, or fear. The weakest minds have generally the greatest share of it, for which reason none are more compassionate than women and children. It must be owned that of all our weaknesses it is the most amiable, and bears the greatest resemblance to virtue; nay, without a considerable mixture of it the society could hardly subsist. But as it is an impulse of nature that consults neither the public interest nor our own reason, it may produce evil as well as good. It has helped to destroy the honour of virgins, and corrupted the integrity of judges; and whoever acts from it as a principle, what good soever he may bring to the society, has nothing to boast of but that he has indulged a passion that has happened to be beneficial to the public. There is no merit in saving an innocent babe ready to drop into the fire. The action is neither good nor bad, and what benefit soever the infant received, we only obliged ourselves; for to have seen it fall, and not strove to hinder it, would have caused a pain which self-preservation compelled us to prevent: Nor has a rich prodigal, that happens to be of a commiserating temper and loves to gratify his passions, greater virtue to boast of when he relieves an object of compassion with what to himself is a trifle.

But such men as without complying with any weakness of their own can part from what they value themselves, and from no other motive but their love of goodness perform a worthy action in silence; such men, I confess, have acquired more refined notions of virtue than those I have hitherto spoke of; yet even in these (with which the world has yet never swarmed) we may discover no small symptoms of pride, and the humblest man alive must confess, that the reward of a virtuous action, which is the satisfaction that ensues upon it, consists in a certain pleasure he procures to himself by contemplating on his own worth: Which pleasure, together with the occasion of it, are as certain signs of pride, as looking pale and trembling at any imminent danger, are the symptoms of fear.

If the too scrupulous Reader should at first view condemn these notions concerning the origin of moral virtue, and think them perhaps offensive to Christianity, I hope he'll forbear his censures, when he shall consider that nothing can render the unsearchable depth of the divine wisdom more conspicuous than that man, whom providence had designed for society, should not only by his own frailties and imperfections be led into the road to temporal happiness, but likewise receive, from a seeming necessity of natural causes, a tincture of the knowledge in which he was afterwards to be made perfect by the true religion, to his eternal welfare.

An Enquiry into the Origin of Honour

THE PREFACE

It is taken for granted that a Christian is not bound to believe anything to have been of divine institution[2] that has not been declared to be such in Holy Writ. Yet great offence has been taken at an essay in the First Part of *The Fable of the Bees,* called "An Enquiry into the Origin of Moral Virtue"; notwithstanding the great caution it is wrote with. Since then, it is thought criminal to surmise that even heathen virtue was of human invention, and the reader, in the following dialogues, will find me to persist in the opinion that it was. I beg his patience to peruse what I have to say for myself on this head, which is all I shall trouble him with here.

The word "morality" is either synonymous with "virtue" or signifies that part of philosophy which treats of it and teaches the regulation of manners; and by the words "moral virtue" I mean the same thing which I believe everybody else does. I am likewise fully persuaded that to govern ourselves according to the dictates of reason is far better than to indulge the passions without stop or control, and consequently that virtue is more beneficial than vice, not only for the peace and real happiness of society but likewise for the temporal felicity of every individual member of it, abstract from the consideration of a future state, I am moreover convinced that all wise men ever were and ever will be of this opinion; and I shall never oppose anybody who shall be pleased to call this an eternal truth. . . .

. . . But to call virtue itself eternal cannot be done without a strangely figurative way of speaking. There is no doubt but all mathematical truths are eternal, yet they are taught; and some of them are very abstruse, and the knowledge of them was never acquired without great labor and depth of thought. Euclid had his merit, and it does not appear that the doctrine of fluxions[3] was known before Sir Isaac Newton invented that concise way of computation; and it is not impossible that there should be another method as yet unknown, still more compendious, that may not be found out these thousand years.

All propositions not confined to time or place that are once true are always true, must be always so, even in the silliest and most abject things in the world; as for example, "It is wrong to underroast mutton for people who love to have their meat well done." The truth of this, which is the most trifling thing I can readily think on, is as much eternal as that of the sublimest virtue. If you ask me where this truth was before there was mutton or people to dress or eat it, I answer, in the same place where chastity was before there were any creatures that had an appetite to procreate their species. . . .

There is no virtue that has a name but it curbs, regulates, or subdues some passion that is peculiar to human nature; and therefore to say that God has all the virtues in the highest perfection wants as much the apology that it is an expression accommodated to vulgar capacities as that he has hands and feet and is angry. For as God has not a body nor anything that is corporeal belonging to his essence, so he is entirely free from passions and frailties. With what propriety then can we attribute anything to him that was invented, or least signifies a strength or ability, to conquer or govern passions and frailties? The holiness of God and all his perfections, as well as the beatitude he exists in, belong to his nature, and there is no virtue but what is acquired. It signifies nothing to add that God has those virtues in the highest perfection. Let them be what they will as to perfection, they must still be virtues, which, for the aforesaid reasons it is impertinent to ascribe to the deity. . . .

I recommend the foregoing paragraph to the consideration of the advocates for the eternity and divine original of virtue, assuring them that if I am mistaken it is not owing to any perverseness of my will but want of understanding.

The opinion that there can be virtue without self-denial is more advantageous to society than the contrary doctrine, which is a vast inlet to hypocrisy. . . . Yet I am willing to allow that men may contract a habit of virtue so as to practise it without being sensible of self-denial, and even that they may take pleasure in actions that would be impracticable to the vicious. But then it is manifest that this habit is the work of art, education and custom, and it never was acquired where the conquest over the passions had not already been made. There is no virtuous man of forty years but he may remember the conflict he had with some natural appetites before he was twenty. How natural seem all civilities to be to a gentleman! Yet time was that he would not have made his bow if he had not been bid. . . .

Editor's Notes

1. "The Grumbling Hive," on which the present essay is a commentary.
2. That is, commanded or initiated by God.
3. The calculus, which Newton invented.

Further Reading

The modern edition of Mandeville's *Fable of the Bees* is by F. B. Kaye, 2 vols. (Oxford: Oxford University Press, 1924). It has an extensive commentary and contains all of Mandeville's writings directly related to the *Fable*. There is also a modern edition of *An Enquiry into the Origin of Honour,* by M. M. Goldsmith (London: Cass, 1971).

M. M. Goldsmith, *Private Vices, Public Benefits: Bernard Mandeville's Social and Political Thought* (Cambridge, England: Cambridge University Press, 1985), is an excellent study, with a full bibliography of both Mandeville's works and the literature concerning him. Irwin Primer, ed., *Mandeville Studies* (The Hague: Nijhoff, 1975), contains essays on many aspects of Mandeville's thought, its context, and its influence, including some bearing directly on his ethics. D. H. Monro, *The Ambivalence of Mandeville* (Oxford: Clarendon Press, 1975), is a valuable study. John Colman, "Bernard Mandeville and the Reality of Virtue," *Philosophy* 47 (1972): 125–39, offers a careful philosophical discussion of the ethics. F. A. Hayek, "Dr. Bernard Mandeville," *Proceedings of the British Academy* 52 (1967), is informed by deep knowledge of the history of thought and of economics. Mandeville is treated in passing in the fascinating book by Albert O. Hirschman, *The Passions and the Interests: Political Arguments for Capitalism Before Its Triumph* (Princeton, N.J.: Princeton University Press, 1977). Finally, a distinguished anthropologist, Louis Dumont, considers Mandeville in his *From Mandeville to Marx* (Chicago: University of Chicago Press, 1977), chap. 5.

John Gay

Introduction

John Gay was born in 1699 and died in 1745. He taught briefly at Cambridge and spent most of his life as pastor in a country parish. His dissertation "Concerning the Fundamental Principle of Virtue or Morality" was published in 1731 as a preface to a translation of a Latin treatise on the problem of evil. Although Gay wrote one other philosophical essay, it is for the dissertation that he is remembered.

Gay's essay is an attempt to solve a problem concerning morality and our motivation to act as morality requires. Like Gassendi, Hobbes (in some of his statements), Mandeville, and many others, Gay thought that all voluntary actions are undertaken for the sake of some benefit to the agent. With Hutcheson, however, he believed that virtue requires us to act for the sake of the good of others. He also accepted Hutcheson's antiegoistic claim about the way our motivation at least seems to us: that we do in fact sometimes act for the sake of bringing good to others. Thus Gay's psychology apparently makes virtue impossible and contradicts the plain facts about human motivation. Would it not be reasonable, then, to abandon the theory? Gay, however, did something more interesting.

He agreed with Hutcheson's data regarding how our motivation seems to us but denied that they were ultimate. Our apparently disinterested motivation therefore can be analyzed into self-interest as it is affected by special circumstances leading us to associate the idea of helping others with the idea of attaining our own good. Because we can see that it pays us to help others, we find ourselves constantly thinking of our own good when we think of helping others. In time the two ideas become associated and then blended. Then we think that we are immediately desirous of helping others. It is like the miser's love of money. He loves it initially for what it can buy, but then the love becomes associated directly with the thought of the money, the idea of purchasing drops out, and the love is transformed into love of the money itself.

For empiricists working with the Lockean distinction between simple and complex ideas, Gay's version of associationism seemed to open the way to a more fully scientific psychology than Locke alone enabled them to produce. In Gay's view, the distinction between simple and complex ideas did not have to be an introspectively obvious one. Moreover, complex ideas might have some features that the simple ideas of which they consist do not have and that are produced by the blending of the simple constituents. We could explain these emergent and apparently simple features of complex ideas by tracing their genesis through time.

Gay's essay was remarkably influential in the development of both psychological and ethical theory. A full associationist psychology was first developed by David

399

Hartley (1705–57), who, after acknowledging a great debt to Gay, tried to show that association can explain a whole range of ideas that seemed to philosophers to be simple but that reveal themselves as complex once their genesis is studied. The moral theories of both Paley and Bentham also have points in common with Gay's view. James Mill worked out his own psychology along associationist lines; John Stuart Mill accepted essentially the same kind of theory; and both of the Mills used their psychology to defend and support their utilitarian moral theories. The tie between utilitarianism and associationism became so common that in the nineteenth century they seemed to be inseparable. It was not until the work of Henry Sidgwick in the last quarter of the century that British utilitarianism broke definitively with Gay's model.

The following is almost the whole of Gay's dissertation. The text is that of the fifth edition, 1781, with some changes in the spelling, capitalization, and punctuation.

Concerning the Fundamental Principle of Virtue or Morality

Though all writers of morality have in the main agreed what particular actions are virtuous and what otherwise, yet they have, or at least seem to have differed very much, both concerning the *criterion* of virtue, viz., what it is which denominates any action virtuous; or, to speak more properly, what it is by which we must try any action to know whether it be virtuous or no; and also concerning the *principle*, or *motive*, by which men are induced to pursue virtue.

As to the former, some have placed it in acting agreeably to nature, or reason; others in the fitness of things; others in a conformity with truth; others in promoting the common good; others in the will of God, etc. This disagreement of moralists concerning the rule or criterion of virtue in general, and at the same time their almost perfect agreement concerning the particular branches of it, would be apt to make one suspect, either that they had a different criterion (though they did not know or attend to it) from what they professed; or (which perhaps is the true as well as the more favorable opinion) that they only talk a different language, and that all of them have the same criterion in reality, only they have expressed it in different words.

And there will appear the more room for this conjecture, if we consider the ideas themselves about which morality is chiefly conversant, viz., that they are all mixed modes, or compound ideas, arbitrarily put together, having at first no archetype or original existing, and afterwards no other than that which exists in other men's minds. Now since men, unless they have these their compound ideas, which are signified by the same name, made up precisely of the same simple ones, must necessarily talk a different language; and since this difference is so difficult, and in some cases impossible to be avoided, it follows that greater allowance and indulgence ought to be given to these writers than any other: and that (if we have a mind to understand them) we should not always take their words in the common acceptation, but in the sense in which we find that particular author which we are reading used them. And if a man interpret the writers of morality with this due candor, I believe their seeming inconsistencies and disagreements about the *criterion* of virtue, would in a great measure vanish; and he would find that acting agreeably to nature, or reason, (when rightly understood) would perfectly coincide with the fitness of things; the fitness of things (as far as these words have any meaning) with truth; truth with the common good; and the common good with the will of God.

But whether this difference be real, or only verbal, a man can scarce avoid observing from it, that mankind have the ideas of most particular virtues, and also a confused notion of virtue in general, before they have any notion of the *criterion* of it; or ever did, neither perhaps can they, deduce all or any of those virtues from their idea of virtue in general, or upon any rational grounds shew how those actions (which the world call moral, and most, if not all men evidently have ideas of) are distinguished from other actions, or why they approve of those actions called moral ones, more than others.

However, since the idea of virtue among all men (notwithstanding their difference in other respects) includes either tacitly or expressly, not only the idea of approbation as the consequence of it; but also that it is to everyone, and in all circumstances, an object of choice; it is incumbent on all writers of morality, to shew that [that] in which they place virtue, whatever it be, not only always will or ought to meet with approbation, but also that it is always an object of choice; which is the other great dispute among moralists, viz., what is the *principle* or *motive* by which men are induced to pursue virtue.

For some have imagined that that is the only object of choice to a rational creature, which upon the whole will produce more happiness than misery to the chooser; and that men are, and ought to be guided wholly by this principle; and farther, that virtue will produce more happiness than misery, and therefore is always an object of choice: and whatever is an object of choice, that we approve of.

But this, however true in theory, is insufficient to account for matter of fact, i.e., that the generality of mankind do approve of virtue, or rather virtuous actions, without being able to give any reason for their approbation; and also, that some pursue it without knowing that it tends to their own private happiness; nay even when it appears to be inconsistent with and destructive of their happiness.

And that this is a matter of fact, the ingenious author of the *Enquiry into the Original of Our Idea of Virtue*[1] has so evidently made appear by a great variety of instances, that a man must either be very little acquainted with the world, or a mere Hobbist in his temper, to deny it.

And therefore to solve these two difficulties, this excellent author has supposed (without proving, unless by shewing the insufficiency of all other schemes) a moral sense to account for the former, and a public or benevolent affection for the latter: And these, viz., the moral sense and public affection, he supposes to be implanted in us like instincts, independent of reason, and previous to any instruction; and therefore his opinion is, that no account can be given, or ought to be expected of them, any more than we pretend to account for the pleasure or pain which arises from sensation; i.e., why any particular motion produced in our bodies should be accompanied with pain rather than pleasure, and *vice versa.*

But this account seems still insufficient, rather cutting the knot than untying it; and if it is not akin to the doctrine of innate ideas, yet I think it relishes too much of that of occult qualities. This ingenious author is certainly in the right in his observations upon the insufficiency of the common methods of accounting for both our election and approbation of moral actions, and rightly infers the necessity of supposing a moral sense (i.e., a power or faculty whereby we may perceive any action to be an object of approbation, and the agent of love) and public affections, to account for the principal actions of human life. But then by calling these instincts, I think he stops too soon, imagining himself at the fountain-head, when he might have traced them much higher even to the true principle of all our actions, our own happiness.

And this will appear by shewing that our approbation of morality, and all affections whatsoever, are finally resolved into reason pointing out private happiness, and are conversant only about things apprehended to be means tending to this end; and that whenever this end is not perceived, they are to be accounted for from the association of ideas and may properly enough be called habits.

For if this be clearly made out, the necessity of supposing a moral sense or public affections to be implanted in us, since it ariseth only from the insufficiency of all other schemes to account for human actions, will immediately vanish. . . .

SECTION I: CONCERNING THE CRITERION OF VIRTUE

The *criterion* of anything is a rule or measure by a conformity with which anything is known to be of this or that sort, or of this or that degree. And in order to determine the criterion of anything, we must first know the thing whose criterion we are seeking after. For a measure presupposes the idea of the thing to be measured, otherwise it could not be known, whether it was fit to measure it or no (since what is the proper measure of one thing is not so of another). Liquids, cloth, and flesh have all different measures; gold and silver different touchstones. This is very intelligible and the method of doing it generally clear, when either the quantity, or kind of any particular substance is thus ascertained.

But when we extend our inquiries after a criterion for abstract, mixed modes,[2] which have no existence but in our minds, and are so very different in different men; we are apt to be confounded, and search after a measure for we know not what. For unless we are first agreed concerning the thing to be measured, we shall in vain expect to agree in our criterion of it, or even to understand one another.

But it may be said, if we are exactly agreed in any mixed mode, what need of any criterion? Or what can we want farther? What we want farther, and what we mean by the criterion of it, is this; viz., to know whether any particular thing do belong to this mixed mode or no. And this is a very proper inquiry. For let a man learn the idea of intemperance from you never so clearly, and if you please let this be the idea, viz., the eating or drinking to that degree as to injure his understanding or health; and let him also be never so much convinced of the obligation to avoid it; yet it is a very pertinent question in him to ask you, how shall I know when I am guilty of intemperance?

And if we examine this thoroughly, we shall find that every little difference in the definition of a mixed mode will require a different criterion, e.g., if murder is defined the willful taking away the life of another, it is evident, that to inquire after the criterion of murder, is to inquire how we shall know when the life of another is taken away willfully; i.e., when one who takes away the life of another does it with that malicious design which is implied by willfulness. But if murder be defined the guilty taking away the life of another, then to inquire after the criterion of murder, is to inquire how it shall be known when guilt is contracted in the willful taking away the life of another. So that the criterion of murder, according to one or other of these definitions, will be different. For willfulness perhaps will be made the criterion of guilt; but willfulness itself, if it want any, must have some farther criterion; it being evident that nothing can be the measure of itself.

If the criterion is contained in the idea itself, then it is merely nominal, e.g., if virtue is defined, the acting agreeably to the will of God: to say the will of God is the criterion of virtue, is only to say, what is agreeable to the will of God is called virtue. But the real criterion, which is of some use, is this, how shall I know what the will of God is in this respect?

From hence it is evident, that the criterion of a mixed mode is neither the definition of it, nor contained in it. For, as has been shewn, the general idea is necessarily to be fixed; and if the particulars comprehended under it are fixed or known also, there remains nothing to be measured; because we measure only things unknown. The general idea then being fixed, the criterion which is to measure or determine inferiors, must be found out and proved to be a proper rule or measure, by comparing it with the general idea only, independent of the inferior things to which it is to be applied. For the truth of the measure must be proved independently of the particulars to be measured, otherwise we shall prove in a circle.

To apply what has been said in general to the case in hand. Great inquiry is made after the criterion of virtue; but it is to be feared that few know distinctly what it is they are inquiring after; and therefore this must be clearly stated. And in order to this, we must (as has been shewn) first fix our idea of virtue, and that exactly; and then our inquiry will be, how we shall know this or that less general or particular action to be comprehended under virtue. For unless our idea of virtue is fixed, we inquire after the criterion of we know not what. And this our idea of virtue, to give any satisfaction, ought to be so general, as to be conformable to that which all or most men are supposed to have. And this general idea, I think, may be thus expressed.

Virtue is the conformity to a rule of life, directing the actions of all rational creatures with respect to each other's happiness; to which conformity everyone in all cases is obliged: and everyone that does so conform, is or ought to be approved of, esteemed and loved for so doing. What is here expressed, I believe most men put into their idea of virtue.

For virtue generally does imply some relation to others: where self is only concerned, a man is called prudent (not virtuous) and an action which relates immediately to God, is styled religious.

I think also that all men, whatever they make virtue to consist in, yet always make it to imply obligation and approbation.

The idea of virtue being thus fixed, to inquire after the criterion of it, is to inquire what that rule of life is to which we are obliged to conform; or how that rule is to be found out which is to direct me in my behavior towards others, which ought always to be pursued, and which, if pursued, will or ought to procure me approbation, esteem, and love.

But before I can answer this inquiry I must first see what is meant by *obligation*.

SECTION II: CONCERNING OBLIGATION

Obligation is the necessity of doing or omitting any action in order to be happy: i.e., when there is such a relation between an agent and an action that the agent cannot be happy without doing or omitting that action, then the agent is said to be obliged to do or omit that action. So that obligation is evidently founded upon the prospect of happiness, and arises from that necessary influence which any action has upon present or future happiness or misery. And no greater obligation can be supposed to be laid upon any free agent without an express contradiction.

This obligation may be considered four ways, according to the four different manners in which it is induced: First, that obligation which ariseth from perceiving the natural consequences of things, i.e. the consequences of things acting according to the fixed laws of nature, may be called *natural*. Secondly, that arising from merit or demerit, as producing the esteem and favor of our fellow creatures, or the contrary, is usually styled *virtuous*. Thirdly, that arising from the authority of the civil magistrate, *civil*. Fourthly, that from the authority of God, *religious*.

Now from the consideration of these four sorts of obligation (which are the only ones) it is evident that a full and complete obligation which will extend to all cases, can only be that arising from the authority of God; because God only can in all cases make a man happy or miserable: and therefore, since we are always obliged to that conformity called virtue, it is evident that the immediate rule or criterion of it, is the will of God.

The next inquiry, therefore, is, what that will of God in this particular is, or what it directs me to do?

Now it is evident from the nature of God, viz. His being infinitely happy in

Himself from all eternity, and from His goodness manifested in His works, that He could have no other design in creating mankind than their happiness; and therefore He wills their happiness; therefore the means of their happiness; therefore that my behavior, as far as it may be a means of the happiness of mankind, should be such. Here then we are got one step farther, or to a new criterion: not to a new criterion of virtue immediately, but to a criterion of the will of God. For it is an answer to the inquiry, how shall I know what the will of God in this particular is? Thus the will of God is the immediate criterion of virtue, and the happiness of mankind the criterion of the will of God; and therefore the happiness of mankind may be said to be the criterion of virtue, but once removed.

And since I am to do whatever lies in my power towards promoting the happiness of mankind, the next inquiry is, what is the criterion of happiness, i.e. how shall I know what in my power is, or is not, for the happiness of mankind?

Now this is to be known only from the relations of things, (which relations, with respect to our present inquiry some have called their fitness and unfitness). For some things and actions are apt to produce pleasure, others pain; some are convenient, others inconvenient for a society; some are for the good of mankind; others tend to the detriment of it; therefore those are to be chosen which tend to the good of mankind, the others to be avoided.

Thus then we are got one step farther, viz. to the criterion of the happiness of mankind. And from this criterion we deduce all particular virtues and vices.

The next inquiry is, how shall I know that there is this fitness and unfitness in things? or if there be, how shall I discover it in particular cases? And the answer is, either from experience or reason. You either perceive the inconveniences of some things and actions when they happen; or you foresee them by contemplating the nature of the things and actions.

Thus the criterion of the fitness or unfitness of things may in general be said to be reason: which reason, when exactly conformable to the things existing, i.e. when it judges of things as they are, is called right reason. And hence also we sometimes talk of the reason of things, i.e. properly speaking, that relation which we should find out by our reason, if our reason was right.

And from hence we may perceive the reason of what I suggested in the beginning of this treatise, viz. that the dispute between moralists about the criterion of virtue is more in words than meaning; and that this difference between them has been occasioned by their dropping the immediate criterion, and choosing some a more remote, some a less remote one. And from hence we may see also the inconvenience of defining any mixed mode by its criterion. For that in a great measure has occasioned all this confusion; as may easily be made [to] appear in all the pretended criteria of virtue above mentioned.

Thus those who either expressly exclude, or don't mention the will of God, making the immediate criterion of virtue to be the good of mankind, must either allow that virtue is not in all cases obligatory (contrary to the idea which all or most men have of it) or they must say that the good of mankind is a sufficient obligation. But how can the good of mankind be any obligation to me, when perhaps in particular cases, such as laying down my life, or the like, it is contrary to my happiness? . . .

What has been said concerning the criterion of virtue as including our constant obligation to it, may perhaps be allowed to be true; but still it will be urged, that it is insufficient to account for matter of fact, viz. that most persons, who are either ignorant of, or never considered these deductions, do however pursue virtue themselves, and approve of it in others. I shall in the next place therefore give some account of our approbations and affections.

Section III: Concerning Approbation and Affection

Man is not only a sensible creature; not only capable of pleasure and pain, but capable also of foreseeing this pleasure and pain in the future consequences of things and actions; and as he is capable of knowing, so also of governing or directing the causes of them, and thereby in a great measure enabled to avoid the one and to procure the other: whence the principle of all action. And therefore, as pleasure and pain are not indifferent to him, nor out of his power, he pursues the former and avoids the latter; and therefore also those things which are causes of them are not indifferent, but he pursues or avoids them also, according to their different tendency. That which he pursues for its own sake, which is only pleasure, is called an *end;* that which he apprehends to be apt to produce pleasure, he calls *good,* and approves of, i.e., judges a proper means to attain his end, and therefore looks upon it as an object of choice; and that which is pregnant with misery he disapproves of and styles evil. And this good and evil are not only barely approved of, or the contrary; but whenever viewed in imagination (since man considers himself as existing hereafter, and is concerned for his welfare then as well as now) they have a present pleasure or pain annexed to them, proportionable to what is apprehended to follow them in real existence; which pleasure or pain arising from the prospect of future pleasure or pain is properly called *passion,* and the desire consequent thereupon, *affection.*

And as by reflecting upon pleasure there arises in our minds a desire of it; and on pain, an aversion from it (which necessarily follows from supposing us to be sensible creatures, and is no more than saying, that all things are not physically indifferent to us) so also by reflecting upon good or evil, the same desires and aversions are excited, and are distinguished into love and hatred. And from love and hatred variously modified, arise all those other desires and aversions which are promiscuously styled passions or affections; and are generally thought to be implanted in our nature originally, like the power of receiving sensitive pleasure or pain. And when placed on inanimate objects, are these following: hope, fear, despair and its opposite, for which we want a name.

SECTION IV: APPROBATION AND AFFECTION CONSIDERED WITH REGARD TO MERIT, OR THE LAW OF ESTEEM

If a man in the pursuit of pleasure or happiness (by which is meant the sum total of pleasure) had to do only with inanimate creatures, his approbation and affections would be as described in the foregoing section. But, since he is dependent with respect to his happiness, not only on these, but also on all rational agents, creatures like himself, which have the power of governing or directing good and evil, and of acting for an end; there will arise different means of happiness, and consequently different pursuits, though tending to the same end, happiness; and therefore different approbations and affections, and the contrary; which deserve particularly to be considered.

That there will arise different means of happiness, is evident from hence, viz. that rational agents, in being subservient to our happiness, are not passive, but voluntary. And therefore since we are in pursuit of that, to obtain which we apprehend the concurrence of their wills necessary, we cannot but approve of whatever is apt to procure this concurrence. And that can be only the pleasure or pain expected from it by them. And therefore as I perceive that my happiness is dependent on others, I cannot but judge whatever I apprehend to be proper to excite them to endeavor to promote my happiness, to be a means of happiness, i.e. I cannot but approve it. And since the annexing pleasure to their endeavors to promote my happiness is the only thing in my power to this end, I cannot but approve of the annexing pleasure to such actions of theirs as are undertaken upon my account. Hence to approve of a rational agent as a means of happiness, is different from the approbation of any other means; because it implies an approbation also of an endeavor to promote the happiness of that agent, in order to excite him and others to the same concern for my happiness for the future.

And because what we approve of we also desire (as has been shewn above) hence also we desire the happiness of any agent that has done us good. And therefore love or hatred, when placed on a rational object, has this difference from the love and hatred of other things, that it implies a desire of, and consequently a pleasure in the happiness of the object beloved; or if hated, the contrary.

The foundation of this approbation and love (which, as we have seen, consists in this voluntary contributing to our happiness) is called the *merit* of the agent so contributing, i.e. that whereby he is entitled (upon supposition that we act like rational, sociable creatures; like creatures, whose happiness is dependent on each other's behavior) to our approbation and love: demerit the contrary.

And this affection or quality of any action which we call merit, is very consistent with a man's acting ultimately for his own private happiness. For any particular action that is undertaken for the sake of another, is meritorious, i.e. deserves esteem, favor, and approbation from him for whose sake it was undertaken, towards the doer of it. Since the presumption of such esteem, etc. was the only motive to that action; and if such esteem, etc. does not follow, or is presumed not to follow it, such a person is reckoned unworthy of any favor, because he shews by his actions that he is incapable of being obliged by favors.

The mistake which some have run into, viz. that merit is inconsistent with acting upon private happiness, as an ultimate end, seems to have arisen from hence, viz. that they have not carefully enough distinguished between an inferior, and ultimate end; the end of a particular action, and the end of action in general: which may be explained thus. Though happiness, private happiness, is the proper or ultimate end of all our actions whatever, yet this particular means of happiness which any particular action is chiefly adapted to procure, or the thing chiefly aimed at by that action; the thing which, if possessed, we would not undertake that action, may [be] and generally is called the *end* of that action. As therefore happiness is the general end of all actions, so each particular action may be said to have its proper and peculiar end: thus the end of a beau[3] is to please by his dress; the end of study, knowledge. But neither pleasing by dress, nor knowledge, are ultimate ends, they still tend or ought to tend to something farther; as is evident from hence, viz. that a man may ask and expect a reason why either of them are pursued: now to ask the *reason* of any action or pursuit, is only to inquire into the *end* of it: but to expect a reason, i.e. an end, to be assigned for an *ultimate* end, is absurd. To ask why I pursue happiness, will admit of no other answer than an explanation of the terms.

Why inferior ends, which in reality are only means, are too often looked upon and acquiesced in as ultimate, shall be accounted for hereafter.

Whenever therefore the particular end of any action is the happiness of another (though the agent designed thereby to procure to himself esteem and favor, and looked upon that esteem and favor as a means of private happiness) that action is meritorious. And the same may be said, though we design to please God, by endeavoring to promote the happiness of others. But when an agent has a view in any particular action distinct from my happiness, and that view is his only motive to that action, though that action promote my happiness to never so great a degree, yet that agent acquires no merit, i.e. he is not thereby entitled to any favor or esteem. . . .

But it is far otherwise when my happiness is the sole end of that particular action, i.e. (as I have explained myself above) when the agent endeavors to promote my happiness as a means to procure my favor, i.e. to make me subservient to his happiness as his ultimate end: though I know he aims at my happiness only a means of his own, yet this lessens not the obligation.

Now from the various combinations of this which we call merit, and its contrary, arise all those various approbations and aversions; all those likings and dislikings which we call *moral*.

As therefore from considering those beings which are the involuntary means of our happiness or misery, there were produced in us the passions or affections of love, hatred, hope, fear, despair and its contrary: so from considering those beings which voluntarily contribute to our happiness or misery, there arise the following. Love and hatred (which are different from that love or hatred placed on involuntary beings; that placed on involuntary beings being only a desire to possess or avoid the thing beloved or hated; but this on voluntary agents being a desire to give pleasure or pain to the agent beloved or hated), gratitude, anger, (sometimes called by one name, resentment) generosity, ambition, honor, shame, envy, benevolence: and if there be any other, they are only, as these are, different modifications of love and hatred.

Love and hatred, and the foundation of them (viz. the agent beloved or hated being apprehended to be instrumental in our happiness) I have explained above. Gratitude is that desire of promoting the happiness of another upon account of some former kindness received. Anger, that desire of thwarting the happiness of another, on account of some former diskindness or injury received. Both these take place, though we hope for, or fear nothing farther from the objects of either of them, and this is still consistent with acting upon a principle of private happiness.

For though we neither hope for, nor fear anything farther from these particular beings; yet the disposition shewn upon these occasions is apprehended to influence the behavior of other beings towards us; i.e. other beings will be moved to promote our happiness or otherwise, as they observe how we resent favors or injuries.

Ambition is a desire of being esteemed. Hence a desire of being thought an object of esteem; hence of being an object of esteem; hence of doing laudable, i.e. useful actions. Generosity and benevolence are species of it. Ambition in too great a degree is called pride, of which there are several species. The title to the esteem of others, which ariseth from any meritorious action, is called honor. The pleasure arising from honor being paid to us, i.e. from others acknowledging that we are entitled to their esteem, is without a name. Modesty is the fear of losing esteem. The uneasiness or passion which ariseth from a sense that we have lost it, is called shame. So that ambition, and all those other passions and affections belonging to it, together with shame, arise from the esteem of others: which is the reason why this tribe of affections operate more strongly on us than any other, viz. because we perceive that as our happiness is chiefly dependent on the behavior of others, so we perceive also that this behavior is dependent on the esteem which others have conceived of us; and consequently that our acquiring or losing esteem, is in effect acquiring or losing happiness, and in the highest degree. And the same may be said concerning all our other affections and passions, to enumerate which, what for want of names to them, and what by the confusion of language about them, is almost impossible.

Envy will be accounted for hereafter, for a reason which will then be obvious.

Thus having explained what I mean by obligation and approbation; and shewn that they are founded on and terminate in happiness: having also pointed out that the difference between our approbations and affections as placed on involuntary and voluntary means of happiness; and farther proved that these approbations and affections are not innate or implanted in us by way of instinct, but are all acquired, being fairly deducible from supposing only sensible and rational creatures dependent on each other for their happiness, as explained above: I shall in the next place endeavor to answer a grand objection to what has here been said concerning approbations and affections arising from a prospect of private happiness.

The objection is this.

The reason or end of every action is always known to the agent; for nothing can move a man but what is perceived; but the generality of mankind love and hate, approve and disapprove, immediately, as soon as any moral character either occurs in life, or is proposed to them, without considering whether their private happiness is affected with it or not: or if they do consider any moral character in relation to their own happiness, and find themselves, as to their private happiness, unconcerned in it; or even find their private happiness lessened by it in some particular instance, yet they still approve the moral character, and love the agent: nay they cannot do otherwise. Whatever reason may be assigned by speculative men why we should be grateful to a benefactor, or pity the distressed; yet if the grateful or compassionate mind never thought of that reason, it is no reason to him. The inquiry is not why he ought to be grateful, but why he is so. These after-reasons therefore rather shew the wisdom and providence of our Maker, in implanting the immediate powers of these approbations (i.e. in Mr. Hutcheson's language, a moral sense) and these public affections in us, than give any satisfactory account of their origin. And therefore these public affections, and this moral sense, are quite independent on private happiness, and in reality act upon us as mere instincts.

Answer.

The matter of fact contained in this argument, in my opinion, is not to be contested; and therefore it remains either that we make the matter of fact consistent with what we have before laid down, or give up the cause.

Now, in order to shew this consistency, I beg leave to observe, that as in the pursuit of truth we do not always trace every proposition whose truth we are examining, to a first principle or axiom, but acquiesce, as soon as we perceive it deducible from some known or presumed truth; so in our conduct we do not always travel to the ultimate end of our actions, happiness: but rest contented, as soon as we perceive any action subservient to a known or presumed means of happiness. And these presumed truths and means of happiness, whether real or otherwise, always influence us after the same manner as if they were real. The undeniable consequences of mere prejudices are as firmly adhered to as the consequences of real truths or arguments; and what is subservient to a false (but imagined) means of happiness, is as industriously pursued as what is subservient to a true one.

Now every man, both in his pursuit after truth, and in his conduct, has settled and fixed a great many of these in his mind, which he always acts upon, as upon principles, without examining. And this is occasioned by the narrowness of our understandings: we can consider but a few things at once; and therefore, to run everything to the fountainhead would be tedious, through a long series of consequences: to avoid this we choose out certain truths and means of happiness, which we look upon as *resting places*, in which we may safely acquiesce, in the conduct both of our understanding and practice; in relation to the one, regarding them as axioms; in the other, as ends. And we are more easily inclined to this, by imagining that we may safely rely upon what we call habitual knowledge, thinking it needless to examine what we are already satisfied in. And hence it is that prejudices, both speculative and practical, are difficult to be rooted out, viz. few will examine them.

These *resting places* are so often used as principles, that at last, letting that slip out of our minds which first inclined us to embrace them, we are apt to imagine them, not as they really are, the substitutes of principles, but, principles themselves.

And from hence, as some men have imagined innate ideas, because they forget how they came by them; so others have set up almost as many distinct instincts as there are acquired principles of acting. And I cannot but wonder why the pecuniary sense, a sense of power and party, etc. were not mentioned, as well as the moral, that of honor, order, and some others.

The case is really this. We first perceive or imagine some real good, i.e. fitness to promote our natural happiness, in those things which we love and approve of. Hence (as was above explained) we annex pleasure to those things. Hence those things and pleasure are so tied together and associated in our minds, that one cannot present itself, but the other will also occur. And the association remains even after that which at first gave them the connection is quite forgot, or perhaps does not exist; but the contrary. An instance or two may perhaps make this clear. How many men are there in the world who have as strong a taste for money as others have for virtue; who count so much money, so much happiness; nay, even sell their happiness for money; or to speak more properly, make the having money, without any design or thought of using it, their ultimate end? But was this propensity to money, born with them, or rather, did not they at first perceive a great many advantages from being possessed of money, and from thence conceive a pleasure of having it, thence desire it, thence endeavor to obtain it, thence receive an actual pleasure in obtaining it, thence desire to preserve the possession of it? Hence by dropping the intermediate steps between money and happiness, they join money and happiness immediately together, and content themselves with the fantastical pleasure of having it, and make that which was at first pursued only as a means, be to them a real end, and what their real happiness or misery consists in. Thus the connection between money and happiness remains in the mind; though it has long since ceased between the things themselves.

The same might be observed concerning the thirst after knowledge, fame, etc., the delight in reading, building, planting, and most of the various exercises and entertainments of life. These were at first entered on with a view to some farther end, but at length became habitual amusements; the idea of pleasure is associated with them, and leads us on still in the same eager pursuit of them, when the first reason is quite vanished, or at least out of our minds. Nay, we find this power of association so great as not only to transport our passions and affections beyond their proper bounds, both as to intenseness and duration; as is evident from daily instances of avarice, ambition, love, revenge, etc., but also that it is able to transfer them to improper objects, and such as are of a quite different nature from those to which our reason had at first directed them. Thus being accustomed to resent an injury done to our body by a retaliation of the like to him that offered it, we are apt to conceive the same kind of resentment, and often express it in the same manner, upon receiving hurt from a stock or a stone; whereby the hatred which we are used to place on voluntary beings, is substituted in the room of that aversion which belongs to involuntary ones. The like may be observed in most of the other passions above mentioned.

From hence also, viz. from the continuance of this association of ideas in our minds, we may be enabled to account for that (almost diabolical) passion called envy, which we promised to consider.

Mr. Locke observes,[4] and I believe very justly, that there are some men entirely unacquainted with this passion. For most men that are used to reflection, may remember the very time when they were first under the dominion of it.

Envy is generally defined to be that pain which arises in the mind from observing the prosperity of others: not of all others indefinitely, but only of some particular persons. Now the examining who those particular persons whom we are apt to envy are, will lead us to the true origin of this passion. And if a man will be at the pains to consult his mind, or to look into the world, he'll find that these particular persons are always such as upon some account or other he has had a rivalship with. For when two or more are competitors for the same thing, the success of the one must necessarily tend to the detriment of the other, or others: hence the success of my rival and misery or pain are joined together in my mind; and this connection or association remaining in my mind, even after the rivalship ceases, makes me always affected with pain whenever I hear of his success, though in affairs which have no manner of relation to the rivalship; much more in those that bring that to my remembrance, and put me in mind of what I might have enjoyed had it not been for him.

Thus also we are apt to envy those persons that refuse to be guided by our judgments, and persuaded by us. For this is nothing else than a rivalship about the superiority of judgment; and we take a secret pride, both to let the world see, and in imagining ourselves, that we are in the right.

There is one thing more to be observed in answer to this objection, and that is, that we do not always (and perhaps not for the most part) make this association ourselves, but learn it from others, i.e., that we annex pleasure or pain to certain actions because we see others do it, and acquire principles of action by imitating those whom we admire, or whose esteem we would procure: Hence the son too often inherits both the vices and the party of his father, as well as his estate: Hence national virtues and vices, dispositions and opinions: and from hence we may observe how easy it is to account for what is generally called the prejudice of education; how soon we catch the temper and affections of those whom we daily converse with; how almost insensibly we are taught to live, admire or hate; to be grateful, generous, compassionate or cruel, etc.

What I say then in answer to the forementioned objection is this: That though it be necessary in order to solve the principal actions of human life to suppose a moral sense (or what is signified by that name) and also public affections; yet I deny that this moral sense, or these public affections, are innate or implanted in us. They are acquired either from our own observation or the imitation of others.

Editor's Notes

1. Francis Hutcheson; for selections, see Part IV.
2. A Lockean notion, mixed modes are complex ideas formed by the mind itself by actively assembling several simple ideas it has passively received from experience. The unity of an idea that is a mixed mode comes only from the act of the mind and is generally signified by giving one name to the complex. As instances, Locke gives obligation, drunkenness, and hypocrisy. See John Locke, *An Essay Concerning Human Understanding*, bk. II, chap. XXII.
3. A fop or dandy, one who loves to show off his fine clothing.
4. In the *Essay*, bk. II, chap. XX, §14.

Further Reading

There is a brief discussion of Gay in Ernest Albee, *A History of English Utilitarianism* (London: Allen & Unwin, 1901). Otherwise there seems to be no extended discussion of him. Gay is mentioned in Elie Halévy, *The Growth of Philosophical Radicalism*, trans. Mary Morris (London: Faber & Faber, 1928), and he receives passing notice in histories of psychology.

Claude Adrien Helvétius

Introduction

Helvétius was born in 1715 into a family of physicians. His grandfather had become wealthy through a Parisian practice, and his father had treated Louis XIV and Louis XV and was physician to the queen. In 1738 family connections enabled Helvétius to obtain a lucrative post as tax collector. He acquired a small fortune within a decade and thereupon retired to devote himself to writing and to companionship with the advanced intellectuals of the day. From about 1750 until 1757 he worked painstakingly on *De l'Esprit* (*On the Mind*), which was published in 1758. The book caused a storm of criticism. Personal, philosophical, religious, and political attacks were launched against Helvétius, and it was only thanks to his official and family connections that he escaped prison or worse. He thought for a time of abandoning his writing, but returned to it after a while, eventually completing a second work, *De l'Homme* (*On Man*), which was published in 1772, a year after his death.

On the Mind is divided into four sections: the first lays out a general psychology and epistemology; the second concerns ethics and politics; the third explains Helvétius's ideas on education; and the final section offers a miscellany of thoughts, largely about aesthetics.

In his psychology, which he learned from a number of French contemporaries who drew much of their inspiration from Locke, Helvétius held that all our ideas come from bodily sensations. Judgment, or combining of ideas, is the act of comparing remembered sensations; the emotions spring from our reactions of pleasure or pain to what we perceive or think. Because he regarded sensation as bodily feeling, Helvétius tacitly implied that there is no need for any notion of a separate soul or mind. Other views of his that were offensive to established religious opinion were slipped in (in Chapter VII of Essay I), on the excuse that he was showing how misleading language can be. Thus Helvétius criticized la Rochefoucauld's Augustinian attack on self-love as "pride and vanity," by noting that the term "self-love" means "nothing more than a sentiment implanted in us by nature" that, depending on the circumstances, can produce either pride or modesty. And he dismissed discussion of free will by saying that the idea of liberty is easy to explain. "A man at liberty," he observed, "is a person neither in chains, under confinement, nor intimidated like a slave by the fear of punishment." But the term has no other meaning. In particular, "no idea can be formed of the word Liberty, when applied to the will." The theory behind this is Hobbesian, but Hobbes would not have agreed that the fear of punishment limits freedom.

If these were not particularly original ideas, neither were the elements of what Helvétius had to say about morality. He presented an egoistic psychology, wavering a

414

little about whether all voluntary action is necessarily self-interested or whether there might be some extraordinary people who are genuinely disinterested. And he offered an egoistic morality. Agents pursue what they take to be good for themselves, and no other good is a reasonable object of individual pursuit. Hence what we praise as virtue or moral goodness is always what we think is useful to us. Nicole had said as much, and similar conclusions can be drawn from Mandeville. But Helvétius had something new to add.

This novelty hinges first on Helvétius's view of what we take to be in our own interest. People tend to think of themselves not as isolated individuals but as members of groups. Initially we identify with small groups, but we can come to identify ourselves through our membership in larger groups and can even see ourselves mainly as members of our nation. If we reach this point, what we take to be good for ourselves will be whatever is good for the whole nation. (Helvétius thought it impossible to identify with a group comprising everyone in the world.)

On the basis of his sensationist psychology, Helvétius argued that all people are equal in innate mental ability, differing only as a result of their experiences. Education in a broad sense is the most important of these formative experiences, and Helvétius contended that it is possible to educate people so that everyone identifies with the nation and knows what is useful to the nation as a whole. In this way education can form people who would act virtuously, that is, in a way that, because it benefits everyone else in the country as well as themselves, would be praised by everyone.

What stands in the way of increasing human happiness without limit, then, is ignorance and identification with small groups. Helvétius was particularly concerned with the small groups that already have power. They find it in their own interest to prevent the masses from being given a proper education, as such a system would ultimately deprive them of the group power in which they could find their own good. Those who already identify with the good of the whole nation must therefore break the hold of these narrower groups and institute a new mode of education. As Helvétius did not hesitate to make clear – and in a Catholic country like France, where the Jesuits dominated the educational system, it could hardly have been overlooked had he not done so – the church was the prime culprit. But the nobility was not far behind.

These ideas were not likely to win Helvétius much favor with his highly placed erstwhile friends, and in the climate of the time they seemed much more dangerous than he perhaps intended them to be. In January 1757 there had been an attempt to assassinate Louis XV, and in the aftermath it was proclaimed that anyone who was convicted of having written anything critical of religion or of the state would be punished with death. Accordingly, Helvétius managed to publish his book only after complicated maneuvers with the censors, and the outraged response to it from those in power affected others besides himself. Because he was closely associated with Diderot and the other enlightened *philosophes* who were producing the great *Encyclopedia* – which was designed to spread scientific knowledge and up-to-date social thought to everyone – publication of the *Encyclopedia* was halted, persecution and prosecution of its editors and their friends ran rampant, and on both sides everyone was furious at Helvétius. After all, the *philosophes* asserted, we all publish anonymously and secretly; why couldn't Helvétius have done so as well?

The uproar passed without having any lasting effect, but this was not true of Helvétius's ideas. His view that people could be made virtuous only by political changes – not by the church, not by grace – and that political changes would have to augment the happiness people experience here and now if they were to be effective in increasing virtue was taken up three decades later by Jeremy Bentham, a lawyer and philosopher who was also a practical reformer. If Helvétius's moral theory did not survive in the form in which he proposed it, it nonetheless lived on in a theory that is still influential.

The following selections are from *De l'Esprit; or Essays on the Mind*, an anonymous translation originally issued in 1759 and republished in 1810.

On the Mind

PREFACE

The subject I propose to examine in this work is new and interesting. People have hitherto considered the Mind only under some of its views: for great writers have no more than cast a rapid glance over it; and this has emboldened me to treat of the subject.

The knowledge of the Mind, when we consider it in its utmost extent, is so closely connected with the knowledge of the heart, and of the passions of men, that it was impossible to write on this subject, without treating of that part of morality at least, which is common to men of all nations, and which in all governments can have no other object in view than the public advantage.

The principles I establish on this subject are, I think, conformable to the general interest, and to experience. It is by facts that I have ascended to causes. I imagined that morality ought to be treated like all the other sciences, and founded on experiment, as well as natural philosophy. I have adhered to this idea, from the persuasion that all morality, where its principles are of use to the public, is necessarily conformable to the morals of religion, which are only the perfection of human morals. For the rest, if I am deceived, and if, contrary to my expectation, some of my principles are not conformable to the general interest, this proceeds from an error of my judgment, and not of my heart; and I declare, beforehand, that I disown them.

ESSAY II

Chapter II: Of Probity Relatively to an Individual

It is not real Probity; that is Probity, with regard to the public, that I consider in this chapter; but merely Probity, considered relatively to each individual.[1]

In this point of view, I say, that each individual calls Probity in another only the habitude of actions which are useful to him: I say habitude, because it is not one single honest action, more than one single ingenious idea, that will gain us the title of virtuous and witty. There is not that penurious wretch on earth which has not once behaved with generosity; nor a liberal person who has not once been parsimonious; no villain who has not done a good action; no person so stupid who has not uttered one smart sentence; and, in fine, no man who, on inspecting certain actions of his life, will not seem possessed of all the opposite virtues and vices. A greater uniformity in the behaviour of men would suppose in them a continuity of attention which they are incapable of; differing from one another only more or less. The man of absolute uniformity has no existence; for that no perfection, either with regard to vice or virtue, is to be found on the earth.

It is therefore to the habitude of actions advantageous to him, that an individual gives the name of Probity: I say of actions, because we cannot judge of intentions. How is it possible? It is seldom or never that action is the effect of a sentiment; we ourselves are often ignorant of the motives by which we are determined. A rich man bestows a comfortable subsistence on a worthy man reduced to poverty. Doubtless he does a good action; but is this action simply the effect of a desire of rendering a man happy? Pity, the hopes of gratitude, vanity itself, all these different motives, separately or aggregately, may they not, unknown to himself, have determined him to that commendable action? Now if a man be, in general, ignorant himself of the motives of his generous action, how can the public be acquainted with them? Thus it is only from the actions of men, that the public can judge of their probity. A man, for instance, has twenty degrees of passion for virtue; but he has thirty degrees of love for a woman; and this woman would instigate him to be guilty of murder. Upon this supposition, it is certain, that this person is nearer guilt than he, who, with only ten degrees of passion for virtue, has only five degrees of love for so wicked a woman. Hence I conclude, that of two men, the more honest in his actions has sometimes the less passion for virtue.

Every philosopher also agrees, that the virtue of men greatly depends on the circumstances in which they are placed. Virtuous men have too often sunk under a strange series of unhappy events.

He who will warrant his virtue in every possible situation, is either an impostor or a fool; characters equally to be mistrusted.

After determining the idea I affix to this word Probity, considered in relation to every individual, we must, to assure ourselves of the propriety of this definition, have recourse to observation; and this will inform us, that there are men whom a happy disposition, a strong desire of glory and esteem, inspire with the same love for justice and virtue, which men in general have for riches and honours.

The actions personally advantageous to these virtuous men are so truly just, that they tend to promote the general welfare, or, at least, not to lessen it.

But the number of these men is so small, that I only mention them in honour of humanity. And the most numerous class, which alone comprehends the far greater part of mankind, is that of men so entirely devoted to their own interest, that they never consider the welfare of the whole. Concentrated, if I may be allowed the expression, in their own happiness; these men call those actions only honest, which are advantageous to themselves. A judge acquits a criminal, a minister prefers an unworthy person; yet both are just, if those they have favoured may be credited. But should the judge punish, and the minister refuse, the criminal, and the party denied, will always consider them as unjust. . . .

In effect, what man, if he sacrifices the pride of stiling himself more virtuous than others, to the pride of being more sincere; and if, with a scrupulous attention, he searches all the recesses of his soul; will not perceive that his virtues and vices are wholly owing to the different modifications of personal interest;* that all equally tend to their happiness; that it is the diversity of the passions and tastes, of which some are agreeable, and others contrary to the public interest, which terms our actions either virtues or vices? Instead of despising the vicious man, we should pity him, rejoice in our own happy disposition, thank heaven for not having given us any of those tastes and passions, which would have forced us to have sought our happiness in the misery of another. For, after all, interest is always obeyed; hence the injustice of all our judgments, and the appellations of just and unjust are lavished on the same actions, according to the advantage resulting from them to particulars.

If the physical universe be subject to the laws of motion, the moral universe is equally so to those of interest. Interest is, on earth, the mighty magician, which to the eyes of every creature changes the appearance of all objects. . . .

This principle is so agreeable to experience, that, without entering into a farther discussion, I think myself warranted to conclude, that personal interest is the only and universal estimator of the merit of human actions; and therefore, that Probity, with regard to an individual is, according to my definition, nothing more than the habitude of actions personally advantageous to this individual.

Chapter V: Of Probity in Relation to Private Societies

Under this point of view, I say, that probity is only a more or less distinguished habit of performing actions particularly useful to this little society. Certain virtuous societies indeed frequently appear to lay aside their own interest to judge the actions of men, in conformity to the interest of the public; but in this they only gratify the passion which an enlightened pride gives them for virtue; and consequently, like all other societies, obey the law of personal interest. What other motive can determine men to generous actions? It is as impossible to love virtue for the sake of virtue as to love vice for the sake of vice.†

---

* The humane man is he to whom the sight of another's misfortunes is insupportable, and who, to remove this afflicting spectacle, is, as it were, forced to relieve the wretched. The cruel man, on the contrary, is he to whom the sight of another's misfortunes gives a secret pleasure; and it is to prolong that pleasure, that he refuses all relief to the wretched. Now these two persons, so very opposite, both equally tend to their pleasures, and are actuated by the same spring. . . .

† The continual declamations of moralists against the malignity of mankind are a proof of their knowing but little of human nature. Men are not cruel and perfidious, but carried away by their own interest. The declamations of the moralist will certainly make no change in this moral spring of the universe. They ought not therefore to complain of the wickedness of mankind, but of the ignorance of the legislators, who have always placed private interest in opposition to the general interest. . . .

Chapter VI: Of the Means of Securing Virtue

A man is just when all his actions tend to the public welfare. Doing well is not all that is requisite to merit the title of virtuous. A prince has a thousand places to bestow; he must fill them up; and he cannot avoid rendering a thousand people happy. Here then his virtue depends only on the justice and injustice of his choice. If, when a place of importance is vacant, he gives it from friendship, from weakness, from solicitation, or from indolence, to a man of moderate abilities, in preference to another of superior talents, he ought to be considered as unjust, whatever praises others may bestow on his probity.

In the affair of probity, he ought only to consult and listen to the public interest, and not to the men by whom he is surrounded; for personal interest too often leads him into an illusion.

We ought then, in order to be virtuous, to blend the light of knowledge with greatness of soul. Whoever assembles within himself these different gifts of nature, always directs his course by the compass of the public utility. This utility is the principle on which all human virtues are founded, and the basis of all legislations. It ought to inspire the legislator with the resolution to force the people to submit to his laws; to this principle, in short, he ought to sacrifice all his sentiments, and even those of humanity itself.

Public humanity is sometimes void of pity for individuals. When a vessel is surprised by long calms, and famine has, with an imperious voice, commanded the mariners to draw lots for the unfortunate victim who is to serve as a repast to his companions, they kill him without remorse: this vessel is the emblem of a nation; every thing becomes lawful, and even virtuous, that procures the public safety.

The conclusion of what I have just said is, that in the case of probity counsel is not to be taken from private connections, but only from the interest of the public: he who constantly consults it will have all his actions directed either immediately to the public utility, or to the advantage of individuals, without their being detrimental to the state.

Chapter XI: Of Probity in Relation to the Public

I shall not in this chapter treat of Probity, with respect to a particular person, or a private society; but of true probity; of probity considered in relation to the public. This kind of probity is the only one that really merits, and has in general obtained the name. It is only considering it in this point of view, that we can form clear ideas of honesty, and discover a guide to virtue.

Now, under this aspect, I say that the public, like particular societies, is only determined in its judgments by motives of interest; that it does not give the name of noble to great and heroic actions, but to those that are of public use; and that the esteem of the public, for such and such an action, is not proportioned to the degree of strength, courage, or generosity, necessary to execute it, but to the importance of that action, and the public advantage derived from it.

In fact, when encouraged by the presence of an army, one man alone fights three men who are wounded: this is doubtless a brave action; but it is what a thousand of our grenadiers are capable of, and for which they will never be mentioned in history; but when the safety of an empire formed to subdue the universe, depends on the success of this battle, Horatius is an hero,[2] he is the admiration of his fellow-citizens, and his name, celebrated in history, is handed down to the most distant ages.

Two persons threw themselves into a gulf; this was an action common to Sappho[3] and Curtius;[4] but the first did it to put an end to the torments of love, and the other to save Rome; Sappho was therefore a fool, and Curtius a hero. In vain have some philosophers given the name of folly to each of these actions; the public sees clearer than they, and never gives the name of fool to those from whom it receives advantage.

Chapter XIII: Of Probity in Relation to Various Ages and Nations

In all ages and nations, probity can be only an habit of performing actions that are of use to our country. However certain this proposition may be, to render this truth the more evident, I shall endeavor to give a clear and full idea of this virtue.

To this purpose, I shall examine two sentiments on this subject, that have hitherto divided the moralists.

Some maintain, that we have an idea of virtue absolutely independent of different ages and governments; and that virtue is always one and the same. The others maintain, on the contrary, that every nation forms a different idea of it.

The first bring, in proof of their opinions, the ingenious, but unintelligible dreams of the Platonists. Virtue, according to them, is nothing but the idea of order, harmony, and essential beauty. But this beauty is a mystery of which they can convey no fixed ideas: they therefore do not establish their system on the knowledge which history affords us of the human heart, and the powers of the mind.

The second, and amongst them Montaigne,[5] with arms more strangely tempered than those of reasoning, that is, with facts, attack the opinion of the first; prove that an action virtuous in the north, is vicious in the south; and from thence conclude, that the idea of virtue is merely arbitrary.

Such are the opinions of these two sects of philosophers. Those, from their not having consulted history err, in a metaphysical labyrinth of words: these, from their not having examined with sufficient depth the facts presented by history, have thought that caprice alone decided the goodness or turpitude of human actions. These two philosophical sects are deceived; but they would both have escaped error, had they, with an attentive eye, considered the history of the world. They would then have perceived, that time must necessarily produce, in the physical and moral world, revolutions that change the face of empires; that, in the great catastrophes of kindgoms, the people always experience great changes; that the same actions may successively become useful and prejudicial, and consequently, by turns, assume the name of virtuous and vicious.

If, in consequence of this observation, they would have been willing to form a mere abstract idea of virtue, independent of practice, they would have acknowledged, that, by the word Virtue can only be understood, a desire of general happiness; that, consequently, the public welfare is the object of virtue; and that the actions it enjoins, are the means it makes use of to accomplish that end; that, therefore, the idea of virtue is not arbitrary; that, in different ages and countries, all men, at least those who live in society, ought to form the same idea of it; and, in short, if the people represent it under different forms, it is because they take for virtue the various means they employ to accomplish the end.

This definition of virtue, I think, gives an idea of it that is at once clear, simple, and conformable to experience; a conformity that alone can establish the truth of an opinion. . . .

However stupid we suppose mankind, it is certain that, enlightened by their own interest, they have not, without motives, adopted the ridiculous customs we find estabished amongst some of them; the fantasticalness of these customs proceed, then, from the diversity of the interests of different nations; and, in fact, if they have always, though confusedly, understood by the word virtue the desire of the public happiness; if they have consequently given the name of honesty only to actions useful to the nation; and if the idea of utilty has always been secretly connected with the idea of virtue, we may assert, that the most ridiculous, and even the most cruel customs, have always had, for their foundation, as I am going to shew by some examples, either a real or apparent utility with respect to the public welfare.

Chapter XV: Of the Use Accruing to Morality, from the Knowledge of the Principles Laid Down in the Preceding Chapters

If morality hitherto has little contributed to the happiness of mankind, it is not owing to any want of perspicuity or beauty of stile, or propriety and loftiness of sentiment, in the moralists: but amidst all their superior talents, it must be owned, that they have not often enough considered the different vices of nations as necessarily resulting from the different form of their government; yet, it is only by considering morality in this point of light, that it can become of any real use to men. What have hitherto been the effects of all the splendid maxims of morality? If some individuals have been corrected by them of faults which perhaps they reproached themselves with, no change in the manners of nations have been produced. What is this to be imputed to? It is because the vices of a people, if I may presume to say so, always lie at the bottom of its legislation. There he must search, who would pluck up the root whence its vices arise. He who wants either penetration, or courage, for such an undertaking, is, in this respect, of little or no use to the universe. To attempt extinguishing the vices annexed to the legislation of a people, without making any change in this legislation, is no less than rejecting the just consequences after admitting the principles. . . .

From what I have said, it follows that no change in the ideas of a people is to be hoped for, till after a change in its legislation; that the reformation of manners is to be begun by the reformation of laws, and declamations against a vice useful in the present form of government, would politically be detrimental, were they not found fruitless. But so they will always be, for it is only the force of the laws that can ever act on the bulk of a nation. Besides, let me be allowed cursorily to observe, that, among the moralists there are very few who, by setting our passions at variance, know how to avail themselves of them, so as to procure their opinions to be adopted. Most of their admonitions are too dogmatical and imperious; yet they should be sensible that invectives will never prevail against sentiments; that it is only a passion which can get the better of a passion. . . .

By thus substituting the soft language of interest, instead of the peremptory clamour of invective, the moralists may establish their maxims. I shall not enlarge farther on this head, but return to my subject; and I say, that all men tend only towards their happiness; that it is a tendency from which they cannot be diverted; that the attempt would be fruitless, and even the success dangerous; consequently, it is only by incorporating personal and general interest, that they can be rendered virtuous. This being granted, morality is evidently no more than a frivolous science, unless blended with policy and legislation: whence I conclude that, if philosophers would be of use to the world, they should survey objects from the same point of view as the legislator. Though not invested with the same power, they are to be actuated by the same principle. The moralist is to indicate the laws, of which the legislator insures the execution, by stamping them with the seal of his authority.

Among the moralists, there are doubtless but few duly impressed with this truth, even of those whose minds are capable of the most exalted ideas; many in the study of morality and the portraits of vices are animated only by personal interest and private contentions; consequently they confine themselves only to the representations of such vices as molest society; and their mind gradually contracting itself within the narrow circle of their interest, soon loses the force necessary for soaring to sublime ideas. In the science of morality, the elevation of the thought often depends on the elevation of the soul. To fix on such moral truths as are of real advantage to men, there must be a warm passion for the general good; and unhappily morality, like religion, is not without hypocrites.

Chapter XVII: Of the Advantages That Result from the Principles Above Established

I pass with rapidity over the advantages that would be obtained by individuals; these would consist in their having clear ideas of morality; the principles of which have been hitherto so ambiguous and contradictory, that they permitted the most senseless persons constantly to justify the folly of their conduct by some of its maxims.

Besides, the individual being better informed of his duties, would be less dependent on the opinion of his friends. Sheltered from the injustice wherein, unknown to himself, he might be frequently involved by those with whom he converses, he would be freed from the puerile fear of ridicule; a phantom that banishes reason, and is the terror of those timid and ignorant souls who sacrifice their inclinations, their pleasures, their repose, and sometimes even their virtues, to the humour and caprice of those splenetic mortals whose criticism we cannot escape, when we have the misfortune to be known.

A person solely subject to reason and virtue might then brave every prejudice, and arm himself with those manly and courageous sentiments that form the distinguishing character of a virtuous man; sentiments desirable in every citizen, and which we have a right to expect from the great. How shall the person, raised to the highest posts, remove the obstacles to the general welfare, which certain prejudices raise against it, and resist the menaces and cabals of men in power, often interested in the public misfortune, if his soul is not inaccessible to all kinds of solicitations, fears, and prejudices?

It appears then that the knowledge of the above principles procures at least these advantages to the individual; it gives him a clear and certain idea of honesty; saves him from all inquietude on this subject, secures the peace of his conscience, and consequently procures him the inward secret pleasure blended with the practice of virtue.

As to the advantages the public would derive from it, they would doubtless be more considerable. In consequence of these principles, we might, if I may venture to use the expression, compose a catechism of probity, the maxims of which being simple, true, and level to all understandings, would teach the people that virtue, though invariable in the object it proposes, is not so in the means it makes use of; that, consequently, we ought to consider actions as indifferent in themselves; to be sensible, that it is the business of the state to determine those that are worthy of esteem or contempt; and, in fine, that it is the office of the legislator to fix, from his knowledge of the public interest, the instant when an action ceases to be virtuous, and becomes vicious.

These principles being once received, with what facility would the legislator extinguish the torches of fanaticism and superstition, suppress abuses, reform barbarous customs, perhaps useful at their establishment, but since become fatal to the world? Customs that subsist only from the fear of not being able to abolish them, without causing an insurrection among people, who are always accustomed to take the practice of certain actions for virtue itself, without kindling long and bloody wars; and in short, without occasioning those seditions which are always dangerous to the common people, and can really be neither foreseen nor subdued but by men of firmness and great abilities.

It is then by weakening the stupid veneration of the people for ancient laws and customs, that sovereigns would be enabled to purge the earth of most of the evils that lay it waste, and be furnished with the means of securing the possession of their crowns.

Chapter XXIII: Of the Causes That Have Hitherto Retarded the Progress of Morality

If poetry, geometry, astronomy, and, in general, all the sciences, advance more or less rapidly towards perfection, while morality seems scarcely to have left its cradle, it is because men, being forced to unite in society, and to give themselves laws, were obliged to form a system of morality before they had learnt, from observation, its true principles. The system being formed, no farther notice was taken of it; thus we have, in a manner, the morals of the world in its infancy, and how shall it be brought to perfection?

The progress of a science does not solely depend on its being of use to the public: every citizen of which a nation is composed ought to reap some advantage from its improvement. Now in the revolutions that have taken place among all the nations of the earth, the public interest, which is that of the majority, among whom the principles of sound morality ought to find its support, not being always agreeable to the interest of those most in power, the latter being indifferent with respect to the progress of all sciences, must effectually oppose that of morality.

The ambitious man, who is raised above his fellow-citizens; the tyrant who tramples them under his feet; and the fanatic, who keeps them prostrate; all these several scourges of the human race, all these different kinds of flagitious men, forced by their private interest to establish laws contrary to the general good, have been very sensible, that their power had no other foundation than the ignorance and weakness of mankind: they have therefore imposed silence on whosoever, by discovering to the people the true principles of morality, would have opened their eyes with respect to their misfortunes and their rights, and have armed them against injustice.

But, it is replied, if in the first ages of the world, when despotic princes held the nations in subjection, and ruled them with a rod of iron, it was then their interest to conceal from the people the true principles of morality; principles, which by animating them against tyrants, would have made revenge the duty of each citizen; yet now, when the sceptre is not purchased with guilt, but placed by unanimous consent in the hand of a prince, and supported by the love of the people; when the glory and happiness of a nation, reflecting on the sovereign, adds to his grandeur and felicity; what enemies of the human race are there still to oppose the progress of morality?

This is no longer done by kings, but by two other sorts of men in power. The first are the fanatics, whom I shall not confound with the men truly pious. These last support the maxims of religion, and the others are their destroyers: the one are the friends of humanity; the other, who are outwardly mild but within barbarous, have the voice of Jacob and the hands of Esau: they are indifferent with respect to worthy actions; they judge virtuous not what is done, but what is believed; and the credulity of men is, according to them, the only standard of their probity. They mortally hate, said queen Christina,[6] all who are not their dupes; and to this they are led by their interest. Being ambitious, hypocritical, and artful, they imagine that, to enslave the people they ought to put out their eyes: thus, these impious wretches are incessantly setting up the cry of impiety against every man born to enlighten the nations: every new truth is suspected by them, and they resemble infants that are terrified at every thing in the dark.

The second species of men in power who oppose the progress of morality are the half-politicians. Among these are some naturally disposed to truth, who are enemies to newly discovered truths only from their indolence, and their being unwilling to apply the attention necessary to examine them. There are others animated by dangerous motives, and these are most to be feared. These are the men whose minds are without abilities, and whose souls are destitute of virtues; they want not the courage of being greatly wicked; and, incapable of new and elevated views, they believe that their importance demands a weak or dissembled respect for all the received opinions and errors countenanced by them. Furious against every man who would stagger the empire, they arm against him even those passions and prejudices which they despise; and, without ceasing, terrify weak minds with the cry of novelty.

But may we not make the nations sensible of the advantages they would obtain from an excellent system of morality? and might we not hasten the progress of that science, by conferring greater honours on those who improve it? Considering the importance of this subject, I shall run the hazard of a digression, in order to treat it more fully.

Chapter XXIV: Of the Means of Perfecting Morality

It would be sufficient for this purpose to remove the obstacles placed against its progress by the two kinds of men I have mentioned. The only means of succeeding in this, is to pull off their masks, and to shew that the protectors of ignorance are the most cruel enemies of human beings; to shew the nations, that men are in general more stupid than wicked; that, in curing them of their errors, we should cure them of most of their vices; and that opposing their cure is committing the crime of treason against human nature.

Every man, who considers the picture of public miseries exhibited in history, soon perceives that ignorance, which is still more barbarous than self-love, has caused most of the calamities that have overflowed the earth. Struck with this truth, we are ready to cry out, Happy the nation where the citizens are permitted to perpetrate only the crimes that flow from self-love! How are they multiplied by ignorance, and what blood has been spilt on its altars! However, man is made to be virtuous; and, in fact, if force essentially reside in the greater number, and justice consist in the practice of actions useful to the greater number, it is evident that justice is in its own nature always armed with a power sufficient to suppress vice, and place men under the necessity of being virtuous.

If audacious and powerful wickedness so often puts justice and virtue in chains, and oppresses the nations, this is only done by the assistance of ignorance, which conceals from every nation its true interest, hinders the action and union of its strength, and by that means shields the guilty from the sword of justice.

To what contempt ought he to be condemned, who would hold the people in the darkness of ignorance? This truth has not hitherto been insisted upon with sufficient force: no, all the altars of error must one day be overthrown. I know with what precaution we ought to advance a new opinion. I know, that in destroying prejudices, we ought to treat them with respect; and that, before we attack an error generally received, we ought to send, like the doves from the ark, some truths on the discovery, to see if the deluge of prejudices does not yet cover the face of the earth; if error begins to subside, and if there can be perceived here and there some isles where virtue and truth may find rest for their feet, and communicate themselves to mankind.

But so many precautions are only to be taken with those prejudices that are not very dangerous. What respect do we owe to the man who, jealous of dominion, would besot the people, in order to tyrannize over them? We must with a bold hand break the talisman of imbecility, to which is attached the power of these malevolent genii; to discover to nations the true principles of morality; to teach them that, being insensibly drawn towards happiness, either apparent or real, grief and pleasure are the only movers of the moral universe; and that the sensation of self-love is the only basis on which we can place the foundations of an useful morality. . . .

It is then only by good laws that we can form virtuous men. All the art therefore of the legislator consists in forcing them by self-love to be always just to each other. Now, in order to compose such laws, it is necessary that the human heart should be known, and in the first place, that we should be convinced that men having sensibility for themselves, and indifference with respect to others, are neither good nor bad, but ready to be either, according as a common interest unites or divides them; that self-love, a sensation necessary to the preservation of the species, is engraven by Nature in a manner not to be erased; that a physical sensibility has produced in us a love of pleasure and a hatred of pain; that pleasure and pain have at length produced and opened in all hearts the buds of self-love, which by unfolding themselves give birth to the passions, whence spring all our virtues and vices.

By contemplating these preliminary ideas, we learn why the passions, of which the forbidden tree is, according to some, only an ingenious image, bear equally on it branches of good and evil fruit; we perceive the mechanism employed by them in the production of our virtues and vices; and, in short, a legislator discovers the means of laying men under a necessity of being virtuous, and causing the passions to bear no other fruit than probity and wisdom.

Now, if the examination of these ideas, so proper to render men virtuous, be forbidden by the two species of men in power above-mentioned, the only means of hastening the progress of morality will be, as I have already said, to shew that these protectors of stupidity are the most cruel enemies of human nature, and to snatch from their hands the sceptre of ignorance, by which they are authorized to command a stupid people. Upon which I shall observe, that this, simple and easy as it appears in speculation, is extremely difficult in the execution. Indeed, there are men who have great and judicious minds, united to the virtue and strength of soul: there are men, who, being persuaded that a citizen without courage is also without virtue, are sensible that the fortune, and even the life of every individual is not his own, but is in a manner a deposit, which he ought always to be ready to deliver up when the safety of the public makes it necessary; but the number of such men is always too few for them to enlighten the public: besides, virtue must ever be of little weight, when the manners of an age fix upon it the rust of ridicule. Thus morality and the legislation, which I consider as one and the same science, can only make an insensible progress.

E S S A Y III

Chapter XVI: To What Cause Ought We to Attribute the Indifference of Certain Nations with Regard to Virtue?

. . . The most exalted virtue, as well as the most shameful vice, is the effect of the greater or less intenseness of the pleasure it affords us.

Thus we can form no exact idea of the degree of our virtue, till we have discovered, by a scrupulous examination, the number and degrees of those pains which a passion, as for instance, the love of justice or of glory, may enable us to support. The person to whom esteem is every thing, and life nothing, will, like Socrates, submit rather to suffer death, than meanly to beg for life. He who is become the soul of a republican state, in which pride and glory render him passionately desirous of the public welfare, will, like Cato,[7] prefer death to the mortification of seeing himself and his country submit to the yoke of arbitrary power. But such actions are the effect of the greatest love of glory. This is the highest pitch to which the strongest passions can attain, and here nature has fixed the bounds of human virtue.

In vain would we deceive ourselves; we necessarily become the enemies of men, when we can no otherwise be happy than by their misfortunes. It is the pleasing conformity we find between our own interest and that of the public, a conformity generally produced by the desire of esteem, that gives us those tender sentiments that are rewarded by their affection. He who to be virtuous must always conquer his inclinations, must necessarily be a wicked man. The meritorious virtues are never certain and infallible virtues. It is impossible in practice for a man to deliver himself up, in a manner, daily to a war with the passions, without losing many battles.

Being always forced to yield to the most powerful interest some of that love for esteem, we never sacrifice any great pleasure to it, but those it procures. If, on certain occasions, sacred personages have sometimes exposed themselves to the contempt of the public, it is because they would not sacrifice their salvation to their glory; and if some women resist the solicitations of a prince, it is because they believe, that his conquest would not recompence them for the loss of their esteem: thus, there are few insensible to the love of a king, who is young and charming; and none who resist such beneficent, amiable, and powerful, beings as we paint the sylphs and genii, who, by a thousand allurements, can at once intoxicate all the senses of a mortal.

This truth, founded on self-love, is not only known, but even acknowledged, by the legislators.

Convinced that self-love is, in general, the strongest passion of mankind, the legislators have never pronounced it criminal, for a man to kill another in his own defence, nor blamed a citizen for not devoting himself to death, like Decius[8] for the preservation of his country.

The virtuous man is not then he who sacrifices his pleasures, habits, and strongest passions, to the public welfare, since it is impossible that such a man should exist; but he whose strongest passion is so conformable to the general interest, that he is almost constantly necessitated to be virtuous. For this reason, he approaches nearer to perfection, and has a greater claim to the name of being a virtuous man, who requires stronger motives of pleasure, and a more powerful interest, in order to determine him to do a bad action, than are necessary to his performing a good one, and consequently supposes that he has a greater passion for virtue than for vice. . . .

We are on the contrary less virtuous, as less powerful motives lead us to the commission of a crime. . . .

This is what distinguishes the virtuous from the vicious man, in a manner the most clear, precise, and conformable, to experience; on this plan the public might make an exact thermometer, which would shew the various degrees of virtue and vice in each citizen, if, by penetrating to the bottom of the heart, we could discover there the value that each sets on his virtue. But the impossibility of arriving at this knowledge forces us to judge of men only by their actions – a judgment extremely faulty in every particular, but on the whole sufficiently conformable to the general interest, and almost as useful as if it were just.

After having inquired into the influence of the passions, and explained the cause of that mixture of virtue and vice observable in all men; having stated the limits of virtue, and at length fixed the idea that belongs to the word virtuous; we are now at liberty to judge, if we ought to attribute the indifference of certain nations for virtue to nature, or to a particular legislation.

If pleasure be the only object of man's pursuit, we need only imitate nature, in order to inspire a love of virtue. Pleasure informs us of what she would have done, and pain what she forbids, and man will readily obey her mandates. Why may not the legislature, armed with the same power, produce the same effects? Were men without passions, there would be no means of producing a reformation; but the love of pleasure, against which men, possessed of a probity more venerable than enlightened, have constantly exclaimed, is a bridle by which the passions of the individuals might always be directed to the public good. The hatred most men have for virtue is not then the effect of the corruption of their nature, but of the imperfection of the legislation. It is the legislation, if I may venture to say so, that excites us to vice, by mingling it with pleasure; the great art of the legislator is that of separating them, and making no proportion between the advantage the villain can receive from his crime, and the pain to which he exposes himself. If among the rich men, who are often less virtuous than the indigent, we see few robbers and assassins, it is because the profit obtained by robbery is never to a rich man proportionable to the hazard of a capital punishment: but this is not the case with respect to the indigent; for the disproportion falling infinitely short of being so great with respect to him, virtue and vice are in a manner placed in an equilibrium. Not that I would here pretend to insinuate, that men ought to be driven as with a rod of iron. In an excellent legislation, and among a virtuous people, contempt, which deprives man of all consolation, and leaves him desolate in the midst of his native country, is a motive sufficient to form virtuous minds. Every other kind of punishment renders men timid, inactive, and stupid. The kind of virtue produced by the fear of punishment resembles its origin; this virtue is pusillanimous, and without knowledge; or rather fear, which only smothers vice, but produces no virtues. True virtue is founded on the love of esteem and glory, and the fear of contempt, which is more terrible than death itself.

Editor's Notes

1. Helvétius uses the term *probité*, meaning "integrity," as a general term for a morally praiseworthy disposition.
2. Horatius is the hero of a Roman legend. During the Roman struggle against the Etruscans, toward the end of the sixth century B.C.E., Horatius single-handedly held a bridge against the Etruscan army.
3. The Greek poetess, who according to one legend threw herself off a rock into the sea because of thwarted love.
4. The soldier Marcus Curtius, according to Roman legend, leapt with his horse and all his weapons into a chasm that opened in the Roman forum, in order to do what the soothsayers indicated was needed to save Rome.
5. Montaigne's skeptical outlook is most fully expressed in his "Apology for Raymond Sebond," selections from which are given in the Prolegomena in Volume I of this anthology.
6. Queen Christina of Sweden (1626–89), regarded as an enlightened ruler; she corresponded with Descartes and brought him to Sweden to teach her philosophy.
7. Cato of Utica (95–46 B.C.E.), often held up as embodying the ideal of the Stoic sage, took his own life on seeing that his political cause was lost.
8. Roman emperor (c. 200–51) who died after valiantly defending his country against invaders.

Further Reading

There are no recent translations of Helvétius, but the old translations of *On the Mind* and of *On Man* are adequate.

Two books by Lester Crocker discuss Helvétius in the general context of French Enlightenment thought: *An Age of Crisis, Man and World in Eighteenth Century French Thought* (Baltimore: Johns Hopkins University Press, 1959); and *Nature and Culture: Ethical Thought in the French Enlightenment* (Baltimore: Johns Hopkins University Press, 1963). The former examines metaphysical issues including free will, and the latter looks at moral issues; mention of Helvétius is scattered throughout both. Ira O. Wade comments on Helvétius at various places in his two-volume study *The Structure and Form of the French Enlightenment* (Princeton, N.J.: Princeton University Press, 1977); see especially vol. 2, pp. 262–97, which summarizes Helvétius's main work and Diderot's criticism.

Ian Cumming, *Helvétius: His Life and Place in the History of Educational Thought* (London: Routledge & Kegan Paul, 1955), studies an issue of considerable importance to Helvétius but does not give adequate attention to his ethics. Irving L. Horowitz, *Claude Helvétius: Philosopher of Democracy and Enlightenment* (New York: Paine–Whitman, 1954), is a more general treatment from a Marxist perspective. There is an excellent study of the background of, and response to, *On Man* in D. W. Smith, *Helvétius, a Study in Persecution* (Oxford: Clarendon Press, 1965), which also covers the philosophy.

Paul Henri Thiry, Baron d'Holbach

Introduction

Holbach was born in 1723 in a small town in Germany and named Paul Heinrich Dietrich. A wealthy uncle provided for his education, brought him to Paris, and left him a fortune and the title under which he became famous – or notorious – as the most persistent and outspoken opponent of religion among the Enlightenment writers. Educated as a chemist and fluent in several languages, Holbach was brought into contact with the advanced thinkers of Paris by Diderot, who wanted him to write scientific articles for the *Encyclopedia*. Holbach wrote several hundred of them and then branched out into other fields. His views were so radical for his times that they could not be published openly. Consequently, he had many of his manuscripts published in Holland, either anonymously or under assumed names. Holbach translated numerous anti-Christian books from English, wrote many others, and supported the authors of still other works that, like his, supported materialism, atheism, and hedonism and attacked the power of organized religion.

No one is quite sure exactly what or how much Holbach wrote himself, but a number of works are commonly assumed to be his. One of the earliest is *Christianity Unveiled* (1761). It was followed by, among others, *The Sacred Contagion; or Natural History of Superstition* (1768) and *Critical History of Jesus Christ* (1770). In 1770 Holbach also published his major philosophical work, the *System of Nature; or On the Laws of the Physical World and the Moral World*. He ended this book with a moral exhortation to man, the general message of which was expanded in a series of volumes including *The Social System; or Natural Principles of Morality and Politics* (1773) and *Universal Morality; or The Duties of Man, Founded on His Nature* (1776). Many of these volumes were immediately translated into English.

Holbach was not only an indefatigable writer and organizer of propagandistic writings by others; he was also the center of a group of intellectuals who met regularly at his house for dinner and discussion. Diderot, Rousseau, Grimm, Helvétius, Condorcet, Turgot, and d'Alembert were among those who attended regularly, and among the many foreigners who came were Gibbon, Hume, Adam Smith, Laurence Sterne, Beccaria, and Benjamin Franklin. If the group was not a consciously controlled secret society of advanced thinkers, it certainly was a forum for exchange of radical ideas and for untrammeled criticism of existing institutions.

For all his radicalism, Holbach was happily married, fond of his children, comfortable with his great wealth, and happy to be a generous patron to those in need. Although his books aroused considerable outcry, he managed to escape punishment and busily continued undermining the credibility of established French institutions until his death in 1789.

The moral philosophy Holbach propagated was simple and unoriginal. We are self-interested in all our actions; the best means to achieve our own good is to work for the good of everyone; but ignorance keeps us from doing so, and ignorance is itself sustained by those in power, who fear losing their superiority over others. This view is built on naturalism. Matter in motion is all that exists; humans are simply a part of nature; their bodies are machines; and their thoughts are determined by their movements. For these ideas Holbach drew not only on Hobbes, Spinoza, and Hume but also on several French writers, such as Diderot and La Mettrie, who held similar views. Although Holbach was perhaps more systematic in his exposition of some of these themes than others were, he was also more repetitive and far more rhetorical. He was animated by an inexhaustible passion against religion – Christianity first and foremost, but by no means exclusively – and he saw his ideas and his systems as providing the secular standpoint that must replace it if human happiness is ever to be achieved.

I have included Holbach in this anthology so that the reader can see at first hand something of the anger that religion could inspire in its Enlightenment enemies. In turn, this anger helps us understand the meaning of the appeals to nature and to self-interest that pervade so much of the writing of this period. Nature is what is not supernatural. Self-interest is what does not postpone human happiness to another life: for these writers it was not, as it was for some, what enables us to defer our reward until we reach another world. Materialism is the refusal to believe in a self divided in ways that would warrant both the postponement of happiness and the hegemony of a privileged spiritual elite entitled to direct us in the meantime.

In his preface to the *System of Nature* Holbach observed that "the most important of our duties is to seek means by which we may destroy delusions that can never do more than mislead us." To a greater extent than his enlightened French allies, Holbach believed that philosophical ideas systematically organized and disseminated to as large an audience as possible provide those means. It is worth seeing just how he tried to work this out.

For the first selection here I have translated parts of Holbach's *Universal Morality*, which outlines his moral philosophy with – for him – unusual concision. The second selection is from Chapter IX of the *System of Nature*, showing Holbach's attitude toward religion. The writer to whom the book was attributed on its first publication was "M. de Mirabaud," a member of the French Academy who had been dead for a decade. The translation is by Samuel Wilkinson.

Universal Morality; or, The Duties of Man, Founded on Nature

FIRST SECTION: GENERAL PRINCIPLES AND DEFINITIONS

Chapter I: Of Morality, Duties, Moral Obligation

Morality [*la morale*] is the science of the relations among men and of the duties that flow from these relations. Or, if you wish, morality is the knowledge of what must necessarily be done or avoided by intelligent and reasonable beings who wish to preserve themselves and to live happily in society.

To be universal, morality should be formed according to the nature of man in general, that is, founded on his essence, on the properties and qualities constantly found in all beings of the species and by which it is distinguished from other animals. From this we see that morality presupposes the science of human nature.

Science can only be the fruit of experience. To know something is to have experienced the effects it produces, the manner in which it acts, and the different points of view from which one may envisage it. The science of manners [*des moeurs*], in order to be certain, should be nothing but the consequence of constant, reiterated, invariable experiences, which alone can provide true knowledge of the relations among beings of the human species.

The relations among men are the different ways in which they act on one another or by which they influence their reciprocal well-being.

The duties of morality are the means that a being who is intelligent and susceptible to experience should use in order to gain the happiness toward which his nature ceaselessly forces him to move. Walking is a duty for whoever wishes to go from one place to another; to be useful is a duty for whoever wishes to deserve the affection and esteem of his fellowmen; to abstain from doing ill is a duty for whoever fears to draw on himself the hatred and resentment of those whom he knows can contribute to his own happiness. In a word, duty is the fitness of means to the end that one proposes for oneself; wisdom consists in proportioning the means to this end, that is, employing them usefully to obtain the happiness that man is made to desire.

Moral obligation is the necessity of doing or avoiding certain actions for the sake of the well-being that we seek in social life. He who wills the end should will the means. Every being who wants to make himself happy is obliged to follow the route best suited to lead him to happiness and to avoid the one that leads away from his goal, on pain of being unhappy. Knowledge of that route or of the means is the fruit of experience, which alone can let us know the goal we should set ourselves and the surest ways of arriving there.

The bonds that unite men to one another are nothing but the obligations and the duties to which they are submitted in accordance with the relations among them. These obligations and duties are the conditions without which they cannot reciprocally make themselves happy. Such are the bonds that unite fathers and children, sovereigns and subjects, society and its members, and so forth.

These principles suffice to convince us that man does not bring with him from birth the knowledge of the duties of morality and that nothing is more chimerical than the opinion of those who attribute innate moral sentiments to man. The ideas he has of good and ill, of pleasure and pain, of the objects he should seek or flee, desire or fear, can only be the consequence of experience, and he cannot rely on his experiences except when they are constant, reiterated, and accompanied by judgment, reflection, and reason.

On entering the world, man brings with him only the faculty of sensing [*de sentir*], and from his sensibility there flow all the faculties called intellectual. To say that we have moral ideas anterior to experience of the good or ill that objects make us experience is to say that we know the causes without having felt their effects.

Chapter II: Of Man and His Nature

Man is a sensible, intelligent, reasonable, sociable being who at every instant of his life seems uninterruptedly to preserve his existence and render it agreeable.

However prodigious the variety found among individuals of the human species, they have a common nature that never deceives. There is no man who does not propose some good at every moment of his life, none who, using the means he thinks most appropriate, does not seek happiness for himself and to secure himself against pain. We deceive ourselves often about both the goal and the means, because we either lack experience or are not in a condition to use what we have learned. Ignorance and error are the true causes of men's wanderings and of the unhappiness that they draw on themselves. . . .

Chapter IV: Of Pleasure and Pain; of Happiness

. . . Among the impressions or sensations that man receives from the objects that impinge on him, some please him by their conformity with the nature of his machine,[1] and others displease him by the trouble and disarray that they convey to it. As a result, he approves of the one and wishes it would continue or renew itself in him, whereas he disapproves of the other and wishes it to vanish. . . .

To love an object is to desire its presence, to want it to continue to produce on our senses impressions suitable to our nature. . . . We love a friend because his presence, his conversation, his estimable qualities cause us pleasure. . . .

Every agreeable sensation or movement excited in us that we want to persist is called "good" or "pleasure," and the object producing that impression in us is called "good," "useful," or "agreeable." Every sensation that we desire to end because it troubles and disturbs the order of our machine is called "bad" or "pain," and the object that excites it is called "bad," "harmful," "wicked," or "disagreeable." Durable and continued pleasure is called "happiness," "well-being, or "felicity"; continued pain is called "unhappiness" or "misfortune." Happiness is thus a state of continued acquiescence in modes of feeling and being that we find agreeable or conforming to our nature.

Man by his nature must necessarily love pleasure and hate pain. . . .

Pleasure ceases to be a good and becomes an evil as soon as it produces in us, either immediately or by its consequences, effects harmful to conservation and contrary to our permanent well-being. . . .

Only experience can teach us to distinguish the pleasures to which we may yield ourselves without fear or that we should prefer from those that have dangerous consequences for us. . . .

Chapter VI: Of Interest, or of Love of Self

Our desires, excited by real or imaginary needs, constitute interest, a term that designates in general what each man desires because he believes it useful or necessary for his own well-being – in a word, the object in the enjoyment of which each takes his pleasure or happiness to consist. The interest of the voluptuary is in sensual pleasure; the miser places his in the possession of his treasures; . . . the interest of the man of letters consists in deserving glory. . . .

It is thus indubitable that every individual of the human species acts and can only act out of interest. The word "interest," like the word "pleasure," presents to the mind only the love of good, the desire of happiness. One cannot blame men for being interested (which means only having needs and passions) except when they have interests, passion, or needs that are harmful either to themselves or to beings with interests with which theirs do not accord.

It is according to their interests that men are good or evil. . . .

If sometimes love of self seems to have no part in our actions, it is when the heart is troubled, enthusiasm intoxicates, one does not reason, one does not calculate; and in the disorder in which he finds himself he is capable of sacrificing himself for the object with which he was taken only because he found his happiness there. That is how a sincere friend can be brought sometimes to wish to perish for his friend. . . .

Chapter VII: Of the Usefulness of the Passions

. . . Nothing is more useless than to declaim against the passions; nothing, more impractical than the project of destroying them. The moralist should explain the advantages of virtue and the unsuitability of vice. The task of the legislator is to invite, to interest, to compel each individual, out of his own interest, to contribute to the general interest. . . .

Chapter XII: Of Habit, Instruction, Education

. . . Man, becoming what he is only with the aid of his own experience or of that with which others furnish him, education can modify him. From a mass that only senses and an almost inactive machine, he becomes, little by little, with the aid of culture, an experimenting being who knows truth and who, depending on how his first matter is altered, shows in the event more or less reason. . . .

Men's opinions are only the true or false associations of ideas that become habitual by being reiterated in their brains. If from infancy onward the idea of virtue is presented only as joined with ideas of pleasure, happiness, esteem, and veneration; if sad examples do not upset this association of ideas, there is every reason to believe that a child educated in this manner will become a man of good deeds, an estimable citizen. . . .

Reason is only the acquired habit of judging things healthily and of separating promptly what is fitting or harmful to our happiness. What is called moral instinct is the faculty of judging promptly and without hesitation, without reflection making part of our judgment. That instinct or that promptness in judging is due to a habit acquired by frequent exercise. In physical matters we behave instinctively toward objects that can give pleasure to our senses; in moral matters we experience a prompt sentiment of esteem, admiration, love toward virtuous actions, and horror of criminal acts whose tendency and goal we see in an instant.

The quickness with which this instinct or moral tact is exercised by enlightened and virtuous persons has made many moralists believe that the faculty is inherent in man from birth. It is the fruit, however, of reflection, of habituation, of culture. . . . In morality, as in the arts, the taste or aptitude for judging human actions well is a faculty acquired by exercise; it does not exist in the majority of men. The man without cultivation, the savage, and the man of the people have neither the instinct nor the moral taste of which we speak; on the contrary, they commonly judge very badly. . . .

These reflections make us feel the importance of a good education. It alone can form reasonable beings, virtuous by habituation, capable of making themselves happy and of contributing to the happiness of others. . . .

Chapter XIII: Of Conscience

. . . An enlightened conscience is the guide of the moral man. It can only be the fruit of extensive experience, perfect knowledge of truth, cultivated reason, and an education that has suitably modified a temperament suited to receive cultivation. A conscience of that stamp, far from being the effect in man of an inherent moral sense, far from being common to all the members of our species, is infinitely rare and is found only in a small number of select men, well born, provided with a lively imagination or a sensible heart, and fittingly modified. . . .

In most men, one finds only erroneous conscience, that is, one that judges in a manner little in accord with the nature of things or with truth. This comes from the false opinions one has formed or received from others, which make one attach the idea of goodness to actions one would find harmful if one examined them more thoroughly. Many people do ill and even commit crimes with assurance of conscience, because their conscience is falsified by prejudices. . . .

SECOND SECTION: THE DUTIES OF MAN IN THE STATE OF NATURE AND IN THE STATE OF SOCIETY; OF THE SOCIAL VIRTUES

Chapter III: Of Virtue in General

Virtue in general is a disposition or habitual and permanent will to contribute to the constant happiness of the beings with whom we live in society. This disposition can be solidly founded only on experience, reflection, and truth, with the help of which we know our true interests and the interests of those with whom we have relations. . . .

Chapter IV: Of Justice

Morality, properly speaking, has only one virtue to propose to men. The unique duty of a sociable being is to be just. Justice is the paradigmatic virtue. It serves as the basis of all the others. It may be defined as a habitual and permanent will or disposition to maintain men in the enjoyment of their rights and to do for them all that we wish they would do for us.

The rights of men consist in the free use of their wills and their faculties to procure the objects necessary for their own happiness. In the state of nature, isolated man has the right to take all the means he judges suitable to conserve and procure his well-being. . . .

In society, the rights of men, or the liberty of acting, are limited by justice, which shows them that they should act only in a manner suiting the well-being of the society, which is constructed to interest them because they are members of it. Everyone living in society would be unjust if the exercise of his own rights or his liberty were harmful to the rights, liberty, and well-being of those with whom he finds himself associated. Thus the rights of man in society consist in the use of his liberty in conformity with the justice he owes his associates. . . .

System of Nature

Chapter IX: Theological Notions Cannot Be the Basis of Morality – Comparison Between Theological Ethics and Natural Morality – Theology Prejudicial to the Human Mind

. . . Let us examine, without prejudice, if the theological ideas of the Divinity have ever given the solution to any one difficulty. Has the human understanding progressed a single step by the assistance of this metaphysical science? Has it not, on the contrary, had a tendency to obscure the more certain science of morals? Has it not, in many instances, rendered the most essential duties of our nature problematical? Has it not in a great measure confounded the notions of virtue and vice, of justice and injustice? Indeed, what is virtue, in the eyes of the generality of theologians? They will instantly reply, "that which is conformable to the will of the incomprehensible beings who govern nature." But may it not be asked, without offence to the individual opinions of any one, what are these beings, of whom they are unceasingly talking, without having the capacity to comprehend them? How can we acquire a knowledge of their will? They will forthwith reply, with a confidence that is meant to strike conviction on uninformed minds, by recounting what they are not, without even attempting to inform us what they are. If they do undertake to furnish an idea of them, they will heap upon their hypothetical beings a multitude of contradictory, incompatible attributes, with which they will form a whole, at once impossible for the human mind to conceive; or else they will refer to oracles, by which they insist their intentions have been promulgated to mankind. If, however, they are requested to prove the authenticity of these oracles, which are at such variance with each other, they will refer to miracles in support of what they assert: these miracles, independent of the difficulty there must exist to repose in them our faith, when, as we have seen, they are admitted even by the theologians themselves to be contrary to the intelligence, the immutability, to the omnipotence of their immaterial substances, are, moreover, warmly disputed by each particular sect, as being impositions, practised by the others for their own individual advantage. As a last resource, then, it will be necessary to accredit the integrity, to rely on the veracity, to rest on the good faith of the priests, who announce these oracles. On this again, there arise two almost insuperable difficulties: in the *first* place, who shall assure us of their actual mission? are we quite certain none of them may be mistaken? how shall we be justified in giving credence to their powers? are they not these priests themselves, who announce to us that they are the infallible interpreters of a being whom they acknowledge they do not at all know? In the *second* place, which set of these oracular developments are we to adopt? For to give currency to the whole, would, in point of fact, annihilate them entirely; seeing that no two of them run in unison with each other. This granted, the priests, that is to say, men extremely suspicious, but little in harmony with each other, will be the arbiters of morality; they will decide (according to their own uncertain knowledge, after their various passions, in conformity to the different perspectives under which they view these things) on the whole system of ethics; upon which absolutely rests the repose of the world – the sterling happiness of each individual. Would this be a desirable state? . . .

No! Arbitrary, inconclusive, contradictory notions, abstract, unintelligible speculations, can never be the sterling bases of the ethical science! They must be evident, demonstrable principles, deduced from the nature of man, founded upon his wants, inspired by rational education, rendered familiar by habit, made sacred by wholesome laws, that will flash conviction on our mind, render systems useful to mankind, make virtue dear to us – that will people nations with honest men – fill up the ranks with faithful subjects – crowd them with intrepid citizens. Incomprehensible beings can present nothing to our imagination, save vague ideas, which will never embrace any common point of union amongst those who shall contemplate them. . . .

It must be concluded from this, that however these systems are viewed, in whatever manner they are considered, they cannot serve for the basis of morality, which in its very nature is formed to be invariably the same. Irascible systems are only useful to those who find an interest in terrifying the ignorance of mankind, that they may advantage themselves of his fears – profit by his expiations. The nobles of the earth, who are frequently men not gifted with the most exemplary morals – who do not on all occasions exhibit the most perfect specimens of self-denial – who would not, perhaps, be at all times held up as mirrors of virtue, will not see these formidable systems, when they shall be inclined to listen to their passions; to lend themselves to the indulgence of their unruly desires: they will, however, feel no repugnance to make use of them to frighten others, to the end that they may preserve unimpaired their superiority; that they may keep entire their prerogatives; that they may more effectually bind them to servitude. Like the rest of mankind, they will see their God under the traits of his benevolence; they will always believe him indulgent to those outrages they may commit against their fellows, provided they shew due respect for him themselves; superstition will furnish them with easy means to turn aside his wrath; its ministers seldom omit a profitable opportunity, to expiate the crimes of human nature.

Morality is not made to follow the caprices of the imagination, the fury of the passions, the fluctuating interests of men: it ought to possess stability; to be at all times the same, for all the individuals of the human race; it ought neither to vary in one country, nor in one age from another: neither superstition, nor religion, has a privilege to make its immutability subservient to the changeable laws of their systems. There is but one method to give ethics this solidity; it has been more than once pointed out in the course of this work; it is only to be founded upon the nature of man, bottomed upon his duties, rested upon the relations subsisting between intelligent beings, who are in love with their happiness, who are occupied with their own preservation, who live together in society that they may with greater facility ascertain these ends. In short, we must take for the basis of morality the necessity of things.

In weighing these principles, which are self-evident, confirmed by constant experience, approved by reason, drawn from nature herself, we shall have an undeviating tone of conduct; a sure system of morality, that will never be in contradiction with itself. Man will have no occasion to recur to theological speculations to regulate his conduct in the visible world. We shall then be capacitated to reply to those who pretend that without them there can be no morality. If we reflect upon the long tissue of errors, upon the immense chain of wanderings, that flow from the obscure notions these various systems hold forth – of the sinister ideas which superstition in all countries inculcates; it would be much more conformable to truth to say, that all sound ethics, all morality, either useful to individuals or beneficial to society, is totally incompatible with systems which never represent their gods but under the form of absolute monarchs, whose good qualities are continually eclipsed by dangerous caprices. Consequently, we shall be obliged to acknowledge, that to establish morality upon a steady foundation, we must necessarily commence by at least quitting those chimerical systems upon which the ruinous edifice of supernatural morality has hitherto been constructed, which during such a number of ages, has been so uselessly preached up to a great portion of the inhabitants of the earth.

Whatever may have been the cause that placed man in his present abode, that gave him the faculties he possesses; whether the human species be considered as the work of nature, or whether it be supposed that he owes his existence to an intelligent being, distinguished from nature; the existence of man, such as he is, is a fact; we behold in him a being who thinks, who feels, who has intelligence, who loves himself, who tends to his own conservation, who in every moment of his duration strives to render his existence agreeable; who, the more easily to satisfy his wants and to procure himself pleasure, congregates in society with beings similar to himself; of whom his conduct can either conciliate the favour, or draw upon him the disaffection. It is, then, upon these general sentiments, inherent in his nature, which will subsist as long as his race shall endure, that we ought to found morality; which is only a science embracing the duties of men living together in society.

These duties have their spring in our nature, they are founded upon our necessities, because we cannot reach the goal of happiness, if we do not employ the requisite means: these means constitute the moral science. To be permanently felicitous, we must so comport ourselves as to merit the affection, so act as to secure the assistance of those beings with whom we are associated; these will only accord us their love, lend us their esteem, aid us in our projects, labour to our peculiar happiness, but in proportion as our own exertions shall be employed for their advantage. It is this necessity, flowing naturally out of the relations of mankind, that is called MORAL OBLIGATION. It is founded upon reflection, rested upon those motives competent to determine sensible, intelligent beings to pursue that line of conduct which is best calculated to achieve that happiness towards which they are continually verging. These motives in the human species, never can be other than the desire, always regenerating, of procuring good and avoiding evil. Pleasure and pain, the hope of happiness, or the fear of misery, are the only motives suitable to have an efficacious influence on the volition of sensible beings. To impel them towards this end, it is sufficient these motives exist and be understood; to have a knowledge of them, it is only requisite to consider our own constitution: according to this, we shall find we can only love those actions, approve that conduct, from whence result actual and reciprocal utility; this constitutes VIRTUE. In consequence, to conserve ourselves, to make our own happiness, to enjoy security, we are compelled to follow the routine which conducts to this end; to interest others in our own preservation, we are obliged to display an interest in theirs; we must do nothing that can have a tendency to interrupt that mutual co-operation which alone can lead to the felicity desired. Such is the true establishment of moral obligation.

Whenever it is attempted to give any other basis to morality than the nature of man, we shall always deceive ourselves. . . .

The morality of nature is clear, it is evident even to those who outrage it. It is not thus with superstitious morality; this is as obscure as the systems which prescribe it; or rather as fluctuating as the passions, as changeable as the temperaments, of those who expound them; if it was left to the theologians, ethics ought to be considered as the science of all others the most problematical, the most unsteady, the most difficult to bring to a point; it would require the most profound, penetrating genius, the most active, vigorous mind, to discover the principles of those duties man owes to himself, that he ought to exercise towards others; this would render the sources of the moral system attainable by a very small number of individuals; would effectually lock them up in the cabinets of the metaphysicians; place them under the treacherous guardianship of priests: to derive it from those systems, which are in themselves undefinable, with the foundations of which no one is actually acquainted, which each contemplates after his own mode, modifies after his own peculiar ideas, is at once to submit it to the caprice of every individual; it is completely to acknowledge, we know not from whence it is derived, nor whence it has its principles. Whatever may be the agent upon whom they make nature, or the beings she contains, to depend; with whatever power they may suppose him invested, it is very certain that man either does, or does not exist; but as soon as his existence is acknowledged, as soon as it is admitted to be what it actually is, when he shall be allowed to be a sensible being living in society, in love with his own felicity, they cannot without either annihilating him, or new modelling him, cause him to exist otherwise than he does. Therefore, according to his actual essence, agreeable to his absolute qualities, conformable to these modifications which constitute him a being of the human species, morality becomes necessary to him, and the desire of conserving himself will make him prefer virtue to vice, by the same necessity that he prefers pleasure to pain. If, following up the doctrine of the theologians, "that man hath occasion for supernatural grace to enable him to do good," it must be very injurious to sound principles of morality; because he will always wait for "the call from above," to exercise that virtue, which is indispensable to his welfare. . . .

Every thing that has been advanced evidently proves, that superstitious morality is an infinite loser when compared with the morality of nature, with which, indeed, it is found in perpetual contradiction. Nature invites man to love himself, to preserve his existence, to incessantly augment the sum of his happiness: superstition teaches him to be in love only with formidable doctrines, calculated to generate his dislike; to detest himself; to sacrifice to his idols his most pleasing sensations – the most legitimate pleasures of his heart. Nature counsels man to consult reason, to adopt it for his guide; superstition portrays this reason as corrupted, as a treacherous director, that will infallibly lead him astray. Nature warns him to enlighten his understanding, to search after truth, to inform himself of his duties; superstition enjoins him not to examine any thing, to remain in ignorance, to fear truth; it persuades him there are no relations so important to his interest, as those which subsist between himself and systems which he can never understand. Nature tells the being who is in love with his welfare, to moderate his passions, to resist them when they are found destructive to himself, to counteract them by substantive motives collected from experience; superstition desires a sensible being to have no passions, to be an insensible mass, or else to combat his propensities by motives borrowed from the imagination, which are as variable as itself. Nature exhorts man to be sociable, to love his fellow creatures, to be just, peaceable, indulgent, benevolent, to permit his associates to freely enjoy their opinions; superstition admonishes him to fly society, to detach himself from his fellow mortals, to hate them when their imagination does not procure them dreams conformable to his own; to break through the most sacred bonds, to maintain his own opinions, or to frustrate those of his neighbour; to torment, to persecute, to massacre, those who will not be mad after his own peculiar manner. Nature exacts that man in society should cherish glory, labour to render himself estimable, endeavour to establish an imperishable name, to be active, courageous, industrious; superstition tells him to be abject, pusillanimous, to live in obscurity, to occupy himself with ceremonies; it says to him, be useless to thyself, and do nothing for others. Nature proposes to the citizen, for his model, men endued with honest, noble, energetic souls, who have usefully served their fellow citizens; superstition recommends to his imitation mean, cringing sycophants; extols pious enthusiasts, frantic penitents, zealous fanatics, who for the most ridiculous opinions have disturbed the tranquility of empires. . . .

Superstition corrupts princes; these corrupt the law, which, like themselves, becomes unjust; from thence institutions are perverted; education only forms men who are worthless, blinded with prejudice, smitten with vain objects, enamoured of wealth, devoted to pleasures, which they must obtain by iniquitous means: thus nature, mistaken, is disdained; virtue is only a shadow quickly sacrificed to the slightest interest, while superstition, far from remedying these evils to which it has given birth, does nothing more than render them still more inveterate; or else engenders sterile regrets which it presently effaces: thus, by its operation, man is obliged to yield to the force of habit, to the general example, to the stream of those propensities, to those causes of confusion, which conspire to hurry all his species, who are not willing to renounce their own welfare, on to the commission of crime.

Here is the mode by which superstition, united with politics, exert their efforts to pervert, abuse, and poison the heart of man; the generality of human institutions appear to have only for their object to abase the human character, to render it more flagitiously wicked. Do not then let us be at all astonished if morality is almost every where a barren speculation, from which every one is obliged to deviate in practice, if he will not risk the rendering himself unhappy. Man can only have sound morals, when, renouncing his prejudices, he consults his nature; but the continued impulse which his soul is every moment receiving, on the part of more powerful motives, quickly compels him to forget those ethical rules which nature points out to him. He is continually floating between vice and virtue; we behold him unceasingly in contradiction with himself; if, sometimes, he justly appreciates the value of an honest, upright conduct, experience very soon shews him, that this cannot lead him to any thing which he has been taught to desire; on the contrary, that it may be an invincible obstacle to the happiness which his heart never ceases for an instant to search after. In corrupt societies it is necessary to become corrupt, in order to become happy.

Citizens, led astray at the same time both by their spiritual and temporal guides, neither knew reason nor virtue. The slaves both of their superstitious systems, and of men like themselves, they had all the vices attached to a slavery; kept in a perpetual state of infancy, they had neither knowledge nor principles; those who preached virtue to them, knew nothing of it themselves, and could not undeceive them with respect to those baubles in which they had learned to make their happiness consist. In vain they cried out to them to stifle those passions which every thing conspired to unloose: in vain they made the thunder of the gods roll to intimidate men whose tumultuous passions rendered them deaf. It was soon discovered that the gods of the heavens were much less feared than those of the earth; that the favour of the latter procured a much more substantive welfare than the promises of the former; that the riches of this world were more tangible than the treasures reserved for favorites in the next; that it was much more advantageous for men to conform themselves to the views of visible powers than to those of powers who were not within the compass of their visual faculties.

Thus society, corrupted by its priests, guided by their caprice, could only bring forth a corrupt offspring. It gave birth to avaricious, ambitious, jealous, dissolute citizens, who never saw any thing happy but crime; who beheld meanness rewarded; incapacity honoured; wealth adored; debauchery held in esteem; who almost every where found talents discouraged; virtue neglected; truth proscribed; elevation of soul crushed; justice trodden under foot; moderation languishing in misery; liberality of mind obligated to groan under the ponderous bulk of haughty injustice. . . .

If the nature of man was consulted in his politics, which supernatural ideas have so woefully depraved, it would completely rectify those false notions that are entertained equally by sovereigns and by subjects; it would contribute more amply than all the superstitions existing, to render society happy, powerful, and flourishing under rational authority. Nature would teach man, it is for the purpose of enjoying a greater portion of happiness, that mortals live together in society; that it is its own preservation, its own immediate felicity, that society should have for its determinate, unchangeable object: that without equity, a nation only resembles a congregation of enemies; that his most cruel foe, is the man who deceives him in order that he may enslave him; that the scourges most to be feared, are those priests who corrupt his chiefs, who, in the name of the gods assure them of impunity for their crimes: she would prove to him that association is a misfortune under unjust, negligent, destructive governments. . . .

It is, then, I repeat it, only by re-conducting man to nature, that we can procure him distinct notions, evident opinions, certain knowledge; it is only by shewing him his true relations with his fellows, that we can place him on the road to happiness. The human mind, blinded by theology, has scarcely advanced a single step. Man's superstitious systems have rendered him sceptical on the most demonstrable truths. Superstition, while it pervaded every thing, while it had an universal influence, served to corrupt the whole:

philosophy, dragged in its train, although it swelled its triumphant procession, was no longer any thing but an imaginary science: it quitted the real world to plunge into the sinuosities of the ideal, inconceivable labyrinths of metaphysics; it neglected nature, who spontaneously opened her book to its examination, to occupy itself with systems filled with spirits, with invisible powers, which only served to render all questions more obscure; which, the more they were probed, the more inexplicable they became: which took delight in promulgating that which no one was competent to understand. In all difficulties it introduced the Divinity; from thence things only became more and more perplexed, until nothing could be explained. Theological notions appear only to have been invented to put man's reason to flight; to confound his judgment; to deceive his mind; to overturn his clearest ideas in every science. In the hands of the theologian, logic, or the art of reasoning, was nothing more than an unintelligible jargon, calculated to support sophism, to countenance falsehood, to attempt to prove the most palpable contradictions. Morality, as we have seen, became wavering and uncertain, because it was founded on ideal systems, never in harmony with themselves, which, on the contrary, were continually contradicting their own most positive assertions. Politics, as we have elsewhere said, were cruelly perverted by the fallacious ideas given to sovereigns of their actual rights. Jurisprudence was determinately submitted to the caprices of superstition, which shackled labour, chained down human industry, controlled activity, and fettered the commerce of nations. Every thing, in short, was sacrificed to the immediate interests of these theologians: in the place of every rational science, they taught nothing but an obscure, quarrelsome metaphysics, which but too often caused the blood of those unhappy people to flow copiously who were incapable of understanding its hallucinations. . . .

Let us then conclude, that theology with its notions, far from being useful to the human species, is the true source of all those sorrows which afflict the earth; of all those errors by which man is blinded; of those prejudices which benumb mankind; of that ignorance which renders him credulous; of those vices which torment him; of those governments which oppress him. Let us be fully persuaded that those theological, supernatural ideas, with which man is inspired from his infancy, are the actual causes of his habitual folly; are the springs of his superstitious quarrels; of his sacred dissensions; of his inhuman persecutions. Let us, at length, acknowledge, that they are these fatal ideas which have obscured morality; corrupted politics; retarded the progress of the sciences; annihilated happiness; banished peace from the bosom of mankind. Then let it be no longer dissimulated, that all those calamities, for which man turns his eyes towards heaven, bathed in tears, have their spring in the imaginary systems he has adopted; let him, therefore, cease to expect relief from them; let him seek in nature, let him search in his own energies, those resources, which superstition, deaf to his cries, will never procure for him. Let him consult the legitimate desires of his heart, and he will find that which he oweth to himself, also that which he oweth to others; let him examine his own essence, let him dive into the aim of society, from thence he will no longer be a slave; let him consult experience, he will find truth, and he will discover, that *error can never possibly render him happy.*

Editor's Note

1. That is, his body.

Further Reading

There are no recent editions or translations of Holbach's works, and the secondary literature on him is scanty. Virgil W. Topazio, *D'Holbach's Moral Philosophy* (Geneva: Institut et Musée Voltaire, 1956), summarizes English and French writers who influenced Holbach and reviews his antireligious and moral thought. The two volumes by Lester Crocker, *An Age of Crisis: Man and World in Eighteenth Century French Thought* (Baltimore: Johns Hopkins University Press, 1959) and *Nature and Culture: Ethical Thought in the French Enlightenment* (Baltimore: Johns Hopkins University Press, 1963), contain discussions of Holbach's views on metaphysical and moral issues. Ira O. Wade, *The Structure and Form of the French Enlightenment* (Princeton, N.J.: Princeton University Press, 1977), also examines Holbach; see especially vol. 2, pp. 298–320. A. C. Kors, *D'Holbach's Coterie* (Princeton, N.J.: Princeton University Press, 1976), provides a good study of Holbach's group of friends and their regular discussions.

William Paley

Introduction

William Paley was not a very original thinker. The philosophical part of his treatise on ethics is an assemblage of ideas developed by others and is presented to be learned by students rather than to be debated by colleagues. But this lack of originality did not stand in the way of Paley's success. His *Principles of Moral and Political Philosophy* (1785) was a required text at Cambridge University until the 1830s and was widely taught elsewhere in Britain and in the United States. Most of the book is taken up by detailed discussion of our duties to God, ourselves, and others. The opening part gives the fullest account available of the position generally known as theological utilitarianism, and as such it is still worthy of study.

Paley was born in 1743 and died in 1805. He studied at Cambridge, graduating in 1763 with great distinction. He taught at a small school near London until he was called back to Cambridge, where for some years he gave instruction in moral philosophy, divinity, and the Greek testament. Through personal connections Paley obtained various positions in the Church of England, the highest of which was that of archdeacon of Carlisle. His *Moral and Political Philosophy* was based on lectures he had given at Cambridge, and his later works were defenses of Christianity. The *View of the Evidences of Christianity* (1794) defended the credibility of miracles. The *Natural Theology* (1802) is an elaborate restatement of the argument from design, the claim that empirically observable features of the world in which we live show so many marks of having been designed for a purpose that we cannot resist the conclusion that the universe must have been created by a superior intelligence. Hume had written a devastating attack on all such arguments many years before Paley published, but Paley did not try to reply to it. His theological books, however, were popular with the clergy, were widely read and taught, and brought him further profitable positions in the church.

It is worth noting that Paley's *Moral and Political Philosophy* was published before Bentham's *Introduction to the Principles of Morals and Legislation*. Indeed, Paley's success is said to have finally stirred Bentham to publish his book, which had been written some years earlier. For decades, moreover, Bentham's work went unnoticed and Paley was accepted as the orthodox representative of utilitarianism.

The *Moral and Political Philosophy* opens with the declaration that "Moral Philosophy, Morality, Ethics, Casuistry, Natural Law, all mean the same thing; namely, that science which teaches men their duty and the reasons of it." As this suggests, and as the reader will see, Paley was not much interested in the subtleties of the science. But he did make some noteworthy points. His attack on all possible positions other than utilitarianism is similar in outline to a kind of criticism that Bentham worked out more fully and that is still used by contemporary utilitarians, and Paley paid considerable attention to the importance of rules in a utilitarian ethic – a matter concerning which he seems to have had more sophisticated views than Bentham did.

Paley based his moral principle on theological considerations that Bentham did not use. And there are differences in addition to this one in the versions of utilitarianism that the two developed. Most notably, Paley did not share Bentham's total rejection of the language of rights. Rather, he simply adopted the natural law vocabulary, attributing a wide variety of rights to humankind but making no attempt to show that this attribution was directed by his utilitarian principle.

Paley's acceptance of rights did not lead him to political and social views that were consistently reformist. He was strongly opposed to the slave trade and argued – before it was fashionable to do so – that it should be abolished. Paley also produced a once-notorious image of property that sounds as if it should have caused him to be quite radical in his thoughts on ownership. In the chapter entitled "Of Property," which opens Book III of his *Moral and Political Philosophy*, he wrote:

If you should see a flock of pigeons in a field of corn; and if (instead of each picking where and what it liked . . .) you should see ninety-nine of them gathering all they got into a heap, reserving nothing for themselves but the chaff and refuse; keeping this heap for one, and that the weakest, perhaps the worst, pigeon of the flock; sitting round, and looking on, all the winter, whilst this one was devouring, throwing about, and wasting it; and if a pigeon more hardy or hungry than the rest, touched a grain of the hoard, all the others flying upon it, and tearing it to pieces; if you should see this, you would see nothing more than is every day practised and established among men.

Nonetheless, Paley drew no radical conclusions. He gave utilitarian reasons for holding that the distribution of property must simply accord with the positive laws of each country, and he wrote a pamphlet during the French Revolution entitled "Reasons for Contentment, Addressed to the Labouring Part of the British Public," urging British working-class pigeons not to emulate their French counterparts. The reader may wish to ask what, if anything, this shows about the usefulness of the principle of utility for morals and politics.

The following selections are from the *Moral and Political Philosophy*.

Moral and Political Philosophy

Book I: Preliminary Considerations

Chapter V: The Moral Sense

Upon the whole, it seems to me, either that there exist no such instincts as compose what is called the moral sense, or that they are not now to be distinguished from prejudices and habits; on which account they cannot be depended upon in moral reasoning: I mean that it is not a safe way of arguing, to assume certain principles as so many dictates, impulses, and instincts of nature, and then to draw conclusions from these principles, as to the rectitude or wrongness of actions, independent of the tendency of such actions, or of any other consideration whatever.

Aristotle lays down, as a fundamental and self-evident maxim, that nature intended barbarians to be slaves;[1] and proceeds to deduce from this maxim a train of conclusions, calculated to justify the policy which then prevailed. And I question whether the same maxim be not still self-evident to the company of merchants trading to the coast of Africa.

Nothing is so soon made as a maxim; and it appears from the example of Aristotle, that authority and convenience, education, prejudice, and general practice, have no small share in the making of them; and that the laws of custom are very apt to be mistaken for the order of nature.

For which reason, I suspect, that a system of morality, built upon instincts, will only find out reasons and excuses for opinions and practices already established, – will seldom correct or reform either.

But further, suppose we admit the existence of these instincts; what, it may be asked, is their authority? No man, you say, can act in deliberate opposition to them, without a secret remorse of conscience. But this remorse may be borne with: and if the sinner chuse to bear with it, for the sake of the pleasure or the profit which he expects from his wickedness; or finds the pleasure of the sin to exceed the remorse of conscience, of which he alone is the judge, and concerning which, when he feels them both together, he can hardly be mistaken, the moral-instinct man, so far as I can understand, has nothing more to offer.

For if he allege that these instincts are so many indications of the will of God, and consequently presages of what we are to look for hereafter; this, I answer, is to resort to a rule and a motive ulterior to the instincts themselves, and at which rule and motive we shall by-and-by arrive by a surer road: – I say *surer,* so long as there remains a controversy whether there be any instinctive maxims at all; or any difficulty in ascertaining what maxims are instinctive.

The celebrated question therefore becomes in our system a question of pure curiosity; and as such, we dismiss it to the determination of those who are more inquisitive, than we are concerned to be, about the natural history and constitution of the human species.

Chapter VII: Virtue

Virtue is "*the doing good to mankind, in obedience to the will of God, and for the sake of everlasting happiness.*"

According to which definition, "the good of mankind" is the subject; the "will of God," the rule; and "everlasting happiness," the motive, of human virtue.

Virtue has been divided by some moralists into *benevolence, prudence, fortitude,* and *temperance. Benevolence* proposes good ends; *prudence* suggests the best means of attaining them; *fortitude* enables us to encounter the difficulties, danger, and discouragements, which stand in our way in the pursuit of these ends; *temperance* repels and overcomes the passions that obstruct it. *Benevolence,* for instance, prompts us to undertake the cause of an oppressed orphan; *prudence* suggests the best means of going about it; *fortitude* enables us to confront the danger, and bear up against the loss, disgrace, or repulse, that may attend our undertaking; and *temperance* keeps under the love of money, of ease, or amusement, which might divert us from it.

Virtue is distinguished by others into two branches only, *prudence* and *benevolence: prudence,* attentive to our own interest; *benevolence,* to that of our fellow-creatures: both directed to the same end, the increase of happiness in nature; and taking equal concern in the future as in the present.

The four CARDINAL virtues are, *prudence, fortitude, temperance,* and *justice.*

But the division of virtue, to which we are in modern times most accustomed, is into duties: –

Towards *God;* as piety, reverence, resignation, gratitude, &c.

Towards *other men* (or relative duties); as justice, charity, fidelity, loyalty, &c.

Towards *ourselves;* as chastity, sobriety, temperance, preservation of life, care of health, &c.

More of these distinctions have been proposed, which it is not worth while to set down.

BOOK II: MORAL OBLIGATION

Chapter I: The Question, "Why Am I Obliged to Keep My Word?" Considered

Why am I obliged to keep my word?

Because it is right, says one. – Because it is agreeable to the fitness of things, says another. – Because it is conformable to reason and nature, says a third. – Because it is conformable to truth, says a fourth. – Because it promotes the public good, says a fifth. – Because it is required by the will of God, concludes a sixth.

Upon which different accounts, two things are observable: –

First, that they all ultimately coincide.

The fitness of things means their fitness to produce happiness; the nature of things means that actual constitution of the world, by which some things, as such and such actions, for example, produce happiness, and others misery. Reason is the principle, by which we discover or judge of this constitution: truth is this judgment expressed or drawn out into propositions. So that it necessarily comes to pass, that what promotes the public happiness, or happiness on the whole, is agreeable to the fitness of things, to nature, to reason, and to truth: and such (as will appear by and by) is the divine character, that what promotes the general happiness is required by the will of God, and what has all the above properties must needs be *right;* for right means no more than conformity to the rule we go by, whatever that rule be.

And this is the reason that moralists, from whatever different principles they set out, commonly meet in their conclusions; that is, they enjoin the same conduct, prescribe the same rules of duty, and, with a few exceptions, deliver upon dubious cases the same determinations.

Secondly, it is to be observed, that these answers all leave the matter *short;* for the inquirer may turn round upon his teacher with a second question, in which he will expect to be satisfied, namely, *Why* am I obliged to do what is right; to act agreeably to the fitness of things; to conform to reason, nature, or truth; to promote the public good, or to obey the will of God?

The proper method of conducting the inquiry is, First, to examine what we mean, when we say a man is *obliged* to do anything; and then to show *why* he is obliged to do the thing which we have proposed as an example, namely, "to keep his word."

Chapter II: What We Mean When We Say a Man Is "Obliged" to Do a Thing

A man is said to be *obliged, "when he is urged by a violent motive resulting from the command of another."*

I. "The motive must be violent." If a person, who has done me some little service, or has a small place in his disposal, ask me upon some occasion for my vote, I may possibly give it to him, from a motive of gratitude or expectation: but I should hardly say that I was *obliged* to give it him; because the inducement does not rise high enough. Whereas if a father or a master, any great benefactor, or one on whom my fortune depends, require my vote, I give it him of course: and my answer to all who ask me why I voted so and so is, that my father or my master *obliged* me; that I had received so many favours from, or had so great a dependence upon, such a one, that I was *obliged* to vote as he directed me.

Secondly, "It must result from the command of another." Offer a man a gratuity for doing anything, for seizing, for example, an offender, he is not *obliged* by your offer to do it; nor would he say he is; though he may be *induced, persuaded, prevailed upon, tempted.* If a magistrate or the man's immediate superior command it, he considers himself as *obliged* to comply, though possibly he would lose less by a refusal in this case than in the former.

I will not undertake to say that the words *obligation* and *obliged* are used uniformly in this sense, or always with this distinction: nor is it possible to tie down popular phrases to any constant signification: but wherever the motive is violent enough, and coupled with the idea of command, authority, law, or the will of a superior, there, I take it, we always reckon ourselves to be *obliged.*

And from this account of obligation it follows, that we can be obliged to nothing, but what we ourselves are to gain or lose something by; for nothing else can be a "violent motive" to us. As we should not be obliged to obey the laws, or the magistrate, unless rewards or punishments, pleasure or pain, somehow or other, depended upon our obedience; so neither should we, without the same reason, be obliged to do what is right, to practise virtue, or to obey the commands of God.

Chapter III: The Question, "Why Am I Obliged to Keep My Word?" *Resumed*

Let it be remembered, that to be *obliged,* is "to be urged by a violent motive, resulting from the command of another."

And then let it be asked, Why am I *obliged* to keep my word? and the answer will be, "because I am urged to do so by a violent motive" (namely the expectation of being after this life rewarded, if I do, or punished for it if I do not), "resulting from the command of another" (namely of God).

This solution goes to the bottom of the subject, as no further question can reasonably be asked.

Therefore, private happiness is our motive, and the will of God our rule.

When I first turned my thoughts to moral speculations, an air of mystery seemed to hang over the whole subject; which arose, I believe, from hence, – that I supposed, with many authors whom I read, that to be *obliged* to do a thing, was very different from being induced only to do it; and that the obligation to practise virtue, to do what is right, just, &c., was quite another thing, and of another kind, than the obligation which a soldier is under to obey his officer, a servant his master; or any of the civil and ordinary obligations of human life. Whereas, from what has been said it appears, that moral obligation is like all other obligations; and that *obligation* is nothing more than an *inducement* of sufficient strength, and resulting, in some way, from the command of another.

There is always understood to be a difference between an act of *prudence* and an act of *duty.* Thus, if I distrust a man who owed me a sum of money, I should reckon it an act of prudence to get another person bound with him; but I should hardly call it an act of duty. On the other hand, it would be thought a very unusual and loose kind of language to say, that, as I had made such a promise, it was *prudent* to perform it; or that, as my friend, when he went abroad, placed a box of jewels in my hands, it would be *prudent* in me to preserve it for him till he returned.

Now in what, you will ask, does the difference consist? inasmuch as, according to our account of the matter, both in the one case and the other, – in acts of duty as well as acts of prudence, – we consider solely what we ourselves shall gain or lose by the act.

The difference, and the only difference, is this; that in the one case, we consider what we shall gain or lose in the present world: in the other case, we consider also what we shall gain or lose in the world to come.

They who establish a system of morality, independent of a future state, must look out for some different idea of moral obligation, unless they can show that virtue conducts the possessor to certain happiness in this life, or to a much greater share of it than he could attain by a different behaviour.

To us there are two great questions:

I. Will there be after this life any distribution of rewards and punishments at all?

II. If there be, what actions will be rewarded, and what will be punished?

The first question comprises the credibility of the Christian religion, together with the presumptive proofs of a future retribution from the light of nature. The second question comprises the province of morality. Both questions are too much for one work. The affirmative therefore of the first, although we confess that it is the foundation upon which the whole fabric rests, must in this treatise be taken for granted.

Chapter IV: The Will of God

As the will of God is our rule; to inquire what is our duty, or what we are obliged to do, in any instance, is, in effect, to inquire what is the will of God in that instance? which consequently becomes the whole business of morality.

Now there are two methods of coming at the will of God on any point:

I. By his express declarations, when they are to be had, and which must be sought for in Scripture.

II. By what we can discover of his designs and disposition from his works; or, as we usually call it, the light of nature.

And here we may observe the absurdity of separating natural and revealed religion from each other. The object of both is the same, – to discover the will of God, – and, provided we do but discover it, it matters nothing by what means.

An ambassador, judging by what he knows of his sovereign's disposition, and arguing from what he has observed of his conduct, or is acquainted with of his designs, may take his measures in many cases with safety, and presume with great probability how his master would have him act on most occasions that arise: but if he have his commission and instructions in his pocket, it would be strange not to look into them. He will be directed by both rules: when his instructions are clear and positive, there is an end to all further deliberation (unless indeed he suspect their authenticity); where his instructions are silent or dubious, he will endeavour to supply or explain them, by what he has been able to collect from other quarters, of his master's general inclination or intentions.

Mr. Hume, in his fourth Appendix to his *Principles of Morals*,[2] has been pleased to complain of the modern scheme of uniting Ethics with the christian Theology. They who find themselves disposed to join in this complaint, will do well to observe what Mr. Hume himself has been able to make of morality without this union. And for that purpose, let them read the second part of the ninth section of the above essay; which part contains the practical application of the whole treatise, – a treatise which Mr. Hume declares to be "incomparably the best he ever wrote." When they have read it over, let them consider, whether any motives there proposed are likely to be found sufficient to withhold men from the gratification of lust, revenge, envy, ambition, avarice; or to prevent the existence of these passions. Unless they rise up from this celebrated essay with stronger impressions upon their minds than it ever left upon mine, they will acknowledge the necessity of additional sanctions. But the necessity of these sanctions is not now the question. If they be *in fact established,* if the rewards and punishments held forth in the Gospel will actually come to pass, they *must* be considered. Such as reject the christian Religion, are to make the best shift they can to build up a system, and lay the foundation of morality, without it. But it appears to me a great inconsistency in those who receive Christianity, and expect something to come out of it, to endeavour to keep all such expectations out of sight in their reasonings concerning human duty.

The method of coming at the will of God concerning any action, by the light of nature, is to inquire into "the tendency of the action to promote or diminish the general happiness." This rule proceeds upon the presumption, that God Almighty wills and wishes the happiness of his creatures; and, consequently, that those actions, which promote that will and wish, must be agreeable to him; and the contrary.

As this presumption is the foundation of our whole system, it becomes necessary to explain the reasons upon which it rests.

Chapter V: The Divine Benevolence

When God created the human species, either He wished their happiness, or He wished their misery, or He was indifferent and unconcerned about both.

If He had wished our misery, He might have made sure of his purpose, by forming our senses to be so many sores and pains to us, as they are now instruments of gratification and enjoyment; or by placing us amidst objects so ill-suited to our perceptions, as to have continually offended us, instead of ministering to our refreshment and delight. He might have made, for example, everything we tasted, bitter; everything we saw, loathsome; everything we touched, a sting; every smell, a stench; and every sound, a discord.

If He had been indifferent about our happiness or misery, we must impute to our good fortune (as all design by this supposition is excluded) both the capacity of our senses to receive pleasure, and the supply of external objects fitted to produce it. But either of these (and still more both of them) being too much to be attributed to accident, nothing remains but the first supposition, that God, when He created the human species, wished their happiness; and made for them the provision which He has made, with that view, and for that purpose.

The same argument may be proposed in different terms, thus: Contrivance proves design; and the predominant tendency of the contrivance indicates the disposition of the designer. The world abounds with contrivances: and all the contrivances which we are acquainted with, are directed to beneficial purposes. Evil, no doubt, exists; but is never, that we can perceive, the object of contrivance. Teeth are contrived to eat, not to ache; their aching now and then, is incidental to the contrivance, perhaps inseparable from it: or even, if you will, let it be called a defect in the contrivance; but it is not the *object* of it. This is a distinction which well deserves to be attended to. In describing implements of husbandry, you would hardly say of the sickle, that it is made to cut the reaper's fingers, though from the construction of the instrument, and the manner of using it, this mischief often happens. But if you had occasion to describe instruments of torture or execution, this engine, you would say, is to extend the sinews; this to dislocate the joints; this to break the bones; this to scorch the soles of the feet. Here, pain and misery are the very *objects* of the contrivance. Now, nothing of this sort is to be found in the works of nature. We never discover a train of contrivance to bring about an evil purpose. No anatomist ever discovered a system of organization calculated to produce pain and disease; or, in explaining the parts of the human body, ever said, this is to irritate; this to inflame; this duct is to convey the gravel to the kidneys; this gland to secrete the humour which forms the gout: if by chance he come at a part of which he knows not the use, the most he can say is, that it is useless: no one ever suspects that it is put there to incommode, to annoy, or to torment. Since then God hath called forth his consummate wisdom to contrive and provide for our happiness, and the world appears to have been constituted with this design at first; so long as this constitution is upholden by Him, we must in reason suppose the same design to continue.

The contemplation of universal nature rather bewilders the mind than affects it. There is always a bright spot in the prospect, upon which the eye rests; a single example, perhaps, by which each man finds himself more *convinced* than by all others put together. I seem, for my own part, to see the benevolence of the Deity more clearly in the pleasures of very young children, than in anything in the world. The pleasures of grown persons may be reckoned partly of their own procuring; especially if there has been any industry, or contrivance, or pursuit, to come at them; or if they are founded, like music, painting, &c. upon any qualification of their own acquiring. But the pleasures of a healthy infant are so manifestly provided for it by *another*, and the benevolence of the provision is so unquestionable, that every child I see at its sport, affords to my mind a kind of sensible evidence of the finger of God, and of the disposition which directs it.

But the example, which strikes each man most strongly, is the true example for him: and hardly two minds hit upon the same; which shows the abundance of such examples about us.

We conclude, therefore, that God wills and wishes the happiness of his creatures. And this conclusion being once established, we are at liberty to go on with the rule built upon it, namely, "that the method of coming at the will of God, concerning any action by the light of nature, is to inquire into the tendency of that action to promote or diminish the general happiness."

Chapter VI: Utility

So then actions are to be estimated by their tendency.* Whatever is expedient, is right. It is the utility of any moral rule alone, which constitutes the obligation of it.

But to all this there seems a plain objection, *viz.* that many actions are useful, which no man in his senses will allow to be right. There are occasions, in which the hand of the assassin would be very useful. The present possessor of some great estate employs his influence and fortune, to annoy, corrupt, or oppress, all about him. His estate would devolve, by his death, to a successor of an opposite character. It is useful, therefore, to dispatch such a one as soon as possible out of the way; as the neighbourhood will exchange thereby a pernicious tyrant for a wise and generous benefactor. It might be useful to rob a miser, and give the money to the poor: as the money, no doubt, would produce more happiness, by being laid out in food and clothing for half a dozen distressed families, than by continuing locked up in a miser's chest. It may be useful to get possession of a place, a piece of preferment, or of a seat in parliament, by bribery or false swearing: as by means of them we may serve the public more effectually than in our private station. What then shall we say? Must we admit these actions to be right, which would be to justify assassination, plunder, and perjury; or must we give up our principle, that the criterion of right is utility?

It is not necessary to do either.

The true answer is this; that these actions, after all, are not useful, and for that reason, and that alone, are not right.

To see this point perfectly, it must be observed that the bad consequences of actions are twofold, *particular* and *general.*

The particular bad consequence of an action, is the mischief which that single action directly and immediately occasions.

The general bad consequence is, the violation of some necessary or useful *general* rule.

Thus, the particular bad consequence of the assassination above described, is the fright and pain which the deceased underwent; the loss he suffered of life, which is as valuable to a bad man, as to a good one, or more so; the prejudice and affliction, of which his death was the occasion, to his family, friends, and dependents.

The general bad consequence is the violation of this necessary general rule, that no man be put to death for his crimes but by public authority.

Although, therefore, such an action have no particular bad consequences, or greater particular good consequences, yet it is not useful, by reason of the gen-

---

* Actions in the abstract are right or wrong, according to their *tendency;* the agent is virtuous or vicious, according to his *design.* Thus, if the question be, Whether relieving common beggars be right or wrong? we inquire into the *tendency* of such a conduct to the public advantage or inconvenience. If the question be, Whether a man remarkable for this sort of bounty is to be esteemed virtuous for that reason? we inquire into his *design,* whether his liberality sprang from charity or from ostentation? It is evident that our concern is with actions in the abstract.

eral consequence, which is of more importance, and which is evil. And the same of the other two instances, and of a million more which might be mentioned.

But as this solution supposes, that the moral government of the world must proceed by general rules, it remains that we show the necessity of this.

Chapter VII: The Necessity of General Rules

You cannot permit one action and forbid another, without showing a difference between them. Consequently, the same sort of actions must be generally permitted or generally forbidden. Where, therefore, the general permission of them would be pernicious, it becomes necessary to lay down and support the rule which generally forbids them.

Thus, to return once more to the case of the assassin. The assassin knocked the rich villain on the head, because he thought him better out of the way than in it. If you allow this excuse in the present instance, you must allow it to all who act in the same manner, and from the said motive; that is, you must allow every man to kill any one he meets, whom he thinks noxious or useless; which, in the event, would be to commit every man's life and safety to the spleen, fury, and fanaticism, of his neighbour; – a disposition of affairs which would soon fill the world with misery and confusion; and ere long put an end to human society, if not to the human species.

The necessity of general rules in human government is apparent: but whether the same necessity subsist in the divine economy, – in that distribution of rewards and punishments to which a moralist looks forward, – may be doubted.

I answer, that general rules are necessary to every moral government: and by moral government I mean any dispensation, whose object is to influence the conduct of reasonable creatures.

For if, of two actions perfectly similar, one be punished, and the other be rewarded or forgiven, which is the consequence of rejecting general rules, the subjects of such a dispensation would no longer know either what to expect or how to act. Rewards and punishments would cease to be such, – would become accidents. Like the stroke of a thunderbolt, or the discovery of a mine, like a blank or a benefit-ticket in a lottery, they would occasion pain or pleasure when they happened; but, following in no known order, from any particular course of action, they could have no previous influence or effect upon the conduct.

An attention to general rules, therefore, is included in the very idea of reward and punishment. Consequently, whatever reason there is to expect future reward and punishment at the hand of God, there is the same reason to believe, that He will proceed in the distribution of it by general rules.

Before we prosecute the consideration of general consequences any further, it may be proper to anticipate a reflection, which will be apt enough to suggest itself, in the progress of our argument.

As the general consequence of an action, upon which so much of the guilt of a bad action depends, consists in the *example;* it should seem, that if the action be done with perfect secrecy, so as to furnish no bad example, that part of the guilt drops off. In the case of suicide, for instance, if a man can so manage matters, as to take away his own life, without being known or suspected to have done so, he is not chargeable with any mischief from the example; nor does his punishment seem necessary, in order to save the authority of any general rule.

In the first place, those who reason in this manner do not observe, that they are setting up a general rule, of all others the least to be endured; namely, that secrecy, whenever secrecy is practicable, will justify any action.

Were such a rule admitted, for instance, in the case above produced; is there not reason to fear that people would be *disappearing* perpetually?

In the next place, I would wish them to be well satisfied about the points proposed in the following queries:

1. Whether the Scriptures do not teach us to expect that, at the general judgment of the world, the most secret actions will be brought to light.

2. For what purpose can this be, but to make them the objects of reward and punishment?

3. Whether, being so brought to light, they will not fall under the operation of those equal and impartial rules, by which God will deal with his creatures?

They will then become examples, whatever they be now; and require the same treatment from the judge and governor of the moral world, as if they had been detected from the first.

Chapter IX: Of Right

Right and obligation are reciprocal; that is, wherever there is a right in one person, there is a corresponding obligation upon others. If one man has a "right" to an estate; others are "obliged" to abstain from it: – If parents have a "right" to reverence from their children; children are "obliged" to reverence their parents: – and so in all other instances.

Now, because moral *obligation* depends, as we have seen, upon the will of God; *right,* which is correlative to it, must depend upon the same. Right therefore signifies, *consistency with the will of God.*

But if the divine will determine the distinction of right and wrong, what else is it but an identical proposition to say of God, that He acts *right?* or how is it possible to conceive even that He should act *wrong?* Yet these assertions are intelligible and significant. The case is this: By virtue of the two principles, that God wills the happiness of his creatures, and that the will of God is the measure of right and wrong, we arrive at certain conclusions; which conclusions become rules; and we soon learn to pronounce actions right or wrong, according as they agree or disagree with our rules, without looking any further: and when the habit is once established of stopping at the rules, we can go back and compare with these rules even the divine conduct itself: and yet it may be true (only not observed by us at the time) that the rules themselves are deduced from the divine will.

Right is a quality of persons or of actions.

Of persons; as when we say, such a one has a "right" to this estate; parents have a "right" to reverence from their children; the king to allegiance from his subjects; masters have a "right" to their servants' labour; a man has not a "right" over his own life.

Of actions; as in such expressions as the following: it is "right" to punish murder with death; his behaviour on that occasion was "right"; it is not "right" to send an unfortunate debtor to gaol; he did or acted "right," who gave up his place rather than vote against his judgment.

In this latter set of expressions, you may substitute the definition of right above given, for the term itself: *e.g.* it is "consistent with the will of God" to punish murder with death; – his behaviour on that occasion was "consistent with the will of God" – it is not "consistent with the will of God" to send an unfortunate debtor to gaol; – he did, or acted, "consistently with the will of God," who gave up his place rather than vote against his judgment.

In the former set, you must vary the construction a little, when you introduce the definition instead of the term. Such a one has a "right" to this estate, that is, it is "consistent with the will of God" that such a one should have it; – parents have a "right" to reverence from their children, that is, it is "consistent with the will of God" that children should reverence their parents; – and the same of the rest.

Editor's Notes

1. In the *Politics* I.5, Aristotle stated that it is not difficult to answer the question whether some men are intended by nature to be slaves. Just as there is a natural and expedient rule of the soul over the body, and of the male over the female, so when one man is as superior to another as the soul is to the body, "the lower sort are by nature slaves, and it is better for them as for all inferiors that they should be under the rule of a master" (1254b20–21, Jowett translation).
2. David Hume, *Enquiry Concerning the Principles of Morals*, app. IV, in which Hume debated whether talents and moral virtues are to be sharply distinguished. He held that the distinction is merely verbal, that theological ethics, with its insistence on rewards and punishments, made more of a distinction between talent and virtue than was warranted.

Further Reading

Paley's works, though reprinted innumerable times in the nineteenth century, have not been dignified with a modern edition, and relatively little has been written about him. M. L. Clark, *Paley* (Toronto: University of Toronto Press, 1974), is a good general study of his philosophy and theology. D. L. LeMahieu, *The Mind of William Paley* (Lincoln: University of Nebraska Press, 1976), concentrates on his natural theology. His moral theory figures here and there in Elie Halévy, *The Growth of Philosophic Radicalism*, trans. Mary Morris (London: Faber & Faber, 1928), and Paley shares a chapter with Bentham in Ernest Albee, *A History of English Utilitarianism* (London: Allen & Unwin, 1902). Somewhat more attention is paid to Paley's ethics in J. B. Schneewind, *Sidgwick's Ethics and Victorian Moral Philosophy* (Oxford: Clarendon Press, 1977); consult the index. Sir Ernest Barker has a chapter, "Paley and His Political Philosophy," in *Traditions of Civility* (Cambridge, England: Cambridge University Press, 1948).

Jeremy Bentham

Introduction

Born in 1748 into a prosperous middle-class family, Jeremy Bentham was sent to Oxford when he was only twelve (he never got over his dislike of, and contempt for, the mindless life there), and by the time he was twenty-one he was a full-fledged lawyer. Bentham did not intend to practice law; rather, he intended to provide a rational basis for law as a whole. He had a small private income and so was able to devote himself to his chosen task. In 1776 he published *A Fragment on Government*, which brought him to the attention of political leaders. Thereafter he mixed political activity with incessant writing, publishing much but writing so much more that neither he nor his many disciples and followers could prepare it all for the press during his lifetime. Books assembled from his manuscripts were translated into many languages, earning him honors abroad, and his practical projects and those of the Benthamites who worked with him earned him notoriety at home. One of his most devoted and most influential followers was James Mill, whose son John Stuart Mill was trained to be a Benthamite and at the age of seventeen edited a massive treatise by Bentham on constitutional law. Bentham died in 1832.

Bentham was a reformer, proposing changes in the laws of England, the courts, the colonial system, the Church of England, the schools, the banks, the prisons, and innumerable matters of daily life, ranging from grammar to sewage. To support his proposals he used a clear and simple test by which ordinary people as well as politicians could judge whether an action was right or an institution or law justified. The test was what Bentham called "utility," which meant usefulness. Usefulness, then, for what? For human happiness: whatever hinders human happiness more than it advances it is wrong; whatever advances it more than it hinders it is right. With this simple test Bentham thought he could justify the reforms that he quite correctly believed were needed in much of English life. His moral philosophy was thus his attempt to explain and support this principle and to spell out its bearing on reform.

Many of Bentham's ideas led to significant changes, thanks in large part to the energetic, intelligent, and devoted group of followers who developed and carried out his suggestions. His philosophy also attracted followers, who, like John Austin and James Mill, wanted to extend and improve it. The controversies caused by his practical reforms have long since died down. The controversies aroused by his philosophy are still with us.

The problem with England, Bentham held, was that too many of its institutions and customs were unreasonable. Humans aim at happiness; laws, courts, and social institutions generally therefore should serve to bring about happiness, but too often they do not. Most people would not accept these unreasonable arrangements if they clearly understood how detrimental they were. Moreover, rationality serves everyone alike, whereas custom and superstition serve only the hidden interests of powerful minorities. Bentham wanted to make society rational. He thought a philosophy would help him do this, because he believed that the irrationality of vested interests masked itself behind philosophical as well as religious slogans.

To clear the philosophical way for his reforms, Bentham developed a way of undermining the claims of his opponents. He attacked their positions using a theory of meaning. Like Hobbes before him and the logical positivists after him, Bentham thought that much damage was done by failure to pay attention to language. Language, he held, can be used to mystify and sanctify legal and political institutions. We must be able to see them for what they are if we are to make them serve the interests of everyone alike. A method of analyzing words to see what they really mean is therefore needed, and Bentham had one.

His method was not a new one. It had originated with John Locke. When you want to know what a word means, Bentham held, find out what in our experience it refers to. Whatever is real is something we can experience with our senses, and the names for such things are those of realities. Our immediate perceptions – the images, tastes, and feelings we receive through our senses, and our inner sensations such as pain or pleasure – have the best claim to be called "real." Everything else we can mean must somehow relate to them. We need to talk about much else besides these perceptions. But anything we wish to talk or think about in addition to what we directly experience should be considered a fictitious entity. It is in fact made up of some combination of sensory experiences. But it is given a name that makes it seem to be an existing entity all by itself, and then we are puzzled, as we cannot tell just what sort of entity it is. To clarify the name of a fictitious entity, therefore, what we must do is find the perceptions to which it refers. If there are none, the name is nonsense.

Bentham applied this method to clarifying the fictions central to the discussion of law and morals. Among the central ones are "good" and "obligation." If we clarify them, we will see that moral language is really about pleasure and pain. We all want whatever is good. But "good" can mean only "pleasure and the absence of pain," and this is all that "happiness" can mean as well. The fictional name "obligation" can refer only to some act we are directed to do, under the condition that if we fail to do it we will suffer some pain. So pleasure and pain are the realities underlying both "obligation" and "good," and the pursuit of pleasure must thus be the core of morality.

Bentham applied his reductive technique to all the traditional theories that disagreed with his view, thereby attempting to show that none of them can provide a rational way of settling moral issues. His own principle, he asserted, offers just such a procedure. It tells us to maximize pleasure and minimize pain for as many people as possible, that is, to bring about the greatest happiness for the greatest number.

Bentham believed his principle to have an advantage lacking in any other. Because everyone wants happiness and because Bentham's principle directs us to maximize it, he held that we all have a motive for doing what his principle directs. He could not see how we could be motivated to follow any other principle. And because a principle that no one can follow is entirely pointless, he thought that the confluence of his motivational theory with his moral principle was yet another argument for the thorough rationality of his position.

Philosophers before Bentham had offered to explain morality in terms of its conduciveness to happiness. Bentham himself saw David Hume as the first to make utility the basic notion in an account of morality, and Helvétius, Hartley, and Priestley as other forerunners. But Bentham clearly made the principle of utility into a directive to be used in conscious deliberation about what to do, and this was a radical departure from Hume. In fact, what distinguishes Bentham's moral outlook is precisely its unremitting insistence on testing every act and every institution by the principle of utility, together with its assurance that a quantitatively based answer to any moral question can always be attained.

The claim that we can deliberately direct all our moral decisions by methodically using a formula had not previously been made so powerfully. At about the time Bentham was working out his views, Kant in Germany was developing his. Like Bentham, Kant thought he had found a directive that anyone could use to make moral decisions and that each of us always has a motive to obey. Kant's views were constructed independently of Bentham's and were antithetical to his. But the radical difference of their principles accompanies an underlying commonality of belief, that it is the task of moral philosophy to show that there is a method that each person can use to arrive at justified moral decisions, and to show how we are motivated to act accordingly. They were arguing, albeit in quite different ways, that it is possible for humans to be autonomous moral agents.

The first set of selections given here is from Bentham's *Introduction to the Principles of Morals and Legislation*, set in type in 1781 but not published until 1789. I have omitted some of the footnotes; those I have left contain some important points. The second set of selections comes from Bentham's *Theory of Legislation* (London, 1864), a work assembled and translated into French from Bentham's own manuscripts by a Genevan disciple, Etienne Dumont, and translated back into English by an American follower, Richard Hildreth. In the first part of the book, "Principles of Legislation," Bentham repeats, sometimes word for word, much of the material published in the earlier *Introduction*, but he gives a better and sometimes fuller exposition of certain moral aspects of his theory.

An Introduction to the Principles of Morals and Legislation

CHAPTER I: OF THE PRINCIPLE OF UTILITY

I. Nature has placed mankind under the governance of two sovereign masters, *pain* and *pleasure*. It is for them alone to point out what we ought to do, as well as to determine what we shall do. On the one hand the standard of right and wrong, on the other the chain of causes and effects, are fastened to their throne. They govern us in all we do, in all we say, in all we think: every effort we can make to throw off our subjection, will serve but to demonstrate and confirm it. In words a man may pretend to abjure their empire: but in reality he will remain subject to it all the while. The *principle of utility* recognises this subjection, and assumes it for the foundation of that system, the object of which is to rear the fabric of felicity by the hands of reason and of law. Systems which attempt to question it, deal in sounds instead of sense, in caprice instead of reason, in darkness instead of light.

But enough of metaphor and declamation: it is not by such means that moral science is to be improved.

II. The principle of utility is the foundation of the present work: it will be proper therefore at the outset to give an explicit and determinate account of what is meant by it. By the principle of utility is meant that principle which approves or disapproves of every action whatsoever, according to the tendency which it appears to have to augment or diminish the happiness of the party whose interest is in question: or, what is the same thing in other words, to promote or to oppose that happiness. I say of every action whatsoever; and therefore not only of every action of a private individual, but of every measure of government.

III. By utility is meant that property in any object, whereby it tends to produce benefit, advantage, pleasure, good, or happiness, (all this in the present case comes to the same thing) or (what comes again to the same thing) to prevent the happening of mischief, pain, evil, or unhappiness to the party whose interest is considered: if that party be the community in general, then the happiness of the community: if a particular individual, then the happiness of that individual.

IV. The interest of the community is one of the most general expressions that can occur in the phraseology of morals: no wonder that the meaning of it is often lost. When it has a meaning, it is this. The community is a *fictitious body*,[1] composed of the individual persons who are considered as constituting as it were its *members*. The interest of the community then is, what? – the sum of the interests of the several members who compose it.

V. It is in vain to talk of the interest of the community, without understanding what is the interest of the individual.* A thing is said to promote the interest, or to be *for* the interest, of an individual, when it tends to add to the sum total of his pleasures: or, what comes to the same thing, to diminish the sum total of his pains.

VI. An action then may be said to be conformable to the principle of utility, or, for shortness sake, to utility, (meaning with respect to the community at large) when the tendency it has to augment the happiness of the community is greater than any it has to diminish it.

VII. A measure of government (which is but a particular kind of action, performed by a particular person or persons)[2] may be said to be conformable to or dictated by the principle of utility, when in like manner the tendency which it has to augment the happiness of the community is greater than any which it has to diminish it.

VIII. When an action, or in particular a measure of government, is supposed by a man to be conformable to the principle of utility, it may be convenient, for the purposes of discourse, to imagine a kind of law or dictate, called a law or dictate of utility: and to speak of the action in question, as being conformable to such law or dictate.

IX. A man may be said to be a partizan of the principle of utility, when the approbation or disapprobation he annexes to any action, or to any measure, is

---

* Interest is one of those words, which not having any superior *genus*, cannot in the ordinary way be defined.

determined by and proportioned to the tendency which he conceives it to have to augment or to diminish the happiness of the community: or in other words, to its conformity or unconformity to the laws or dictates of utility.

X. Of an action that is conformable to the principle of utility one may always say either that it is one that ought to be done, or at least that it is not one that ought not to be done. One may say also, that it is right it should be done; at least that it is not wrong it should be done: that it is a right action; at least that it is not a wrong action. When thus interpreted, the words *ought*, and *right* and *wrong*, and others of that stamp, have a meaning: when otherwise, they have none.

XI. Has the rectitude of this principle been ever formally contested? It should seem that it had, by those who have not known what they have been meaning. Is it susceptible of any direct proof? it should seem not: for that which is used to prove every thing else, cannot itself be proved: a chain of proofs must have their commencement somewhere. To give such proof is as impossible as it is needless.

XII. Not that there is or ever has been that human creature breathing, however stupid or perverse, who has not on many, perhaps on most occasions of his life, deferred to it. By the natural constitution of the human frame, on most occasions of their lives men in general embrace the principle, without thinking of it: if not for the ordering of their own actions, yet for the trying of their own actions, as well as of those of other men. There have been, at the same time, not many, perhaps, even of the most intelligent, who have been disposed to embrace it purely and without reserve. There are even few who have not taken some occasion or other to quarrel with it, either on account of their not understanding always how to apply it, or on account of some prejudice or other which they were afraid to examine into, or could not bear to part with. For such is the stuff that man is made of: in principle and in practice, in a right track and in a wrong one, the rarest of all human qualities is consistency.

XIII. When a man attempts to combat the principle of utility, it is with reasons drawn, without his being aware of it, from that very principle itself. His arguments, if they prove any thing, prove not that the principle is *wrong*, but that, according to the applications he supposes to be made of it, it is *misapplied*. Is it possible for a man to move the earth? Yes; but he must first find out another earth to stand upon.

XIV. To disprove the propriety of it by arguments is impossible; but, from the causes that have been mentioned, or from some confused or partial view of it, a man may happen to be disposed not to relish it. Where this is the case, if he thinks the settling of his opinions on such a subject worth the trouble, let him take the following steps, and at length, perhaps, he may come to reconcile himself to it.

1. Let him settle with himself, whether he would wish to discard this principle altogether; if so, let him consider what it is that all his reasonings (in matters of politics especially) can amount to?

2. If he would, let him settle with himself, whether he would judge and act without any principle, or whether there is any other he would judge and act by?

3. If there be, let him examine and satisfy himself whether the principle he thinks he has found is really any separate intelligible principle; or whether it be not a mere principle in words, a kind of phrase, which at bottom expresses neither more nor less than the mere averment of his own unfounded sentiments; that is, what in another person he might be apt to call caprice?

4. If he is inclined to think that his own approbation or disapprobation, annexed to the idea of an act, without any regard to its consequences, is a sufficient foundation for him to judge and act upon, let him ask himself whether his sentiment is to be a standard of right and wrong, with respect to every other man, or whether every man's sentiment has the same privilege of being a standard to itself?

5. In the first case, let him ask himself whether his principle is not despotical, and hostile to all the rest of [the] human race?

6. In the second case, whether it is not anarchial, and whether at this rate there are not as many different standards of right and wrong as there are men? and whether even to the same man, the same thing, which is right to-day, may not (without the least change in its nature) be wrong to-morrow? and whether the same thing is not right and wrong in the same place at the same time? and in either case, whether all argument is not at an end? and whether, when two men have said, "I like this," and "I don't like it," they can (upon such a principle) have any thing more to say?

7. If he should have said to himself, No: for that the sentiment which he proposes as a standard must be grounded on reflection, let him say on what particulars the reflection is to turn? if on particulars having relation to the utility of the act, then let him say whether this is not deserting his own principle, and borrowing assistance from that very one in opposition to which he sets it up: or if not on those particulars, on what other particulars?

8. If he should be for compounding the matter, and adopting his own principle in part, and the principle of utility in part, let him say how far he will adopt it?

9. When he has settled with himself where he will stop, then let him ask himself how he justifies to himself the adopting it so far? and why he will not adopt it any farther?

10. Admitting any other principle than the principle of utility to be a right principle, a principle that it is right for a man to pursue; admitting (what is not true) that the word *right* can have a meaning without reference to utility, let him say whether there is any such thing as a *motive* that a man can have to pursue the dictates of it: if there is, let him say what that motive is, and how it is to be distinguished from those which enforce the dictates of utility: if not, then lastly let him say what it is this other principle can be good for?

Chapter II: Of Principles Adverse to That of Utility

I. If the principle of utility be a right principle to be governed by, and that in all cases, it follows from what has been just observed, that whatever principle differs from it in any case must necessarily be a wrong one. To prove any other principle, therefore, to be a wrong one, there needs no more than just to show it to be what it is, a principle of which the dictates are in some point or other different from those of the principle of utility: to state it is to confute it.

II. A principle may be different from that of utility in two ways: 1. By being constantly opposed to it: this is the case with a principle which may be termed the principle of *asceticism*.[3] 2. By being sometimes opposed to it, and sometimes not, as it may happen: this is the case with another, which may be termed the principle of *sympathy* and *antipathy*.

III. By the principle of asceticism I mean that principle, which, like the principle of utility, approves or disapproves of any action, according to the tendency which it appears to have to augment or diminish the happiness of the party whose interest is in question; but in an inverse manner: approving of actions in as far as they tend to diminish his happiness; disapproving of them in as far as they tend to augment it.

IV. It is evident that any one who reprobates any the least particle of pleasure, as such, from whatever source derived, is *pro tanto* a partizan of the principle of asceticism. It is only upon that principle, and not from the principle of utility, that the most abominable pleasure which the vilest of malefactors ever reaped from his crime would be to be reprobated, if it stood alone. The case is, that it never does stand alone; but is necessarily followed by such a quantity of pain (or, what comes to the same thing, such a chance for a certain quantity of pain) that the pleasure in comparison of it, is as nothing: and this is the true and sole, but perfectly sufficient, reason for making it a ground for punishment.

V. There are two classes of men of very different complexions, by whom the principle of asceticism appears to have been embraced; the one a set of moralists, the other a set of religionists. Different accordingly have been the motives which appear to have recommended it to the notice of these different parties. Hope, that is the prospect of pleasure, seems to have animated the former: hope, the aliment of philosophic pride: the hope of honour and reputation at the hands of men. Fear, that is the prospect of pain, the latter: fear, the offspring of superstitious fancy: the fear of future punishment at the hands of a splenetic and revengeful Deity. I say in this case fear: for of the invisible future, fear is more powerful than hope. These circumstances characterize the two different parties among the partizans of the principle of asceticism; the parties and their motives different, the principle the same. . . .

VIII. The principle of asceticism, however, with whatever warmth it may have been embraced by its partizans as a rule of private conduct, seems not to have been carried to any considerable length, when applied to the business of government. In a few instances it has been carried a little way by the philosophical party: witness the Spartan regimen. Though then, perhaps, it may be considered as having been a measure of security: and an application, though a precipitate and perverse application, of the principle of utility. Scarcely in any instances, to any considerable length, by the religious: for the various monastic orders, and the societies of the Quakers, Dumplers, Moravians,[4] and other religionists, have been free societies, whose regimen no man has been astricted to without the intervention of his own consent. Whatever merit a man may have thought there would be in making himself miserable, no such notion seems ever to have occurred to any of them, that it may be a merit, much less a duty, to make others miserable: although it should seem, that if a certain quantity of misery were a thing so desirable, it would not matter much whether it were brought by each man upon himself, or by one man upon another.

IX. The principle of asceticism seems originally to have been the reverie of certain hasty speculators, who having perceived, or fancied, that certain pleasures, when reaped in certain circumstances, have, at the long run, been attended with pains more than equivalent to them, took occasion to quarrel with every thing that offered itself under the name of pleasure. Having then got thus far, and having forgot the point which they set out from, they pushed on, and went so much further as to think it meritorious to fall in love with pain. Even this, we see, is at bottom but the principle of utility misapplied.

X. The principle of utility is capable of being consistently pursued; and it is but tautology to say, that the more consistently it is pursued, the better it must ever be for humankind. The principle of asceticism never was, nor ever can be, consistently pursued by any living creature. Let but one tenth part of the inhabitants of this earth pursue it consistently, and in a day's time they will have turned it into a hell.

XI. Among principles adverse to that of utility, that which at this day seems to have most influence in matters of government, is what may be called the principle of sympathy and antipathy. By the principle of sympathy and antipathy, I mean that principle which approves or disapproves of certain actions, not on account of their tending to augment the happiness, nor yet on account of their tending to diminish the happiness of the party whose interest is in question, but merely because a man finds himself disposed to approve or disapprove of them: holding up that approbation or disapprobation as a sufficient reason for itself, and disclaiming the necessity of looking out for any extrinsic ground. Thus far in the general department of morals: and in the particular department of politics, measuring out the quantum (as well as determining the ground) of punishment, by the degree of the disapprobation.

XII. It is manifest, that this is rather a principle in name than in reality: it is not a positive principle of itself, so much as a term employed to signify the negation of all principle. What one expects to find in a principle is something that points out some external consideration, as a means of warranting and guiding the internal sentiments of approbation and disapprobation: this expectation is but ill fulfilled by a proposition, which does neither more nor less than hold up each of those sentiments as a ground and standard for itself.

XIII. In looking over the catalogue of human actions (says a partizan of this principle) in order to determine which of them are to be marked with the seal of disapprobation, you need but to take counsel of your own feelings: whatever you find in yourself a propensity to condemn, is wrong for that very reason. For the same reason it is also meet for punishment: in what proportion it is adverse to utility, or whether it be adverse to utility at all, is a matter that makes no difference. In that same *proportion* also is it meet for punishment: if you hate much, punish much: if you hate little, punish little: punish as you hate. If you hate not at all, punish not at all: the fine feelings of the soul are not to be overborne and tyrannized by the harsh and rugged dictates of political utility.

XIV. The various systems that have been formed concerning the standard of right and wrong, may all be reduced to the principle of sympathy and antipathy.[5] One account may serve for all of them. They consist all of them in so many contrivances for avoiding the obligation of appealing to any external standard, and for prevailing upon the reader to accept of the author's sentiment or opinion as a reason for itself. The phrases different, but the principle the same.[†]

---

† It is curious enough to observe the variety of inventions men have hit upon, and the variety of phrases they have brought forward, in order to conceal from the world, and, if possible, from themselves, this very general and therefore very pardonable self-sufficiency.

1. One man says, he has a thing made on purpose to tell him what is right and what is wrong; and that it is called a *moral sense:* and then he goes to work at his ease, and says, such a thing is right, and such a thing is wrong – why? "because my moral sense tells me it is."

2. Another man comes and alters the phrase: leaving out *moral*, and putting in *common*, in the room of it. He then tells you, that his common sense teaches him what is right and wrong, as surely as the other's moral sense did: meaning by common sense, a sense of some kind or other, which, he says, is possessed by all mankind: the sense of those, whose sense is not the same as the author's, being struck out of the account as not worth taking. This contrivance does better than the other; for a moral sense, being a new thing, a man may feel about him a good while without being able to find it out: but common sense is as old as the creation; and there is no man but would be ashamed to be thought not to have as much of it as his neighbours. It has another great advantage: by appearing to share power, it lessens envy: for when a man gets up upon this ground, in order to anathematize those who differ from him, it is not by a *sic volo sic jubeo*, but by a *velitis jubeatis*.

3. Another man comes, and says, that as to a moral sense indeed, he cannot find that he has any such thing: that however he has an *understanding*, which will do quite as well. This understanding, he says, is the standard of right and wrong: it tells him so and so. All good and wise men understand as he does: if other men's understandings differ in any point from him, so much the worse for them: it is a sure sign they are either defective or corrupt.

4. Another man says, that there is an eternal and immutable Rule of Right: that that rule of right dictates so and so: and then he begins giving you his sentiments upon any thing that comes uppermost: and these sentiments (you are to take for granted) are so many branches of the eternal rule of right.

5. Another man, or perhaps the same man (it's no matter) says, that there are certain practices conformable, and others repugnant, to the Fitness of Things; and then he tells you, at his leisure, what practices are conformable and what repugnant: just as he happens to like a practice or dislike it.

6. A great multitude of people are continually talking of the Law of Nature; and then they go

XV. It is manifest, that the dictates of this principle will frequently coincide with those of utility, though perhaps without intending any such thing. Probably more frequently than not: and hence it is that the business of penal justice is carried on upon that tolerable sort of footing upon which we see it carried on in common at this day. For what more natural or more general ground of hatred to a practice can there be, than the mischievousness of such practice? What all men are exposed to suffer by, all men will be disposed to hate. It is far yet, however, from being a constant ground: for when a man suffers, it is not always that he knows what it is he suffers by. A man may suffer grievously, for instance, by a new tax, without being able to trace up the cause of his sufferings to the injustice of some neighbour, who has eluded the payment of an old one.

XVI. The principle of sympathy and antipathy is most apt to err on the side of severity. It is for applying punishment in many cases which deserve none: in many cases which deserve some, it is for applying more than they deserve. There is no incident imaginable, be it ever so trivial, and so remote from mischief, from which this principle may not extract a ground of punishment. Any difference in taste: any difference in opinion: upon one subject as well as upon another. No disagreement so trifling which perseverance and altercation will not render serious. Each becomes in the other's eyes an enemy, and, if laws permit, a criminal. This is one of the circumstances by

on giving you their sentiments about what is right and what is wrong: and these sentiments, you are to understand, are so many chapters and sections of the Law of Nature. . . .

The mischief common to all these ways of thinking and arguing (which, in truth, as we have seen, are but one and the same method, couched in different forms of words) is their serving as a cloke, and pretence, and aliment, to despotism: if not a despotism in practice, a despotism however in disposition: which is but too apt, when pretence and power offer, to show itself in practice. The consequence is, that with intentions very commonly of the purest kind, a man becomes a torment either to himself or his fellow-creatures. If he be of the melancholy cast, he sits in silent grief, bewailing their blindness and depravity: if of the irascible, he declaims with fury and virulence against all who differ from him; blowing up the coals of fanaticism, and branding with the charge of corruption and insincerity, every man who does not think, or profess to think, as he does.

If such a man happens to possess the advantages of style, his book may do a considerable deal of mischief before the nothingness of it is understood.

These principles, if such they can be called, it is more frequent to see applied to morals than to politics: but their influence extends itself to both. In politics, as well as morals, a man will be at least equally glad of a pretence for deciding any question in the manner that best pleases him, without the trouble of inquiry. If a man is an infallible judge of what is right and wrong in the actions of private individuals, why not in the measures to be observed by public men in the direction of those actions? accordingly (not to mention other chimeras) I have more than once known the pretended law of nature set up in legislative debates, in opposition to arguments derived from the principle of utility.

"But is it never, then, from any other considerations than those of utility, that we derive our notions of right and wrong?" I do not know: I do not care. Whether a moral sentiment can be originally conceived from any other source than a view of utility, is one question: whether upon examination and reflection it can, in point of fact, be actually persisted in and justified on any other ground, by a person reflecting within himself, is another: whether in point of right it can properly be justified on any other ground, by a person addressing himself to the community, is a third. The two first are questions of speculation: it matters not, comparatively speaking, how they are decided. The last is a question of practice: the decision of it is of as much importance as that of any can be. . . .

which the human race is distinguished (not much indeed to its advantage) from the brute creation.

XVII. It is not, however, by any means unexampled for this principle to err on the side of lenity. A near and perceptible mischief moves antipathy. A remote and imperceptible mischief, though not less real, has no effect. . . .

XVIII. It may be wondered, perhaps, that in all this while no mention has been made of the *theological* principle; meaning that principle which professes to recur for the standard of right and wrong to the will of God. But the case is, this is not in fact a distinct principle. It is never any thing more or less than one or other of the three before-mentioned principles presenting itself under another shape. The *will* of God here meant cannot be his revealed will, as contained in the sacred writings: for that is a system which nobody ever thinks of recurring to at this time of day, for the details of political administration: and even before it can be applied to the details of private conduct, it is universally allowed, by the most eminent divines of all persuasions, to stand in need of pretty ample interpretations; else to what use are the works of those divines? And for the guidance of these interpretations, it is also allowed, that some other standard must be assumed. The will then which is meant on this occasion, is that which may be called the *presumptive* will: that is to say, that which is presumed to be his will on account of the conformity of its dictates to those of some other principle. What then may be this other principle? it must be one or other of the three mentioned above: for there cannot, as we have seen, be any more. It is plain, therefore, that, setting revelation out of the question, no light can ever be thrown upon the standard of right and wrong, by any thing that can be said upon the question, what is God's will. We may be perfectly sure, indeed, that whatever is right is conformable to the will of God: but so far is that from answering the purpose of showing us what is right, that it is necessary to know first whether a thing is right, in order to know from thence whether it be conformable to the will of God.‡

XIX. There are two things which are very apt to be confounded, but which it imports us carefully to distinguish: – the motive or cause, which, by operating on the mind of an individual, is productive of any act: and the ground or reason which warrants a legislator, or other by-stander, in regarding that act

‡ The principle of theology refers every thing to God's pleasure. But what is God's pleasure? God does not, he confessedly does not now, either speak or write to us. How then are we to know what is his pleasure? By observing what is our own pleasure, and pronouncing it to be his. Accordingly, what is called the pleasure of God, is and must necessarily be (revelation apart) neither more nor less than the good pleasure of the person, whoever he be, who is pronouncing what he believes, or pretends, to be God's pleasure. How know you it to be God's pleasure that such or such an act should be abstained from? whence come you even to suppose as much? "Because the engaging in it would, I imagine, be prejudicial upon the whole to the happiness of mankind"; says the partizan of the principle of utility: "Because the commission of it is attended with a gross and sensual, or at least with a trifling and transient satisfaction"; says the partizan of the principle of asceticism: "Because I detest the thoughts of it; and I cannot, neither ought I to be called upon to tell why"; says he who proceeds upon the principle of antipathy. In the words of one or other of these must that person necessarily answer (revelation apart) who professes to take for his standard the will of God.

with an eye of approbation. When the acts happens, in the particular instance in question, to be productive of effects which we approve of, much more if we happen to observe that the same motive may frequently be productive, in other instances, of the like effects, we are apt to transfer our approbation to the motive itself, and to assume, as the just ground for the approbation we bestow on the act, the circumstance of its originating from that motive. It is in this way that the sentiment of antipathy has often been considered as a just ground of action. Antipathy, for instance, in such or such a case, is the cause of an action which is attended with good effects: but this does not make it a right ground of action in that case, any more than in any other. Still farther. Not only the effects are good, but the agent sees beforehand that they will be so. This may make the action indeed a perfectly right action: but it does not make antipathy a right ground of action. For the same sentiment of antipathy, if implicitly deferred to, may be, and very frequently is, productive of the very worst effects. Antipathy, therefore, can never be a right ground of action. No more, therefore, can resentment, which, as will be seen more particularly hereafter, is but a modification of antipathy. The only right ground of action, that can possibly subsist, is, after all, the consideration of utility, which, if it is a right principle of action, and of approbation, in any one case, is so in every other. Other principles in abundance, that is, other motives, may be the reasons why such and such an act *has* been done: that is, the reasons or causes of its being done: but it is this alone that can be the reason why it might or ought to have been done. Antipathy or resentment requires always to be regulated, to prevent its doing mischief: to be regulated by what? always by the principle of utility. The principle of utility neither requires nor admits of any other regulator than itself.

CHAPTER III: OF THE FOUR SANCTIONS OR SOURCES OF PAIN AND PLEASURE

I. It has been shown that the happiness of the individuals, of whom a community is composed, that is their pleasures and their security, is the end and the sole end which the legislator ought to have in view: the sole standard, in conformity to which each individual ought, as far as depends upon the legislator, to be *made* to fashion his behaviour. But whether it be this or any thing else that is to be *done*, there is nothing by which a man can ultimately be *made* to do it, but either pain or pleasure. Having taken a general view of these two grand objects (*viz.* pleasure, and what comes to the same thing, immunity from pain) in the character of *final* causes; it will be necessary to take a view of pleasure and pain itself, in the character of *efficient* causes or means.

II. There are four distinguishable sources from which pleasure and pain are in use to flow: considered separately, they may be termed the *physical*, the *political*, the *moral*, and the *religious:* and inasmuch as the pleasures and pains belonging to each of them are capable of giving a binding force to any law or rule of conduct, they may all of them be termed *sanctions*.[§]

III. If it be in the present life, and from the ordinary course of nature, not purposely modified by the interposition of the will of any human being, nor by any extraordinary interposition of any superior invisible being, that the pleasure or the pain takes place or is expected, it may be said to issue from or to belong to the *physical sanction*.

IV. If at the hands of a *particular* person or set of persons in the community, who under names correspondent to that of *judge*, are chosen for the particular purpose of dispensing it, according to the will of the sovereign or supreme ruling power in the state, it may be said to issue from the *political sanction*.

V. If at the hands of such *chance* persons in the community, as the party in question may happen in the course of his life to have concerns with, according to each man's spontaneous disposition, and not according to any settled or concerted rule, it may be said to issue from the *moral* or *popular sanction*.

VI. If from the immediate hand of a superior invisible being, either in the present life, or in a future, it may be said to issue from the *religious sanction*.

VII. Pleasures or pains which may be expected to issue from the *physical, political,* or *moral* sanctions, must all of them be expected to be experienced, if ever, in the *present* life: those which may be expected to issue from the *religious* sanction, may be expected to be experienced either in the *present* life or in a *future*.

VIII. Those which can be experienced in the present life, can of course be no others than such as human nature in the course of the present life is susceptible of: and from each of these sources may flow all the pleasures or pains of which, in the course of the present life, human nature is susceptible. With regard to these then (with which alone we have in this place any concern) those of them which belong to any one of those sanctions, differ not ultimately in kind from those which belong to any one of the other three: the only difference there is among them lies in the circumstances that accompany their production. A suffering which befalls a man in the natural and spontaneous course of things, shall be styled, for instance, a *calamity;* in which case, if it be supposed to befall him through any imprudence of his, it may be styled a punishment issuing from the physical sanction. Now this same suffering, if

---

[§] Sanctio, in Latin, was used to signify the *act of binding,* and, by a common grammatical transition, *any thing which serves to bind a man:* to wit, to the observance of such or such a mode of conduct. According to a Latin grammarian, the import of the word is derived by rather a far-fetched process (such as those commonly are, and in a great measure indeed must be, by which intellectual ideas are derived from sensible ones) from the word *sanguis,* blood: because, among the Romans, with a view to inculcate into the people a persuasion that such or such a mode of conduct would be rendered obligatory upon a man by the force of what I call the religious sanction (that is, that he would be made to suffer by the extraordinary interpolation of some superior being, if he failed to observe the mode of conduct in question) certain ceremonies were contrived by the priests: in the course of which ceremonies the blood of victims was made use of.

A Sanction then is a source of obligatory powers or *motives* that is, of *pains* and *pleasures;* which, according as they are connected with such or such modes of conduct, operate, and are indeed the only things which can operate, as *motives*. . . .

inflicted by the law, will be what is commonly called a *punishment;* if incurred for want of any friendly assistance, which the misconduct, or supposed misconduct, of the sufferer has occasioned to be withholden, a punishment issuing from the *moral* sanction; if through the immediate interposition of a particular providence, a punishment issuing from the religious sanction. . . .

XI. Of these four sanctions the physical is altogether, we may observe, the ground-work of the political and the moral: so is it also of the religious, in as far as the latter bears relation to the present life. It is included in each of those other three. This may operate in any case, (that is, any of the pains or pleasures belonging to it may operate) independently of *them:* none of *them* can operate but by means of this. In a word, the powers of nature may operate of themselves; but neither the magistrate, nor men at large, *can* operate, nor is God in the case in question *supposed* to operate, but through the powers of nature.

XII. For these four objects, which in their nature have so much in common, it seemed of use to find a common name. It seemed of use, in the first place, for the convenience of giving a name to certain pleasures and pains, for which a name equally characteristic could hardly otherwise have been found: in the second place, for the sake of holding up the efficacy of certain moral forces, the influence of which is apt not to be sufficiently attended to. Does the political sanction exert an influence over the conduct of mankind? The moral, the religious sanctions do so too. In every inch of his career are the operations of the political magistrate liable to be aided or impeded by these two foreign powers: who, one or other of them, or both, are sure to be either his rivals or his allies. Does it happen to him to leave them out in his calculations? he will be sure almost to find himself mistaken in the result. Of all this we shall find abundant proofs in the sequel of this work. It behoves him, therefore, to have them continually before his eyes; and that under such a name as exhibits the relation they bear to his own purposes and designs.

Chapter IV: Value of a Lot of Pleasure or Pain, How to Be Measured

I. Pleasures then, and the avoidance of pains, are the *ends* which the legislator has in view: it behoves him therefore to understand their *value.* Pleasures and pains are the *instruments* he has to work with: it behoves him therefore to understand their force, which is again, in other words, their value.

II. To a person considered *by himself,* the value of a pleasure or pain considered *by itself,* will be greater or less, according to the four following circumstances:

1. Its *intensity.*
2. Its *duration.*
3. Its *certainty* or *uncertainty.*
4. Its *propinquity* or *remoteness.*

III. These are the circumstances which are to be considered in estimating a pleasure or a pain considered each of them by itself. But when the value of any pleasure or pain is considered for the purpose of estimating the tendency of any *act* by which it is produced, there are two other circumstances to be taken into the account; these are,

5. Its *fecundity,* or the chance it has of being followed by sensations of the *same* kind: that is, pleasures, if it be a pleasure: pains, if it be a pain.

6. Its *purity,* or the chance it has of *not* being followed by sensations of the *opposite* kind: that is, pains, if it be a pleasure: pleasures, if it be a pain.

These two last, however, are in strictness scarcely to be deemed properties of the pleasure or the pain itself; they are not, therefore, in strictness to be taken into the account of the value of that pleasure or that pain. They are in strictness to be deemed properties only of the act, or other event, by which such pleasure or pain has been produced; and accordingly are only to be taken into the account of the tendency of such act or such event.

IV. To a *number* of persons, with reference to each of whom the value of a pleasure or a pain is considered, it will be greater or less, according to seven circumstances: to wit, the six preceding ones; *viz.*

1. Its *intensity.*

2. Its *duration.*

3. Its *certainty* or *uncertainty.*

4. Its *propinquity* or *remoteness.*

5. Its *fecundity.*

6. Its *purity.*

And one other; to wit:

7. Its *extent;* that is, the number of persons to whom it *extends;* or (in other words) who are affected by it.

V. To take an exact account then of the general tendency of any act, by which the interests of a community are affected, proceed as follows. Begin with any one person of those whose interests seem most immediately to be affected by it: and take an account,

1. Of the value of each distinguishable *pleasure* which appears to be produced by it in the *first* instance.

2. Of the value of each *pain* which appears to be produced by it in the *first* instance.

3. Of the value of each pleasure which appears to be produced by it *after* the first. This constitutes the *fecundity* of the first *pleasure* and the *impurity* of the first *pain.*

4. Of the value of each *pain* which appears to be produced by it after the first. This constitutes the *fecundity* of the first *pain,* and the *impurity* of the first pleasure.

5. Sum up all the values of all the *pleasures* on the one side, and those of all the pains on the other. The balance, if it be on the side of pleasure, will give the *good* tendency of the act upon the whole, with respect to the interests of that *individual* person; if on the side of pain, the *bad* tendency of it upon the whole.

6. Take an account of the *number* of persons whose interests appear to be concerned; and repeat the above process with respect to each. *Sum up* the number expressive of the degrees of *good* tendency, which the act has, with

respect to each individual, in regard to whom the tendency of it is *good* upon the whole: do this again with respect to each individual, in regard to whom the tendency of it is *good* upon the whole: do this again with respect to each individual, in regard to whom the tendency of it is *bad* upon the whole. Take the *balance;* which, if on the side of *pleasure,* will give the general *good tendency* of the act, with respect to the total number or community of individuals concerned; if on the side of pain, the general *evil tendency,* with respect to the same community.

VI. It is not to be expected that this process should be strictly pursued previously to every moral judgment, or to every legislative or judicial operation. It may, however, be always kept in view: and as near as the process actually pursued on these occasions approaches to it, so near will such process approach to the character of an exact one.

VII. The same process is alike applicable to pleasure and pain, in whatever shape they appear: and by whatever denomination they are distinguished: to pleasure, whether it be called *good* (which is properly the cause or instrument of pleasure) or *profit* (which is distant pleasure, or the cause or instrument of distant pleasure,) or *convenience,* or *advantage, benefit, emolument, happiness,* and so forth: to pain, whether it be called *evil,* (which corresponds to *good*) or *mischief,* or *inconvenience,* or *disadvantage,* or *loss,* or *unhappiness,* and so forth.

VIII. Nor is this a novel and unwarranted, any more than it is a useless theory. In all this there is nothing but what the practice of mankind, wheresoever they have a clear view of their own interest, is perfectly conformable to. An article of property, an estate in land, for instance, is valuable, on what account? On account of the pleasures of all kinds which it enables a man to produce, and what comes to the same thing the pains of all kinds which it enables him to avert. But the value of such an article of property is universally understood to rise or fall according to the length or shortness of the time which a man has in it: the certainty or uncertainty of its coming into possession: and the nearness or remoteness of the time at which, if at all, it is to come into possession. As to the *intensity* of the pleasures which a man may derive from it, this is never thought of, because it depends upon the use which each particular person may come to make of it; which cannot be estimated till the particular pleasures he may come to derive from it, or the particular pains he may come to exclude by means of it, are brought to view. For the same reason, neither does he think of the *fecundity* or *purity* of those pleasures. . . .

Theory of Legislation

CHAPTER XII: THE LIMITS WHICH SEPARATE MORALS FROM LEGISLATION

Morality in general is the art of directing the actions of men in such a way as to produce the greatest possible sum of good.

Legislation ought to have precisely the same object.

But although these two arts, or rather sciences, have the same end, they differ greatly in extent. All actions, whether public or private, fall under the jurisdiction of morals. It is a guide which leads the individual, as it were, by the hand through all the details of his life, all his relations with his fellows. Legislation cannot do this; and, if it could, it ought not to exercise a continual interference and dictation over the conduct of men.

Morality commands each individual to do all that is advantageous to the community, his own personal advantage included. But there are many acts useful to the community which legislation ought not to command. There are also many injurious actions which it ought not to forbid, although morality does so. In a word, legislation has the same centre with morals, but it has not the same circumference.

There are two reasons for this difference: 1st. Legislation can have no direct influence upon the conduct of men, except by punishments. Now these punishments are so many evils, which are not justifiable except so far as there results from them a greater sum of good. But, in many cases in which we might desire to strengthen a moral precept by a punishment, the evil of the punishment would be greater than the evil of the offence. The means necessary to carry the law into execution would be of a nature to spread through society a degree of alarm more injurious than the evil intended to be prevented.

2nd. Legislation is often arrested by the danger of overwhelming the innocent in seeking to punish the guilty. Whence comes this danger? From the difficulty of defining an offence, and giving a clear and precise idea of it. For example, hard-heartedness, ingratitude, perfidy, and other vices which the popular sanction punishes, cannot come under the power of the law, unless they are defined as exactly as theft, homicide, or perjury.

But, the better to distinguish the true limits of morals and legislation, it will be well to refer to the common classification of moral duties.

Private morality regulates the actions of men, either in that part of their conduct in which they alone are interested, or in that which may affect the interests of others. The actions which affect a man's individual interest compose a class called, perhaps improperly, *duties to ourselves;* and the quality or disposition manifested in the accomplishment of those duties receives the name of *prudence*. That part of conduct which relates to others composes a class of actions called *duties to others*. Now there are two ways of consulting the happiness of others: the one negative, abstaining from diminishing it; the other positive, labouring to augment it. The first constitutes *probity;* the second is *beneficence.*

Morality upon these three points needs the aid of the law; but not in the same degree, nor in the same manner.

I. The rules of prudence are almost always sufficient of themselves. If a man fails in what regards his particular private interest, it is not his will which is in fault, it is his understanding. If he does wrong, it can only be through mistake.

The fear of hurting himself is a motive of repression sufficiently strong; it would be useless to add to it the fear of an artificial pain.

Does any one object, that facts show the contrary? That excesses of play, those of intemperance, the illicit intercourse between the sexes, attended so often by the greatest dangers, are enough to prove that individuals have not always sufficient prudence to abstain from what hurts them?

Confining myself to a general reply, I answer, in the first place, that, in the greater part of these cases, punishment would be so easily eluded, that it would be inefficacious; secondly, that the evil produced by the penal law would be much beyond the evil of the offence. . . .

As a general rule, the greatest possible latitude should be left to individuals, in all cases in which they can injure none but themselves, for they are the best judges of their own interests. If they deceive themselves, it is to be supposed that the moment they discover their error they will alter their conduct. The power of the law need interfere only to prevent them from injuring each other. It is there that restraint is necessary; it is there that the application of punishments is truly useful, because the rigour exercised upon an individual becomes in such a case the security of all.

II. It is true that there is a natural connection between prudence and probity; for our own interest, well understood, will never leave us without motives to abstain from injuring our fellows.

Let us stop a moment at this point. I say that, independently of religion and the laws, we always have some natural motives – that is, motives derived from our own interest for consulting the happiness of others. 1st. The motive of pure benevolence, a sweet and calm sentiment which we delight to experience, and which inspires us with a repugnance to be the cause of suffering. 2nd. The motives of private affection, which exercise their empire in domestic life, and within the particular circle of our intimacies. 3rd. The desire of good repute, and the fear of blame. This is a sort of calculation of trade. It is paying, to have credit; speaking truth, to obtain confidence; serving, to be served. It is thus we must understand that saying of a wit, *that, if there were no such thing as honesty, it would be a good speculation to invent it, as a means of making one's fortune.*

A man enlightened as to his own interest will not indulge himself in a secret offence through fear of contracting a shameful habit, which sooner or later will betray him; and because the having secrets to conceal from the prying curiosity of mankind leaves in the heart a sediment of disquiet, which corrupts every pleasure. All he can acquire at the expense of security cannot make up for the loss of that; and, if he desires a good reputation, the best guarantee he can have for it is his own esteem.

But, in order that an individual should perceive this connection between the interests of others and his own, he needs an enlightened spirit and a heart free from seductive passions. The greater part of men have neither sufficient light, sufficient strength of mind, nor sufficient moral sensibility to place their honesty above the aid of the laws. The legislator must supply the feebleness of this natural interest by adding to it an artificial interest, more steady and more easily perceived.

More yet. In many cases morality derives its existence from the law; that is, to decide whether the action is morally good or bad, it is necessary to know whether the laws permit or forbid it. It is so of what concerns property. A manner of selling or acquiring, esteemed dishonest in one country, would be irreproachable in another. It is the same with offences against the state. The state exists only by law, and it is impossible to say what conduct in this behalf morality requires of us before knowing what the legislator has decreed. There are countries where it is an offence to enlist into the service of a foreign power, and others in which such a service is lawful and honourable.*

III. As to beneficence some distinctions are necessary. The law may be extended to general objects, such as the care of the poor; but, for details, it is necessary to depend upon private morality. Beneficence has its mysteries, and loves best to employ itself upon evils so unforeseen or so secret that the law cannot reach them. Besides, it is to individual free-will that benevolence owes its energy. If the same acts were commanded, they would no longer be benefits, they would lose their attraction and their essence. It is morality, and especially religion, which here form the necessary complement to legislation, and the sweetest tie of humanity.

However, instead of having done too much in this respect, legislators have not done enough. They ought to erect into an offence the refusal or the omission of a service of humanity when it would be easy to render it, and when some distinct ill clearly results from the refusal; such, for example, as abandoning a wounded man in a solitary road without seeking any assistance for him; not giving information to a man who is ignorantly meddling with poisons; not reaching out the hand to one who has fallen into a ditch from which he cannot extricate himself; in these, and other similar cases, could any fault be found with a punishment, exposing the delinquent to a certain degree of shame, or subjecting him to a pecuniary responsibility for the evil which he might have prevented?

I will add, that legislation might be extended further than it is in relation to the interests of the inferior animals. I do not approve the laws of the Hindus on this subject. There are good reasons why animals should serve for the nourishment of man, and for destroying those which incommode us. We are the better for it, and they are not the worse; for they have not, as we have, long and cruel anticipations of the future; and the death which they receive at our hands may always be rendered less painful than that which awaits them in the inevitable course of nature. But what can be said to justify the useless torments they are made to suffer; the cruel caprices which are exercised upon

---

* Here we touch upon one of the most difficult of questions. If the law is not what it ought to be; if it openly combats the principle of utility; ought we to obey it? Ought we to violate it? Ought we to remain neuter between the law which commands an evil, and morality which forbids it? The solution of this question involves considerations both of prudence and benevolence. We ought to examine if it is more dangerous to violate the law than to obey it; we ought to consider whether the probable evils of obedience are less or greater than the probable evils of disobedience.

them? Among the many reasons which might be given for making criminal such gratuitous cruelties, I confine myself to that which relates to my subject. It is a means of cultivating a general sentiment of benevolence, and of rendering men more mild; or at least of preventing that brutal depravity, which, after fleshing itself upon animals, presently demands human suffering to satiate its appetite.

Editor's Notes

1. Bentham thought that the word "community" stood for a fiction because it may mislead us into thinking that there is some existing entity called the "community" which is other than the group of perceptible people who really are all that there is to a community.
2. Here "measure of government" is treated as a fiction.
3. An ascetic is one who practices severe self-denial, denying satisfaction of desires and needs. Bentham added a polemical footnote about monks who live ascetically in the hope of being rewarded many times over in heaven.
4. Bentham treated these sects as if they were Protestant counterparts of the Catholic monks he so disliked.
5. In the next footnote, Bentham dismissed the bulk of previous Western moral philosophy as resting on the objectionable principle of sympathy and antipathy. Most of the views he rejected are represented in these volumes, although Bentham's description does not always identify a specific author.

Further Reading

Modern editions of Bentham's writings are appearing in J. H. Burns, John Dinwiddy, and F. Rosen, eds., *The Collected Works of Jeremy Bentham* (Oxford: Oxford University Press 1968–   ). The only previous attempt at a complete edition is the unsatisfactory *Works* edited by John Bowring, 1843. Bentham elaborated his views on morality in a late work, the *Deontology*, now available in Amnon Goldworth, ed., *Collected Works* (Oxford: Oxford University Press, 1983). This book contains Bentham's thoughts on virtue and his ideas on other topics not covered in the *Introduction to the Principles of Morals and Legislation*, but it is a frustrating and rather eccentric work. For Bentham's views of language, the best work to consult is C. K. Ogden, ed., *Bentham's Theory of Fictions* (London: Routledge & Kegan Paul, 1932).

The literature on Bentham, Benthamism, and utilitarianism is immense. One of the best places to begin is the brilliant essay "Bentham" by his sometime disciple John Stuart Mill, in Mill's *Collected Works*, vol. 10, ed. John M. Robson (Toronto: University of Toronto Press, 1969). The first volume of Sir Leslie Stephen, *The English Utilitarians* (London: Duckworth, 1900), devoted to Bentham, is still worth reading. For the development of Bentham's thought, the great work by Elie Halévy, *The Growth of Philosophical Radicalism*, trans. Mary Morris (London: Faber & Faber, 1928), is indispensable.

John Dinwiddy, *Bentham* (Oxford: Oxford University Press, 1989), gives a concise survey, taking advantage of recent research. Ross Harrison, *Bentham* (London: Routledge & Kegan Paul, 1983), is especially good on Bentham's theory of meaning. David Lyons, *In the Interest of the Governed* (Oxford: Clarendon Press, 1973), proposes an interesting but controversial reading. David Baumgardt, *Bentham and the Ethics of*

Today (Princeton N.J.: Princeton University Press, 1952), is a long and diffuse study that draws on much manuscript material.

H. L. A. Hart's *Essays on Bentham* (Oxford: Oxford University Press, 1982) – though primarily about Bentham on jurisprudence and political theory – is of great value to the student of Bentham's ethics. Gerald J. Postema, *Bentham and the Common Law Tradition* (Oxford: Oxford University Press, 1986), studies Bentham's legal theory in its jurisprudential context. James Steintrager, *Bentham* (Ithaca, N.Y.: Cornell University Press, 1977), is helpful on Bentham's political thought.

Finally, the journal *Utilitas* publishes studies of Bentham and of the utilitarian tradition generally.

Part IV.
Autonomy and Responsibility

The Earl of Shaftesbury

Introduction

Anthony Ashley Cooper, who became the third earl of Shaftesbury upon the death of his father in 1699, was born in 1671. His grandfather, the first earl, was a central figure in the Whig party during the seventeenth century. The first earl took charge of his grandson's education, placing him under the tutelage of John Locke, who was the household physician and adviser to the whole family. As a young man, Cooper traveled on the Continent for several years, and in 1695 he was elected to a seat in Parliament. He served for three years and continued to attend sessions when he was elevated to the House of Lords, but his poor health made it necessary for him to stay away from London as much as possible. Eventually he was forced to move to Italy in the hope that he could survive in the warmer climate. But in 1713 he died in Naples, leaving behind a widow and one son.

His chief work is a series of essays, collected first in three volumes under the title *Characteristics of Men, Manners, Opinions, Times* (1711). The most overtly philosophical of these essays is the one of most significance in the history of ethics, the *Inquiry Concerning Virtue or Merit*. The other essays deal with art, morals, religion, literature, politics, and the proper manner of living. In an elaborate style, often playful, often mocking, sometimes exhortative, sometimes biting and trenchant, they expose the reader not so much to a system as to a personality. Their influence was enormous. They made Shaftesbury the founder of a distinctive school of ethical thought, the moral sense, or sentimentalist, school. And in art and literature the essays, translated into French and German, were a major factor in forming subsequent sensibilities on the Continent as well as in Britain.

The problems of politics, inseparable from religious issues during the seventeenth century, were a part of Shaftesbury's life from its beginning. In addition to this family inheritance, a number of other influences helped shape his mind. Shaftesbury was educated after childhood by John Locke. Although Shaftesbury admired Locke personally, he came to dislike profoundly his views of morality, in particular Locke's voluntarism, his belief that God is perfectly free to establish for us any moral laws he pleases, as there is no measure of morality other than God's will. Hobbes, Shaftesbury thought, had held similar views, but he had had too low a character to exercise any real influence, whereas Locke had to be taken seriously and opposed. This opposition is evident in much of Shaftesbury's work.

In Amsterdam in 1698 Shaftesbury met the great skeptical writer Pierre Bayle. Bayle, a Huguenot refugee living in Holland, was one of the first to argue that a society of atheists could be as virtuous as a society of religious believers. Our actions are

483

determined by our feelings rather than by our opinions, Bayle believed, and feelings left to themselves would not divide us as opinion does. Hence there are no practical grounds for persecuting those who do not accept orthodox views. And because we have no absolute knowledge of religious truth, we have no theoretical basis for suppressing what we believe are mistaken opinions. Consequently, we should be tolerant of diversity of belief, in the assurance that religious beliefs by themselves make little or no real difference to morality. Shaftesbury himself later championed religious tolerance and developed a moral psychology in which feelings play a major role.

Shaftesbury was associated with a group of politically influential noblemen who advocated the theories that Harrington had proposed in his *Oceana* in 1656. One of Shaftesbury's closest friends was Robert Viscount Molesworth, a leader of the group trying to make the ideas of classical republicanism into an effective political program. (See the section "The Classical Republic" in the Introduction to this anthology.) Shaftesbury was also connected with a free-lance political writer and pamphleteer named John Toland, who edited Harrington's works and was responsible for the first publication of a draft of Shaftesbury's first long essay on morals. It appeared in 1699 under the title *An Inquiry Concerning Virtue*, without naming its author – but possibly with his assent. The classical republic could be a reality only if its citizens were concerned about sustaining the common good. Shaftesbury's interest in showing how people can have this concern may have one of its roots here.

Finally, Shaftesbury knew the work of the Cambridge Platonists. (For a brief sketch of their views, see the introduction to the selections from Ralph Cudworth in Part II of this anthology.) In fact, Shaftesbury's first publication was an edition of sermons by their most admired member, Benjamin Whichcote, from a manuscript that Shaftesbury owned. Shaftesbury's preface makes clear his detestation of Hobbes and his contempt for those who, as he put it, portray humans as mean and selfish in order to show that there is need for a religious revelation to set them straight. Whichcote, he commented, saw that men are naturally sociable and loving, that Christianity is preeminently the religion in which love is enjoined, not one whose basis of morality is law backed by terror. Views like these occupied a central place in Shaftesbury's own mature thinking.

Shaftesbury did not, however, express his views in a Christian vocabulary. Rather, he looked back to classical antiquity for his language – not to Epicureanism, which was too close to Hobbes's position to be acceptable, but to Stoicism, a suitable outlook for the politically active man of integrity, the citizen of a classical republic. Virtue will lead one to act for the general good; virtue is sufficient as an end, as it consists in having one's inner life in proper order, and happiness itself is no more than such order. One can therefore act as one sees fit, regardless of the political consequences for oneself. There is a God, for Shaftesbury, but he is rather aloof, not a God from whom to expect miraculous help but a God who simply ensures the good order of the universe and who does not need to intervene to make things go well. People can be left to run their lives by themselves.

Shaftesbury used the phrase "moral sense" to identify the mental ability that guides us, but he did not use it often; still less did he worry about exactly how that sense functions – whether it gives us knowledge or provides us with a feeling. He was more concerned with showing that the object of the moral faculty is itself something inner, that is, our own feelings and desires or motives. Shaftesbury was a sentimentalist in morals not simply because of the presence of a moral sense in his theory but also because he trusted human sentiments to move us to act appropriately and relied on our reflexive awareness of those sentiments as a sufficient guide to what is or is not appropriate. Inner order, for him, is not constituted by conformity to what external laws or perfections require. It exists when our active principles are in an harmonious relation to one another, as judged by the moral faculty. Bringing oneself into moral order is like composing a work of art; each of us must be an independent artist.

In the following selections I have given most of the space to excerpts from the *Inquiry Concerning Virtue or Merit*, which Shaftesbury first published under his own name and in its present form in the 1711 edition of the *Characteristics*. These selections are preceded by short excerpts from two other essays, "*Sensus communis:* An Essay on the Freedom of Wit and Humour" (1709) and "Soliloquy; or, Advice to an Author" (1710). These passages indicate, however inadequately, something of Shaftesbury's broader aims and interests. The texts are from John M. Robertson's edition of the *Characteristics*, 2 vols., London, 1900.

Sensus communis: *An Essay on the Freedom of Wit and Humour*

A public spirit can come only from a social feeling or sense of partnership with human kind. Now there are none so far from being partners in this sense, or sharers in this common affection, as they who scarcely know an equal, nor consider themselves as subject to any law of fellowship or community. And thus morality and good government go together. There is no real love of virtue, without the knowledge of public good. And where absolute power is, there is no public.

They who live under a tyranny, and have learnt to admire its power as sacred and divine, are debauched as much in their religion as in their morals. Public good, according to their apprehension, is as little the measure or rule of government in the universe as in the State. They have scarce a notion of what is good or just, other than as mere will and power have determined. Omnipotence, they think, would hardly be itself, were it not at liberty to dispense with the laws of equity, and change at pleasure the standard of moral rectitude.[1]

But notwithstanding the prejudices and corruptions of this kind, 'tis plain there is something still of a public principle, even where it is most perverted and depressed. The worst of magistracies, the mere despotic kind, can show sufficient instances of zeal and affection towards it. Where no other government is known, it seldom fails of having that allegiance and duty paid it which is owing to a better form. The Eastern countries, and many barbarous nations, have been and still are examples of this kind. The personal love they bear their prince, however severe towards them, may show how natural an affection there is towards government and order among mankind. If men have really no public parent, no magistrate in common to cherish and protect them, they will still imagine they have such a one; and, like new-born creatures who have never seen their dam, will fancy one for themselves, and apply (as by Nature prompted) to some like form, for favour and protection. In the room of a true foster-father and chief, they will take after a false one; and in the room of a legal government and just prince, obey even a tyrant, and endure a whole lineage and succession of such.

As for us Britons, thank Heaven, we have a better sense of government delivered to us from our ancestors. We have the notion of a public, and a constitution; how a legislative and how an executive is modelled. We understand weight and measure in this kind, and can reason justly on the balance of power and property. The maxims we draw from hence, are as evident as those in mathematics. Our increasing knowledge shows us every day, more and more, what common sense is in politics; and this must of necessity lead us to understand a like sense in morals, which is the foundation.

Soliloquy; or, Advice to an Author

Thus is every one convinced of the reality of a better self, and of the cult or homage which is due to it. The misfortune is, we are seldom taught to comprehend this self by placing it in a distinct view from its representative or counterfeit. In our holy religion, which for the greatest part is adapted to the very meanest capacities, 'tis not to be expected that a speculation of this kind should be openly advanced. 'Tis enough that we have hints given us of a nobler self than that which is commonly supposed the basis and foundation of our actions. Self-interest is there taken as it is vulgarly conceived. Though on the other side there are, in the most sacred characters, examples given us of the highest contempt of all such interested views, of a willingness to suffer without recompense for the sake of others, and of a desire to part even with life and being itself on account of what is generous and worthy. But in the same manner as the celestial phænomena are in the sacred volumes generally treated according to common imagination and the then current system of Astronomy and Natural Science, so the moral appearances are in many places preserved without alteration, according to vulgar prejudice and the general conception of interest and self-good. Our real and genuine self is sometimes supposed that ambitious one which is fond of power and glory, sometimes that childish one which is taken with vain show, and is to be invited to obedience by promise of finer habitations, precious stones and metals, shining garments, crowns, and other such dazzling beauties, by which another earth or material city is represented. . . .

But whatever may be the proper effect or operation of religion, 'tis the known province of philosophy to teach us ourselves, keep us the self-same persons, and so regulate our governing fancies, passions, and humours, as to make us comprehensible to ourselves, and knowable by other features than those of a bare countenance. For 'tis not certainly by virtue of our face merely that we are ourselves. 'Tis not we who change when our complexion or shape changes. But there is that, which being wholly metamorphosed and converted, we are thereby in reality transformed and lost.

. . . When from a noted liberality we change perhaps to as remarkable a parsimony; when from indolence and love of rest we plunge into business, or from a busy and severe character, abhorrent from the tender converse of the fair sex, we turn on a sudden to a contrary passion, and become amorous or uxorious; we acknowledge the weakness, and charging our defect on the general want of philosophy we say (sighing) "that, indeed, we none of us truly know ourselves." And thus we recognise the authority and proper object of philosophy; so far at least, that though we pretend not to be complete philosophers, we confess "that as we have more or less of this intelligence or comprehension of ourselves we are accordingly more or less truly men, and either more or less to be depended on in friendship, society, and the commerce of life."

The fruits of this science are indeed the fairest imaginable, and upon due trial are found to be as well relished and of as good favour with mankind. . . .

This is the philosophy which by Nature has the pre-eminence above all other science or knowledge. Nor can this surely be of the sort called vain or deceitful, since it is the only means by which I can discover vanity and deceit.[2] This is not of that kind which depends on genealogies or traditions,[3] and ministers questions and vain jangling.[4] It has not its name, as other philosophies, from the mere subtlety and nicety of the speculation, but by way of excellence, from its being superior to all other speculations, from its presiding over all other sciences and occupations, teaching the measure of each, and assigning the just value of everything in life. By this science religion itself is judged, spirits are searched, prophecies proved, miracles distinguished: the sole measure and standard being taken from moral rectitude, and from the discernment of what is sound and just in the affections. For if the tree is known only by its fruits, my first endeavour must be to distinguish the true taste of fruits, refine my palate, and establish a just relish in the kind. So that to bid me judge authority by morals, whilst the rule of morals is supposed dependent on mere authority and will, is the same in reality as to bid me see with my eyes shut, measure without a standard, and count without arithmetic.

And thus Philosophy, which judges both of herself and of everything besides, discovers her own province and chief command, teaches me to distinguish between her person and her likeness, and shows me her immediate and real self, by that sole privilege of teaching me to know myself and what belongs to me. She gives to every inferior science its just rank; leaves some to measure sounds, others to scan syllables, others to weigh vacuums, and define spaces and extensions; but reserves to herself her due authority and majesty, keeps her state and ancient title of vitae dux, virtutis indagatrix,[5] . . .

Should a writer upon music, addressing himself to the students and lovers of the art, declare to them "that the measure or rule of harmony was caprice or will, humour or fashion," 'tis not very likely he should be heard with great attention or treated with real gravity. For harmony is harmony by nature, let men judge ever so ridiculously of music. So is symmetry and proportion founded still in nature, let men's fancy prove ever so barbarous, or their fashions ever so Gothic in their architecture, sculpture, or whatever other designing art. 'Tis the same case where life and manners are concerned. Virtue has the same fixed standard. The same numbers, harmony, and proportion will have place in morals, and are discoverable in the characters and affections of mankind; in which are laid the just foundations of an art and science superior to every other of human practice and comprehension.

This, I suppose therefore, is highly necessary that a writer should comprehend. For things are stubborn and will not be as we fancy them, or as the fashion varies, but as they stand in nature. Now whether the writer be poet, philosopher, or of whatever kind, he is in truth no other than a copyist after nature.

An Inquiry Concerning Virtue or Merit

Book I

Part II

Section I

When we reflect on any ordinary frame or constitution either of Art or Nature, and consider how hard it is to give the least account of a particular part without a competent knowledge of the whole, we need not wonder to find ourselves at a loss in many things relating to the constitution and frame of Nature herself. For to what end in Nature many things, even whole species of creatures, refer, or to what purpose they serve, will be hard for any one justly to determine; but to what end the many proportions and various shapes of parts in many creatures actually serve, we are able, by the help of study and observation, to demonstrate with great exactness.

We know that every creature has a private good and interest of his own, which Nature has compelled him to seek, by all the advantages afforded him within the compass of his make. We know that there is in reality a right and a wrong state of every creature, and that his right one is by nature forwarded and by himself affectionately sought. There being therefore in every creature a certain interest or good, there must be also a certain end to which everything in his constitution must naturally refer. To this end if anything, either in his appetites, passions, or affections, be not conducing but the contrary, we must of necessity own it ill to him. And in this manner he is ill with respect to himself, as he certainly is with respect to others of his kind, when any such appetites or passions make him anyway injurious to them. Now, if by the natural constitution of any rational creature, the same irregularities of appetite which make him ill to others, make him ill also to himself, and if the same regularity of affections which causes him to be good in one sense, causes him to be good also in the other, then is that goodness by which he is thus useful to others a real good and advantage to himself. And thus virtue and interest may be found at last to agree.

If therefore in the structure of this or any other animal, there be anything which points beyond himself, and by which he is plainly discovered to have relation to some other being or nature besides his own, then will this animal undoubtedly be esteemed a part of some other system. For instance, if an animal has the proportions of a male, it shows he has relation to a female. And the respective proportions both of the male and female will be allowed, doubtless, to have a joint relation to another existence and order of things beyond themselves. So that the creatures are both of them to be considered as parts of another system, which is that of a particular race or species of living creatures, who have some one common nature, or are provided for by some one order or constitution of things subsisting together, and co-operating towards their conservation and support.

In the same manner, if a whole species of animals contribute to the existence or well-being of some other, then is that whole species, in general, a part only of some other system. . . .

Now, if the whole system of animals, together with that of vegetables, and all other things in this inferior world, be properly comprehended in one system of a globe or earth, and if, again, this globe or earth itself appears to have a real dependence on something still beyond, as, for example, either on its sun, the galaxy, or its fellow-planets, then is it in reality a part only of some other system. And if it be allowed that there is in like manner a system of all things, and a universal nature, there can be no particular being or system which is not either good or ill in that general one of the universe; for if it be insignificant and of no use, it is a fault or imperfection, and consequently ill in the general system.

Therefore if any being be wholly and really ill, it must be ill with respect to the universal system; and then the system of the universe is ill or imperfect. But if the ill of one private system be the good of others; if it makes still to the good of the general system (as when one creature lives by the destruction of another; one thing is generated from the corruption of another; or one planetary system or vortex may swallow up another), then is the ill of that private system no real ill in itself, any more than the pain of breeding teeth is ill in a system or body which is so constituted that, without this occasion of pain, it would suffer worse by being defective.

So that we cannot say of any being that it is wholly and absolutely ill, unless we can positively show and ascertain that what we call ill is nowhere good besides, in any other system, or with respect to any other order or economy whatsoever.

But were there in the world any entire species of animals destructive to every other, it may be justly called an ill species, as being ill in the animal system. And if in any species of animals (as in men, for example) one man is of a nature pernicious to the rest, he is in this respect justly styled an ill man.

We do not, however, say of any one that he is an ill man because he has the plague-spots upon him, or because he has convulsive fits which make him strike and wound such as approach him. Nor do we say on the other side that he is a good man when, having his hands tied up, he is hindered from doing the mischief he designs; or (which is in a manner the same) when he abstains from executing his ill purpose through a fear of some impending punishment, or through the allurement of some exterior reward.

So that in a sensible creature that which is not done through any affection at all makes neither good nor ill in the nature of that creature, who then only is supposed good when the good or ill of the system to which he has relation is the immediate object of some passion or affection moving him.

Since it is therefore by affection merely that a creature is esteemed good or ill, natural or unnatural, our business will be to examine which are the good and natural, and which the ill and unnatural affections.

Section III

But to proceed from what is esteemed mere goodness, and lies within the reach and capacity of all sensible creatures, to that which is called virtue or merit, and is allowed to man only.

In a creature capable of forming general notions of things, not only the outward beings which offer themselves to the sense are the objects of the affection, but the very actions themselves, and the affections of pity, kindness, gratitude, and their contraries, being brought into the mind by reflection, become objects. So that, by means of this reflected sense, there arises another kind of affection towards those very affections themselves, which have been already felt, and are now become the subject of a new liking or dislike.

The case is the same in the mental or moral subjects as in the ordinary bodies or common subjects of sense. The shapes, motions, colours, and proportions of these latter being presented to our eye, there necessarily results a beauty or deformity, according to the different measure, arrangement, and disposition of their several parts. So in behaviour and actions, when presented to our understanding, there must be found, of necessity, an apparent difference, according to the regularity or irregularity of the subjects.

The mind, which is spectator or auditor of other minds, cannot be without its eye and ear, so as to discern proportion, distinguish sound, and scan each sentiment or thought which comes before it. It can let nothing escape its censure. It feels the soft and harsh, the agreeable and disagreeable in the affections; and finds a foul and fair, a harmonious and a dissonant, as really and truly here as in any musical numbers or in the outward forms or representations of sensible things. Nor can it withhold its admiration and ecstasy, its aversion and scorn, any more in what relates to one than to the other of these subjects. So that to deny the common and natural sense of a sublime and beautiful in things, will appear an affectation merely, to any one who considers duly of this affair.

Now as in the sensible kind of objects the species or images of bodies, colours, and sounds are perpetually moving before our eyes, and acting on our senses even when we sleep; so in the moral and intellectual kind, the forms and images of things are no less active and incumbent on the mind, at all seasons, and even when the real objects themselves are absent.

In these vagrant characters or pictures of manners, which the mind of necessity figures to itself and carries still about with it, the heart cannot possibly remain neutral; but constantly takes part one way or other. However false or corrupt it be within itself, it finds the difference, as to beauty and comeliness, between one heart and another, one turn of affection, one behaviour, one sentiment and another; and accordingly, in all disinterested cases, must approve in some measure of what is natural and honest, and disapprove what is dishonest and corrupt.

Thus the several motions, inclinations, passions, dispositions, and consequent carriage and behaviour of creatures in the various parts of life, being in several views or perspectives represented to the mind, which readily discerns the good and ill towards the species or public, there arises a new trial or exercise of the heart, which must either rightly and soundly affect what is just and right, and disaffect what is contrary, or corruptly affect what is ill and disaffect what is worthy and good.

And in this case alone it is we call any creature worthy or virtuous, when it can have the notion of a public interest, and can attain the speculation or science of what is morally good or ill, admirable or blamable, right or wrong. For though we may vulgarly call an ill horse vicious, yet we never say of a good one, nor of any mere beast, idiot, or changeling,[6] though ever so good-natured, that he is worthy or virtuous.

So that if a creature be generous, kind, constant, compassionate, yet if he cannot reflect on what he himself does, or sees others do, so as to take notice of what is worthy or honest, and make that notice or conception of worth and honesty to be an object of his affection, he has not the character of being virtuous; for thus, and no otherwise, he is capable of having a sense of right or wrong, a sentiment or judgment of what is done through just, equal, and good affection, or the contrary.

Whatsoever is done through any unequal affection is iniquitous, wicked, and wrong. If the affection be equal, sound, and good, and the subject of the affection such as may with advantage to society be ever in the same manner prosecuted or affected, this must necessarily constitute what we call equity and right in any action. For wrong is not such action as is barely the cause of harm (since at this rate a dutiful son aiming at an enemy, but by mistake or ill chance happening to kill his father, would do a wrong), but when anything is done through insufficient or unequal affection (as when a son shows no concern for the safety of a father; or, where there is need of succour, prefers an indifferent person to him) this is of the nature of wrong.

Neither can any weakness or imperfection in the senses be the occasion of iniquity or wrong; if the object of the mind itself be not at any time absurdly framed, nor any way improper, but suitable, just, and worthy of the opinion and affection applied to it. For if we will suppose a man who, being sound and entire both in his reason and affection, has nevertheless so depraved a constitution or frame of body that the natural objects are, through his organs of sense, as through ill glasses, falsely conveyed and misrepresented, 'twill be soon observed, in such a person's case, that since his failure is not in his principal or leading part, he cannot in himself be esteemed iniquitous or unjust.

Tis otherwise in what relates to opinion, belief, or speculation. For as the extravagance of judgment or belief is such that in some countries even monkeys, cats, crocodiles, and other vile or destructive animals have been esteemed holy, and worshipped even as deities; should it appear to any one of the religion or belief of those countries that to save such a creature as a cat, preferably to a parent, was right, and that other men who had not the same religious opinion were to be treated as enemies till converted; this would be certainly wrong and wicked in the believer; and every action, grounded on this belief, would be an iniquitous, wicked, and vicious action.

And thus whatsoever causes a misconception or misapprehension of the worth or value of any object, so as to diminish a due, or raise any undue, irregular or unsocial affection, must necessarily be the occasion of wrong. . . .

A mistake therefore, in fact, being no cause or sign of ill affection, can be no cause of vice. But a mistake of right being the cause of unequal affection, must of necessity be the cause of vicious action in every intelligent or rational being.

But as there are many occasions where the matter of right may even to the most discerning part of mankind appear difficult, and of doubtful decision, 'tis not a slight mistake of this kind which can destroy the character of a virtuous or worthy man. But when, either through superstition or ill custom, there come to be very gross mistakes in the assignment or application of the affection; when the mistakes are either in their nature so gross, or so complicated and frequent, that a creature cannot well live in a natural state, nor with due affections, compatible with human society and civil life; then is the character of virtue forfeited.

And thus we find how far worth and virtue depend on a knowledge of right and wrong, and on a use of reason, sufficient to secure a right application of the affections; that nothing horrid or unnatural, nothing unexemplary, nothing destructive of that natural affection by which the species or society is upheld, may on any account, or through any principle or notion of honour or religion, be at any time affected or prosecuted as a good and proper object of esteem. For such a principle as this must be wholly vicious; and whatsoever is acted upon it can be no other than vice and immorality. And thus if there be anything which teaches men either treachery, ingratitude, or cruelty, by divine warrant or under colour and pretence of any present or future good to mankind; if there be anything which teaches men to persecute their friends through love, or to torment captives of war in sport, or to offer human sacrifice, or to torment, macerate, or mangle themselves in a religious zeal before their God, or to commit any sort of barbarity or brutality as amiable or becoming; be it custom which gives applause, or religion which gives a sanction; this is not, nor ever can be, virtue of any kind, or in any sense, but must remain still horrid depravity, notwithstanding any fashion, law, custom or religion which may be ill and vicious itself, but can never alter the eternal measures and immutable independent nature of worth and virtue.

Section IV

Upon the whole. As to those creatures who are only capable of being moved by sensible objects, they are accordingly good or vicious as the sensible affections stand with them. 'Tis otherwise in creatures capable of framing rational objects of moral good. For in one of this kind, should the sensible affections stand ever so much amiss, yet if they prevail not, because of those other rational affections spoken of, 'tis evident the temper still holds good in the main, and the person is with justice esteemed virtuous by all men. . . .

Part III

Section I

. . . 'Tis impossible to suppose a mere sensible creature originally so ill-constituted and unnatural as that, from the moment he comes to be tried by sensible objects, he should have no one good passion towards his kind, no foundation either of pity, love, kindness, or social affection. 'Tis full as impossible to conceive that a rational creature coming first to be tried by rational objects, and receiving into his mind the images or representations of justice, generosity, gratitude, or other virtue, should have no liking of these or dislike of their contraries, but be found absolutely indifferent towards whatsoever is presented to him of this sort. A soul, indeed, may as well be without sense as without admiration in the things of which it has any knowledge. Coming therefore to a capacity of seeing and admiring in this new way, it must needs find a beauty and a deformity as well in actions, minds, and tempers, as in figures, sounds, or colours. If there be no real amiableness or deformity in moral acts, there is at least an imaginary one of full force. Though perhaps the thing itself should not be allowed in Nature, the imagination or fancy of it must be allowed to be from Nature alone. Nor can anything besides art and strong endeavour, with long practice and meditation, overcome such a natural prevention[7] or prepossession of the mind in favour of this moral distinction.

Sense of right and wrong therefore being as natural to us as natural affection itself, and being a first principle in our constitution and make, there is no speculative opinion, persuasion, or belief, which is capable immediately or directly to exclude or destroy it. That which is of original and pure nature, nothing beside contrary habit and custom (a second nature) is able to displace. And this affection being an original one of earliest rise in the soul or affectionate part, nothing beside contrary affection, by frequent check and control, can operate upon it, so as either to diminish it in part or destroy it in the whole. . . .

Section II

. . . For whoever thinks there is a God, and pretends formally to believe that he is just and good, must suppose that there is independently such a thing as justice and injustice, truth and falsehood, right and wrong, according to which he pronounces that God is just, righteous, and true. If the mere will, decree, or law of God he said absolutely to constitute right and wrong, then are these latter words of no significancy at all. For thus, if each part of a contradiction were affirmed for truth by the Supreme Power, they would consequently become true. Thus if one person were decreed to suffer for another's fault, the sentence would be just and equitable. And thus, in the same manner, if arbitrarily and without reason some beings were destined to endure perpetual ill, and others as constantly to enjoy good, this also would pass under the same denomination. But to say of anything that it is just or unjust on such a foundation as this, is to say nothing, or to speak without a meaning.

And thus it appears that where a real devotion and hearty worship is paid to a Supreme Being, who in his history or character is represented otherwise than as really and truly just and good, there must ensue a loss of rectitude, a disturbance of thought, and a corruption of temper and manners in the believer. His honesty will of necessity be supplanted by his zeal, whilst he is thus unnaturally influenced, and rendered thus immorally devout.

To this we need only add, that as the ill character of a God does injury to the affections of men, and disturbs and impairs the natural sense of right and wrong, so, on the other hand, nothing can more highly contribute to the fixing of right apprehensions, and a sound judgment or sense of right and wrong, than to believe a God who is ever and on all accounts represented such as to be actually a true model and example of the most exact justice and highest goodness and worth. Such a view of divine providence and bounty extended to all, and expressed in a constant good affection towards the whole, must of necessity engage us, within our compass and sphere, to act by a like principle and affection. And having once the good of our species or public in view, as our end or aim, 'tis impossible we should be misguided by any means to a false apprehension or sense of right or wrong. . . .

Section III
   . . . That it is possible for a creature capable of using reflection to have a liking or dislike of moral actions, and consequently a sense of right and wrong, before such time as he may have any settled notion of a God, is what will hardly be questioned; it being a thing not expected, or any way possible, that a creature such as man, arising from his childhood slowly and gradually to several degrees of reason and reflection, should at the very first be taken up with those speculations or more refined sort of reflections, about the subject of God's existence.

Let us suppose a creature who, wanting reason and being unable to reflect, has notwithstanding many good qualities and affections, as love to his kind, courage, gratitude, or pity. 'Tis certain that if you give to this creature a reflecting faculty, it will at the same instant approve of gratitude, kindness, and pity; be taken with any show or representation of the social passion, and think nothing more amiable than this, or more odious than the contrary.

And this is to be capable of virtue, and to have a sense of right and wrong. . . .

BOOK II

Part I

Section I

We have considered what virtue is and to whom the character belongs. It remains to inquire, what obligation there is to virtue, or what reason to embrace it.

We have found that, to deserve the name of good or virtuous, a creature must have all his inclinations and affections, his dispositions of mind and temper, suitable, and agreeing with the good of his kind, or of that system in which he is included, and of which he constitutes a part. To stand thus well affected, and to have one's affections right and entire, not only in respect of oneself but of society and the public, this is rectitude, integrity, or virtue. And to be wanting in any of these, or to have their contraries, is depravity, corruption, and vice. . . .

There being allowed therefore in a creature such affections as these towards the common nature or system of the kind, together with those other which regard the private nature or self-system, it will appear that in following the first of these affections, the creature must on many occasions contradict and go against the latter. How else should the species be preserved? Or what would signify that implanted natural affection, by which a creature through so many difficulties and hazards preserves its offspring and supports its kind? . . .

Now that this is in reality quite otherwise, we shall endeavour to demonstrate, so as to make appear that what men represent as an ill order and constitution in the universe, by making moral rectitude appear the ill, and depravity the good or advantage of a creature, is in Nature just the contrary. That to be well affected towards the public interest and one's own is not only consistent but inseparable; and that moral rectitude or virtue must accordingly be the advantage, and vice the injury and disadvantage of every creature.

Section III

It has been shown before, that no animal can be said properly to act otherwise than through affections or passions, such as are proper to an animal. For in convulsive fits, where a creature strikes either himself or others, 'tis a simple mechanism, an engine, or piece of clockwork, which acts, and not the animal.

Whatsoever therefore is done or acted by any animal as such, is done only through some affection or passion, as of fear, love, or hatred moving him.

And as it is impossible that a weaker affection should overcome a stronger, so it is impossible but that where the affections or passions are strongest in the main, and form in general the most considerable party, either by their force or number, thither the animal must incline: and according to this balance he must be governed and led to action.

The affections or passions which must influence and govern the animal are either –

1. The natural affections, which lead to the good of the public.

2. Or the self affections, which lead only to the good of the private.

3. Or such as are neither of these, nor tending either to any good of the public or private, but contrariwise; and which may therefore be justly styled unnatural affections.

So that according as these affections stand, a creature must be virtuous or vicious, good or ill.

The latter sort of these affections, 'tis evident, are wholly vicious. The two former may be vicious or virtuous according to their degree.

It may seem strange, perhaps, to speak of natural affections as too strong, or of self affections as too weak. But to clear this difficulty we must call to mind what has been already explained, "That natural affection may, in particular cases, be excessive, and in an unnatural degree." As when pity is so overcoming as to destroy its own end, and prevent the succour and relief required; or as when love to the offspring proves such a fondness as destroys the parent, and consequently the offspring itself. . . .

And thus the affections towards private good become necessary and essential to goodness. For though no creature can be called good or virtuous merely for possessing these affections, yet since it is impossible that the public good or good of the system can be preserved without them, it follows that a creature really wanting in them is in reality wanting in some degree to goodness and natural rectitude, and may thus be esteemed vicious and defective. . . .

But having shown what is meant by a passion's being in too high or in too low a degree; and that to have any natural affection too high, or any self affection too low, though it be often approved as virtue, is yet, strictly speaking, a vice and imperfection; we come now to the plainer and more essential part of vice, and which alone deserves to be considered as such; that is to say –

1. When either the public affections are weak or deficient.

2. Or the private and self affections too strong.

3. Or that such affections arise as are neither of these, nor in any degree tending to the support either of the public or private system.

Otherwise than thus, it is impossible any creature can be such as we call ill or vicious. So that if once we prove that it is really not the creature's interest to be thus viciously affected, but contrariwise, we shall then have proved that it is his interest to be wholly good and virtuous, since in a wholesome and sound state of his affections, such as we have described, he cannot possibly be other than sound, good, and virtuous in his action and behaviour.

Our business, therefore, will be to prove –

1. That to have the natural, kindly, or generous affections strong and power-

ful towards the good of the public, is to have the chief means and power of self-enjoyment; and that to want them, is certain misery and ill.

2. That to have the private or self affections too strong, or beyond their degree of subordinacy to the kindly and natural, is also miserable.

3. And that to have the unnatural affections (viz. such as are neither founded on the interest of the kind or public, nor of the private person or creature himself) is to be miserable in the highest degree.

Part II

Section I

To begin therefore with this proof, That to have the natural affections (such as are founded in love, complacency, good-will, and in a sympathy with the kind or species) is to have the chief means and power of self-enjoyment; and that to want them is certain misery and ill. . . .

How much the social pleasures are superior to any other may be known by visible tokens and effects. The very outward features, the marks and signs which attend this sort of joy, are expressive of a more intense, clear, and undisturbed pleasure than those which attend the satisfaction of thirst, hunger, and other ardent appetites. But more particularly still may this superiority be known from the actual prevalence and ascendency of this sort of affection over all besides. Wherever it presents itself with any advantage, it silences and appeases every other motion of pleasure. No joy, merely of sense, can be a match for it. Whoever is judge of both the pleasures will ever give the preference to the former. But to be able to judge of both, 'tis necessary to have a sense of each. The honest man indeed can judge of sensual pleasure, and knows its utmost force. For neither is his taste or sense the duller; but, on the contrary, the more intense and clear on the account of his temperance and a moderate use of appetite. But the immoral and profligate man can by no means be allowed a good judge of social pleasure, to which he is so mere a stranger by his nature. . . .

It may be considered, withal, as a thing impossible, that they who esteem or love by any other rule than that of virtue, should place their affection on such subjects as they can long esteem or love. 'Twill be hard for them, in the number of their so beloved friends, to find any in whom they can heartily rejoice, or whose reciprocal love or esteem they can sincerely prize and enjoy. Nor can those pleasures be sound or lasting which are gathered from a self-flattery and false persuasion of the esteem and love of others who are incapable of any sound esteem or love. It appears therefore how much the men of narrow or partial affection must be losers in this sense, and of necessity fall short in this second principal part of mental enjoyment.

Meanwhile entire affection has all the opposite advantages. It is equal, constant, accountable to itself, ever satisfactory and pleasing. It gains applause and love from the best, and in all disinterested cases from the very worst of men. We may say of it with justice, that it carries with it a consciousness of merited love and approbation from all society, from all intelligent creatures, and from whatever is original to all other intelligence. And if there be in Nature any such original, we may add that the satisfaction which attends entire affection is full and noble in proportion to its final object, which contains all perfection, according to the sense of theism above noted.[8] For this, as has been shown, is the result of virtue. And to have this entire affection or integrity of mind is to live according to Nature, and the dictates and rules of supreme wisdom. This is morality, justice, piety, and natural religion. . . .

There are two things which to a rational creature must be horridly offensive and grievous, viz. to have the reflection in his mind of any unjust action or behaviour which he knows to be naturally odious and ill-deserving; or of any foolish action or behaviour which he knows to be prejudicial to his own interest or happiness.

The former of these is alone properly called Conscience, whether in a moral or religious sense. For to have awe and terror of the Deity does not, of itself, imply conscience. No one is esteemed the more conscientious for the fear of evil spirits, conjurations, enchantments, or whatever may proceed from any unjust, capricious, or devilish nature. Now to fear God any otherwise than as in consequence of some justly blamable and imputable act, is to fear a devilish nature, not a divine one. Nor does the fear of hell or a thousand terrors of the Deity imply conscience, unless where there is an apprehension of what is wrong, odious, morally deformed, and ill-deserving. And where this is the case, there conscience must have effect, and punishment of necessity be apprehended, even though it be not expressly threatened.

And thus religious conscience supposes moral or natural conscience. And though the former be understood to carry with it the fear of divine punishment, it has its force however from the apprehended moral deformity and odiousness of any act with respect purely to the Divine Presence, and the natural veneration due to such a supposed being. For in such a presence the shame of villainy or vice must have its force, independently on that further apprehension of the magisterial capacity of such a being, and his dispensation of particular rewards or punishments in a future state.

It has been already said, that no creature can maliciously and intentionally do ill without being sensible at the same time that he deserves ill. And in this respect, every sensible creature may be said to have conscience. For with all mankind, and all intelligent creatures, this must ever hold, that what they know they deserve from every one, that they necessarily must fear and expect from all. And thus suspicious and ill apprehensions must arise, with terror both of men and of the Deity. But besides this, there must in every rational creature be yet farther conscience, viz. from sense of deformity in what is thus ill-deserving and unnatural, and from a consequent shame or regret of incurring what is odious and moves aversion.

There scarcely is, or can be, any creature whom consciousness of villainy, as such merely, does not at all offend; nor anything opprobrious or heinously imputable move or affect. If there be such a one, 'tis evident he must be absolutely indifferent towards moral good or ill. If this indeed be his case, 'twill be allowed he can be no way capable of natural affection; if not of that, then neither of any social pleasure or mental enjoyment as shown above, but on the contrary, he must be subject to all manner of horrid, unnatural, and ill affection. So that to want conscience, or natural sense of the odiousness of crime and injustice, is to be most of all miserable in life; but where conscience or sense of this sort remains, there, consequently, whatever is committed against it must of necessity, by means of reflection, as we have shown, be continually shameful, grievous, and offensive. . . . And thus we have demonstrated that as, on one side, to have the natural and good affections is to have the chief means and power of self-enjoyment; so, on the other side, to want them is certain misery and ill.

Section II

We are now to prove, that by having the self-passions too intense or strong, a creature becomes miserable.

In order to [do] this we must, according to method, enumerate those home-affections which relate to the private interest or separate economy of the creature, such as love of life; resentment of injury; pleasure, or appetite towards nourishment and the means of generation; interest, or desire of those conveniences by which we are well provided for and maintained; emulation, or love of praise and honour; indolence, or love of ease and rest. These are the affections which relate to the private system, and constitute whatever we call interestedness or self-love.

Now these affections, if they are moderate and within certain bounds, are neither injurious to social life nor a hindrance to virtue; but being in an extreme degree, they become cowardice, revengefulness, luxury, avarice, vanity and ambition, sloth; and as such are owned vicious and ill with respect to human society. How they are ill also with respect to the private person, and are to his own disadvantage as well as that of the public, we may consider as we severally examine them. . . .

Conclusion

Thus have we endeavoured to prove what was proposed in the beginning. And since in the common and known sense of vice and illness, no one can be vicious or ill except either –

1. By the deficiency or weakness of natural affections;

Or, 2. By the violence of the selfish;

Or, 3. By such as are plainly unnatural;

It must follow that, if each of these are pernicious and destructive to the creature, insomuch that his completest state of misery is made from hence, to be wicked or vicious is to be miserable and unhappy.

And since every vicious action must in proportion, more or less, help towards this mischief and self-ill, it must follow that every vicious action must be self-injurious and ill.

On the other side, the happiness and good of virtue has been proved from the contrary effect of other affections, such as are according to Nature and the economy of the species or kind. We have cast up all those particulars from whence (as by way of addition and subtraction) the main sum or general account of happiness is either augmented or diminished. And if there be no article exceptionable in this scheme of moral arithmetic, the subject treated may be said to have an evidence as great as that which is found in numbers or mathematics. For let us carry scepticism ever so far, let us doubt, if we can, of everything about us, we cannot doubt of what passes within ourselves. Our passions and affections are known to us. They are certain, whatever the objects may be on which they are employed. Nor is it of any concern to our argument how these exterior objects stand: whether they are realities or mere illusions; whether we wake or dream. For ill dreams will be equally disturbing; and a good dream (if life be nothing else) will be easily and happily passed. In this dream of life, therefore, our demonstrations have the same force; our balance and economy hold good, and our obligation to virtue is in every respect the same.

Upon the whole there is not, I presume, the least degree of certainty wanting in what has been said concerning the preferableness of the mental pleasures to the sensual; and even of the sensual, accompanied with good affection, and under a temperate and right use, to those which are no ways restrained, nor supported by anything social or affectionate.

Nor is there less evidence in what has been said of the united structure and fabric of the mind, and of those passions which constitute the temper or soul, and on which its happiness or misery so immediately depend. It has been shown that in this constitution the impairing of any one part must instantly tend to the disorder and ruin of other parts, and of the whole itself, through the necessary connection and balance of the affections; that those very passions through which men are vicious are of themselves a torment and disease; and that whatsoever is done which is knowingly ill must be of ill consciousness; and in proportion as the act is ill must impair and corrupt social enjoyment, and destroy both the capacity of kind affection and the consciousness of meriting any such. So that neither can we participate thus in joy or happiness with others, nor receive satisfaction from the mutual kindness or imagined love of others, on which, however, the greatest of all our pleasures are founded.

If this be the case of moral delinquency, and if the state which is consequent to this defection from Nature be of all other the most horrid, oppressive, and miserable, 'twill appear that to yield or consent to anything ill or immoral is a breach of interest, and leads to the greatest ills, and that on the other side, everything which is an improvement of virtue, or an establishment of right affection and integrity, is an advancement of interest, and leads to the greatest and most solid happiness and enjoyment.

Thus the wisdom of what rules, and is first and chief in Nature, has made it to be according to the private interest and good of every one to work towards the general good, which if a creature ceases to promote, he is actually so far wanting to himself, and ceases to promote his own happiness and welfare. He is on this account directly his own enemy, nor can he any otherwise be good or useful to himself than as he continues good to society, and to that whole of which he is himself a part. So that virtue, which of all excellences and beauties is the chief and most amiable; that which is the prop and ornament of human affairs; which upholds communities, maintains union, friendship, and correspondence amongst men; that by which countries, as well as private families, flourish and are happy, and for want of which everything comely, conspicuous, great, and worthy, must perish and go to ruin; that single quality, thus beneficial to all society, and to mankind in general, is found equally a happiness and good to each creature in particular, and is that by which alone man can be happy, and without which he must be miserable.

And thus the virtue is the good, and vice the ill of every one.

Editor's Notes

1. Shaftesbury here is taking a slap at voluntarist theories of the divine origin of morality.
2. Col. 2:8 – "Beware lest any man spoil you through philosophy and vain deceit."
3. Titus 3:9.
4. 1 Tim. 1:4, 6.
5. Guide to life, investigator of virtue; a tag from Cicero.
6. Here in an archaic sense, meaning not a child substituted for another but an imbecile or half-wit.
7. Here in the sense of "prejudice," an opinion coming before "art and strong endeavour."
8. In Part III, Section II, Shaftesbury distinguished between an arbitrary and unjust deity and a just and lovable one. The latter must be an object of love to the virtuous person, and the latter, not the former, conforms to the theist's idea of God.

Further Reading

A new edition of the works of Shaftesbury is in progress, edited by Gerd Hemmerich, Wolfram Benda, and Ulrich Schödlbauer. The volume containing the *Inquiry Concerning Virtue or Merit* (giving the 1699 text as well as the later text) and several others are published by Frommann-Holzboog, Stuttgart. Robert Voitle, *The Third Earl of Shaftesbury, 1671–1713* (Baton Rouge: Louisiana State University Press, 1983), is an excellent biography.

For a brief survey of Bayle's thought, see Elizabeth Labrousse, *Bayle* (Oxford: Oxford University Press, 1983). Bayle's main book in defense of toleration, the *Philosophical Commentary*, was translated by Amie Goodman Tannenbaum (Bern: Peter Lang, 1987).

Ernst Cassirer, *The Platonic Renaissance in England*, trans. James Pettegrove (Austin: University of Texas Press, 1953), accompanies a valuable study of the Cambridge

Platonists with some discussion of Shaftesbury. Stanley Grean, *Shaftesbury's Philosophy of Religion and Ethics* (Athens: Ohio University Press, 1967), has a good bibliography up to its date. The first chapter of John Andrew Bernstein, *Shaftesbury, Rousseau, and Kant* (London: Associated University Presses, 1980), is directly relevant. Two articles by Ernest Tuveson help place Shaftesbury in his times: "The Origin of the Moral Sense," *Huntington Library Quarterly* 11 (1947–8):241–59; and "The Importance of Shaftesbury," *Journal of English Literary History* 20 (1953): 267–79.

There is a brilliant discussion of Shaftesbury, shedding light on his ethics, in David Marshall, *The Figure of Theater* (New York: Columbia University Press, 1986). See also John A. Dussinger, " 'The Lovely System of Lord Shaftesbury': An Answer to Locke . . . ?" *Journal of the History of Ideas* 62 (1981); Bernard Peach, "Shaftesbury's Moral *Arithmeticks*," *The Personalist* 39 (1958); Irwin Primer, "Mandeville and Shaftesbury: Some Facts and Problems," in Irwin Primer, ed., *Mandeville Studies* (The Hague: Nijhoff, 1975); and Gregory Trianosky, "On the Obligation to Be Virtuous: Shaftesbury and the Question, Why Be Moral?" *Journal of the History of Philosophy* 16 (1978).

Francis Hutcheson

Introduction

Francis Hutcheson was born in 1694 into a family of Scottish emigrés in northern Ireland. Educated first in Ireland, he then studied theology in Glasgow and, like his grandfather and father, became a Presbyterian minister. Hutcheson subsequently returned to Ireland, where he spent some years in Dublin teaching in a Presbyterian academy. He soon attracted the attention of several leaders of opinion, in particular Robert Viscount Molesworth, one of the foremost advocates of classical republicanism as a guide to current politics. (See the section "The Classical Republic" in the Introduction to this anthology.) Hutcheson spent much time in the Molesworth circle, and Molesworth encouraged him to publish his first book, the *Inquiry into the Original of Our Ideas of Beauty and Virtue* (1725).

In two later short works, published together in 1728 as *An Essay on the Nature and Conduct of the Passions, with Illustrations on the Moral Sense,* Hutcheson elaborated on his moral psychology, defended his views, and attacked opposing positions with considerable acuity. He was then called to the professorship of philosophy at the University of Glasgow, where he remained until his death in 1746. Hutcheson's early preaching in Ireland had drawn protests against its unorthodoxy; more formal accusations of heresy were made while he was at Glasgow, but he was not officially censured. He belonged to the moderate group in the Scottish church, taking a more lenient view of grace and predestination than had been traditional and showing less concern about abstruse points of the theology of the trinity.

Hutcheson's moral philosophy reflects both his departure from the sterner Calvinism of his forebears and his abiding commitment to Christianity. It also shows the marks of his philosophical education, which took place under the aegis of Gershom Carmichael, one of Hutcheson's predecessors in the chair at Glasgow. Carmichael had produced an annotated edition of Pufendorf's short version of his system of natural law, the *Duty of Man and Citizen,* and had taught his students Locke. Both of these philosophers were important to shaping Hutcheson's thought, as were the writings of the third earl of Shaftesbury, who, like Hutcheson, had enjoyed a close friendship with Molesworth.

Widely read in Britain during his lifetime, Hutcheson attracted a number of philosophical followers and admirers. Not the least of these was David Hume, whose ethics was much influenced by Hutcheson's. Adam Smith was a student of Hutcheson's at the university, and Thomas Reid discussed him in his early work. Hutcheson's first book was translated into French in 1749; his posthumous *System of Moral Philosophy* (1755) was promptly translated into German by the great literary critic Lessing, and both his earlier books appeared in German a few years later. Kant also read and admired Hutcheson, referring to him regularly in his lectures as the most notable representative of the moral sense school. In the British colonies in North America Hutcheson exercised considerable influence, especially as a political thinker.

Although Shaftesbury spoke occasionally of a "moral sense," he gave no careful account of what he meant by the phrase. Hutcheson, by contrast, made an account of the moral sense one of the main points of his ethical theory. Locke's theory of the origins of our ideas underlies Hutcheson's view. The Lockean holds that ideas must ultimately be derived from experience, each kind of idea arising from a separate kind of experience. Hutcheson argued at length that moral ideas are unique and irreducible and concluded that there must be a special source of the experience from which the ideas arise: our ideas of colors, sounds, and so on are attributed to the various external senses; Locke attributed our ideas of mental operations and of feelings to reflexive senses; and Hutcheson added a moral sense to be the source of our moral ideas.

What sort of idea do we get from the moral sense? The usual answer is that Hutcheson was a "sentimentalist" in morals, one who held, as Shaftesbury was taken to believe, that morality is ultimately a matter of feeling rather than of knowledge. What we obtain from the moral sense is feelings of approval and disapproval, which are special feelings of love for some people and of dislike for others. Morality is thus fundamentally one of the ways that we feel about one another, rather than one of the ways the mind obtains knowledge of the world.

The task of the scientific student of morals is, then, to say just what gives rise to our feelings of approval and disapproval. Like Shaftesbury, Hutcheson took the answer to be that it is, in the first instance, inner feelings and dispositions. He devoted much argument to showing, against Hobbes and Mandeville, that we are moved by disinterested benevolent feelings and not only by desires for our own good. Approval is aroused by desires and dispositions that lead us to do good to others; disapproval, by motives that lead us to harm others. Self-interested motives are considered by themselves to be morally indifferent. Because benevolent concern for the good of others is real, there also is a real foundation in our nature for morality. Hence, in Hutcheson's view, there is no place for moral skepticism. Although moral approval is an affective response to the world rather than itself a cognition of the world, it arises from cognition and is built into our own nature. We are not left doubting what in general is amiable or odious in behavior, nor are we without motives to do the one and avoid the other.

The Calvinists taught that original sin has so badly flawed our nature that we can hope to act rightly only if grace transforms us, enabling us to escape the domination of our feelings. Hutcheson rejected this doctrine and defended our natural passions, instincts, and affections as sources of virtuous action. Reason shows us the way to attain certain ends, but if the ends are not attractive to us, we will not act to obtain them. A benevolent instinct is what makes the good of others attractive. Why should not action from that instinct be counted as virtuous? In insisting that the appropriate final end of human action must be something we are motivated to attain, Hutcheson was repudiating the older Protestant notion that the law was established to show us what we ought to do and at the same time to show us that we cannot do it. (See the section "Luther and Calvin" in the Introduction to this anthology.) Both in making benevolence the sole motive we approve and in construing approval as a form of love, Hutcheson provided a philosophical equivalent of the gospel teaching that the law is summed up in the commandment to love God above all else and one's neighbor as oneself.

Hutcheson has long been considered to be a forerunner of utilitarianism. He was the first to use a phrase that Bentham later made famous: "That action is best," Hutcheson stated, "which procures the greatest happiness for the greatest numbers" (*Inquiry* 3.viii). But he held that the moral judgment of motives is prior to the moral judgment of actions or results, and he used the "greatest happiness" principle to explain our approvals and disapprovals rather than to give us a procedure for making decisions. On both these points his view is crucially different from the utilitarianism of Bentham and his followers.

Recently, some scholars have argued that it is a mistake to regard Hutcheson as a sentimentalist. Rather, they think, he was a moral realist, carrying on a natural law tradition that goes back beyond Pufendorf to Hooker and ultimately to Saint Thomas. And it is certainly true that Hutcheson tried to incorporate some natural law concepts into his own view. He considered laws, obligations, and rights to be important to the moral life, and in the *Inquiry* he offered accounts of them, in terms of the ideas furnished us by the moral sense. Whether or not the realist and natural law readings of Hutcheson can be sustained, they deserve serious attention (references to the main sources are given in the list of further readings). They show at least that for a full understanding of Hutcheson's views, and of the views of those whom he influenced, knowledge of the Continental natural law tradition is indispensable.

The following selections are from Hutcheson's *Inquiry into the Original of Our Ideas of Beauty and Virtue, in Two Treatises . . . II. Concerning Moral Good and Evil*, 4th ed., 1737. I have modernized some of the spelling and punctuation.

An Inquiry into the Original of Our Ideas of Beauty and Virtue

II. Concerning Moral Good and Evil

The Preface

. . . In reflecting upon our external senses, we plainly see that our perceptions[1] of pleasure or pain do not depend directly on our will. Objects do not please us according as we incline they should. The presence of some objects necessarily pleases us, the presence of others as necessarily displeases us. Nor can we, by our will, any otherwise procure pleasure or avoid pain than by procuring the former kind of objects and avoiding the latter. By the very frame of our nature the one is made the occasion of delight and the other of dissatisfaction.

The same observation will hold in all our other pleasures and pains. For there are many other sorts of objects which please or displease us as necessarily as material objects do when they operate upon our organs of sense. There is scarcely any object which our minds are employed about which is not thus constituted the necessary occasion of some pleasure or pain. Thus we find ourselves pleased with a regular form, a piece of architecture or painting, a composition of notes, a theorem, an action, an affection, a character. And we are conscious that this pleasure necessarily arises from the contemplation of the idea which is then present to our minds, with all its circumstances, although some of these ideas have nothing of what we commonly call sensible perception in them; and in those which have, the pleasure arises from some uniformity, order, arrangement, imitation; and not from the simple ideas of colour, or sound, or mode of extension separately considered.

These determinations to be pleased with any forms or ideas which occur to our observation, the author[2] chooses to call senses; distinguishing them from the powers which commonly go by that name by calling our power of perceiving the beauty of regularity, order, harmony, an internal sense; and that determination to approve affections, actions, or characters of rational agents, which we call virtuous, he marks by the name of a moral sense.

His principal design is to shew that human nature was not left quite indifferent in the affair of virtue, to form to itself observations concerning the advantage or disadvantage of actions and accordingly to regulate its conduct. The weakness of our reason, and the avocations arising from the infirmities and necessities of our nature are so great that very few men could ever have formed those long deductions of reason which shew some actions to be in the whole advantageous to the agent, and their contraries pernicious. The author of nature has much better furnished us for a virtuous conduct than our moralists seem to imagine, by almost as quick and powerful instructions as we have for the preservation of our bodies. He has given us strong affections to be the springs of each virtuous action; and made virtue a lovely form, that we might easily distinguish it from its contrary, and be made happy by the pursuit of it. . . .

Introduction

The word moral goodness, in this treatise, denotes our idea of some quality apprehended in actions which procures approbation attended with desire of the agent's happiness. Moral evil denotes our idea of a contrary quality, which excites condemnation or dislike. Approbation and condemnation are probably simple ideas, which cannot be farther explained. We must be contented with these imperfect descriptions until we discover whether we really have such ideas, and what general foundation there is in nature for this difference of actions as morally good or evil. These descriptions seem to contain an universally acknowledged difference of moral good and evil, from natural. All men who speak of moral good acknowledge that it procures approbation and good-will toward those we apprehend possessed of it; whereas natural good does not. In this matter men must consult their own breasts. How differently are they affected toward these they suppose possessed of honesty, faith, generosity, kindness; and those who are possessed of the natural goods, such as houses, lands, gardens, vineyards, health, strength, sagacity? We shall find that we necessarily love and approve the possessors of the former; but the possession of the latter procures no approbation or good-will at all toward the possessor, but often contrary affections of envy and hatred. In the same manner, whatever quality we apprehend to be morally evil raises our dislike toward the person in whom we observe it, such as treachery, cruelty, ingratitude; whereas we heartily love, esteem, and pity many who are exposed to natural evils, such as pain, poverty, hunger, sickness, death.

Now the first question on this subject is, whence arise these different ideas of actions? . . .

Section I: Of the Moral Sense by Which We Perceive Virtue and Vice, and Approve or Disapprove Them in Others

I. That the perceptions of moral good and evil are perfectly different from those of natural good or advantage, every one must convince himself by reflecting upon the different manner in which he finds himself affected when these objects occur to him. Had we no sense of good distinct from the advantage or interest arising from the external senses and the perceptions of beauty and harmony, the sensations and affections toward a fruitful field or commodious habitation would be much the same with what we have toward a generous friend or any noble character; for both are or may be advantageous to us. And we should no more admire any action or love any person in a distant country or age, whose influence could not extend to us, than we love the mountains of Peru while we are unconcerned in the Spanish trade. We should have the same sentiments and affections toward inanimate beings which we have toward rational agents, which yet every one knows to be false. Upon comparison, we say, "Why should we approve or love inanimate beings? They have no intention of good to us, or to any other person; their nature makes them fit for our uses, which they neither know nor study to serve. But it is not so with rational agents: they study the interest and desire the happiness of other beings with whom they converse."

We are all then conscious of the difference between that approbation or perception of moral excellence which benevolence excites toward the person in whom we observe it, and that opinion of natural goodness which only raises desire of possession toward the good object. Now what should make this difference, if all approbation or sense of good be from prospect of advantage? Do not inanimate objects promote our advantage as well as benevolent persons who do us offices of kindness and friendship? Should we not then have the same endearing approbation of both? or only the same cold opinion of advantage in both? The reason why it is not so must be this, that we have a distinct perception of beauty or excellence in the kind affections of rational agents, whence we are determined to admire and love such characters and persons.

Suppose we reap the same advantage from two men, one of whom serves us from an ultimate desire of our happiness or good-will toward us, the other from views of self-interest, or by constraint. Both are in this case equally beneficial or advantageous to us, and yet we shall have quite different sentiments of them. We must then certainly have other perceptions of moral actions than those of advantage. And that power of receiving these perceptions may be called a moral sense since the definition agrees to it, *viz.* a determination of the mind to receive any idea from the presence of an object which occurs to us independent on our will. . . .

II. In our sentiments of actions which affect ourselves, there is indeed a mixture of the ideas of natural and moral good which require some attention to separate them. But when we reflect upon the actions which affect other persons only, we may observe the moral ideas unmixed with those of natural good or evil. For let it be here observed that those senses by which we perceive pleasure in natural objects whence they are constituted advantageous could never raise in us any desire of public good, but only of what was good to ourselves in particular. Nor could they ever make us approve an action merely because of its promoting the happiness of others. And yet as soon as any action is represented to us as flowing from love, humanity, gratitude, compassion, a study of the good of others, and an ultimate desire of their happiness, although it were in the most distant part of the world or in some past age, we feel joy within us, admire the lovely action, and praise its author. And on the contrary, every action represented as flowing from ill-will, desire of the misery of others without view to any prevalent good to the public, or ingratitude, raises abhorrence and aversion.

It is true indeed that the actions we approve in others are generally imagined to tend to the natural good of mankind or of some parts of it. But whence this secret chain between each person and mankind? How is my interest connected with the most distant parts of it? And yet I must admire actions which show good-will toward them, and love the author. Whence this love, compassion, indignation and hatred toward even feigned characters in the most distant ages, and nations, according as they appear kind, faithful, compassionate, or of the opposite disposition, toward their imaginary contemporaries? If there is no moral sense which makes benevolent actions appear beautiful; if all approbation be from the interest of the approver,

What's Hecuba to us, or we to Hecuba?[3] . . .

IV. Some moralists, who will rather twist self-love into a thousand shapes than allow any other principle of approbation than interest, may tell us that whatever profits one part without detriment to another profits the whole, and then some small share will resound to each individual; that those actions which tend to the good of the whole, if universally performed, would most effectually secure to each individual his own happiness; and that consequently we may approve such actions, from the opinion of their tending ultimately to our own advantage.

We need not trouble these gentlemen to show by their nice train of consequences and influences of actions by way of precedent in particular instances that we in this age reap any advantage from Orestes' killing the treacherous Aegysthus,[4] or from the actions of Codrus[5] or Decius.[6] Allow their reasonings to be perfectly good, they only prove that after long reflection and reasoning we may find out some ground to judge certain actions advantageous to us which every man admires as soon as he hears of them; and that too under a quite different conception.

Should any of our travellers find some old Grecian treasure, the miser who hid it certainly performed an action more to the traveller's advantage, than Codrus or Orestes; for he must have but a small share of benefit from their actions, whose influence is so dispersed and lost in various ages and nations. Surely then this miser must appear to the traveller a prodigious hero in virtue! For self-interest will recommend men to us only according to the good they do to our selves, and not give us high ideas of public good but in proportion to our share of it. But must a man have the reflection of Cumberland or Pufendorf[7] to admire generosity, faith, humanity, gratitude? Or reason so nicely to apprehend the evil in cruelty, treachery, ingratitude? Do not the former excite our admiration and love and study of imitation, where-ever we see them, almost at first view, without any such reflection, and the latter, our contempt and abhorrence? Unhappy would it be for mankind if a sense of virtue was of as narrow an extent, as a capacity for such metaphysics. . . .

It may perhaps be alleged that in those actions of our own which we call good, there is this constant advantage, superior to all others, which is the ground of our approbation, and the motive to them from self-love, *viz.* that we suppose the deity will reward them. . . . At present it is enough to observe that many have high notions of honour, faith, generosity, justice, who have scarce any opinions about the deity or any thoughts of future regards; and abhor any thing which is treacherous, cruel, or unjust, without any regard to future punishments. . . .

This is the second thing to be considered: whether our sense of the moral good or evil in the actions of others can be overbalanced or bribed by views of interest. Now I may indeed easily be capable of wishing that another would do an action I abhor as morally evil, if it were very advantageous to me. Interest in that case may overbalance my desire of virtue in another. But no interest to myself will make me approve an action as morally good which without that interest to myself would have appeared morally evil, if upon computing its whole effects it appears to produce as great a moment of good in the whole, when it is not beneficial to me, as it did before, when it was. In our sense of moral good or evil, our own private advantage or loss is of no more moment than the advantage or loss of a third person to make an action appear good or evil. This sense therefore cannot be overbalanced by interest. How ridiculous an attempt would it be to engage a man by rewards or threatenings into a good opinion of an action which was contrary to his moral notions? We may procure dissimulation by such means, and that is all. . . .

VII. If what is said makes it appear that we have some other amiable idea of actions than that of advantageous to ourselves, we may conclude that this perception of moral good is not derived from custom, education, example, or study. These give us no new ideas. They might make us see private advantage in actions whose usefulness did not at first appear, or give us opinions of some tendency of actions to our detriment, by some nice deductions of reason or by a rash prejudice, when upon the first view of the action we should have observed no such thing: but they never could have made us apprehend actions as amiable or odious without any consideration of our own advantage.

VIII. It remains then that as the Author of Nature has determined us to receive, by our external senses, pleasant or disagreeable ideas of objects according as they are useful or hurtful to our bodies, and to receive from uniform objects the pleasures of beauty and harmony, to excite us to the pursuit of knowledge and to reward us for it, or to be an argument to us of his goodness, as the uniformity itself proves his existence, whether we had a sense of beauty in uniformity or not; in the same manner he has given us a moral sense to direct our actions, and to give us still nobler pleasures. So that while we are only intending the good of others, we undesignedly promote our own greatest private good.

We are not to imagine this moral sense, more than the other senses, supposes any innate ideas, knowledge, or practical proposition. We mean by it only a determination of our minds to receive the simple ideas of approbation or condemnation from actions observed antecedent to any opinions of advantage or loss to redound to ourselves from them; even as we are pleased with a regular form or an harmonious composition without having any knowledge of mathematics, or seeing any advantage in that form or composition, different from the immediate pleasure. . . .

Section II: Concerning the Immediate Motive to Virtuous Actions

The motives of human actions, or their immediate causes, would be best understood after considering the passions and affections; but here we shall only consider the springs of the actions which we call virtuous, as far as it is necessary to settle the general foundation of the moral sense.

I. Every action which we apprehend as either morally good or evil is always supposed to flow from some affection toward sensitive natures; and whatever we call virtue or vice is either some such affection or some action consequent upon it. Or it may perhaps be enough to make an action or omission appear vicious if it argues the want of such affection toward rational agents as we expect in characters counted morally good. All the actions counted religious in any country are supposed, by those who count them so, to flow from some affections toward the deity; and whatever we call social virtue we still suppose to flow from affections toward our fellow-creatures. For in this all seem to agree, that external motions, when accompanied with no affections toward God or man, or evidencing no want of the expected affections toward either, can have no moral good or evil in them.

Ask, for instance, the most abstemious hermit if temperance of itself would be morally good, supposing it showed no obedience toward the deity, made us no fitter for devotion, or the service of mankind, or the search after truth, than luxury; and he will easily grant that it would be no moral good, though still it might be naturally good or advantageous to health. And mere courage or contempt of danger, if we conceive it to have no regard to the defence of the innocent, or repairing of wrongs or self-interest, would only entitle its possessor to Bedlam.[8] When such sort of courage is sometimes admired it is upon some secret apprehension of a good intention in the use of it or as a natural ability capable of an useful application. Prudence, if it was only employed in promoting private interest, is never imagined to be a virtue. And justice, or observing a strict equality, if it has no regard to the good of mankind, the preservation of rights and securing peace, is a quality properer for its ordinary gestamen,[9] a beam and scales, than for a rational agent. So that these four qualities, commonly called cardinal virtues, obtain that name because they are dispositions universally necessary to promote public good, and denote affections toward rational agents; otherwise there would appear no virtue in them.

II. Now, if it can be made appear that none of these affections which we approve as virtuous are either self-love, or desire or private interest; since all virtue is either some such affections, or actions consequent upon them; it must necessarily follow that virtue springs from some other affection than self-love, or desire of private advantage. And where self-interest excites to the same action, the approbation is given only to the disinterested principle.

The affections which are of most importance in morals are commonly included under the names love and hatred. Now in discoursing of love, we need not be cautioned not to include that love between the sexes, which, when no other affections accompany it, is only desire of pleasure and is never counted a virtue. Love toward rational agents is subdivided into love of complacence[10] or esteem, and love of benevolence: And hatred is subdivided into hatred of displicence[11] or contempt, and hatred of malice. Complacence denotes approbation of any person by our moral sense; and is rather a perception than an affection; tho' the affection of good-will is ordinarily subsequent to it. Benevolence is the desire of the happiness of another. Their opposites are called dislike and malice. Concerning each of these separately we shall consider whether they can be influenced by motives of self-interest. . . .

III. As to the love of benevolence, the very name excludes self-interest. We never call that man benevolent who is in fact useful to others, but at the same time only intends his own interest without any ultimate desire of the good of others. If there be any benevolence at all, it must be disinterested; for the most useful action imaginable loses all appearance of benevolence as soon as we discern that it only flowed from self-love or interest. . . .

But it must be here observed that as all men have self-love, as well as benevolence, these two principles may jointly excite a man to the same action; and then they are to be considered as two forces impelling the same body to motion; sometimes they conspire, sometimes are indifferent to each other, and sometimes are in some degree opposite. Thus, if a man have such strong benevolence as would have produced an action without any views of self-interest, that such a man has also in view private advantage along with public good as the effect of his action does no way diminish the benevolence of the action. When he would not have produced so much public good, had it not been for prospect of self-interest, then the effect of self-love is to be deducted, and his benevolence is proportioned to the remainder of good which pure benevolence would have produced. When a man's benevolence is hurtful to himself then self-love is opposite to benevolence, and the benevolence is proportioned to the sum of the good produced, added to the resistance of self-love surmounted by it. In most cases it is impossible for men to know how far their fellows are influenced by the one or other of these principles; but yet the general truth is sufficiently certain, that this is the way in which the benevolence of actions is to be computed. . . .

VI. If anyone should ask: . . . to what purpose serves our moral sense, our sense of pleasure from the happiness of others? To what purpose serves the wise order of nature, by which virtue is even made generally advantageous in this life? To what end are eternal rewards appointed and revealed? The answer to these questions was given partly already: all these motives may make us desire to have benevolent affections, and consequently turn our attention to those qualities in objects which excite them; they may overbalance all apparent contrary motives and all temptations to vice. But farther, I hope it will be still thought an end worthy of the deity to make the virtuous happy, by a wise constitution of nature, whether the virtues were in every action intending to obtain this happiness or not. Beneficent actions tend to the public good; it is therefore good and kind to give all possible additional motives to them, and to excite men who have some weak degrees of good affection to promote the public good more vigorously by motives of self-interest; or even to excite those who have no virtue at all to external acts of beneficence, and to restrain them from vice.*

From the whole it may appear that there is in human nature a disinterested ultimate desire of the happiness of others, and that our moral sense determines us to approve actions as virtuous which are apprehended to proceed partly at least from such desire. . . .

X. Having removed these false springs of virtuous actions, let us next establish the true one, *viz.* some determination of our nature to study the good of others or some instinct, antecedent to all reason from interest, which influences us to the love of others; even as the moral sense, above explained, determines us to approve the actions which flow from this love in ourselves or others. This disinterested affection may appear strange to men impressed with notions of self-love as the sole spring of action, from the pulpit, the schools, the systems, and conversations regulated by them: but let us consider it in its strongest and simplest kinds, and when we see the possibility of it in these instances, we may easily discover its universal extent.

An honest farmer will tell you that he studies the preservation and happiness of his children, and loves them without any design of good to himself. But, say some of our philosophers, "The happiness of their children gives

---

* . . . Whoever would appeal to the general strain of the Christian exhortation will find disinterested love more inculcated and motives of gratitude more frequently suggested than any others.

parents pleasure, and their misery gives them pain; and therefore to obtain the former and avoid the latter, they study, from self-love, the good of their children." Suppose several merchants joined in partnership of their whole effects. One of them is employed abroad in managing the stock of the company; his prosperity occasions gain to all, and his losses give them pain for their share in the loss. Is this then the same kind of affection with that of parents to their children? Is there the same tender, personal regard? I fancy no parent will say so. In this case of merchants there is a plain conjunction of interest; but whence the conjunction of interest between the parent and child? Do the child's sensations give pleasure or pain to the parent? Is the parent hungry, thirsty, sick, when his children are so? No; but his naturally implanted desire of their good and aversion to their misery makes him be affected with joy or sorrow from their pleasures or pains. This desire then is antecedent to the conjunction of interest, and the cause of it, not the effect. It then must be disinterested. "No," says another sophist, "children are parts of ourselves, and in loving them we but love ourselves in them." A very good answer! Let us carry it as far as it will go. How are they parts of ourselves? Not as a leg or an arm: We are not conscious of their sensations. "But their bodies were formed from parts of ours." So is a fly, or a maggot, which may breed in any discharged blood or humour – very dear insects surely! There must be something else then which makes children parts of ourselves; and what is this but that affection which nature determines us to have toward them? This love makes them parts of ourselves, and therefore does not flow from their being so before. This is indeed a good metaphor; and wherever we find a determination among several rational agents to mutual love, let each individual be looked upon as a part of a great whole, or system, and concern himself in the public good of it. . . .

Section III: The Sense of Virtue, and the Various Opinions About It, Reducible to One General Foundation. The Manner of Computing the Morality of Actions

I. If we examine all the actions which are counted amiable anywhere, and inquire into the grounds upon which they are approved, we shall find that in the opinion of the person who approves them they always appear as benevolent, or flowing from good-will to others and a study of their happiness, whether the approver be one of the persons beloved or profited or not, so that all those kind affections which incline us to make others happy and all actions supposed to flow from such affections appear morally good, if, while they are benevolent towards some persons, they be not pernicious to others. Nor shall we find any thing amiable in any action whatsoever where there is no benevolence imagined; nor in any disposition, or capacity which is not supposed applicable to, and designed for, benevolent purposes. Nay, as was before observed, the actions which in fact are exceedingly useful shall appear void of moral beauty if we know they proceeded from no kind intentions towards others; and yet an unsuccessful attempt of kindness, or of promoting public good, shall appear as amiable as the most successful if it flowed from as strong benevolence.

II. Hence those affections which would lead us to do good to our benefactor shall appear amiable, and the contrary affections odious, even when our actions cannot possibly be of any advantage or hurt to him. Thus a sincere love and gratitude toward our benefactor, a cheerful readiness to do whatever he shall require, how burdensome soever, a hearty inclination to comply with his intentions and contentment with the state he has placed us in, are the strongest evidences of benevolence we can show to such a person; and therefore they must appear exceedingly amiable. And under these is included all the rational devotion or religion toward a deity apprehended as good which we can possibly perform. . . .

As to external performances of religion, they are no doubt very various in different nations and ages; and education may give men opinions that certain actions are pleasing and others displeasing to the deity. But then wherever any external rite of worship is approved there also it is looked upon to proceed from love toward the deity or some other affection necessarily joined with love, as reverence, repentance, or sorrow to have offended. So that the general principle of love is the foundation of all the apparent moral excellence, even in the most fantastic rites of worship which were ever approved. For as to rites designed only to appease a furious being, no mortal, I fancy, apprehends there is any virtue or excellence in them, but that they are chosen only as the dishonourable means of avoiding a greater evil. Now as there are various speculative opinions about what is acceptable to the deity, it necessarily follows that, accordingly, practices and approbation must be various, though all the moral goodness of actions is still presumed to flow from love.

III. Again, that we may see how benevolence is the foundation of all apprehended excellence in social virtues, let us only observe that amidst the diversity of sentiments on this head among various sects, this is still allowed to be the way of deciding the controversy about any disputed practice, *viz.* to inquire whether this conduct or the contrary will most effectually promote the public good. The morality is immediately adjusted when the natural tendency or influence of the action upon the universal natural good of mankind is agreed upon. That which produces more good than evil in the whole is acknowledged good; and what does not is counted evil. In this case we no other way regard the good of the actor, or that of those who are thus inquiring, than as they make a part of the great system. . . .

V. The actions which flow solely from self-love and yet evidence no want of benevolence, having no hurtful effects upon others, seem perfectly indifferent in a moral sense and neither raise the love or hatred of the observer. Our reason can indeed discover certain bounds within which we may not only act from self-love, consistently with the good of the whole; but every mortal's acting thus within these bounds for his own good is absolutely necessary for the good of the whole; and the want of such self-love would be universally pernicious. Hence, he who pursues his own private good, with an intention also to concur with that constitution which tends to the good of the whole, and much more he who promotes his own good with a direct view of making himself more capable of serving God, or doing good to mankind, acts not only innocently but also honourably and virtuously. For in both these cases benevolence concurs with self-love to excite him to the action. And thus a neglect of our own good may be morally evil and argue a want of benevolence toward the whole. But when self-love breaks over the bounds above-mentioned and leads us into actions detrimental to others and to the whole, or makes us insensible of the generous kind affections, then it appears vicious and is disapproved. So also, when upon small injuries or sudden resentment or any weak superstitious suggestions, our benevolence becomes so faint as to let us entertain odious conceptions of men or any part of them without just ground, as if they were wholly evil or malicious, or as if they were a worse sort of beings than they really are, these conceptions must lead us into malevolent affections or at least weaken our good ones and makes us really vicious.

VI. Here we must also observe that every moral agent justly considers himself as a part of this rational system which may be useful to the whole; so that he may be, in part, an object of his own benevolence. Nay, farther, as was hinted above, he may see that the preservation of the system requires every one to be innocently solicitous about himself. Hence he may conclude that an action which brings greater evil to the agent than good to others, however it may evidence strong benevolence or a virtuous disposition in the agent, yet it must be founded upon a mistaken opinion of its tendency to public good, when it has no such tendency: so that a man who reasoned justly and considered the whole would not be led into it, were his benevolence ever so strong. . . .

VIII. In comparing the moral qualities of actions in order to regulate our election among various actions proposed, or to find which of them has the greatest moral excellency, we are led by our moral sense of virtue to judge thus: that in equal degrees of happiness expected to proceed from the action the virtue is in proportion to the number of persons to whom the happiness shall extend (and here the dignity, or moral importance of persons, may compensate numbers); and in equal numbers, the virtue is as the quantity of the happiness or natural good; or that the virtue is in a compound ratio of the quantity of good and number of enjoyers. In the same manner, the moral evil or vice is as the degree of misery and number of sufferers; so that that action is best, which procures the greatest happiness for the greatest numbers; and that worst, which in like manner occasions misery.

Again, when the consequences of actions are of a mixed nature, partly advantageous and partly pernicious, that action is good whose good effects preponderate[12] the evil by being useful to many, and pernicious to few, and that evil, which is otherwise. Here also the moral importance of characters, or dignity of persons may compensate numbers,[13] as may also the degrees of happiness or misery. For to procure an inconsiderable good to many, but an immense evil to few, may be evil; and an immense good to few may preponderate a small evil to many.

But the consequences which affect the morality of actions are not only the direct and natural effects of the actions themselves, but also all those events which otherwise would not have happened. For many actions which have no immediate or natural evil effects, nay, which actually produce good effects, may be evil, if a man foresees that the evil consequences which will probably flow from the folly of others upon his doing of such actions are so great as to overbalance all the good produced by those actions, or all the evils which would flow from the omission of them. And in such cases the probability is to be computed on both sides. Thus if an action of mine will probably, through the mistake or corruption of others, be made a precedent in unlike cases to very evil actions, or when my action, though good in itself, will probably provoke men to very evil actions, upon some mistaken notion of their right; any of these considerations foreseen by me may make such an action of mine evil, whenever the evils which will probably be occasioned by the action are greater than the evils occasioned by the omission.

And this is the reason that many laws prohibit actions in general even when some particular instances of those actions would be very useful; because an universal allowance of them, considering the mistakes men would probably fall into, would be more pernicious than an universal prohibition; nor could there be any more special boundaries fixed between the right and wrong cases. In such cases, it is the duty of persons to comply with the generally useful constitution; or if in some very important instances the violation of the law would be of less evil consequence than obedience to it, they must patiently resolve to undergo those penalties which the state has, for valuable ends to the whole, appointed. And this disobedience will have nothing criminal in it. . . .

XI. To find a universal rule to compute the morality of any actions, with all their circumstances, when we judge of the actions done by ourselves or by others, we must observe the following propositions or axioms.

1. The moral importance of any agent, or the quantity of public good he produces, is in a compound proportion of his benevolence and abilities. For 'tis plain that his good offices depend upon these two jointly. In like manner, the quantity of private good which any agent obtains for himself is in a like compound proportion of his selfish principles and his abilities. We speak here only of the external goods of this world, which one pursues from some selfish principles. For as to internal goods of the mind, these are most effectually obtained by the exercise of other affections than those called selfish, even those which carry the agent beyond himself toward the good of others.

2. In comparing the virtues of different agents, when the abilities are equal, the moments of public good are proportioned to the goodness of the temper or the benevolence; and when the tempers are equal, the quantities of good are as the abilities.

3. The virtue then or goodness of temper is directly as the moment of good

when other circumstances are equal, and inversely as the abilities. That is to say, where the abilities are greatest, there is less virtue evidenced in any given moment of good produced.

4. But as the natural consequences of our actions are various, some good to ourselves and evil to the public, and others evil to ourselves and good to the public, or either useful both to ourselves and others, or pernicious to both; the entire spring of good actions is not always benevolence alone; or of evil, malice alone (nay, sedate malice is rarely found); but in most actions we must look upon self-love as another force, sometimes conspiring with benevolence and assisting it, when we are excited by views of private interest as well as public good; and sometimes opposing benevolence when the good action is any way difficult or painful in the performance or detrimental in its consequences to the agent.

These selfish motives . . . we may in general denote . . . by the word interest, which when it concurs with benevolence in any action capable of increase or diminution must produce a greater quantity of good than benevolence alone in the same abilities; and therefore when the moment of good in an action partly intended for the good is but equal to the moment of good in the action of another agent influenced only by benevolence, the former is less virtuous; and in this case the interest must be deducted to find the true effect of the benevolence or virtue. In the same manner, when interest is opposite to benevolence and yet is surmounted by it, this interest must be added to the moment to increase the virtue of the action, or the strength of the benevolence. By interest, in this last case, is understood all the advantage which the agent might have obtained by omitting the action, which is a negative motive to it; and this, when subtracted, becomes positive. . . .

The sixth axiom only explains the external marks by which men must judge, who do not see into each other's hearts; for it may really happen in many cases that men may have benevolence sufficient to surmount any difficulty and yet they may meet with none at all. And in that case it is certain there is as much virtue in the agent, though he does not give such proof of it to his fellow-creatures, as if he had surmounted difficulties in his kind actions. And this too must be the case with the deity, to whom nothing is difficult.

Since then in judging of the goodness of temper in any agent, the abilities must come into computation, as is above-mentioned, and none can act beyond their natural abilities; that must be the perfection of virtue where the moment of good produced equals the ability, or when the being acts to the utmost of his power for the public good; and hence the perfection of virtue, in this case, is as unity. . . .

From the preceding reasonings we shall only draw this one inference, which seems the most joyful imaginable, even to the lowest rank of mankind, *viz.* that no external circumstances of fortune, no involuntary disadvantages, can exclude any mortal from the most heroic virtue. For how small soever the moment of public good be which any one can accomplish, yet if his abilities are proportionably small, the virtue may be as great as any whatsoever. Thus, not only the prince, the statesman, the general, are capable of true heroism, though these are the chief characters whose fame is diffused through various nations and ages, but when we find in an honest trader, the kind friend, the faithful prudent adviser, the charitable and hospitable neighbour, the tender husband and affectionate parent, the sedate yet cheerful companion, the generous assistant of merit, the cautious allayer of contention and debate, the promoter of love and good understanding among acquaintances; if we consider that these were all the good offices which his station in the world gave him an opportunity of performing to mankind, we must judge this character really as amiable as those whose external splendor dazzles an injudicious world into an opinion that they are the only heroes in virtue. . . .

Section VI: Concerning the Importance of This Moral Sense to the Present Happiness of Mankind, and Its Influence on Human Affairs

I. It may now probably appear that notwithstanding the corruption of manners so justly complained of everywhere, this moral sense has a greater influence on mankind than is generally imagined, although it is often directed by very partial imperfect views of public good, and often overcome by self-love. But we shall offer some farther considerations to prove that it gives us more pleasure and pain than all our other faculties. And to prevent repetitions, let us observe that wherever any morally good quality gives pleasure from reflection, or from honour, the contrary evil one will give proportionable pain, from remorse and shame. Now we shall consider the moral pleasures, not only separately but as they are the most delightful ingredient in the ordinary pleasures of life.

All men seem persuaded of some excellency in the possession of good morals which is superior to all other enjoyments; and on the contrary look upon a state of moral evil as worse and more wretched than any other whatsoever. We must not form our judgment in this matter from the actions of men; for however they may be influenced by moral sentiments, yet it is certain that self-interested passions frequently overcome them, and partial views of the tendency of actions make us do what is really morally evil, apprehending it to be good. But let us examine the sentiments which men universally form of the state of others when they are no way immediately concerned; for in these sentiments human nature is calm and undisturbed and shows its true face.

Now should we imagine a rational creature in a sufficiently happy state, whose mind was without interruption wholly occupied with pleasant sensations of smell, taste, touch, etc. if at the same time all other ideas were excluded? Should we not think the state low, mean, and sordid, if there were no society, no love or friendship, no good offices? What then must that state be wherein there are no pleasures but those of the external senses, with such long intervals as human nature at present must have? Do these short fits of pleasure make the luxurious happy? How insipid and joyless are the reflections on past pleasure! And how poor a recompense is the return of the transient sensation for the nauseous satieties, and languors in the intervals! This frame of our nature, so incapable of long enjoyments of the external senses, points out to us that there must be some other more durable pleasure, without such tedious interruptions, and nauseous reflections. . . .

II. Let us in the same manner examine our sentiments of the happiness of others in common life. Wealth and external pleasures bear no small bulk in our imaginations; but does there not always accompany this opinion of happiness in wealth some supposed beneficent intention of doing good offices to persons dear to us, at least to our families or kinsmen? And in our imagined happiness from external pleasure, are not some ideas always included of some moral enjoyments of society, some communication of pleasure, something of love, of friendship, of esteem, of gratitude? Who ever pretended to a taste of these pleasures without society? Or if any seem violent in pursuit of them, how base and contemptible do they appear to all persons, even to those who could have no expectation of advantage from their having a more generous notion of pleasure?

Now, were there no moral sense, no happiness in benevolence, and did we act from no other principle than self-love, sure there is no pleasure of the external senses which we could not enjoy alone with less trouble and expense than in society. But a mixture of the moral pleasures is what gives the alluring relish; 'tis some appearance of friendship, of love, of communicating pleasure to others, which preserves the pleasures of the luxurious from being nauseous and insipid. And this partial imagination of some good morals, some benevolence, in actions which have many cruel, inhuman, and destructive consequences toward others, is what has kept vice more in countenance than any other consideration.

But to convince us farther wherein the happiness of wealth and external pleasure lies, let us but suppose malice, wrath, revenge, or only solitude, absence of friendship, of love, of society, of esteem, joined with the possession of them; and all the happiness vanishes like a dream. And yet love, friendship, society, humanity, though accompanied with poverty and toil, nay even with smaller degrees of pain, such as do not wholly occupy the mind, are not only the object of love from others but even of a sort of emulation; which plainly shows that virtue is the chief happiness in the judgment of all mankind. . . .

Section VII: A Deduction of Some Complex Moral Ideas; Viz. of Obligation, and Right, Perfect, Imperfect, and External, Alienable, and Unalienable, from This Moral Sense

I. To conclude this subject, we may, from what has been said, see the true original of moral ideas, *viz.* this moral sense of excellence in every appearance or evidence of benevolence. It remains to be explained how we acquire more particular ideas of virtue and vice, abstracting from any law, human, or divine.

If anyone ask, can we have any sense of obligation, abstracting from the laws of a superior? We must answer according to the various senses of the word obligation. If by obligation we understand a determination, without regard to our own interest to approve actions and to perform them, which determination shall also make us displeased with ourselves and uneasy upon having acted contrary to it; in this meaning of the word obligation there is naturally an obligation upon all men to benevolence; and they are still under its influence even when by false or partial opinions of the natural tendency of their actions, this moral sense leads them to evil; unless by long inveterate habits it be exceedingly weakened; for it scarce seems possible wholly to extinguish it. Or, which is to the same purpose, this internal sense and instinct of benevolence will either influence our actions or make us very uneasy and dissatisfied; and we shall be conscious that we are in a base unhappy state even without considering any law whatsoever, or any external advantages lost, or disadvantages impending from its sanctions. And farther, there are still such indications given us of what is in the whole beneficent, and what not, as may probably discover to us the true tendency of every action, and let us see, some time or other, the evil tendency of what upon a partial view appeared good. Or if we have no friends so faithful as to admonish us, the persons injured will not fail to upbraid us. So that no mortal can secure to himself a perpetual serenity, satisfaction, and self-approbation, but by a serious inquiry into the tendency of his actions and a perpetual study of universal good according to the justest notions of it.

But if, by obligation, we understand a motive from self-interest sufficient to determine all those who duly consider it and pursue their own advantage wisely to a certain course of actions; we may have a sense of such an obligation, by reflecting on this determination of our nature to approve virtue, to be pleased and happy when we reflect upon our having done virtuous actions, and to be uneasy when we are conscious of having acted otherwise; and also by considering how much superior we esteem the happiness of virtue to any other enjoyment. We may likewise have a sense of this sort of obligation by considering those reasons which prove a constant course of benevolent and social actions to be the most probable means of promoting the natural good of every individual, as Cumberland and Pufendorf have proved. And all this without relation to a law.

But farther, if our moral sense be supposed exceedingly weakened and the selfish passions grown strong, either through some general corruption of nature or inveterate habits; if our understanding be weak and we be often in danger of being hurried by our passions into precipitate and rash judgments that malicious actions shall promote our advantage more than beneficence; in such a case, if it be inquired what is necessary to engage men to beneficent actions or induce a steady sense of an obligation to act for the public good; then, no doubt, a law with sanctions, given by a superior being of sufficient power to make us happy or miserable, must be necessary to counterbalance those apparent motives of interest, to calm our passions, and give room for the recovery of our moral sense, or at least for a just view of our interest.

II. Now the principal business of the moral philosopher is to shew, from solid reasons, that universal benevolence tends to the happiness of the benevolent, either from the pleasures of reflection, honour, natural tendency to engage the good offices of men, upon whose aid we must depend for our happiness in this world, or from the sanctions of divine laws discovered to us by the constitution of the universe; that so no apparent views of interest may counteract this natural inclination; but not to attempt proving that prospects of our own advantage of any kind can raise in us the virtuous benevolence toward others. Let the obstacles from self-love be only removed, and Nature itself will incline us to benevolence. Let the misery of excessive selfishness be only removed and all its passions be but once explained so that self-love may cease to counteract our natural propensity to benevolence; and when this noble disposition gets loose from these bonds of ignorance and false views of interest, it shall be assisted even by self-love and grow strong enough to make a noble virtuous character. Then he is to inquire by reflection upon human affairs what course of action does most effectually promote the universal good, what universal rules or maxims are to be observed, and in what circumstances the reason of them alters, so as to admit exceptions; that so our good inclinations may be directed by reason and a just knowledge of the interests of mankind. But virtue itself, or good dispositions of mind, are not directly taught or produced by instruction; they must be originally implanted in our nature by its great Author, and afterwards strengthened and confirmed by our own cultivation.

III. We are often told that there is no need of supposing such a sense of morality given to men, since reflection and instruction would recommend the same actions from arguments of self-interest, and engage us from the acknowledged principle of self-love to the practice of them, without this unintelligible determination to benevolence or the occult quality of a moral sense.

It is perhaps true that reflection and reason might lead us to approve the same actions as advantageous. But would not the same reflection and reason likewise generally recommend the same meats to us which our taste represents as pleasant? And shall we thence conclude that we have no sense of tasting, or that such a sense is useless? No, the use is plain in both cases. Notwithstanding the mighty reason we boast of above other animals, its processes are too slow, too full of doubt and hesitation, to serve us in every exigency, either for our own preservation, without the external senses, or to influence our actions for the good of the whole, without this moral sense. Nor could we be so strongly determined at all times to what is most conducive to either of these ends without these expeditious monitors and importunate solicitors; nor so nobly rewarded when we act vigorously in pursuit of these ends by the calm dull reflections of self-interest, as by those delightful sensations. . . .

V. But that our first ideas of moral good depend not on laws may plainly appear from our constant inquiries into the justice of laws themselves; and that not only of human laws but of the divine. What else can be the meaning of that universal opinion that the laws of God are just, and holy, and good? Human laws may be called good because of their conformity to the divine. But to call the laws of the supreme deity good, or holy, or just, if all goodness, holiness, and justice be constituted by laws, or the will of a superior any way revealed, must be an insignficant tautology, amounting to no more than this, that God wills what he wills.

It must then first be supposed that there is something in actions which is apprehended absolutely good; and this is benevolence, or desire of the public natural happiness of rational agents; and that our moral sense perceives this excellence. And then we call the laws of the deity good when we imagine that they are contrived to promote the public good in the most effectual and impartial manner. And the deity is called good, in a moral sense, when we apprehend that his whole providence tends to the universal happiness of his creatures; whence we conclude his benevolence, and desire [for] their happiness.

Some tell us that the goodness of the divine laws consists in their conformity to some essential rectitude of his nature. But they must excuse us from assenting to this, till they make us understand the meaning of this metaphor, essential rectitude; and till we discern whether any thing more is meant by it than a perfectly wise, uniform, impartial benevolence.

Hence we may see the difference between constraint and obligation. There is indeed no difference between constraint and the second sense of the word obligation, *viz.* a constitution which makes an action eligible from self-interest, if we only mean external interest distinct from the delightful consciousness which arises from the moral sense. The reader need scarcely be told that by constraint we do not understand an external force moving our limbs without our consent; for in that case we are not agents at all; but that constraint which arises from the threatening and presenting some evil in order to make us act in a certain manner. And yet there seems an universally acknowledged difference between even this sort of constraint and obligation. We never say we are obliged to do an action which we count base, but we may be constrained to it. We never say that the divine laws, by their sanctions, constrain us, but oblige us; nor do we call obedience to the deity constraint, unless by a metaphor, though many own they are influenced by fear of punishments. And yet supposing an almighty evil being should require, under grievous penalties, treachery, cruelty, ingratitude, we would call this constraint. The difference is plainly this. When any sanctions co-operate with our moral sense in exciting us to actions which we count morally good, we say we are obliged; but when sanctions of rewards or punishments oppose our moral sense, then we say we are bribed or constrained. In the former case we call the lawgiver good, as designing the public happiness; in the latter we call him evil, or unjust, for the supposed contrary intention. But were all our ideas of moral good or evil derived solely from opinions of private advantage or loss in actions, I see no possible difference which could be made in the meaning of these words.

VI. From this sense too we derive our ideas of rights. Whenever it appears to us that a faculty of doing, demanding, or possessing any thing, universally allowed in certain circumstances, would in the whole tend to the general good, we say that one in such circumstances has a right to do, possess, or demand that thing. And according as this tendency to the public good is greater or less, the right is greater or less. . . .

XII. If it be here inquired, "Could not the deity have given us a different or contrary determination of mind, *viz.* to approve actions upon another foundation than benevolence?" There seems nothing in this surpassing the natural power of the deity. But, as in the first treatise,[14] we resolved the constitution of our present sense of beauty into the divine goodness, so with much more obvious reason may we ascribe the present constitution of our moral sense to his goodness. For if the deity be really benevolent, and desires the happiness of others, he could not rationally act otherwise or give us a moral sense upon another foundation without counteracting his own benevolent intentions. . . .

Editor's Notes

1. Hutcheson uses the term "perception" in a very broad sense, meaning by it roughly what Locke meant by idea, that is, whatever is before the mind when the mind thinks. Pleasure and pains are therefore perceptions, as are ideas of the qualities of external objects and of the operations of our own minds, including feeling, thinking, remembering, and the like.
2. Hutcheson here was speaking of himself in the third person.
3. A slight misquotation of Shakespeare's *Hamlet*, act 2, sc. 2. An actor has given a passionate speech at Hamlet's request concerning Hecuba, who has lost a daughter; Hamlet wonders at the actor's ability to feign such passion.
4. Orestes, helped by his sister Electra, slew Aegysthus, who had seduced their mother, Clytemnestra, while their father, Agamemnon, was leading the Greek armies at Troy and then had joined Clytemnestra in murdering Agamemnon on his return.
5. A legendary king of Athens, reputed to have sacrificed himself for his country in order to save it from an invasion.
6. A Roman consul who saved his city by leading his troops to battle at the cost of his own life.
7. For Cumberland and Pufendorf, see the selections in Part I of this anthology.
8. An asylum for the insane, originally called "Bethlehem," of which the word "*Bedlam*" is a corruption.
9. Latin, "that which carries," as the balance – the "beam and scales" – symbolically carries justice.
10. Its ordinary meaning was "satisfaction or pleasure in one's own condition," but Hutcheson is giving it a broader sense, "satisfaction or pleasure in anyone's condition."
11. Its usual meaning was "dissatisfaction or displeasure with one's condition," but, as with "complacence," Hutcheson gives it a broader meaning.
12. Outweigh.
13. Hutcheson is saying that good done or evil avoided in regard to a very small number of persons whose activity is important to a society (e.g., a group of military leaders in time of war) may outweigh good or evil involving larger numbers of persons of less importance to the society.
14. That is, the *Inquiry Concerning the Original of Our Idea of Beauty*, bound with this treatise.

Further Reading

There is no good modern edition of Hutcheson's collected works, although eighteenth-century copies of his writings have been reprinted. His important *Illustrations on the Moral Sense*, 1728, was edited by Bernard Peach (Cambridge, Mass.: Harvard University Press, 1971), with a good introduction. For his life, the study by W. R. Scott, *Francis Hutcheson* (Cambridge, England: Cambridge University Press, 1900), is still indispensable. For Hutcheson and the classical republican tradition, see Caroline Robbins, *The Eighteenth Century Commonwealthman* (Cambridge, Mass.: Harvard University Press, 1959).

For Gershom Carmichael, Hutcheson's teacher, see James Moore and Michael Silverthorne, "Gershom Carmichael and the Natural Jurisprudence Tradition in Eighteenth Century Scotland," in Istvan Hont and Michael Ignatieff, eds., *Wealth and Virtue* (Cambridge, England: Cambridge University Press, 1983). There are several essays pertaining to Hutcheson in R. H. Campbell and Andrew S. Skinner, eds., *The Origin and Nature of the Scottish Enlightenment* (Edinburgh: John Donald, 1982).

William Frankena's important article "Hutcheson's Moral Sense Theory," *Journal of the History of Ideas* 16 (1955), stimulated much of the recent discussion of the proper interpretation of Hutcheson. William T. Blackstone, *Francis Hutcheson and Contemporary Moral Theory* (Athens: University of Georgia Press, 1965), is analytical rather than historical. Henning Jensen, *Motivation and the Moral Sense in Francis Hutcheson's Ethical Theory* (The Hague: Nijhoff, 1971), contains some very controversial interpretations. David Fate Norton initiated the reading of Hutcheson as a moral realist. The second chapter of his book, *David Hume* (Princeton, N.J.: Princeton University Press, 1982), argues for this position, drawing on his earlier publications. "Hutcheson's Moral Sense Theory Reconsidered," *Dialogue* 13 (1974), and "Hutcheson on Perception and Moral Perception," *Archiv für Geschichte der Philosophie* 59 (1977). Norton argued in part against Frankena and in part against the influential reading of Hutcheson given by Norman Kemp Smith in his *Philosophy of David Hume* (London: Macmillan, 1941), chap. 2. Kenneth P. Winkler criticized Norton's position in "Hutcheson's Alleged Realism," *Journal of the History of Philosophy* 23 (1985), and Norton replied in a later issue of the same journal during the same year. See also Joel J. Kupperman, "Francis Hutcheson: Morality and Nature," *History of Philosophy Quarterly* 2 (1985). In a series of important papers, Knud Haakonssen discussed the thesis of Hutcheson's moral realism and built it into an impressive interpretation of the course of moral and political thought from Pufendorf through Reid. See especially his "Moral Philosophy and Natural Law: From the Cambridge Platonists to the Scottish Enlightenment," *Political Science* 40 (1988), and "Natural Law and Moral Realism: The Scottish Synthesis," in M. A. Stewart, ed., *Oxford Studies in the History of Philosophy*, vol. 1: *The Philosophy of the Scottish Enlightenment* (Oxford: Oxford University Press, 1989). Hutcheson figures importantly in both these essays, which will steer the interested reader to additional secondary material.

There is a chapter on Hutcheson in Alasdair MacIntyre, *Whose Justice? Which Rationality?* (Notre Dame, Ind.: University of Notre Dame Press, 1988). The best book on Hutcheson is Wolfgang Leidhold, *Ethik und Politik bei Francis Hutcheson* (Munich: Verlag Karl Alber, 1985), which contains a good bibliography.

Joseph Butler

Introduction

Joseph Butler, born in 1692 into a family of Dissenters – Protestants who were not members of the Church of England – studied at a Dissenting academy until 1714. During this time he corresponded with Samuel Clarke about the latter's proofs of the existence of God; Clarke admired the letters enough to publish the exchange in later editions of his own work. Butler then went to Oxford to prepare for ordination in the Church of England. He became a priest soon after he graduated in 1718 and was appointed preacher at the Rolls Chapel in London. It was here that he delivered the *Fifteen Sermons* (1726) on which his importance as a moral philosopher rests. In 1736 he wrote a lengthy attack on deism, the view that a fully adequate religion can be developed by natural reason without the aid of any revelation and that faith in the distinctive doctrines of Christianity is not essential to religion. Butler's work *The Analogy of Religion, Natural and Revealed, to the Constitution and the Course of Nature* (1736) was used in the education of Church of England clergy through the remainder of the eighteenth century and much of the nineteenth. It was generally thought to have destroyed the deistic position and stopped it from gathering adherents. Butler devoted the rest of his life to his work in the church. He was the bishop first of Bristol and then, late in life, of Durham. He died in 1752.

The *Sermons* are among the most influential English writings on ethics. Although they did not receive much acclaim when they were published, by mid-century they had begun to be more widely noticed, and some of the most powerful of later moral philosophers – in particular, Richard Price and Thomas Reid, in the eighteenth century, and William Whewell and Henry Sidgwick, in the nineteenth – considered themselves to be, in one way or another, Butlerians. Densely written, the *Sermons* repay the careful study they require.

It was characteristic of Butler to stress the complexity of human nature and the moral life. Against Hobbes (and others of the period) he developed classic arguments to show that human motivation cannot be reduced to any single desire or principle. Egoistic psychology was his target because he supposed, rightly or wrongly, that Hobbes held that all voluntary human actions are self-interested and because Mandeville had proposed a variant of that view. But Butler's arguments would apply to any alleged reduction of all desires and impulses to a single motivation.

Butler also emphasized the complexities of the principles that guide us in deciding which of our desires and passions to act on. He noted two kinds of complexity. The first is that some practical principles are superior to others not simply in strength but also in what Butler called "authority." Some principles claim the right to govern

525

others. For example, if fear prompts us to refuse to go the dentist, self-interest will prompt us to go, and we will all agree, Butler thought, that we ought to go. It is only reasonable to do so, even if the desire to stay away is stronger than the desire to go. This illustrates the *idea* of authority, and Butler believed that we could then see that conscience has a similar authority over all the other practical principles.

Principles are complex in another way. There is no single rule or principle from which we can obtain all the guidance we need. In fact, Butler asserted, no honest person needs a rule (Sermon III.4). Conscience gives us sufficient direction in each case as it comes. But conscience may be led astray, owing to personal failings, and if it is, no abstract rule will set it right. Butler particularly attacked the idea – proposed by Hutcheson – that virtue might be wholly contained in benevolence, so that the directive "Do as much good as possible" would suffice. A principle like that, Butler allowed, might express the mode in which God works, but it cannot be our principle. In resisting the Hutchesonian view, Butler presented some of the more incisive criticisms of what much later came to be known as utilitarianism.

Conscience must thus be our final arbiter. Yet Butler did not give us a detailed analysis of conscience. He ignored the Thomistic account of conscience as a synderesis, or repository of rules, together with the power of applying the rules to instances, although this account had been accepted by most of his predecessors in the Church of England. And he put nothing definite in its place. Butler used a perplexing variety of terms to refer to conscience, and consequently there has been considerable discussion of whether he thought of it as a feeling or as an instrument of knowledge. The fact is that he was not interested in theories about such matters. His concern was to remind us that we all are aware of this source of inner guidance and its authority, however we describe it. For practical purposes, we do not need any theory about it.

Yet another complexity in the moral life is emphasized in the *Sermons*. Butler held that it is as appropriate to be concerned for one's own long-range good as it is to be concerned for the good of others. Both self-interest and benevolence are reasonable principles of action, but Butler declined to rank them in relation to each other or to justice or veracity. The ordinary person is perfectly capable of seeing, in specific contexts, what is to be done, and no more is needed.

In one of the first histories of moral philosophy in English, William Whewell said that Butler had done more to make us aware of the facts of the moral life than had any of his predecessors but that he had not developed an adequate theory to explain the complex data he uncovered. Whewell plainly thought this a defect. But in refusing to suppose that theory must play a practical part in daily life, Butler was making a strongly Protestant reaffirmation of the immediate responsibility of all individuals for their own actions and for the condition of their own character. His understanding of morality grew from his religious beliefs. God, in Butler's view, has given each of us a conscience that is adequate for our practical needs. Advice from a minister or confessor is not necessary for ordinary people to live decent lives, and neither is philosophy. Butler's strong assertion of our capacity for self-direction inevitably raises a question: if we are capable of living decently without the guidance of other people, might not conscience be adequate even without God? The reader will wish to consider how important religious assumptions are to Butler's general outlook.

The selections from the *Sermons* reprinted here are from J. H. Bernard, ed., *The Works of Joseph Butler*, London, 1900, vol. 1, which gives the text of the second edition of 1729. The best way of referring to Butler's works is by sermon number and paragraph number, and so I have included Bernard's numbering in brackets. The brief excerpt from the "Dissertation on Virtue," published as an appendix to the *Analogy of Religion*, is from the second volume of the same edition.

Sermons

Sermon I: Upon Human Nature

For as we have many members in one body, and all members have not the same office: so we, being many, are one body in Christ, and every one members one of another. (Rom. 12:4, 5)

[4.] The relation which the several parts or members of the natural body have to each other and to the whole body, is here compared to the relation which each particular person in society has to other particular persons and to the whole society; and the latter is intended to be illustrated by the former. And if there be a likeness between these two relations, the consequence is obvious: that the latter shows us we were intended to do good to others, as the former shews us that the several members of the natural body were intended to be instruments of good to each other and to the whole body. . . .

[5.] From this review and comparison of the nature of man as respecting self, and as respecting society, it will plainly appear, that there are as real and the same kind of indications in human nature, that we were made for society and to do good to our fellow-creatures; as that we were intended to take care of our own life and health and private good: and that the same objections lie against one of these assertions, as against the other. For,

[6.] First, There is a natural principle of *benevolence** in man; which is in

---

* Suppose a man of learning to be writing a grave book upon *human nature*, and to shew in several parts of it that he had an insight into the subject he was considering; amongst other things, the following one would require to be accounted for; the appearance of benevolence or good-will in men towards each other in the instances of natural relation, and in others (Hobbes, *Of Human Nature*, c. ix. § 7). Cautious of being deceived with outward show, he retires within himself to see exactly, what that is in the mind of man from whence this appearance proceeds; and, upon deep reflection, asserts the principle in the mind to be only the love of power, and delight in the exercise of it. Would not every body think here was a mistake of one word for another? that the philosopher was contemplating and accounting for some other human actions, some other behaviour of man to man? And could any one be thoroughly satisfied, that what is commonly called benevolence or good-will was really the affection meant, but only by being made to understand that this learned person had a general hypothesis, to which the appearance of good-will could no otherwise be reconciled? That what has this appearance is often nothing but ambition; that delight in superiority often (suppose always) mixes itself with benevolence, only makes it more specious to call it ambition than hunger, of the two: but in reality that passion does no more account for the whole appearances of good-will, than this appetite does. Is there not often the appearance of one man's wishing that good to another, which he knows himself unable to procure him; and rejoicing in it, though bestowed by a third person? And can love of power any way possibly come in to account for this desire or delight? Is there not often the appearance of men's distinguishing between two or more persons, preferring one before another, to do good to, in cases where love of power cannot in the least account for the distinction and preference? For this principle can no otherwise distinguish between objects, than as it is a greater instance and exertion of power to do good to one rather than to another. Again, suppose good-will in the mind of man to be nothing but delight in the exercise of power: men might indeed be restrained by distant and accidental considerations; but these restraints being removed, they would have a disposition to, and delight in mischief as

some degree to *society,* what *self-love* is to the *individual.* And if there be in mankind any disposition to friendship; if there be any such thing as compassion, for compassion is momentary love; if there be any such thing as the paternal or filial affections; if there be any affection in human nature, the object and end of which is the good of another; this is itself benevolence, or the love of another. Be it ever so short, be it in ever so low a degree, or ever so unhappily confined; it proves the assertion, and points out what we were designed for, as really as though it were in a higher degree and more extensive. I must however remind you that though benevolence and self-love are different; though the former tends most directly to public good, and the latter to private: yet they are so perfectly coincident, that the greatest satisfactions to ourselves depend upon our having benevolence in a due degree, and that self-love is one chief security of our right behaviour towards society. It may be added, that their mutual coinciding, so that we can scarce promote one without the other, is equally a proof that we were made for both.

[7.] Secondly, This will further appear, from observing that the *several passions and affections,* which are distinct† both from benevolence and self-

an exercise and proof of power: and this disposition and delight would arise from, or be the same principle in the mind, as a disposition to, and delight in charity. Thus cruelty, as distinct from envy and resentment, would be exactly the same in the mind of man as good-will: that one tends to the happiness, the other to the misery of our fellow-creatures, is, it seems, merely an accidental circumstance, which the mind has not the least regard to. These are the absurdities which even men of capacity run into, when they have occasion to belie their nature, and will perversely disclaim that image of God which was originally stamped upon it, the traces of which, however faint, are plainly discernible upon the mind of man.

If any person can in earnest doubt, whether there be such a thing as good-will in one man towards another; (for the question is not concerning either the degree or extensiveness of it, but concerning the affection itself:) let it be observed, that whether man be thus, or otherwise constituted, what is the inward frame in this particular, is a mere question of fact or natural history, not provable immediately by reason. It is therefore to be judged of and determined in the same way other facts or matters of natural history are: by appealing to the external senses, or inward perceptions, respectively, as the matter under consideration is cognizable by one or the other: by arguing from acknowledged facts and actions; for a great number of actions in the same kind, in different circumstances, and respecting different objects, will prove, to a certainty what principles they do not, and, to the greatest probability, what principles they do proceed from: and lastly, by the testimony of mankind. Now that there is some degree of benevolence amongst men, may be as strongly and plainly proved in all these ways, as it could possibly be proved, supposing there was this affection in our nature. And should any one think fit to assert, that resentment in the mind of man was absolutely nothing but reasonable concern for our own safety, the falsity of this, and what is the real nature of that passion, could be shewn in no other ways than those in which it may be shewn, that there is such a thing in some degree as real good-will in man towards man. It is sufficient that the seeds of it be implanted in our nature by God. There is, it is owned, much left for us to do upon our own heart and temper; to cultivate, to improve, to call it forth, to exercise it in a steady, uniform manner. This is our work: this is virtue and religion.

† Every body makes a distinction between self-love, and the several particular passions, appetites, and affections; and yet they are often confounded again. That they are totally different, will be seen by any one who will distinguish between the passions and appetites themselves, and endeavouring after the means of their gratification. Consider the appetite of hunger, and the desire of esteem: these being the occasion both of pleasure and pain, the coolest self-love, as well as the appetites and passions themselves, may put us upon making use of the proper methods of obtaining that pleasure, and avoiding that pain; but the feelings themselves, the pain of hunger and shame, and the delight from esteem, are no more self-love than they are anything in the world. Though a man hated himself, he would as much feel the pain of hunger

love, do in general contribute and lead us to *public* good as really as to *private*. It might be thought too minute and particular, and would carry us too great a length, to distinguish between and compare together the several passions or appetites distinct from benevolence, whose primary use and intention is the security and good of society; and the passions distinct from self-love, whose primary intention and design is the security and good of the individual.‡ It is enough to the present argument, that desire of esteem from others, contempt and esteem of them, love of society as distinct from affection to the good of it, indignation against successful vice, that these are public affections or passions; have an immediate respect to others, naturally lead us to regulate our behaviour in such a manner as will be of service to our fellow-creatures. If any or all of these may be considered likewise as private affections, as tending to private good; this does not hinder them from being public affections too, or destroy the good influence of them upon society, and their tendency to public good. . . . The sum is, men have various appetites, passions, and particular affections, quite distinct both from self-love and from benevolence: all of these have a tendency to promote both public and private good, and may be considered as respecting others and ourselves equally and in common: but some of them seem most immediately to respect others, or tend to public good; others of them most immediately to respect self, or tend to private good: as the former are not benevolence, so the latter are not self-love: neither sort are instances of our love either to ourselves or others; but only instances of our Maker's care and love both of the individual and the species, and proofs that He intended we should be instruments of good to each other, as well as that we should be so to ourselves.

as he would that of the gout: and it is plainly supposable there may be creatures with self-love in them to the highest degree, who may be quite insensible and indifferent (as men in some cases are) to the contempt and esteem of those, upon whom their happiness does not in some further respects depend. And as self-love and the several particular passions and appetites are in themselves totally different; so, that some actions proceed from one, and some from the other, will be manifest to any one who will observe the two following very supposable cases. One man rushes upon certain ruin for the gratification of a present desire: nobody will call the principle of this action self-love. Suppose another man to go through some laborious work upon promise of a great reward, without any distinct knowledge what the reward will be: this course of action cannot be ascribed to any particular passion. The former of these actions is plainly to be imputed to some particular passion or affection, the latter as plainly to the general affection or principle of self-love. That there are some particular pursuits or actions concerning which we cannot determine how far they are owing to one, and how far to the other, proceeds from this, that the two principles are frequently mixed together, and run up into each other. This distinction is further explained in the eleventh sermon.

‡ If any desire to see this distinction and comparison made in a particular instance, the appetite and passion now mentioned may serve for one. Hunger is to be considered as a private appetite; because the end for which it was given us is the preservation of the individual. Desire of esteem is a public passion; because the end for which it was given us is to regulate our behaviour towards society. The respect which this has to private good is as remote as the respect that has to public good: and the appetite is no more self-love, than the passion is benevolence. The object and end of the former is merely food; the object and end of the latter is merely esteem: but the latter can no more be gratified, without contributing to the good of society; than the former can be gratified, without contributing to the preservation of the individual.

[8.] Thirdly, There is a principle of reflection[1] in men, by which they distinguish between, approve and disapprove their own actions. We are plainly constituted such sort of creatures as to reflect upon our own nature. The mind can take a view of what passes within itself, its propensions, aversions, passions, affections, as respecting such objects, and in such degrees; and of the several actions consequent thereupon. In this survey it approves of one, disapproves of another, and towards a third is affected in neither of these ways, but is quite indifferent. This principle in man, by which he approves or disapproves his heart, temper, and actions, is conscience; for this is the strict sense of the word, though sometimes it is used so as to take in more. And that this faculty tends to restrain men from doing mischief to each other, and leads them to do good, is too manifest to need being insisted upon. . . . It cannot possibly be denied, that there is this principle of reflection or conscience in human nature. Suppose a man to relieve an innocent person in great distress; suppose the same man afterwards, in the fury of anger, to do the greatest mischief to a person who had given no just cause of offence; to aggravate the injury, add the circumstances of former friendship, and obligation from the injured person; let the man who is supposed to have done these two different actions, coolly reflect upon them afterwards, without regard to their consequences to himself: to assert that any common man would be affected in the same way towards these different actions, that he would make no distinction between them, but approve or disapprove them equally, is too glaring a falsity to need being confuted. There is therefore this principle of reflection or conscience in mankind. It is needless to compare the respect it has to private good, with the respect it has to public; since it plainly tends as much to the latter as to the former, and is commonly thought to tend chiefly to the latter. This faculty is now mentioned merely as another part in the inward frame of man, pointing out to us in some degree what we are intended for, and as what will naturally and of course have some influence. The particular place assigned to it by nature, what authority it has, and how great influence it ought to have, shall be hereafter considered.

[9.] From this comparison of benevolence and self-love, of our public and private affections, of the courses of life they lead to, and of the principle of reflection or conscience as respecting each of them, it is as manifest, that we were made for society, and to promote the happiness of it; as that we were intended to take care of our own life, and health, and private good.

Sermon II: Upon Human Nature

For when the Gentiles, which have not the law, do by nature the things contained in the law, these, having not the law, are a law unto themselves. (Rom. 2:14)

[3.] But it may be said, "What is all this, though true, to the purpose of virtue and religion? these require, not only that we do good to others, when we are led this way, by benevolence or reflection, happening to be stronger than other principles, passions, or appetites; but likewise that the *whole* character be formed upon thought and reflection; that *every* action be directed by some determinate rule, some other rule than the strength and prevalency of any principle or passion. What sign is there in our nature (for the inquiry is only about what is to be collected from thence) that this was intended by its Author? Or how does so various and fickle a temper as that of man appear adapted thereto? It may indeed be absurd and unnatural for men to act without any reflection; nay, without regard to that particular kind of reflection which you call conscience; because this does belong to our nature. For as there never was a man but who approved one place, prospect, building, before another: so it does not appear that there ever was a man who would not have approved an action of humanity rather than of cruelty; interest and passion being quite out of the case. But interest and passion do come in, and are often too strong for and prevail over reflection and conscience. Now as brutes have various instincts, by which they are carried on to the end the Author of their nature intended them for: is not man in the same condition; with this difference only, that to his instincts (*i.e.,* appetites and passions) is added the principle of reflection or conscience? And as brutes act agreeably to their nature, in following that principle or particular instinct which for the present is strongest in them: does not man likewise act agreeably to his nature, or obey the law of his creation, by following that principle, be it passion or conscience, which for the present happens to be strongest in him? . . .

[4.] Now all this licentious talk entirely goes upon a supposition, that men follow their nature in the same sense, in violating the known rules of justice and honesty for the sake of a present gratification, as they do in following those rules when they have no temptation to the contrary. And if this were true, that could not be so which St. Paul asserts, that men are "by nature a law to themselves." . . . the objection will be fully answered, and the text before us explained, by observing that *nature* is considered in different views, and the words used in different senses; and by shewing in what view it is considered, and in what sense the word is used, when intended to express and signify that which is the guide of life, that by which men are a law to themselves. I say, the explanation of the term will be sufficient, because from thence it will appear, that in some senses of the word *nature* cannot be, but that in another sense it manifestly is, a law to us.

[5.] I. By nature is often meant no more than some principle in man, without regard either to the kind or degree of it. Thus the passion of anger, and the affection of parents to their children, would be called equally *natural*. And as the same person hath often contrary principles, which at the same time draw contrary ways, he may by the same action both follow and contradict his nature in this sense of the word; he may follow one passion and contradict another.

[6.] II. *Nature* is frequently spoken of as consisting in those passions which are strongest, and most influence the actions; which being vicious ones, mankind is in this sense naturally vicious, or vicious by nature. Thus St. Paul says of the Gentiles, "who were dead in trespasses and sins, and walked according to the spirit of disobedience, that they were by nature the children of wrath."[2] They could be no otherwise *children of wrath* by nature, than they were vicious by nature.

[7.] Here then are two different senses of the word *nature*, in neither of which men can at all be said to be a law to themselves. They are mentioned only to be excluded; to prevent their being confounded, as the latter is in the objection, with another sense of it, which is now to be inquired after and explained.

[8.] III. . . . . What that is in man by which he is *naturally a law to himself,* is explained in the following words: "which shew the work of the law written in their hearts, their conscience also bearing witness, and their thoughts the meanwhile accusing or else excusing one another."[3] If there be a distinction to be made between the *works written in their hearts,* and the *witness of conscience;* by the former must be meant the natural disposition to kindness and compassion, to do what is of good report, to which this apostle often refers: that part of the nature of man, treated of in the foregoing discourse, which with very little reflection and of course leads him to society, and by means of which he naturally acts a just and good part in it, unless other passions or interest lead him astray. Yet since other passions, and regards to private interest, which lead us (though indirectly, yet they lead us) astray, are themselves in a degree equally natural, and often most prevalent; and since we have no method of seeing the particular degrees in which one or the other is placed in us by nature; it is plain the former, considered merely as natural, good and right as they are, can no more be a law to us than the latter. But there is a superior principle of reflection or conscience in every man, which distinguishes between the internal principles of his heart, as well as his external actions: which passes judgment upon himself and them; pronounces determinately some actions to be in themselves just, right, good; others to be in themselves evil, wrong, unjust; which, without being consulted, without being advised with, magisterially exerts itself, and approves or condemns him the doer of them accordingly: and which, if not forcibly stopped, naturally and always of course goes on to anticipate a higher and more effectual sentence, which shall hereafter second and affirm its own.[4] But this part of the office of conscience is beyond my present design explicitly to consider. It is by this faculty, natural to man, that he is a moral agent, that he is a law to himself: by this faculty, I say, not to be considered merely as a principle in his heart, which is to have some influence as well as others; but considered as a faculty in kind and in nature supreme over all others, and which bears its own authority of being so.

[9.] This *prerogative,* this *natural supremacy,* of the faculty which surveys, approves or disapproves the several affections of our mind and actions of our lives, being that by which men *are a law to themselves,* their conformity or disobedience to which law of our nature renders their actions, in the highest and most proper sense, natural or unnatural; it is fit it be further explained to you: and I hope it will be so, if you will attend to the following reflections.

[10.] Man may act according to that principle or inclination which for the present happens to be strongest, and yet act in a way disproportionate to, and violate his real proper nature. Suppose a brute creature by any bait to be allured into a snare, by which he is destroyed. He plainly followed the bent of his nature, leading him to gratify his appetite: there is an entire correspondence between his whole nature and such an action: such action therefore is natural. But suppose a man, foreseeing the same danger of certain ruin, should rush into it for the sake of a present gratification; he in this instance would follow his strongest desire, as did the brute creature: but there would be as manifest a disproportion, between the nature of a man and such an action, as between the meanest work of art and the skill of the greatest master in that art: which disproportion arises, not from considering the action singly in *itself*, or in its *consequences;* but from comparison of it with the nature of the agent. And since such an action is utterly disproportionate to the nature of man, it is in the strictest and most proper sense unnatural; this word expressing that disproportion. Therefore instead of the words *disproportionate to his nature*, the word *unnatural* may now be put; this being more familiar to us: but let it be observed, that it stands for the same thing precisely.

[11.] Now what is it which renders such a rash action unnatural? Is it that he went against the principle of reasonable and cool self-love, considered *merely* as a part of his nature? No: for if he had acted the contrary way, he would equally have gone against a principle, or part of its nature, namely, passion or appetite. But to deny a present appetite, from foresight that the gratification of it would end in immediate ruin or extreme misery, is by no means an unnatural action: whereas to contradict or go against cool self-love for the sake of such gratification, is so in the instance before us. Such an action then being unnatural; and its being so not arising from a man's going against a principle or desire barely, nor in going against that principle or desire which happens for the present to be strongest; it necessarily follows, that there must be some other difference or distinction to be made between these two principles, passion and cool self-love, than what I have yet taken notice of. And this difference, not being a difference in strength or degree, I call a difference in *nature* and in *kind*. And since, in the instance still before us, if passion prevails over self-love, the consequent action is unnatural; but if self-love prevails over passion, the action is natural: it is manifest that self-love is in human nature a superior principle to passion. This may be contradicted without violating that nature; but the former cannot. So that, if we will act conformably to the economy of man's nature, reasonable self-love must govern. Thus, without particular consideration of conscience, we may have a clear conception of the *superior nature* of one inward principle to another; and see that there really is this natural superiority, quite distinct from degrees of strength and prevalency.

[13.] Passion or appetite implies a direct simple tendency towards such and such objects, without distinction of the means by which they are to be obtained. Consequently it will often happen there will be a desire of particular objects, in cases where they cannot be obtained without manifest injury to others. Reflection or conscience comes in, and disapproves the pursuit of them in these circumstances; but the desire remains. Which is to be obeyed, appetite or reflection? Cannot this question be answered, from the economy and constitution of human nature merely, without saying which is strongest? Or need this at all come into consideration? Would not the question be intelligibly and fully answered by saying, that the principle of reflection or conscience being compared with the various appetites, passions, and affections in men, the former is manifestly superior and chief, without regard to strength? And how often soever the latter happens to prevail, it is mere usurpation: the former remains in nature and in kind its superior; and every instance of such prevalence of the latter is an instance of breaking in upon and violation of the constitution of man.

[14.] All this is no more than the distinction, which everybody is acquainted with, between *mere power* and *authority:* only instead of being intended to express the difference between what is possible, and what is lawful in civil government; here it has been shewn applicable to the several principles in the mind of man. Thus that principle, by which we survey, and either approve or disapprove our own heart, temper, and actions, is not only to be considered as what is in its turn to have some influence; which may be said of every passion, of the lowest appetites: but likewise as being superior; as from its very nature manifestly claiming superiority over all others: insomuch that you cannot form a notion of this faculty, conscience, without taking in judgment, direction, superintendency. This is a constituent part of the idea, that is, of the faculty itself: and to preside and govern, from the very economy and constitution of man, belongs to it. Had it strength, as it has right; had it power, as it has manifest authority, it would absolutely govern the world.

SERMON III: UPON HUMAN NATURE

For when the Gentiles, which have not the law, do by nature the things contained in the law, these, having not the law, are a law unto themselves. (Rom. 2:14)

[1.] The natural supremacy of reflection or conscience being thus established; we may from it form a distinct notion of what is meant by *human nature,* when virtue is said to consist in following it, and vice in deviating from it.

[2.] As the idea of a civil constitution implies in it united strength, various subordinations, under one direction, that of the supreme authority; the different strength of each particular member of the society not coming into the idea; whereas, if you leave out the subordination, the union, and the one direction, you destroy and lose it: so reason, several appetites, passions, and affections, prevailing in different degrees of strength, is not *that* idea or notion of *human nature;* but *that nature* consists in these several principles considered as having a natural respect to each other, in the several passions being naturally subordinate to the one superior principle of reflection or conscience. Every bias, instinct, propension within, is a real part of our nature, but not the whole: add to these the superior faculty, whose office it is to adjust, manage, and preside over them, and take in this its natural superiority, and you complete the idea of human nature. And as in civil government the constitution is broken in upon, and violated by power and strength prevailing over authority; so the constitution of man is broken in upon and violated by the lower faculties or principles within prevailing over that which is in its nature supreme over them all. Thus, when it is said by ancient writers, that tortures and death are not so contrary to human nature as injustice;[5] by this to be sure is not meant, that the aversion to the former in mankind is less strong and prevalent than their aversion to the latter; but that the former is only contrary to our nature considered in a partial view, and which takes in only the lowest part of it, that which we have in common with the brutes; whereas the latter is contrary to our nature, considered in a higher sense, as a system and constitution contrary to the whole economy of man.

[3.] And from all these things put together, nothing can be more evident, than that, exclusive of revelation, man cannot be considered as a creature left by his Maker to act at random, and live at large up to the extent of his natural power, as passion, humour, wilfulness, happen to carry him; which is the condition brute creatures are in: but that from his make, constitution, or nature, he is in the strictest and most proper sense a law to himself. He hath the rule of right within: what is wanting is only that he honestly attend to it.

[4.] The inquiries which have been made by men of leisure, after some general rule, the conformity to, or disagreement from which, should denominate our actions good or evil, are in many respects of great service. Yet let any plain honest man, before he engages in any course of action, ask himself, Is this I am going about right, or is it wrong? Is it good, or is it evil? I do not in the least doubt, but that this question would be answered agreeably to truth and virtue, by almost any fair man in almost any circumstance. Neither do there appear any cases which look like exceptions to this; but those of superstition, and of partiality to ourselves. Superstition may perhaps be somewhat of an exception: but partiality to ourselves is not; this being itself dishonesty. For a man to judge that to be the equitable, the moderate, the right part for him to act, which he would see to be hard, unjust, oppressive in another; this is plain vice, and can proceed only from great unfairness of mind.

[5.] But allowing that mankind hath the rule of right within himself, yet it may be asked, "What obligations are we under to attend to and follow it?" I answer: it has been proved that man by his nature is a law to himself, without the particular distinct consideration of the positive sanctions of that law; the rewards and punishments which we feel, and those which from the light of reason we have ground to believe are annexed to it. The question then carries its own answer along with it. Your obligation to obey this law, is its being the law of your nature. That your conscience approves of and attests to such a course of action, is itself alone an obligation. Conscience does not only offer itself to shew us the way we should walk in, but it likewise carries its own authority with it, that it is our natural guide; the guide assigned us by the Author of our nature: it therefore belongs to our condition of being, it is our duty to walk in that path, and follow this guide, without looking about to see whether we may not possibly forsake them with impunity.

SERMON XI: UPON THE LOVE OF OUR NEIGHBOUR

And if there be any other commandment, it is briefly comprehended in this saying, namely, Thou shalt love thy neighbour as thyself. (Rom. 13:9)

[5.] Every man hath a general desire of his own happiness; and likewise a variety of particular affections, passions, and appetites to particular external objects. The former proceeds from, or is self-love; and seems inseparable from all sensible creatures, who can reflect upon themselves and their own interest or happiness, so as to have that interest an object to their minds: what is to be said of the latter is, that they proceed from, or together make up that particular nature, according to which man is made. The object the former pursues is somewhat internal, our own happiness, enjoyment, satisfaction; whether we have, or have not, a distinct particular perception what it is, or wherein it consists: the objects of the latter are this or that particular external thing, which the affections tend towards, and of which it hath always a particular idea or perception. The principle we call self-love never seeks anything external for the sake of the thing, but only as a means of happiness or good: particular affections rest in the external things themselves. One belongs to man as a reasonable creature reflecting upon his own interest or happiness. The other, though quite distinct from reason, are as much a part of human nature.

[6.] That all particular appetites and passions are towards *external things themselves*, distinct from the *pleasure arising from them*, is manifested from hence; that there could not be this pleasure, were it not for that prior suitableness between the object and the passion: there could be no enjoyment or delight from one thing more than another, from eating food more than from swallowing a stone, if there were not an affection or appetite to one thing more than another.

[7.] Every particular affection, even the love of our neighbour, is as really our own affection, as self-love; and the pleasure arising from its gratification is as much my own pleasure, as the pleasure self-love would have, from knowing I myself should be happy some time hence, would be my own pleasure. And if, because every particular affection is a man's own, and the pleasure arising from its gratification his own pleasure, or pleasure to himself, such particular affection must be called self-love; according to this way of speaking, no creature whatever can possibly act but merely from self-love; and every action and every affection whatever is to be resolved up into this one principle. But then this is not the language of mankind: or if it were, we should want words to express the difference, between the principle of an action, proceeding from cool consideration that it will be to my own advantage; and an action, suppose of revenge, or of friendship, by which a man runs upon certain ruin, to do evil or good to another. It is manifest the principles of these actions are totally different, and so want different words to be distinguished by: all that they agree in is, that they both proceed from, and are done to gratify an inclination in a man's self. But the principle or inclination in one case is self-love; in the other, hatred or love of another. There is then a distinction between the cool principle of self-love, or general desire of our happiness, as one part of our nature, and one principle of action; and the particular affections towards particular external objects, as another part of our nature, and another principle of action. How much soever therefore is to be allowed to self-love, yet it cannot be allowed to be the whole of our inward constitution; because, you see, there are other parts or principles which come into it.

[8.] Further, private happiness or good is all which self-love can make us desire, or be concerned about: in having this consists its gratification: it is an affection to ourselves; a regard to our own interest, happiness, and private good: and in the proportion a man hath this, he is interested, or a lover of himself. Let this be kept in mind; because there is commonly, as I shall presently have occasion to observe, another sense put upon these words. On the other hand, particular affections tend towards particular external things: these are their objects; having these is their end: in this consists their gratification: no matter whether it be, or be not, upon the whole, our interest or happiness. An action done from the former of these principles is called an interested action. An action proceeding from any of the latter has its denomination of passionate, ambitious, friendly, revengeful, or any other, from the particular appetite or affection from which it proceeds. Thus self-love as one part of human nature, and the several particular principles as the other part, are, themselves, their objects and ends, stated and shewn.

[11.] Self-love and interestedness was stated to consist in or be an affection to ourselves, a regard to our own private good: it is therefore distinct from benevolence, which is an affection to the good of our fellow-creatures. But that benevolence is distinct from, that is, not the same thing with self-love, is no reason for its being looked upon with any peculiar suspicion; because every principle whatever, by means of which self-love is gratified, is distinct from it; and all things which are distinct from each other are equally so. A man has an affection or aversion to another: that one of these tends to, and is gratified by doing good, that the other tends to, and is gratified by doing harm, does not in the least alter the respect which either one or the other of these inward feelings has to self-love. We use the word *property* so as to exclude any other persons having an interest in that of which we say a particular man has the property. And we often use the word *selfish* so as to exclude in the same manner all regards to the good of others. But the cases are not parallel: for though that exclusion is really part of the idea of property; yet such positive exclusion, or bringing this peculiar disregard to the good of others into the idea of self-love, is in reality adding to the idea, or changing it from what it was before stated to consist in, namely, in an affection to ourselves. This being the whole idea of self-love, it can no otherwise exclude good-will or love of others, than merely by not including it, no otherwise, than it excludes love of arts or reputation, or of anything else. Neither on the other hand does benevolence, any more than love of arts or of reputation, exclude self-love. Love of our neighbour then has just the same respect to, is no more distant from, self-love, than hatred of our neighbour, or than love or hatred of anything else. . . .

[12.] Thus it appears that there is no peculiar contrariety between self-love and benevolence; no greater competition between these, than between any other particular affections and self-love. This relates to the affections themselves. Let us now see whether there be any peculiar contrariety between the respective courses of life which these affections lead to; whether there be any greater competition between the pursuit of private and of public good, than between any other particular pursuits and that of private good.

[16.] The short of the matter is no more than this. Happiness consists in the gratification of certain affections, appetites, passions, with objects which are by nature adapted to them. Self-love may indeed set us on work to gratify these: but happiness or enjoyment has no immediate connexion with self-love, but arises from such gratification alone. Love of our neighbour is one of those affections. This, considered as a *virtuous principle,* is gratified by a consciousness of endeavouring to promote the good of others; but considered as a *natural affection,* its gratification consists in the actual accomplishment of this endeavour. Now indulgence or gratification of this affection, whether in that consciousness, or this accomplishment, has the same respect to interest, as indulgence of any other affection; they equally proceed from or do not proceed from self-love, they equally include or equally exclude this principle. Thus it appears, that benevolence and the pursuit of public good hath at least as great respect to self-love and the pursuit of private good, as any other particular passions, and their respective pursuits.

[20.] And to all these things may be added, that religion, from whence arises our strongest obligation to benevolence, is so far from disowning the principle of self-love, that it often addresses itself to that very principle, and always to the mind in that state when reason presides; and there can no access be had to the understanding, but by convincing men, that the course of life we would persuade them to is not contrary to their interest. It may be allowed, without any prejudice to the cause of virtue and religion, that our ideas of happiness and misery are of all our ideas the nearest and most important to us; that they will, nay, if you please, that they ought to prevail over those of order, and beauty, and harmony, and proportion, if there should ever be, as it is impossible there ever should be, any inconsistence between them: though these last too, as expressing the fitness of actions, are real as truth itself. Let it be allowed, though virtue or moral rectitude does indeed consist in affection to and pursuit of what is right and good as such; yet, that when we sit down in a cool hour, we can neither justify to ourselves this or any other pursuit, till we are convinced that it will be for our happiness, or at least not contrary to it.

SERMON XII: UPON THE LOVE OF OUR NEIGHBOUR

And if there be any other commandment, it is briefly comprehended in this saying, namely, Thou shalt love thy neighbour as thyself. (Rom. 13:9)

[1.] Having already removed the prejudices against public spirit, or the love of our neighbour, on the side of private interest and self-love; I proceed to the particular explanation of the precept before us, by shewing, Who is our neighbour: In what sense we are required to love him as ourselves: The influence such love would have upon our behaviour in life: and lastly, How this commandment comprehends in it all others.

[2.] I. The objects and due extent of this affection will be understood by attending to the nature of it, and to the nature and circumstances of mankind in this world. The love of our neighbour is the same with charity, benevolence, or good-will: it is an affection to the good and happiness of our fellow creatures. This implies in it a disposition to produce happiness: and this is the simple notion of goodness, which appears so amiable wherever we meet with it. From hence it is easy to see, that the perfection of goodness consists in love to the whole universe. This is the perfection of Almighty God.

[3.] But as man is so much limited in his capacity, as so small a part of the creation comes under his notice and influence, and as we are not used to consider things in so general a way; it is not to be thought of, that the universe should be the object of benevolence to such creatures as we are. . . .

For this reason moral writers also have substituted a less general object for our benevolence, mankind. But this likewise is an object too general, and very much out of our view. Therefore persons more practical have, instead of mankind, put our country; and made the principle of virtue, of human virtue, to consist in the entire uniform love of our country: and this is what we call a public spirit; which in men of public stations is the character of a patriot. But this is speaking to the upper part of the world. Kingdoms and governments are large; and the sphere of action of far the greatest part of mankind is much narrower than the government they live under: or however, common men do not consider their actions as affecting the whole community of which they are members. There plainly is wanting a less general and nearer object of benevolence for the bulk of men, than that of their country. Therefore the Scripture, not being a book of theory and speculation, but a plain rule of life for mankind, has with the utmost possible propriety put the principle of virtue upon the love of our neighbour; which is that part of the universe, that part of mankind, that part of our country, which comes under our immediate notice, acquaintance, and influence, and with which we have to do.

[4.] This is plainly the true account or reason, why our Saviour places the principle of virtue in the love of our *neighbour;* and the account itself shews who are comprehended under that relation. . . .

[25.] IV. I proceed to consider lastly, what is affirmed of the precept now explained, that it comprehends in it all others; *i.e.*, that to love our neighbour as ourselves includes in it all virtues.

[26.] Now the way in which every maxim of conduct, or general speculative assertion, when it is to be explained at large, should be treated, is, to shew what are the particular truths which were designed to be comprehended under such a general observation, how far it is strictly true; and then the limitations, restrictions, and exceptions, if there be exceptions, with which it is to be understood. But it is only the former of these; namely, how far the assertion in the text holds, and the ground of the preeminence assigned to the precept of it, which in strictness comes into our present consideration.

[27.] However, in almost everything that is said, there is somewhat to be understood beyond what is explicitly laid down, and which we of course supply; somewhat, I mean, which would not be commonly called a restriction, or limitation. Thus, when benevolence is said to be the sum of virtue, it is not spoken of as a blind propension, but as a principle in reasonable creatures, and so to be directed by their reason: for reason and reflection comes into our notion of a moral agent. And that will lead us to consider distant consequences, as well as the immediate tendency of an action: it will teach us, that the care of some persons, suppose children and families, is particularly committed to our charge by Nature and Providence; as also that there are other circumstances, suppose friendship or former obligations, which require that we do good to some, preferably to others. Reason, considered merely as subservient to benevolence, as assisting to produce the greatest good, will teach us to have particular regard to these relations and circumstances; because it is plainly for the good of the world that they should be regarded. And as there are numberless cases, in which, notwithstanding appearances, we are not competent judges, whether a particular action will upon the whole do good or harm; reason in the same way will teach us to be cautious how we act in these cases of uncertainty. It will suggest to our consideration, which is the safer side; how liable we are to be led wrong by passion and private interest; and what regard is due to laws, and the judgment of mankind. All these things must come into consideration, were it only in order to determine which way of acting is likely to produce the greatest good. Thus, upon supposition that it were in the strictest sense true, without limitation, that benevolence includes in it all virtues; yet reason must come in as its guide and director, in order to attain its own end, the end of benevolence, the greatest public good. Reason then being thus included, let us now consider the truth of the assertion itself.

[28.] First, It is manifest that nothing can be of consequence to mankind or any creature, but happiness. This then is all which any person can, in strictness of speaking, be said to have a right to. We can therefore "owe no man anything,"[6] but only further and promote his happiness, according to our abilities. And therefore a disposition and endeavour to do good to all with whom we have to do, in the degree and manner which the different relations we stand in to them require, is a discharge of all the obligations we are under to them.

[29.] As human nature is not one simple uniform thing, but a composition of various parts, body, spirit, appetites, particular passions, and affections; for each of which reasonable self-love would lead men to have due regard, and make suitable provision: so society consists of various parts, to which we stand in different respects and relations; and just benevolence would as surely lead us to have due regard to each of these, and behave as the respective relations require. Reasonable good-will, and right behaviour towards our fellow-creatures, are in a manner the same: only that the former expresseth the principle as it is in the mind; the latter, the principle as it were become external, *i.e.*, exerted in actions.

[30.] And so far as temperance, sobriety, and moderation in sensual pleasures, and the contrary vices, have any respect to our fellow-creatures, any influence upon their quiet, welfare, and happiness; as they always have a real, and often a near influence upon it; so far it is manifest those virtues may be produced by the love of our neighbour, and that the contrary vices would be prevented by it. Indeed if men's regard to themselves will not restrain them from excess; it may be thought little probable, that their love to others will be sufficient: but the reason is, that their love to others is not, any more than their regard to themselves, just, and in its due degree. There are however manifest instances of persons kept sober and temperate from regard to their affairs, and the welfare of those who depend upon them. And it is obvious to every one, that habitual excess, a dissolute course of life, implies a general neglect of the duties we owe towards our friends, our families, and our country.

[31.] From hence it is manifest that the common virtues, and the common vices of mankind, may be traced up to benevolence, or the want of it. And this entitles the precept, "Thou shalt love thy neighbour as thyself," to the preeminence given to it; and is a justification of the Apostle's assertion, that all other commandments are comprehended in it; whatever cautions and restrictions§

---

§ For instance: as we are not competent judges, what is upon the whole for the good of the world, there may be other immediate ends appointed us to pursue, besides that one of doing good, or producing happiness. Though the good of the creation be the only end of the Author of it, yet He may have laid us under particular obligations, which we may discern and feel ourselves under, quite distinct from a perception, that the observance or violation of them is for the happiness or misery of our fellow-creatures. And this is in fact the case. For there are certain dispositions of mind, and certain actions, which are in themselves approved or disapproved by mankind, abstracted from the consideration of their tendency to the happiness or misery of the world; approved or disapproved by reflection, by that principle within, which is the guide of life, the judge of right and wrong. Numberless instances of this kind might be mentioned. There are pieces of treachery, which in themselves appear base and detestable to every one. There are actions, which perhaps can scarce have any other general name given them than indecencies, which yet are odious and shocking to human nature. There is such a thing as meanness, a little mind; which, as it is quite distinct from incapacity, so it raises a dislike and disapprobation quite different from that contempt, which men are too apt to have, of mere folly. On the other hand: what we call greatness of mind is the object of another sort of approbation, than superior understanding. Fidelity, honour, strict justice, are themselves approved in the highest degree, abstracted from the consideration of their tendency. Now, whether it be thought that each of there are, which might require to be considered, if we were to state particularly and at length what is virtue and right behaviour in mankind. But,

[32.] Secondly, it might be added, that in a higher and more general way of consideration, leaving out the particular nature of creatures, and the particular circumstances in which they are placed, benevolence seems in the strictest sense to include in it all that is good and worthy; all that is good, which we have any distinct particular notion of. We have no clear conception of any positive moral attribute in the Supreme Being, but what may be resolved up into goodness. And, if we consider a reasonable creature or moral agent, without regard to the particular relations and circumstances in which he is placed; we cannot conceive anything else to come in towards determining whether he is to be ranked in an higher or lower class of virtuous beings, but the higher or lower degree in which that principle, and what is manifestly connected with it, prevail in him.

[33.] That which we more strictly call piety, or the love of God, and which is an essential part of a right temper, some may perhaps imagine no way connected with benevolence: yet surely they must be connected, if there be indeed in being an object infinitely good. Human nature is so constituted, that every good affection implies the love of itself; *i.e.*, becomes the object of a new affection in the same person. Thus, to be righteous, implies in it the love of righteousness; to be benevolent, the love of benevolence; to be good, the love of goodness; whether this righteousness, benevolence, or goodness, be viewed as in our own mind, or in another's: and the love of God as being perfectly good, is the love of perfect goodness contemplated in a being or person. Thus morality and religion, virtue and piety, will at last necessarily coincide, run up into one and the same point, and love will be in all senses "the end of the commandment."[7]

Dissertation on Virtue

OF THE NATURE OF VIRTUE

[8.] Fifthly, Without inquiring how far, and in what sense, virtue is resolvable into benevolence, and vice into the want of it; it may be proper to observe, that benevolence, and the want of it, singly considered, are in no sort the whole of virtue and vice. For if this were the case, in the review of one's own character, or that of others, our moral understanding and moral sense would be indifferent to everything, but the degrees in which benevolence prevailed, and the degrees in which it was wanting. That is, we should neither approve of

these are connected with benevolence in our nature, and so may be considered as the same thing with it; or whether some of them be thought an inferior kind of virtues and vices, somewhat like natural beauties and deformities; or lastly, plain exceptions to the general rule; thus much however is certain, that the things now instanced in, and numberless others, are approved or disapproved by mankind in general; in quite another view than as conducive to the happiness or misery of the world.

benevolence to some persons rather than to others, nor disapprove injustice and falsehood upon any other account, than merely as an overbalance of happiness was foreseen likely to be produced by the first, and of misery by the second. But now, on the contrary, suppose two men competitors for anything whatever, which would be of equal advantage to each of them; though nothing indeed would be more impertinent, than for a stranger to busy himself to get one of them preferred to the other; yet such endeavour would be virtue, in behalf of a friend or benefactor, abstracted from all consideration of distant consequences: as that examples of gratitude, and the cultivation of friendship, would be of general good to the world. Again, suppose one man should, by fraud or violence, take from another the fruit of his labour, with intent to give it to a third, who he thought would have as much pleasure from it as would balance the pleasure which the first possessor would have had in the enjoyment, and his vexation in the loss of it; suppose also that no bad consequences would follow: yet such an action would surely be vicious. Nay further, were treachery, violence and injustice, no otherwise vicious, than as foreseen likely to produce an overbalance, of misery to society; then, if in any case a man could procure to himself as great advantage by an act of injustice, as the whole foreseen inconvenience, likely to be brought upon others by it, would amount to; such a piece of injustice would not be faulty or vicious at all: because it would be no more than, in any other case, for a man to prefer his own satisfaction to another's in equal degrees. The fact then appears to be, that we are constituted so as to condemn falsehood, unprovoked violence, injustice, and to approve of benevolence to some preferably to others, abstracted from all consideration, which conduct is likeliest to produce an overbalance of happiness or misery. And therefore, were the Author of Nature to propose nothing to Himself as an end but the production of happiness, were His moral character merely that of benevolence; yet ours is not so. Upon that supposition indeed the only reason of His giving us the above-mentioned approbation of benevolence to some persons rather than others, and disapprobation of falsehood, unprovoked violence, and injustice, must be, that He foresaw this constitution of our nature would produce more happiness, than forming us with a temper of mere general benevolence. But still, since this is our constitution; falsehood, violence, injustice, must be vice in us, and benevolence to some, preferably to others, virtue; abstracted from all consideration of the overbalance of evil or good, which they may appear likely to produce.

Editor's Notes

1. "Reflection" is a Lockean term; it refers to an act of mind that presupposes the presence in the mind of ideas or feelings and operates upon them. Ideas of perception, by contrast, come directly from the senses or from inner bodily stimuli and do not presuppose other ideas. For Butler, reflection presupposes the various desires and passes judgment on them.
2. Eph. 2:3.

3. Rom. 2:15.
4. Butler here was hinting that conscience naturally tends to anticipate rewards and punishments in a life after death.
5. For example, Cicero, *De officiis* III.v. 21: "Well then, for a man to take something from his neighbour and to profit by his neighbour's loss is more contrary to Nature than is death or poverty or pain or anything else that can affect either our person or our property." This is standard Stoic teaching, but Butler gives his own meaning to "nature."
6. Rom. 13:8.
7. I Tim. 1:5.

Further Reading

There is a substantial literature on Butler. E. C. Mossner, *Bishop Butler and the Age of Reason* (New York: B. Blom, 1971), is a general study. The best philosophical book on Butler is that by Terence Penelhum, *Butler* (London: Routledge & Kegan Paul, 1985), which has a good bibliography. Penelhum's work is unusual in that it gives an extended account of Butler's religious thought as well as of his ethics. C. D. Broad, in *Five Types of Ethical Theory* (London: Routledge & Kegan Paul, 1930), and more reliably Austin Duncan-Jones, in *Butler's Moral Philosophy* (London: Penguin, 1952), present analytical studies of Butler's ethics. T. A. Roberts, *The Concept of Benevolence* (London: Macmillan, 1973), compares Butler's views on benevolence with those of Hutcheson and Hume.

Butler provokes continued discussion. Of the many articles on Butler, the following are noteworthy:

Jackson, R. "Bishop Butler's Refutation of Psychological Egoism." *Philosophy* 18 (1943).
Raphael, D. D. "Butler's View of Conscience." *Philosophy* 24 (1949).
Rorty, Amelie. "Butler on Benevolence and Conscience." *Philosophy* 53 (1978).
Scott-Taggart, M. J. "Butler on Disinterested Actions." *Philosophical Quarterly* 18 (1968).
Sturgeon, Nicholas. "Nature and Conscience in Butler's Ethics." *Philosophical Review* 85 (1976).

David Hume

Introduction

Hume was born in Edinburgh in 1711. Educated at home and at the University of Edinburgh, he came early to the decision that he wanted a career as a man of letters, and not in a profession like the law. At the age of eighteen he became convinced that he had an idea for a major philosophical work. He brooded constantly on this idea and its ramifications, eventually moving to France in 1734 because there he could live on his small independent income and devote himself to writing down his thoughts. Hume returned to Scotland in 1737 with his book essentially complete. It was published in three volumes in 1739–40 as *A Treatise of Human Nature*. Hume's hope that it would bring him recognition in the literary world was disappointed, however. His book received little attention, and of that most was unfavorable.

As a result, Hume rewrote his book, recasting the first part, which covered epistemology, into the *Philosophical Essays Concerning Human Understanding* (later entitled *An Enquiry Concerning Human Understanding*), published in 1748, and the third part, on ethics, into *An Enquiry Concerning the Principles of Morals* (1751). He also wrote a number of essays on politics, history, economics, aesthetics, and other topics. These, with the rewritten versions of his philosophy, finally brought him literary recognition. During the 1750s Hume wrote his other major philosophical work, the *Dialogues Concerning Natural Religion*, which was not published until 1779, after his death. Its companion piece, the *Natural History of Religion*, was published in 1757. Hume twice tried to get academic appointments but failed. From 1746 to 1749 he served on a diplomatic mission to France. In 1752 he was appointed to direct a library in Edinburgh; while in this post he began writing a many-volumed history of Britain, completed in 1762, which was the most widely read of all his writings. He served in several other political positions after leaving the library in 1757 and in his later years spent much time revising his published works. After a brief illness he died in 1776.

The general aim of Hume's philosophical work was to show that we can explain every facet of human existence without appealing to anything beyond the realm of ordinary natural events related to one another in ways that can be discovered by means of scientific investigation. At a time when the biblical narrative was still accepted as literal history and when many people believed in divine intervention in individual lives, this was a bolder venture than it would be now. Hume tried to explain not only our political and social institutions but even our most basic thought processes and our scientific, moral, and religious beliefs without calling on God, or soul, or any unique mental substance different in kind from material substance. Hobbes had had a similar

545

naturalistic ambition, but Hume carried out the program much more thoroughly and with more sophistication.

Hume was long considered to be primarily a skeptic who aimed at demolishing our confidence in all our ordinary beliefs. Certainly, skepticism is prominent in his major philosophical works. In the first part of the *Treatise* he argued at length that ordinary convictions, such as that the sun will rise tomorrow or that hitting a window with a rock will make it break, cannot be proved. He concluded that reason is not the source of these convictions, because if it were, we could give conclusive rational grounds for them. In the *Dialogues Concerning Natural Religion* Hume examined all the main arguments to show that God exists and offered devastating criticisms of them. Once again he concluded that reason is not the source of belief. Skeptical demonstrations that we do not hold our factual or religious beliefs because we have good reasons for them are not the end of the matter, however. They open the way to the question, What makes us feel so certain of our convictions in these matters?

In answering this question Hume went beyond skepticism, offering a naturalistic account of human belief. In the domain of facts, he held that regular patterns in our experience of objects and the sequences in which they appear to us induce habits of expectation. For example, as it gets less dark, we expect to see the sun; as the rock nears the window, we expect to see shattered glass. These habits of expectation are strongly reinforced by repeated experience, and they are at the core of our factual beliefs. Religious beliefs, by contrast, Hume contended, arise not so much from the observation, in experience, of constant conjunctions and sequences as from the desires and fears that come when we do not have the settled beliefs about the future that we usually call knowledge. We then try to control the future about which we are uncertain, by treating the world and things in it as full of hopes and fears, that is, as animated. We think that things about us will respond as people do to prayers and offerings, and eventually we come to worship the beings that our imagination originally created in order to give us some way of diminishing our fears.

What science does, in Hume's view, is show us which beliefs about sequences of events are reliable. As science shows us more and more of these, our certainties about the world we live in will increase, and our need to make up for lack of them by invoking spirits outside ourselves will diminish. Religious beliefs, in other words, will be replaced by the much firmer factual beliefs that science provides. Religious beliefs can no more be refuted than they can be proved, but in common with many thinkers of the time who thought of themselves as forwarding the enlightenment of mankind, Hume expected that they would slowly disappear.

Where, then, does this leave morality? Does it have a firm basis in experience, like the ordinary factual convictions that we all share because we perceive the same patterns of coexistence and sequence? Is it destined to vanish, like the different religious beliefs that arise from widely varying hopes and fears? Or is it perhaps a matter of rational knowledge?

As the reader will see, Hume began his discussion of morals with arguments to show that we do not have moral knowledge in any strict sense and that morality is, as he put it in the *Treatise,* "more properly felt than judged of." He then proceeded to ask – as Hutcheson before him had asked – just what it is that explains our having the moral feelings we have. Why do we approve and disapprove as we do? The answer constitutes the rest of his ethical theory.

Like Hutcheson, Hume answered that we approve of what is useful or agreeable to people – what increases the amount of good, of what people enjoy. He then tried to make this answer more convincing than Hutcheson did, by going into considerable detail about exactly how it explains our ordinary moral convictions. His treatment of our beliefs about justice – which Hume took to center on our ideas about property – is a prime example. Butler had argued that justice cannot rest on the principle of doing good, because there are many cases in which justice requires us to act in a way that does less good instead of more. One might give as an example that justice requires us to restore money to a wealthy miser instead of leaving it with the worthy poor worker who found it. In working out an answer to this objection, Hume developed a theory of the nature and social function of justice that has not ceased to stimulate both critical and creative thought. He offered similarly insightful and provocative accounts of many of our other common moral beliefs. The reader must decide whether, by doing so, he made his explanation satisfactory.

In a letter to Hutcheson dated March 16, 1740, Hume relayed a view he was about to publish in the third volume of his *Treatise*, that "when you pronounce any action or character to be vicious, you mean nothing but that from the particular constitution of your nature you have a feeling or sentiment of blame from the contemplation of it," and commented: "I wish from my heart I could avoid concluding that, since morality, according to your opinion as well as mine, is determined merely by sentiment, it regards only human nature and human life." Hutcheson might have regretted this implication of their shared opinion; it is doubtful that Hume did. Early in his life he abandoned the religion in which he had been brought up. It was not a disappointment to him that we must give up all claim to know that we are guided by external or divine laws that hold for God and the angels as well as for human beings. It was a liberation from what he took to be the stifling superstitions of the past.

The following selections are from *An Enquiry Concerning the Principles of Morals*, using the 1777 edition – the last one Hume revised – as that is given in Hume's *Works*, edited by T. H. Green and T. H. Grose, London, 1874.

An Enquiry Concerning the Principles of Morals

Section I: Of the General Principles of Morals

Disputes with men, pertinaciously obstinate in their principles, are, of all others, the most irksome; except, perhaps, those with persons, entirely disingenuous, who really do not believe the opinions they defend, but engage in controversy, from affectation, from a spirit of opposition, or from a desire of showing wit and ingenuity, superior to the rest of mankind. The same blind adherence to their own arguments is to be expected in both; the same contempt of their antagonists; and the same passionate vehemence, in inforcing sophistry and falsehood. And as reasoning is not the source, whence either disputant derives his tenets; it is in vain to expect, that any logic, which speaks not to the affections, will ever engage him to embrace sounder principles.

Those who have denied the reality of moral distinctions, may be ranked among the disingenuous disputants; nor is it conceivable, that any human creature could ever seriously believe, that all characters and actions were alike entitled to the affection and regard of every one. The difference, which nature has placed between one man and another, is so wide, and this difference is still so much farther widened, by education, example, and habit, that, where the opposite extremes come at once under our apprehension, there is no scepticism so scrupulous, and scarce any assurance so determined, as absolutely to deny all distinction between them. Let a man's insensibility be ever so great, he must often be touched with the images of RIGHT and WRONG; and let his prejudices be ever so obstinate, he must observe, that others are susceptible of like impressions. The only way, therefore, of converting an antagonist of this kind, is to leave him to himself. For, finding that no body keeps up the controversy with him, it is probable he will, at last, of himself, from mere weariness, come over to the side of common sense and reason.

There has been a controversy started of late, much better worth examination, concerning the general foundation of MORALS; whether they be derived from REASON, or from SENTIMENT; whether we attain the knowledge of them by a chain of argument and induction, or by an immediate feeling and finer internal sense; whether, like all sound judgment of truth and falsehood, they should be the same to every rational intelligent being; or whether, like the perception of beauty and deformity, they be founded entirely on the particular fabric and constitution of the human species. . . .

It must be acknowledged, that both sides of the question are susceptible of specious arguments. Moral distinctions, it may be said, are discernible by pure *reason:* Else, whence the many disputes that reign in common life, as well as in philosophy, with regard to this subject: The long chain of proofs often produced on both sides; the examples cited, the authorities appealed to, the analogies employed, the fallacies detected, the inferences drawn, and the several conclusions adjusted to their proper principles. Truth is disputable; not taste: What exists in the nature of things is the standard of our judgment; what each man feels within himself is the standard of sentiment. Propositions in geometry may be proved, systems in physics may be controverted; but the harmony of verse, the tenderness of passion, the brilliancy of wit, must give immediate pleasure. No man reasons concerning another's beauty; but frequently concerning the justice or injustice of his actions. In every criminal trial the first object of the prisoner is to disprove the facts alleged, and deny the actions imputed to him: The second to prove, that, even if these actions were real, they might be justified, as innocent and lawful. It is confessedly by deductions of the understanding, that the first point is ascertained: How can we suppose that a different faculty of the mind is employed in fixing the other?

On the other hand, those who would resolve all moral determinations into *sentiment,* may endeavour to show, that it is impossible for reason ever to draw conclusions of this nature. To virtue, say they, it belongs to be *amiable,* and vice *odious.* This forms their very nature or essence. But can reason or argumentation distribute these different epithets to any subjects, and pronounce before-hand, that this must produce love, and that hatred? Or what other reason can we ever assign for these affections, but the original fabric and formation of the human mind, which is naturally adapted to receive them?

The end of all moral speculations is to teach us our duty; and, by proper representations of the deformity of vice and beauty of virtue, beget correspondent habits, and engage us to avoid the one, and embrace the other. But is this ever to be expected from inferences and conclusions of the understanding, which of themselves have no hold of the affections or set in motion the active powers of men? They discover truths: But where the truths which they discover are indifferent, and beget no desire or aversion, they can have no influence on conduct and behaviour. What is honourable, what is fair, what is becoming, what is noble, what is generous, takes possession of the heart, and animates us to embrace and maintain it. What is intelligible, what is evident, what is probable, what is true, procures only the cool assent of the understanding; and gratifying a speculative curiosity, puts an end to our researches.

Extinguish all the warm feelings and prepossessions in favour of virtue, and all disgust or aversion to vice: Render men totally indifferent towards these distinctions; and morality is no longer a practical study, nor has any tendency to regulate our lives and actions.

These arguments on each side (and many more might be produced) are so plausible, that I am apt to suspect, they may, the one as well as the other, be solid and satisfactory, and that *reason* and *sentiment* concur in almost all moral determinations and conclusions. The final sentence, it is probable, which pronounces characters and actions amiable or odious, praise-worthy or blameable; that which stamps on them the mark of honour or infamy, approbation or censure; that which renders morality an active principle, and constitutes virtue our happiness, and vice our misery: It is probable, I say, that this final sentence depends on some internal sense or feeling, which nature has made universal in the whole species. For what else can have an influence of this nature? But in order to pave the way for such a sentiment, and give a proper discernment of its object, it is often necessary, we find, that much reasoning should precede, that nice distinctions be made, just conclusions drawn, distant comparisons formed, complicated relations examined, and general facts fixed and ascertained. Some species of beauty, especially the natural kinds, on their first appearance, command our affection and approbation; and where they fail of this effect, it is impossible for any reasoning to redress their influence, or adapt them better to our taste and sentiment. But in many orders of beauty, particularly those of the finer arts, it is requisite to employ much reasoning, in order to feel the proper sentiment; and a false relish may frequently be corrected by argument and reflection. There are just grounds to conclude, that moral beauty partakes much of this latter species, and demands the assistance of our intellectual faculties, in order to give it a suitable influence on the human mind.

But though this question, concerning the general principles of morals, be curious and important, it is needless for us, at present, to employ farther care in our researches concerning it. For if we can be so happy, in the course of this enquiry, as to discover the true origin of morals, it will then easily appear how far either sentiment or reason enters into all determinations of this nature.* In order to attain this purpose, we shall endeavour to follow a very simple method: We shall analyse that complication of mental qualities, which form what, in common life, we call PERSONAL MERIT: We shall consider every attribute of the mind, which renders a man an object either of esteem and affection, or of hatred and contempt; every habit or sentiment or faculty, which, if ascribed to any person, implies either praise or blame, and may enter into any panegyric or satire of his character and manners. The quick sensibility, which, on this head is so universal among mankind, gives a philosopher sufficient assurance, that he can never be considerably mistaken in framing the catalogue, or incur any danger of misplacing the objects of his contemplation: He needs only enter into his own breast for a moment, and consider whether or not he should desire to have this or that quality ascribed to him, and whether such or such an imputation would proceed from a friend or an enemy. The very nature of language guides us almost infallibly in forming a judgment of this nature; and as every tongue possesses one set of words which are taken in a good sense, and another in the opposite, the least acquaintance with the idiom suffices, without any reasoning, to direct us in collecting and arranging the estimable or blameable qualities of men. The only object of reasoning is to discover the circumstances on both sides, which are common to these qualities; to observe that particular in which the estimable qualities agree on the one hand, and the blameable on the other; and thence to reach the foundation of ethics, and find those universal principles, from which all censure or approbation is ultimately derived. As this is a question of fact, not of abstract science, we can only expect success, by following the experimental method, and deducing general maxims from a comparison of particular instances. The other scientific method, where a general abstract principle is first established, and is afterwards branched out into a variety of inferences and conclusions, may be more perfect in itself, but suits less the imperfection of human nature, and is a common source of illusion and mistake in this as well as in other subjects. Men are now cured of their passion for hypotheses and systems in natural philosophy, and will hearken to no arguments but those which are derived from experience. It is full time they should attempt a like reformation in all moral disquisitions; and reject every system of ethics, however subtle or ingenious, which is not founded on fact and observation.

We shall begin our enquiry on this head by the consideration of social virtues, benevolence and justice. The explication of them will probably give us an opening by which others may be accounted for.

SECTION II: OF BENEVOLENCE

Part I

It may be esteemed, perhaps, a superfluous task to prove, that the benevolent or softer affections are ESTIMABLE; and wherever they appear, engage

---

* See Appendix I, "Concerning Moral Sentiment."

the approbation, and good-will of mankind. The epithets *sociable, good-natured, humane, merciful, grateful, friendly, generous, beneficent,* or their equivalents, are known in all languages, and universally express the highest merit, which *human nature* is capable of attaining. Where these amiable qualities are attended with birth and power and eminent abilities, and display themselves in the good government or useful instruction of mankind, they seem even to raise the possessors of them above the rank of *human nature,* and make them approach in some measure to the divine. Exalted capacity, undaunted courage, prosperous success; these may only expose a hero or politician to the envy or ill-will of the public: But as soon as the praises are added of humane and beneficent; when instances are displayed of lenity, tenderness, or friendship: envy itself is silent, or joins the general voice of approbation and applause.

. . . our object here being more the speculative, than the practical part of morals, it will suffice to remark, (what will readily, I believe, be allowed) that no qualities are more intitled to the general good-will and approbation of mankind than benevolence and humanity, friendship and gratitude, natural affection and public spirit, or whatever proceeds from a tender sympathy with others, and a generous concern for our kind and species. These, wherever they appear, seem to transfuse themselves, in a manner, into each beholder, and to call forth, in their own behalf, the same favourable and affectionate sentiments, which they exert on all around.

Part II

We may observe, that, in displaying the praises of any humane, beneficent man, there is one circumstance which never fails to be amply insisted on, namely, the happiness and satisfaction, derived to society from his intercourse and good offices. To his parents, we are apt to say, he endears himself by his pious attachment and duteous care, still more than by the connexions of nature. His children never feel his authority, but when employed for their advantage. With him, the ties of love are consolidated by beneficence and friendship. The ties of friendship approach, in a fond observance of each obliging office, to those of love and inclination. His domestics and dependants have in him a sure resource; and no longer dread the power of fortune, but so far as she exercises it over him. From him the hungry receive food, the naked cloathing, the ignorant and slothful skill and industry. Like the sun, an inferior minister of providence, he cheers, invigorates, and sustains the surrounding world.

If confined to private life, the sphere of his activity is narrower; but his influence is all benign and gentle. If exalted into a higher station, mankind and posterity reap the fruit of his labours.

As these topics of praise never fail to be employed, and with success, where we would inspire esteem for any one; may it not thence be concluded, that the UTILITY, resulting from the social virtues, forms, at least, a *part* of their merit.

and is one source of that approbation and regard so universally paid to them? . . .

In all determinations of morality, this circumstance of public utility is ever principally in view; and wherever disputes arise, either in philosophy or common life, concerning the bounds of duty, the question cannot, by any means, be decided with greater certainty, than by ascertaining, on any side, the true interests of mankind. If any false opinion, embraced from appearances, has been found to prevail; as soon as farther experience and sounder reasoning have given us juster notions of human affairs; we retract our first sentiment, and adjust anew the boundaries of moral good and evil.

Giving alms to common beggars is naturally praised; because it seems to carry relief to the distressed and indigent: But when we observe the encouragement thence arising to idleness and debauchery, we regard that species of charity rather as a weakness than a virtue.

Tyrannicide, or the assassination of usurpers and oppressive princes, was highly extolled in ancient times; because it both freed mankind from many of these monsters, and seemed to keep the others in awe, whom the sword or poinard could not reach. But history and experience having since convinced us, that this practice encreases the jealousy and cruelty of princes, a TIMOLEON and a BRUTUS,[1] though treated with indulgence on account of the prejudices of their times, are now considered as very improper models for imitation. . . .

Upon the whole, then, it seems undeniable, *that* nothing can bestow more merit on any human creature than the sentiment of benevolence in an eminent degree; and *that* a *part*, at least, of its merit arises from its tendency to promote the interests of our species, and bestow happiness on human society. We carry our view into the salutary consequences of such a character and disposition; and whatever has so benign an influence, and forwards so desirable an end, is beheld with complacency and pleasure. The social virtues are never regarded without their beneficial tendencies, nor viewed as barren and unfruitful. The happiness of mankind, the order of society, the harmony of families, the mutual support of friends, are always considered as the result of their gentle dominion over the breasts of men.

How considerable a *part* of their merit we ought to ascribe to their utility, will better appear from future disquisitions,† as well as the reason, why this circumstance has such a command over our esteem and approbation.‡

SECTION III: OF JUSTICE

Part I

That Justice is useful to society, and consequently that *part* of its merit, at least, must arise from that consideration, it would be a superfluous undertaking to prove. That public utility is the *sole* origin of justice, and that reflections

---

† Sect. 3d and 4th, "Of Justice" and "Of Political Society."
‡ Sect. 5th, "Why Utility Pleases."

on the beneficial consequences of this virtue are the *sole* foundation of its merit; this proposition, being more curious and important, will better deserve our examination and enquiry.

Let us suppose, that nature has bestowed on the human race such profuse *abundance* of all *external* conveniences, that, without any uncertainty in the event, without any care or industry on our part, every individual finds himself fully provided with whatever his most voracious appetites can want, or luxurious imagination wish or desire. His natural beauty, we shall suppose, surpasses all acquired ornaments: The perpetual clemency of the seasons renders useless all cloaths or covering: The raw herbage affords him the most delicious fare; the clear fountain, the richest beverage. No laborious occupation required: No tillage: No navigation. Music, poetry, and contemplation, form his sole business: Conservation, mirth, and friendship his sole amusement.

It seems evident, that, in such a happy state, every other social virtue would flourish, and receive tenfold encrease; but the cautious, jealous virtue of justice would never once have been dreamed of. For what purpose make a partition of goods, where every one has already more than enough? Why give rise to property, where there cannot possibly be any injury? Why call this object *mine*, when, upon the seizing of it by another, I need but stretch out my hand to possess myself of what is equally valuable? Justice, in that case, being totally USELESS, would be an idle ceremonial, and could never possibly have place in the catalogue of virtues.

We see, even in the present necessitous condition of mankind, that, wherever any benefit is bestowed by nature in an unlimited abundance, we leave it always in common among the whole human race, and make no subdivisions of right and property. Water and air, though the most necessary of all objects, are not challenged as the property of individuals; nor can any man commit injustice by the most lavish use and enjoyment of these blessings. In fertile extensive countries, with few inhabitants, land is regarded on the same footing. And no topic is so much insisted on by those, who defend the liberty of the seas, as the unexhausted use of them in navigation. Were the advantages, procured by navigation, as inexhaustible, these reasoners had never had any adversaries to refute; nor had any claims ever been advanced of a separate, exclusive dominion over the ocean.

It may happen, in some countries, at some periods, that there be established a property in water, none in land; if the latter be in greater abundance than can be used by the inhabitants, and the former be found, with difficulty, and in very small quantities.

Again; suppose, that, though the necessities of human race continue the same as at present, yet the mind is so enlarged, and so replete with friendship and generosity, that every man has the utmost tenderness for every man, and feels no more concern for his own interest than for that of his fellows: It seems evident, that the USE of justice would, in this case, be suspended by such an extensive benevolence, nor would the divisions and barriers of property and obligation have ever been thought of. Why should I bind another, by a deed or promise, to do me any good office, when I know that he is already prompted, by the strongest inclination, to seek my happiness, and would, of himself, perform the desired service; except the hurt, he thereby receives, be greater than the benefit accruing to me? in which case, he knows, that, from my innate humanity and friendship, I should be the first to oppose myself to his imprudent generosity. Why raise land-marks between my neighbour's field and mine, when my heart has made no division between our interests; but shares all his joys and sorrows with the same force and vivacity as if originally my own? Every man, upon this supposition, being a second self to another, would trust all his interests to the discretion of every man; without jealousy, without partition, without distinction. And the whole human race would form only one family; where all would lie in common, and be used freely, without regard to property; but cautiously too, with as entire regard to the necessities of each individual, as if our own interests were most intimately concerned.

In the present disposition of the human heart, it would, perhaps, be difficult to find compleat instances of such enlarged affections; but still we may observe, that the case of families approaches towards it; and the stronger the mutual benevolence is among the individuals, the nearer it approaches; till all distinction of property be, in a great measure, lost and confounded among them. Between married persons, the cement of friendship is by the laws supposed so strong as to abolish all division of possessions; and has often, in reality, the force ascribed to it. And it is observable, that, during the ardour of new enthusiasms, when every principle is inflamed into extravagance, the community of goods has frequently been attempted: and nothing but experience of its inconveniences, from the returning or disguised selfishness of men, could make the imprudent fanatics adopt anew the ideas of justice and of separate property. So true is it, that this virtue derives its existence entirely from its necessary *use* to the intercourse and social state of mankind.

To make this truth more evident, let us reverse the foregoing suppositions; and carrying every thing to the opposite extreme, consider what would be the effect of these new situations. Suppose a society to fall into such want of all common necessaries, that the utmost frugality and industry cannot preserve the greater number from perishing, and the whole from extreme misery: It will readily, I believe, be admitted, that the strict laws of justice are suspended, in such a pressing emergence, and give place to the stronger motives of necessity and self-preservation. Is it any crime, after a shipwreck, to seize whatever means or instrument of safety one can lay hold of, without regard to former limitations of property? Or if a city besieged were perishing with hunger; can we imagine, that men will see any means of preservation before them, and lose their lives, from a scrupulous regard to what, in other situations, would be the rules of equity and justice? The USE and TENDENCY of that virtue is to procure happiness and security, by preserving order in society: But where the society is ready to perish from extreme necessity, no greater evil can be dreaded from violence and injustice; and every man may now provide for himself by all the means, which prudence can dictate, or humanity permit. The public, even in less urgent necessities, opens granaries, without the consent of proprietors; as justly supposing, that the authority of magistracy may, consistent with equity, extend so far: But were any number of men to assemble, without the tye of laws or civil jurisdiction; would an equal partition of bread in a famine, though effected by power and even violence, be regarded as criminal or injurious?

Suppose likewise, that it should be a virtuous man's fate to fall into the society of ruffians, remote from the protection of laws and government; what conduct must he embrace in that melancholy situation? He sees such a desperate rapaciousness prevail; such a disregard to equity, such contempt of order, such stupid blindness to future consequences, as must immediately have the most tragical conclusion, and must terminate in destruction to the greater number, and in a total dissolution of society to the rest. He, mean while, can have no other expedient than to arm himself, to whomever the sword he seizes, or the buckler, may belong: To make provision of all means of defence and security: And his particular regard to justice being no longer of USE to his own safety or that of others, he must consult the dictates of self-preservation alone, without concern for those who no longer merit his care and attention. . . .

Thus, the rules of equity or justice depend entirely on the particular state and condition, in which men are placed, and owe their origin and existence to that UTILITY, which results to the public from their strict and regular observance. Reverse, in any considerable circumstance, the condition of men: Produce extreme abundance or extreme necessity: Implant in the human breast perfect moderation and humanity, or perfect rapaciousness and malice: By rendering justice totally *useless,* you thereby totally destroy its essence, and suspend its obligation upon mankind.

The common situation of society is a medium amidst all these extremes. We are naturally partial to ourselves, and to our friends; but are capable of learning the advantage resulting from a more equitable conduct. Few enjoyments are given us from the open and liberal hand of nature; but by art, labour, and industry, we can extract them in great abundance. Hence the ideas of property become necessary in all civil society: Hence justice derives its usefulness to the public: And hence alone arises its merit and moral obligation. . . .

Part II

If we examine the *particular* laws, by which justice is directed, and property determined; we shall still be presented with the same conclusion. The good of mankind is the only object of all these laws and regulations. Not only it is requisite, for the peace and interest of society, that men's possessions should be separated; but the rules, which we follow, in making the separation, are such as can best be contrived to serve farther the interests of society. . . .

Thus we seem, upon the whole, to have attained a knowledge of the force of that principle here insisted on, and can determine what degree of esteem or moral approbation may result from reflections on public interest and utility. The necessity of justice to the support of society is the SOLE foundation of that virtue; and since no moral excellence is more highly esteemed, we may conclude, that this circumstance of usefulness has, in general, the strongest energy, and most entire command over our sentiments. It must, therefore, be the source of a considerable part of the merit ascribed to humanity, benevolence, friendship, public spirit, and other social virtues of that stamp; as it is the SOLE source of the moral approbation paid to fidelity, justice, veracity, integrity, and those other estimable and useful qualities and principles. It is entirely agreeable to the rules of philosophy, and even of common reason; where any principle has been found to have a great force and energy in one instance, to ascribe to it a like energy in all similar instances. This indeed is NEWTON's chief rule of philosophizing.[2]

SECTION V: WHY UTILITY PLEASES

Part I

It seems so natural a thought to ascribe to their utility the praise, which we bestow on the social virtues, that one would expect to meet with this principle every where in moral writers, as the chief foundation of their reasoning and enquiry. In common life, we may observe, that the circumstance of utility is always appealed to; nor is it supposed, that a greater eulogy can be given to any man, than to display his usefulness to the public, and enumerate the services, which he has performed to mankind and society. What praise, even of an inanimate form, if the regularity and elegance of its parts destroy not its fitness for any useful purpose! And how satisfactory an apology for any disproportion or seeming deformity, if we can show the necessity of that particular construction for the use intended! . . .

From the apparent usefulness of the social virtues, it has readily been inferred by sceptics, both ancient and modern, that all moral distinctions arise from education, and were, at first, invented, and afterwards encouraged, by the art of politicians, in order to render men tractable, and subdue their natural ferocity and selfishness, which incapacitated them for society. This principle, indeed, of precept and education, must so far be owned to have a powerful influence, that it may frequently encrease or diminish, beyond their natural standard, the sentiments of approbation or dislike; and may even, in particular instances, create, without any natural principle, a new sentiment of this kind; as is evident in all superstitious practices and observances: But that *all* moral affection or dislike arises from this origin, will never surely be allowed by any judicious enquirer. Had nature made no such distinction, founded on the original constitution of the mind, the words, *honourable* and *shameful, lovely* and *odious, noble* and *despicable*, had never had place in any language; nor could politicians, had they invented these tems, ever have been able to render them intelligible, or make them convey any idea to the audience. So that nothing can be more superficial than this paradox of the sceptics; and it were well, if, in the abstruser studies of logic and metaphysics, we could as easily obviate the cavils of that sect, as in the practical and more intelligible sciences of politics and morals.

The social virtues must, therefore, be allowed to have a natural beauty and amiableness, which, at first, antecedent to all precept or education, recommends them to the esteem of uninstructed mankind, and engages their affections. And as the public utility of these virtues is the chief circumstance, whence they derive their merit, it follows, that the end, which they have a tendency to promote, must be some way agreeable to us, and take hold of some natural affection. It must please, either from considerations of self-interest, or from more generous motives and regards.

It has often been asserted, that, as every man has a strong connexion with society, and perceives the impossibility of his solitary subsistence, he becomes, on that account, favourable to all those habits or principles, which promote order in society, and insure to him the quiet possession of so inestimable a blessing. As much as we value our own happiness and welfare, as much must we applaud the practice of justice and humanity, by which alone the social confederacy can be maintained, and every man reap the fruits of mutual protection and assistance.

This deduction of morals from self-love, or a regard to private interest, is an obvious thought, and has not arisen wholly from the wanton sallies and sportive assaults of the sceptics. . . . yet . . . the voice of nature and experience seems plainly to oppose the selfish theory.

We frequently bestow praise on virtuous actions, performed in very distant ages and remote countries; where the utmost subtilty of imagination would not discover any appearance of self-interest, or find any connexion of our present happiness and security with events so widely separated from us.

A generous, a brave, a noble deed, performed by an adversary, commands our approbation; while in its consequences it may be acknowledged prejudicial to our particular interest. . . .

It is but a weak subterfuge, when pressed by these facts and arguments, to say, that we transport ourselves, by the force of imagination, into distant ages and countries, and consider the advantage, which we should have reaped from these characters, had we been contemporaries, and had any commerce with the persons. It is not conceivable, how a *real* sentiment or passion can ever arise from a known *imaginary* interest; especially when our *real* interest is still kept in view, and is often acknowledged to be entirely distinct from the imaginary, and even sometimes opposite to it. . . .

Usefulness is agreeable, and engages our approbation. This is a matter of fact, confirmed by daily observation. But, *useful?* For what? For some body's interest, surely. Whose interest then? Not our own only: For our approbation frequently extends farther. It must, therefore, be the interest of those, who

are served by the character or action approved of; and these we may conclude, however remote, are not totally indifferent to us. By opening up this
principle, we shall discover one great source of moral distinctions.

Part II

Self-love is a principle in human nature of such extensive energy, and the
interest of each individual is, in general, so closely connected with that of the
community, that those philosophers were excusable, who fancied, that all our
concern for the public might be resolved into a concern for our own happiness
and preservation. They saw every moment, instances of approbation or
blame, satisfaction or displeasure towards characters and actions; they denominated the objects of these sentiments, *virtues*, or *vices;* they observed,
that the former had a tendency to encrease the happiness, and the latter the
misery of mankind; they asked, whether it were possible that we could have
any general concern for society, or any disinterested resentment of the welfare
or injury of others; they found it simpler to consider all these sentiments as
modifications of self-love; and they discovered a pretence, at least, for this
unity of principle, in that close union of interest, which is so observable
between the public and each individual.

But notwithstanding this frequent confusion of interests, it is easy to attain
what natural philosophers, after lord BACON,[3] have affected to call the *experi-
mentum crucis*, or that experiment, which points out the right way in any
doubt or ambiguity. We have found instances, in which private interest was
separate from public; in which it was even contrary: And yet we observed the
moral sentiment to continue, notwithstanding this disjunction of interests.
And wherever these distinct interests sensibly concurred, we always found a
sensible encrease of the sentiment, and a more warm affection to virtue, and
detestation of vice, or what we properly call, *gratitude* and *revenge.* Compelled by these instances, we must renounce the theory, which accounts for
every moral sentiment by the principle of self-love. We must adopt a more
public affection, and allow, that the interests of society are not, even on their
own account, entirely indifferent to us. Usefulness is only a tendency to a
certain end; and it is a contradiction in terms, that any thing pleases as means
to an end, where the end itself no wise affects us. If usefulness, therefore, be a
source of moral sentiment, and if this usefulness be not always considered
with a reference to self; it follows, that every thing, which contributes to the
happiness of society, recommends itself directly to our approbation and good-
will. Here is a principle, which accounts, in great part, for the origin of
morality: And what need we seek for abstruse and remote systems, when
there occurs one so obvious and natural?[§]

[§] It is needless to push our researches so far as to ask, why we have humanity or a fellow-feeling
with others. It is sufficient, that this is experienced to be a principle in human nature. We must
stop somewhere in our examination of causes; and there are, in every science, some general
principles, beyond which we cannot hope to find any principle more general. No man is

Have we any difficulty to comprehend the force of humanity and benevolence? Or to conceive, that the very aspect of happiness, joy, prosperity, gives pleasure; that of pain, suffering, sorrow, communicates uneasiness? . . .

A statesman or patriot, who serves our own country, in our own time, has always a more passionate regard paid to him, than one whose beneficial influence operated on distant ages or remote nations; where the good, resulting from his generous humanity, being less connected with us, seems more obscure, and affects us with a less lively sympathy. We may own the merit to be equally great, though our sentiments are not raised to an equal height, in both cases. The judgment here corrects the inequalities of our internal emotions and perceptions; in like manner, as it preserves us from error, in the several variations of images, presented to our external senses. The same object, at a double distance, really throws on the eye a picture of but half the bulk; yet we imagine that it appears of the same size in both situations; because we know, that, on our approach to it, its image would expand on the eye, and that the difference consists not in the object itself, but in our position with regard to it. And, indeed, without such a correction of appearances, both in internal and external sentiment, men could never think or talk steadily on any subject; while their fluctuating situations produce a continual variation on objects, and throw them into such different and contrary lights and positions.‖

The more we converse with mankind, and the greater social intercourse we maintain, the more shall we be familiarized to these general preferences and distinctions, without which our conversation and discourse could scarcely be rendered intelligible to each other. Every man's interest is peculiar to himself, and the aversions and desires, which result from it, cannot be supposed to affect others in a like degree. General language, therefore, being formed for general use, must be moulded on some more general views, and must affix the epithets of praise or blame, in conformity to sentiments, which arise from the general interests of the community. And if these sentiments, in most men, be not so strong as those, which have a reference to private good; yet still they

absolutely indifferent to the happiness and misery of others. The first has a natural tendency to give pleasure; the second, pain. This every one may find in himself. It is not probable, that these principles can be resolved into principles more simple and universal, whatever attempts may have been made to that purpose. But if it were possible, it belongs not to the present subject; and we may here safely consider these principles as original: Happy, if we can render all the consequences sufficiently plain and perspicuous!

‖ For a like reason, the tendencies of actions and characters, not their real accidental consequences, are alone regarded in our determinations or general judgments; though in our real feeling or sentiment, we cannot help paying greater regard to one whose station, joined to virtue, renders him really useful to society, than to one, who exerts the social virtues only in good intentions and benevolent affections. Separating the character from the fortune, by an easy and necessary effort of thought, we pronounce these persons alike, and give them the same general praise. The judgment corrects or endeavours to correct the appearance: But is not able entirely to prevail over sentiment.

Why is this peach-tree said to be better than that other; but because it produces more or better fruit? And would not the same praise be given it, though snails or vermin had destroyed the peaches, before they came to full maturity? In morals too, is not *the tree known by the fruit?* And cannot we easily distinguish between nature and accident, in the one case as well as in the other?

must make some distinction, even in persons the most depraved and selfish; and must attach the notion of good to a beneficent conduct, and of evil to the contrary. Sympathy, we shall allow, is much fainter than our concern for ourselves, and sympathy with persons remote from us, much fainter than that with persons near and contiguous; but for this very reason, it is necessary for us, in our calm judgments and discourse concerning the characters of men, to neglect all these differences, and render our sentiments more public and social. Besides, that we ourselves often change our situation in this particular, we every day meet with persons, who are in a situation different from us, and who could never converse with us, were we to remain constantly in that position and point of view, which is peculiar to ourselves. The intercourse of sentiments, therefore, in society and conversation, makes us form some general unalterable standard, by which we may approve or disapprove of characters and manners. And though the heart takes not part with those general notions, nor regulates all its love and hatred, by the universal, abstract differences of vice and virtue, without regard to self, or the persons with whom we are more intimately connected; yet have these moral differences a considerable influence, and being sufficient, at least, for discourse, serve all our purposes in company, in the pulpit, on the theatre, and in the schools.

Thus, in whatever light we take this subject, the merit, ascribed to the social virtues, appears still uniform, and arises chiefly from that regard, which the natural sentiment of benevolence engages us to pay to the interests of mankind and society. . . .

SECTION VI: OF QUALITIES USEFUL TO OURSELVES

Part I

It seems evident, that where a quality or habit is subjected to our examination, if it appear, in any respect, prejudicial to the person possessed of it, or such as incapacitates him for business and action, it is instantly blamed, and ranked among his faults and imperfections. Indolence, negligence, want of order and method, obstinacy, fickleness, rashness, credulity; these qualities were never esteemed by any one indifferent to a character; much less, extolled as accomplishments or virtues. The prejudice, resulting from them, immediately strikes our eye, and gives us the sentiment of pain and disapprobation.

No quality, it is allowed, is absolutely either blameable or praiseworthy. It is all according to its degree. A due medium, say the PERIPATETICS,[4] is the characteristic of virtue. But this medium is chiefly determined by utility. A proper celerity, for instance, and dispatch in business, is commendable. When defective, no progress is ever made in the execution of any purpose: When excessive, it engages us in precipitate and ill-concerted measures and enterprises: By such reasons, we fix the proper and commendable mediocrity in all moral and prudential disquisitions; and never lose view of the advantages, which result from any character or habit.

Now as these advantages are enjoyed by the person possessed of the character, it can never be *self-love* which renders the prospect of them ageeable to us, the spectators, and prompts our esteem and approbation. . . .

Section IX: Conclusion

Part I

It may justly appear surprising, that any man, in so late an age, should find it requisite to prove, by elaborate reasoning, that PERSONAL MERIT consists altogether in the possession of mental qualities, *useful* or *agreeable* to the *person himself* or to *others*. It might be expected, that this principle would have occurred even to the first rude, unpractised enquirers concerning morals, and been received from its own evidence, without any argument or disputation. Whatever is valuable in any kind, so naturally classes itself under the division of *useful* or *agreeable,* the *utile* or the *dulce,* that it is not easy to imagine, why we should ever seek farther, or consider the question as a matter of nice research or enquiry. And as every thing useful or agreeable must possess these qualities with regard either to the *person himself* or to *others,* the compleat delineation or description of merit seems to be performed as naturally as a shadow is cast by the sun, or an image is reflected upon water. If the ground, on which the shadow is cast, be not broken and uneven; nor the surface, from which the image is reflected, disturbed and confused; a just figure is immediately presented, without any art or attention. And it seems a reasonable presumption, that systems and hypotheses have perverted our natural understanding; when a theory, so simple and obvious, could so long have escaped the most elaborate examination.

But however the case may have fared with philosophy; in common life, these principles are still implicitly maintained, nor is any other topic of praise or blame ever recurred to, when we employ any panegyric or satire, any applause or censure of human action and behaviour. If we observe men, in every intercourse of business or pleasure, in every discourse and conversation; we shall find them no where, except in the schools, at any loss upon this subject. . . .

And as every quality, which is useful or agreeable to ourselves or others, is, in common life, allowed to be a part of personal merit; so no other will ever be received, where men judge of things by their natural, unprejudiced reason, without the delusive glosses of superstition and false religion. Celibacy, fasting, penance, mortification, self-denial, humility, silence, solitude, and the whole train of monkish virtues; for what reason are they every where rejected by men of sense, but because they serve to no manner of purpose; neither advance a man's fortune in the world, nor render him a more valuable member of society; neither qualify him for the entertainment of company, nor increase his power of self-enjoyment? We observe, on the contrary, that they cross all these desirable ends; stupify the understanding and harden the heart, obscure the fancy and sour the temper. We justly, therefore, transfer them to the opposite column, and place them in the catalogue of vices; nor has any superstition force sufficient among men of the world, to pervert entirely these natural sentiments. A gloomy, harebrained enthusiast, after his death, may have a place in the calendar; but will scarcely ever be admitted, when alive, into intimacy and society, except by those who are as delirious and dismal as himself.

It seems a happiness in the present theory, that it enters not into that vulgar dispute concerning the *degrees* of benevolence or self-love, which prevail in human nature; a dispute which is never likely to have any issue, both because men, who have taken part, are not easily convinced, and because the phenomena, which can be produced on either side, are so dispersed, so uncertain, and subject to so many interpretations, that it is scarcely possible accurately to compare them, or draw from them any determinate inference or conclusion. It is sufficient for our present purpose, if it be allowed, what surely, without the greatest absurdity, cannot be disputed, that there is some benevolence, however small, infused into our bosom; some spark of friendship for human kind; some particle of the dove, kneaded into our frame, along with the elements of the wolf and serpent. Let these generous sentiments be supposed ever so weak; let them be insufficient to move even a hand or finger of our body; they must still direct the determinations of our mind, and where every thing else is equal, produce a cool preference of what is useful and serviceable to mankind, above what is pernicious and dangerous. A *moral distinction;* therefore, immediately arises; a general sentiment of blame and approbation; a tendency, however faint, to the objects of the one, and a proportionable aversion to those of the other. . . .

APPENDIX I: CONCERNING MORAL SENTIMENT

If the foregoing hypothesis[5] be received, it will now be easy for us to determine the question first started, concerning the general principles of morals; and though we postponed the decision of that question, lest it should then involve us in intricate speculations, which are unfit for moral discourses, we may resume it at present, and examine how far either *reason* or *sentiment* enters into all decisions of praise or censure.

One principal foundation of moral praise being supposed to lie in the usefulness of any quality or action; it is evident, that *reason* must enter for a considerable share in all decisions of this kind; since nothing but that faculty can instruct us in the tendency of qualities and actions, and point out their beneficial consequences to society and to their possessor. In many cases, this is an affair liable to great controversy: Doubts may arise; opposite interests may occur; and a preference must be given to one side, from very nice views, and a small overbalance of utility. This is particularly remarkable in questions with regard to justice; as is, indeed, natural to suppose, from that species of utility, which attends this virtue. Were every single instance of justice, like that of benevolence, useful to society; this would be a more simple state of the case, and seldom liable to great controversy. But as single instances of justice are often pernicious in their first and immediate tendency, and as the advantage to society results only from the observance of the general rule, and from the concurrence and combination of several persons in the same equitable conduct; the case here becomes more intricate and involved. The various circumstances of society; the various consequences of any practice; the various interests, which may be proposed: These, on many occasions, are doubtful, and subject to great discussion and enquiry. The object of municipal laws is to fix all the questions with regard to justice: The debates of civilians; the reflections of politicians; the precedents of history and public records, are all directed to the same purpose. And a very accurate *reason* or *judgment* is often requisite, to give the true determination, amidst such intricate doubts arising from obscure or opposite utilities.

But though reason, when fully assisted and improved, be sufficient to instruct us in the pernicious or useful tendency of qualities and actions; it is not alone sufficient to produce any moral blame or approbation. Utility is only a tendency to a certain end; and were the end totally indifferent to us, we should feel the same indifference towards the means. It is requisite a *sentiment* should here display itself, in order to give a preference to the useful above the pernicious tendencies. This sentiment can be no other than a feeling for the happiness of mankind, and a resentment of their misery; since these are the different ends which virtue and vice have a tendency to promote. Here, therefore, *reason* instructs us in the several tendencies of actions, and *humanity* makes a distinction in favour to those which are useful and beneficial. . . .

I. It is easy for a false hypothesis to maintain some appearance of truth, while it keeps wholly in generals, makes use of undefined terms, and employs comparisons, instead of instances. This is particularly remarkable in that philosophy, which ascribes the discernment of all moral distinctions to reason alone, without the concurrence of sentiment. It is impossible that, in any particular instance, this hypothesis can so much as be rendered intelligible; whatever specious figure it may make in general declamations and discourses. Examine the crime of *ingratitude,* for instance; which has place, wherever we observe good-will, expressed and known, together with good-offices performed, on the one side, and a return of ill-will or indifference, with ill-offices or neglect on the other: Anatomize all these circumstances, and examine, by your reason alone, in what consists the demerit or blame: You never will come to any issue or conclusion.

Reason judges either of *matter of fact* or of *relations.* Enquire then, *first,* where is that matter of fact, which we here call *crime;* point it out; determine the time of its existence; describe its essence or nature; explain the sense of faculty, to which it discovers itself. It resides in the mind of the person, who is ungrateful. He must, therefore, feel it, and be conscious of it. But nothing is there, except the passion of ill-will or absolute indifference. You cannot say, that these, of themselves, always, and in all circumstances, are crimes. No: They are only crimes, when directed towards persons, who have before expressed and displayed good-will towards us. Consequently, we may infer, that the crime of ingratitude is not any particular individual *fact;* but arises from a complication of circumstances, which, being presented to the spectator, excites the *sentiment* of blame, by the particular structure and fabric of his mind.

This representation, you say, is false. Crime, indeed, consists not in a particular *fact,* of whose reality we are assured by *reason:* But it consists in certain *moral relations,* discovered by reason, in the same manner as we discover, by reason, the truths of geometry or algebra. But what are the relations, I ask, of which you here talk? In the case stated above, I see first good-will and good-offices in one person; then ill-will and ill-offices in the other. Between these, there is the relation of *contrariety.* Does the crime consist in that relation? But suppose a person bore me ill-will or did me ill-offices; and I, in return, were indifferent towards him, or did him good-offices: Here is the same relation of *contrariety;* and yet my conduct is often highly laudable. Twist and turn this matter as much as you will, you can never rest the morality on relation; but must have recourse to the decisions of sentiment.

When it is affirmed, that two and three are equal to the half of ten; this relation of equality, I understand perfectly. I conceive, that if ten be divided into two parts, of which one has as many units as the other; and if any of these parts be compared to two added to three, it will contain as many units as that compound number. But when you draw thence a comparison to moral relations, I own that I am altogether at a loss to understand you. A moral action, a crime, such as ingratitude, is a complicated object. Does morality consist in the relation of its parts to each other? How? After what manner? Specify the relation: Be more particular and explicit in your propositions; and you will easily see their falsehood.

No, say you, the morality consists in the relation of actions to the rule of right; and they are denominated good or ill, according as they agree or disagree with it. What then is this rule of right? In what does it consist? How is it determined? By reason, you say, which examines the moral relations of actions. So that moral relations are determined by the comparison of actions to a rule. And that rule is determined by considering the moral relations of objects. Is not this fine reasoning?

All this is metaphysics, you cry: That is enough: There needs nothing more to give a strong presumption of falsehood. Yes, reply I: Here are metaphysics surely: But they are all on your side, who advance an abstruse hypothesis, which can never be made intelligible, nor quadrate with any particular instance or illustration. The hypothesis which we embrace is plain. It maintains, that morality is determined by sentiment. It defines virtue to be *whatever mental action or quality gives to a spectator the pleasing sentiment of approbation;* and vice the contrary. We then proceed to examine a plain matter of fact, to wit, what actions have this influence: We consider all the circumstances, in which these actions agree: And hence endeavour to extract some general observations with regard to these sentiments. If you call this metaphysics, and find any thing abstruse here, you need only conclude, that your turn of mind is not suited to the moral sciences.

V. It appears evident, that the ultimate ends of human actions can never, in any case, be accounted for by *reason,* but recommend themselves entirely to the sentiments and affections of mankind, without any dependance on the intellectual faculties. Ask a man, *why he uses exercise;* he will answer, *because he desires to keep his health.* If you then enquire, *why he desires health,* he will readily reply, *because sickness is painful.* If you push your enquiries farther, and desire a reason, *why he hates pain,* it is impossible he can ever give any. This is an ultimate end, and is never referred to any other object.

Perhaps, to your second question, *why he desires health,* he may also reply, that *it is necessary for the exercise of his calling.* If you ask, *why he is anxious on that head,* he will answer, *because he desires to get money.* If you demand *Why? It is the instrument of pleasure,* says he. And beyond this it is an absurdity to ask for a reason. It is impossible there can be a progress *in infinitum;* and that one thing can always be a reason, why another is desired. Something must be desirable on its own account, and because of its immediate accord or agreement with human sentiment and affection.

Now as virtue is an end, and is desirable on its own account, without fee or reward, merely, for the immediate satisfaction which it conveys; it is requisite that there should be some sentiment, which it touches; some internal taste or feeling, or whatever you please to call it, which distinguishes moral good and evil, and which embraces the one and rejects the other.

Thus the distinct boundaries and offices of *reason* and of *taste* are easily ascertained. The former conveys the knowledge of truth and falsehood: The latter gives the sentiment of beauty and deformity, vice and virtue. The one discovers objects, as they really stand in nature, without addition or diminution: The other has a productive faculty, and gilding or staining all natural objects with the colours, borrowed from internal sentiment, raises, in a manner, a new creation. Reason, being cool and disengaged, is no motive to action, and directs only the impulse received from appetite or inclination, by showing us the means of attaining happiness or avoiding the misery: Taste, as it gives pleasure or pain, and thereby constitutes happiness or misery, becomes a motive to action, and is the first spring or impulse to desire and volition. From circumstances and relations, known or supposed, the former leads us to the discovery of the concealed and unknown: After all circumstances and relations are laid before us, the latter makes us feel from the whole a new sentiment of blame or approbation. The standard of the one, being founded on the nature of things, is eternal and inflexible, even by the will of the Supreme Being: The standard of the other, arising from the internal frame and constitution of animals, is ultimately derived from that Supreme Will, which bestowed on each being its peculiar nature, and arranged the several classes and orders of existence.

Editor's Notes

1. Timoleon helped other citizens of Corinth assassinate his own brother in about 365 B.C.E. when his brother attempted to become a tyrant. Marcus Junius Brutus joined in the conspiracy to kill his benefactor Julius Caesar in 44 B.C.E. when it was felt that Caesar was becoming tyrannical.
2. In Book III of his *Mathematical Principles of Natural Philosophy*, Newton gave four rules for philosophizing, that is, for proceeding in a scientific treatment of any subject. The first is that "we are to admit no more causes of natural things than such as are both true and sufficient to explain their appearances." The second is that "to the same effects we must, as far as possible, assign the same causes." I quote from the Motte translation of 1729, in the edition by Florian Cajori (Berkeley and Los Angeles: University of California Press, 1947), p. 398.
3. Sir Francis Bacon, *Novum Organum* II.xxxvi, discussed at length the use in science of data of experience that enable one to decide to take one road or another at a crossroads of thought. Such cases are called "instances of the fingerpost."
4. The Aristotelians, who place virtue in a "mean" between two extremes.
5. That is, the hypothesis that we feel moral approval when we perceive a useful trait or disposition in someone.

Further Reading

The standard biography of Hume is that by Ernest C. Mossner, *The Life of David Hume*, 2nd ed. (Oxford: Oxford University Press, 1980). His correspondence is available in J. Y. T. Greig, *The Letters of David Hume* (Oxford: Oxford University Press, 1932); and in Raymond Klibansky and Ernest C. Mossner, *New Letters of David Hume* (Oxford: Oxford University Press, 1954).

A. J. Ayer, *Hume* (Oxford: Oxford University Press, 1980), is a brisk and very brief overview of Hume's entire philosophy. Terence Penelhum, *Hume* (New York: St. Martin's Press, 1975), gives a more detailed study, as does Barry Stroud, *Hume* (London: Routledge & Kegan Paul, 1977). The starting point for modern Hume studies is Norman Kemp Smith, *The Philosophy of David Hume* (London: Macmillan, 1941). Some of Kemp Smith's views are controverted in David Fate Norton, *David Hume: Common-sense Moralist, Sceptical Metaphysician* (Princeton, N.J.: Princeton University Press, 1982), which is itself a controversial study.

Discussion of Hume's philosophy tends to concentrate on the account given in the *Treatise of Human Nature*. There are no separate commentaries on the *Enquiry Concerning the Principles of Morals*, but examination of the ethics presented in the *Treatise* illuminates the later version of the theory. J. L. Mackie, *Hume's Moral Theory* (London: Routledge & Kegan Paul, 1980), is a sympathetic discussion of the main points of Hume's moral psychology and ethics, set in context by brief reviews of his predecessors and successors. Páll Ardal, *Passion and Value in Hume's Treatise* (Edinburgh: Edinburgh University Press, 1966) is a valuable study of the connection between Hume's psychology and his ethics. Jonathan Harrison has written two books on the ethics, both very analytical, frequently to the point of anachronism: *Hume's Moral Epistemology* (Oxford: Oxford University Press, 1976), and *Hume's Theory of Justice* (Oxford: Oxford University Press, 1981). Chapters 9 and 10 of Robert J. Fogelin, *Hume's Skepticism in the Treatise of Human Nature* (London: Routledge & Kegan Paul, 1985), are concerned with his moral psychology and his ethics. For the historical setting of Hume's moral philosophy, Duncan Forbes, *Hume's Philosophical Politics* (Cambridge,

England: Cambridge University Press, 1975), is most valuable. The reader interested in knowing more about the Scottish Enlightenment as the context for Hume should look at two volumes: R. H. Campbell and Andrews S. Skinner, eds., *The Origins and Nature of the Scottish Enlightenment* (Edinburgh: John Donald, 1982); and Istvan Hont and Michael Ignatieff, eds., *Wealth and Virtue* (Cambridge, England: Cambridge University Press, 1983).

The periodical literature on Hume's ethics is very large. Here is a selective list of articles:

Ardal, Páll. "Another Look at Hume's Account of Moral Evaluation." *Journal of the History of Philosophy* 15 (1977).

Baier, Annette. "Frankena and Hume on Points of View." *The Monist* 64 (1981); reprinted in her *Postures of the Mind* (Minneapolis: University of Minnesota Press, 1985).

"Good Men's Women: Hume on Chastity and Trust." *Hume Studies* 5 (1979).

"Hume on Resentment." *Hume Studies* 6 (1980).

"Hume's Account of Our Absurd Passions." *Journal of Philosophy* 79 (1982).

Bricke, John. "Emotion and Thought in Hume's Treatise." *Canadian Journal of Philosophy* 1 (supp.) (1974).

Cottle, Charles F. "Justice as an Artificial Virtue in Hume's *Treatise.*" *Journal of the History of Ideas* 40 (1979).

Davidson, Donald. "Hume's Cognitive Theory of Pride." In his *Essays on Action and Events* (Oxford: Clarendon Press, 1980).

Falk, W. D., "Hume on Is and Ought." *Canadian Journal of Philosophy* 11 (1976).

"Hume on Practical Reason." *Philosophical Studies* 27 (1975).

Gauthier, David. "David Hume, Contractarian." *Philosophical Review* 88 (1979).

MacIntyre, Alasdair. "Hume on Is and Ought." *Philosophical Review* 67 (1959).

Norton, David F. "Hume's Moral Ontology." *Hume Studies*, 1985 supplement.

Snare, Frank. "The Argument from Motivation." *Mind* 84 (1975).

Christian August Crusius

Introduction

Christian August Crusius was born in 1715. He studied theology, philosophy, and other subjects at Leipzig, one of the more advanced of the enlightened German universities, and in 1740 began to teach philosophy there. Between 1744 and 1749 he published his main philosophical works. Among them are *Anweisung, vernünftig zu leben* (*Guide to Rational Living*) (1744), *Entwurf der nothwendigen Vernunft-Wahrheiten* (*Sketch of Necessary Rational Truths*) (1745), and *Weg zur Gewissheit und Zuverlässigkeit der menschlichen Erkenntniss* (*Way to the Certainty and Adequacy of Human Knowledge*) (1747). Thereafter he wrote only on religious and theological topics. Crusius moved to the theological faculty while keeping a position in the philosophical faculty. A popular teacher, he had a successful university career and achieved substantial recognition outside the university. He died in 1775.

The dominant philosophy in Protestant Germany during Crusius's lifetime was that of Christian Wolff. Crusius, a strongly Pietist Lutheran, was opposed to it on religious grounds and came to be known as its most acute and effective critic. As a Pietist he saw personal religious experience and feeling as more important than institutional practices and rituals, and he held that simple and uneducated people could have a richer religious life than could those who were sophisticated and learned. Against Wolff's intellectualism, therefore, which taught that humans are autonomous and which held that the human good consists of the endless increase of knowledge, Crusius stressed the importance of deliberate obedience to God's laws, of which everyone could be aware through feeling, and of reliance on God to look after one's well-being.

In developing these themes Crusius did more than point out problems with Wolff's own position. He began to push in new directions the conventional vocabulary of obligation and moral necessity, established since the time of Pufendorf. One of his aims was to show that each person is wholly responsible to God for his or her own actions. Because Crusius thought Wolff's account of free will an utter failure, he tried to develop a much more radical notion of freedom, and he connected it with the important thought that the will has its own innate structure of laws. He also went beyond previous thinkers in disconnecting moral obligation from the agent's concern with his or her own good and in disconnecting it even from a concern with any good at all. For Crusius, moral obligation – he called it the obligation of virtue – arises simply from our awareness that there are laws that bind us as such, and we can comply with them simply because they are valid laws for us.

Crusius's more general philosophical views stressed the limitations of human knowledge, and the ways in which beliefs that we cannot give up we must accept as true even if we have no proof of them. Crusius was far more aware of the importance of probable empirical evidence than the Wolffians were, and more appreciative of the advances of the mechanistic understanding of the world than his Pietist philosophical forerunners were. Crusius's ethics, in particular, is a vital part of the transition from the philosophy of the earlier German enlightenment to the work of Kant. For in trying to explain how we could be wholly dependent on God and also wholly responsible for our own actions, he worked out some of the conceptual apparatus that Kant was to use for a much stronger assertion of human autonomy than Wolff had presented.

If Crusius is now remembered mainly for his influence on Kant (who in his early years admired Crusius), his work is worth reading for an understanding of the development of the modern vocabulary of morality as well as for insight into the most important of the philosophical controversies in German during the first half of the eighteenth century.

I have translated selections from the *Anweisung vernünftig zu Leben*, using the reprint edition by Giorgio Tonelli (Hildesheim: Olms, 1969). Like Wolff's "German Ethics," this was a book intended for students. It was written in a compact and undecorated style, full of cross-references to earlier and later paragraphs. Although I have kept Crusius's paragraph numbers, I have omitted most of the cross-references and eliminated most of the italicizations and capitalizations.

Guide to Rational Living

Psychology

Chapter I: Of Goals and of the Human Will

§2 By "will" I understand the power of a mind to act according to its ideas. I mean that the will is the efficient cause, whereas the ideas are the model or exemplary cause. One acts according to them when one makes represented things real or tries to do so. . . . my explanation includes everything that belongs to will according to ordinary language. For desire and aversion, including all doing and omitting that come from them, are ascribed to will. In all these cases it is clear that an act of the mind according to ideas comes first. . . .

§4 All minds must have wills. If they had none, they could not act according to their ideas, and these would then be useful neither to them nor to others but quite in vain. But it is altogether contrary to God's perfection to create something wholly useless and in vain.

§6. . . the will, in all finite beings, is a separate basic power, distinguished from the understanding or, to speak more precisely, the essential part of separate basic powers that on account of their common essence are conceived together and called will. . . .

§9 A willing, through which we are moved to make something real that does not yet exist or to bring about its union with ourselves, insofar as the willing is considered an action within the willing mind, is called a desire. . . .

§13 Whatever a mind wants can be called a goal or end in the widest sense.

In the narrower meaning, however, we understand by end only something that one wants consciously and with clear knowledge. Whenever a mind strives for an end, three aspects are to be distinguished in the striving. First of all, there must be an effective willing, which is the efficient power moving us toward something. I will call this the subjective end. . . . Further, a particular thing must be conceived toward which one strives, which is called the objective end. Finally, we must think of a certain relation of that thing to the willing mind seeking to bring it about and for the sake of which the action is undertaken, which is called the formal end. For example, when Alexander went to war against the Persians, the Persian Empire was his objective end. The formal end was that he bring it under his control and rule it. Alexander's desire for mastery was the subjective end. . . .

§22 A willing that one could omit or direct to something else even in identical circumstances is called a free willing, and the power involved is called freedom. The application of freedom to an existing situation, by which one really wills, is called a resolution or decision. . . .

§24 The condition of our soul that arises from the satisfaction of a willing is called pleasant and, if we recognize this consciously, enjoyment. . . .

§26 Whatever accords with the will of a mind we call to that extent good, and likewise what is contrary to it we call to that extent an evil. Accordingly, the goodnesses of things consist in their relation to a will with which they are compared, just as truth rests in a relation to the understanding. If by contrast we call something good that is in accordance with perfection, it is undeniable that this happens because rational minds generally desire perfection in themselves and in other things and insofar as they desire it, as otherwise there would be no reason that one should not also call the imperfect good. . . . The perfection of a thing consists only in the relation of its condition to the sum of the effects for which it is fit; and the more it is fit for and the more fit it is for them, the more perfect it is. So goodness and perfection are not the same.

This concept of good can easily be fitted into the categories of good that philosophers recognize. Insofar as something is found to agree with the natural goals of God – that is, insofar as it is found suited to those effects that God has willed to make possible through the thing's created essence – so far it is metaphysically good. So far as something agrees with the will of created beings, it is physically good. . . . The morally good, however, is what is in accordance with the moral designs of God, that is, those that he wills to have forwarded through the reason and free wills of created minds or, to put it otherwise, the morally good is what agrees with his laws.

Chapter III: Of the Freedom of the Human Will

§38. . . . According to ordinary notions, a free will is a will not outwardly compelled and also not inwardly necessary. It should make man capable of responsibility for his activity, so that one does not only ascribe it to him as the efficient cause but also can think him open to praise or blame or to charges of guilt and can hold him worthy of punishment or reward because he acted this way rather than that. Freedom must be what makes us fit to be subordinated to a law and to obligation and fit for giving a reckoning of the direction of our behavior. If we take together these presupposed properties, then a free being can be nothing but a being who at one time and in one set of circumstances can either do or omit something or in place of it do something else. The power by means of which it is capable of this is called freedom. . . .

§39 Consequently, one may express the essence of freedom also through this concept, that it is a power to determine oneself to an action, without being determined by anything else, whether internal or external. . . .

§40 If one does not include this concept, there would never be an act done without necessity. For even if one indicated an act to which the efficient substance were determined through its own ideas and desires, which one calls spontaneity or spiritual self-activity, still the act would not cease to be necessary, because everything determined, insofar as it is determined, is necessary. It makes no difference through what sort of ideas the effective mind is determined, not even whether or not the determining motives in its understanding are clearly conceived. In such a case, all our virtue would be turned into a mere piece of luck, as it would come about if one had a good nature or were put in such relations to things that one were determined to do actions according with perfection. Vice would be mere misfortune, for which no true guilt could arise, as it would not be up to the agent to improve the situation, but everything would depend on the nature that the creator had given him. . . .

Praise and blame sometimes mean only judgments about whether or not certain properties of a thing agree with perfection. Still, there are two sorts of praise and blame, first the nonmoral, which is nothing but a judgment of the perfection or imperfection of the thing, and [second] the moral, when we hold someone to be the free cause of a characteristic that we recognize as worthy of praise or blame. I will show in what follows that many things that do not now occur completely freely, or even that occur without freedom, can be awarded truly moral praise or blame, because we have earlier brought about their causes. Thus one can admittedly praise a naturally good property. But we must not on that account deny that we are able to praise it on account of voluntarily occasioned acts or properties, and we must not confuse the praise-worthy qualities with one another. . . .

§41 If we reflect on how such a power as freedom, according to this concept of it, is possible, it becomes clear that it must consist in a perfect inner activity. It is a point to be shown in metaphysics that an action or activity must come between an effect and its efficient cause but that the series cannot extend to infinity. Consequently, one must come to first actions or basic activities, for which it is not necessary that another activity of an efficient cause precede but that arise immediately out of the essence of an active basic power. . . . The freedom of the human will must be of this category. So we can determine its concept more fully thus: freedom is the highest degree of activity in a will, by virtue of which it can itself begin, direct, and then break off its effectiveness, regardless of all the necessary conditions, which only make it possible. . . .

§42 You will be convinced by the following that the same freedom that I have explained from the use of language . . . is really present in our soul. We are, first, conscious in many cases that in the same circumstances we can omit an action or direct it otherwise. Therefore we really possess the power. For example, I find within myself that while I write this I could stop and take up another task or walk up and down in the room. . . .

It is further necessary that free minds must exist in any world whatever. Otherwise God could not create any world, because he could have no end, on his side, in doing so. For otherwise it would be as if God did everything himself, and created beings would obtain through their reality no other relation to God than what they already had in the mere condition of possibility, namely, that their being and essence depended on him. He would therefore have had to make them real without the slightest formal end, which contradicts the divine perfection. Now, because divine perfection is necessary, a world without free minds is just as impossible as a four-sided circle or wooden iron is.

Finally, whoever admits that true divine laws exist, whose certainty I will show in its place, must admit also on that account that there is true freedom in us, because that is the sole possible cause that puts us in the condition to be subordinated to a law and to live according to it.

§43 Whenever we freely will something, we decide to do something for which one or several desires already exist in us, and accordingly, the formal end always consists of the relation that a thing has to one or several of our drives. . . . herewith we discover the complete idea of freedom. Freedom consists in an inner perfect activity of will, which is capable of connecting its efficacy with one of the currently activated drives of the will, or of omitting this connection and remaining inactive, or of connecting it with another drive instead of the first one.

§46 . . . From what has been said, we can easily see the goal for whose sake God gave freedom to humans. It should be the ruling power that directs the other powers of soul, which are subordinated to it and are to serve it. Through this the capacities of the soul are transformed into abilities that can be ascribed to the efficacious substance. And thereby the many desires are subordinated to one another and are brought without compulsion or necessity into a system in which exists the perfection that God intended. How much store God sets on such a constitution of rational creatures can be inferred from this, that otherwise he cannot create any world at all. . . .

Chapter V: Of Basic Desires

§89 A desire always has its ground in one or several other desires. But because this series cannot continue to infinity, we must finally come to first desires, which are not due to others and are the ground of all the rest.

§92 Every act of will is an action according to ideas. But a desire is a continuous striving to act in certain ways according to certain ideas. So if there are basic desires, there are also innate ideas that belong to them and that must be assumed to be presupposed and inseparable conditions of them. . . .

§93 The marks of a basic desire are accordingly the following: First, it must not be wicked in and of itself, that is, conflict with divine or human perfection, because otherwise God would not have built it into the human essence. . . . Next, it must be universal. The proof of universality is drawn from experience. . . . Finally, it must not be derivable from any other. . . .

Chapter VI: Of Universal Properties of Desires That Are Themselves Desires

§97 Every desire is a striving to bring certain ideas to reality. If this is to happen, the idea of the desired object must be held vividly in mind. . . . Consequently, all desires include a desire for the clear idea of the object and an inclination to take pleasure in it.

§101 If we are to achieve what we wish, we must ourselves exist and live. . . . Accordingly, all our drives include the desire for our own existence or reality. . . .

§102 Every desire in a rational mind strives also for the assurance of its object and thus is also a desire for the future. . . .

§106 When our desires are satisfied, pleasure ensues. We therefore desire pleasure because we want the satisfaction of our desires. If our desires are not satisfied, pain will ensue, which we therefore avoid. There thus arises out of all desires taken together a longing to see them all satisfied with pleasure and to be free from all pain, and this is called the drive for happiness. Now, we have a desire to live and a desire for perfect assurance of the wanted object, whose satisfaction is also the aim of the drive for happiness. Consequently, the drive for happiness, taken comprehensively, is a drive for an endless life in which all our wishes will continuously be pleasantly satisfied . . . and in which no unhappiness is possible.

We see from this that the drive toward happiness is in fact directed toward an infinite object, that is, toward one that will infinitely satisfy. Now, because the achievement of this is not possible except through the will and power of our creator, it is clear that the drive to happiness is always in error if man strives for his happiness in any order other than that in which he seeks to make himself pleasing to his creator in every part and is assured of grace. Thus the drive to human happiness, rightly understood, always leads to God. . . .

Chapter VII: Of Basic Human Desires

§111 . . . The first basic human desire is the drive for our own perfection, or the urge to see our condition in its appropriate perfection and to make it always more perfect. . . .

§122 The next of the basic human desires is the urge for union with objects in which we perceive perfection, or think we perceive it. It is distinguished from the preceding desire, in that through the former we seek our own perfection, but by means of this we seek union with perfection without any view to ourselves or to the use that we could expect from it. . . .

§132 Finally, the third of the basic human drives is the natural drive to recognize a divine moral law, that is, to believe a rule for human action in which it is determined what God wants done or not done out of obedience because of our dependence and otherwise will punish us. It is one of the natural basic laws of human nature . . . that we compare the concepts of the understanding with our desires to become aware of what in their objects is or is not in conformity with the ideas. From this arises an inclination to judge the morality of our acts, that is, their justice or injustice and, when they are not in accordance with the law, to fear God's wrath and punishment on that account.

We call the judgment of the morality of our acts "conscience." So we shall call the basic drive to recognize the divine moral law that is its ground the "drive of conscience." That conscience is no mere theoretical judgment of the understanding – but must have its ground in a drive of the will – can be seen from the fact that it rejoices us and terrifies us. One should not confuse conscience with consciousness in general or with the awareness of the perfection or imperfection of one's actions in general. For it is one thing to make something a matter of conscience, another to be aware of an imperfection in action and therefore to regret what one did because one is aware that it was in vain or contrary to one's goal. . . .

§133 The motive of conscience is therefore merely a motive to recognize certain indebtednesses [*Schuldigkeiten*], that is, such universal obligations [*Verbindlichkeiten*][1] as one must observe even if one does not wish to consider the advantages and disadvantages deriving from them, whose transgression God will punish and, if his law is not to be in vain, must punish. . . . Here I shall . . . add that to the word indebtedness we attach, by the guidance of nature, the concept I have given. This I shall make clear as follows:

We distinguish what lays an indebtedness on us from motives in general. If we are inclined toward something through motives or are even fully determined to do it, it still does not follow that on that account we have an indebtedness to do it. For there also are motives for evil and for indifferent things.

Further, indebtedness is to be distinguished from all inner and outer compulsions. For whatever we are compelled to do, we have on that account no indebtedness to do. We distinguish indebtedness further from what one does out of fear or hope. For how much does one do from fear, to which one is not obligated [*verbunden*], and how often do we say that this or that would be for our own benefit, but it is also our indebtedness?

Finally, indebtedness is not identical with what is done out of love. For all men agree on this: that an indebtedness may not be the sort of thing in which it depends on our own preference whether or not we are to do it; I mean, so that the essence of indebtedness might disappear through just a change in our will. There remains no alternative, therefore, but that an indebtedness is such an act or omission as we should do out of obedience to God as our highest lord, creator, and sustainer, for the sake of his will.

There exists, therefore, in the motive of conscience the genuine basic essence of legal obligation [*Verbindlichkeit*]. For the obligation of law should be what moves the subordinate to obey the commands of his lord. This, however, can be nothing else but the idea of his dependence on the other. By dependence, among minds, nothing else is to be understood than such a relation of one to the other, that the one has certain goods from the will of the other in such a way that if the will of the other ceased, the goods would also cease. From this it is clear that we depend in all things on God. How could the idea of dependence, all by itself, bring us to execute the commands of our lord, if there were not a natural basic motive existing in us, leading us to act in accordance with our dependence on God?

§134 It is thus not specially necessary to show that the drive of conscience is distinct from the previously distinguished basic drives, as its object is so very different from those of the other drives. It is just as superfluous to try to show its goodness, as it is self-evident that nothing can be good without agreement with divine law. . . .

§135 The universality of the drive of conscience does, however, need a special proof, because owing to its many hindrances and suppressions, it may look as if it is missing in many people. If one first assumes the reality of divine law, which we shall prove later, then one will easily see an a priori reason that there must be an innate drive of conscience. For because God has created basic drives for many lesser ends, which usually serve their ends with considerable certainty, should he not have cared for virtue as his main end but have left men in a condition in which it would be possible to eradicate any idea of a true law of God?

Second, coming to know God and his will through proofs, and judging what is told us by means of clear arguments, is for most people much too roundabout. Most scholars do not get far in doing so, and [so] how could the unlearned get things completely right? But because all men are subordinated to the divine law and will be judged by it hereafter, it is easy to infer that God would create a shorter path to knowledge of it and would make his will evident in such a way that it could come to everyone's knowledge.

§136 Experience agrees with this. All men recognize certain things as right or wrong, proper or improper, under which words nothing but a dark idea of a universal law lies buried. A man of moderate understanding will soon become aware in the hardest and most confused actions of what would be right or wrong, even without being able to give clearly any sufficient grounds for his judgment or even to defend it. From this it is evident that there is a natural sensation of justice and propriety in us that has something more than a mere judgment of the understanding as its ground.

The majority who believe in a divine law can give no correct and unobjectionable proof of it. Indeed, few teachers of morals prove it thoroughly, and it is a common but well-based complaint that one gets nowhere worse proofs than in moral writings. The natural law is something that is contrary to our common inclinations and directs their limitation and improvement. Now, I would like to know whence it comes that whereas men laugh at and reject other unproved claims running against our natural inclinations, nonetheless all decent people approve the law of nature and do not reject it because of the bad proofs of it that they find but, rather, feel themselves required to find better ones. Do we not see here evidently a testimony that the truth of the law is hidden within ourselves?

Scholars are still not agreed on the principle on which we must build natural duties. About the most important duties, however, they all agree. . . . I am convinced that philosophers mostly do not seek basic principles in order that they may learn from them what is right or wrong. Their effort is, rather, only this: to structure into an orderly theory the duties that nature teaches humankind. . . .

§137 Now, if there is a drive in us to recognize a divine law and to act according to it, then there must also be in us an innate idea of the natural law, which is the pattern according to which the drive of conscience strives to direct human action. This need not be taken to imply that the concept of every single duty is implanted in us. It suffices if God has given us a universal rule of action from which the individual cases can be judged. If we pay attention a posteriori to the material duties that conscience teaches, it will become clear that most of them, at least, can be collected in this rule: *do what is in accordance with the perfection of God and your relations to him and further what accords with the essential perfection of human nature, and omit the opposite.* The acts of a mind are said to be in accordance with perfection when one can see from their direction that they recognize mind and keep an eye on it.

Accordingly, we can state the express concept of the drive of conscience thus: the drive of conscience is a natural, basic drive that moves us to do what conforms with divine and human perfection – out of obedience to God's will because of our dependence on him – and, in the contrary case, to fear his anger and punishment. We see here immediately that there must be an innate idea of God.

ETHICS

Chapter I: Of Virtue in General

§156 If we ask how the will should be constituted and wish to answer merely according to the prescriptions of reason . . . we are asking either how the human will should be constituted with a view to divine natural laws, which we see as the ends of the creator, or how it should be constituted with a view to the ends of humans, which they all desire, that is, with a view to the advancement of their perfection and happiness.

§157 I have deliberately linked the condition of perfection with that of happiness. These two concepts speak of one and the same thing. For the perfection of man exists when his condition agrees with all of his ends. Consequently, all his desires must be satisfied as fully as possible. . . .

§159 Now, if we determine the idea of ethics first by saying that it is the science of the rules that show the way to human happiness, we still will have to investigate whether there really are divine laws. Suppose there were; then we would fail to reach happiness if we did not concern ourselves with them. . . .

I can, accordingly, give a fuller description of the *Guide to Rational Living* by saying that it is a science that explains rationally both the divine laws and the rest of the general rules for the achievement of good ends and thus shows the way as far as possible to attain human perfection and happiness.

§160 A "duty" [*Pflicht*], in the broad sense, is an act or omission in which a moral necessity exists. A "moral necessity" is a relation of an act or omission to certain ends such that a rational mind can understand that it should or should not be done. The condition in which a moral necessity for something exists is, in a broad sense, called "obligation" [*Verbindlichkeit*]. Accordingly, morals encompass duties and obligations.

§161 By "prudence" we understand the skill of choosing and applying good means to one's ends. "Virtue," however, is the agreement of the moral condition of a mind with the divine laws. Hence we call each single part of it a virtue. I do not overlook that at times the word "virtue" is used in a broader sense for any praiseworthy property. But this meaning is not serviceable for my purpose, as I want to keep apart essentially different things. I call moral all that brings about its effect by means of a free will. . . .

§162 Now I can indicate the kinds of duties and obligations. . . . To wit, that on which the moral necessity of an act or omission is grounded – I mean from which it should be understood – is either to be sought only in certain ends already desired by us; because we then have to look only at the ends that according to the psychology are essential to human nature, which otherwise one would not be able to achieve; then I will name the duty, insofar as it is grounded on this, a duty of prudence, and similarly I can call the obligation arising out of it the obligation of prudence. Or else the ground of the moral necessity lies in a law and in our owing fulfillment of it; then I will name that duty a duty of virtue. The obligation arising from it, however, can be called legal obligation, or the obligation of virtue, or true obligation in a narrower sense. Accordingly, the obligation of prudence, in ethics, is the relation of an act or omission to certain goals that we desire because of our nature . . . such that if we do not behave in certain ways we will not be able to attain our goal. The obligation of virtue is the relation of an act or omission to a divine law, such that if we do not behave in certain ways the law will be violated. A duty of prudence exists where there is an obligation of prudence. A duty of virtue exists where there is an obligation of virtue. Where an obligation of virtue exists, one may also speak of an indebtedness.

§163 Although I have carefully distinguished duties and obligations of virtue and prudence, it should not be thought that in virtue itself both sorts of obligation are not present, so that a duty of virtue is not also always a duty of prudence. For because, as we shall see, the divine law orders the truest means to our well-being, the essential desires of our soul will be fulfilled when we obey the divine law. [Virtue and prudence] are, however, to be distinguished, so that true legal obligation and the essence of virtue will not be destroyed by the assumption that there is only the obligation of prudence – which, regrettably, seems to occur all too often.

§165 A law is a universal will of a more powerful being who does not have another more powerful being over him, through which an indebtedness springing from this will is imposed on those subordinate to him to do or omit something. The more powerful being who gives the law is called a *superior*. . . . If one does the will of a superior because one is indebted to do so, this is called *obedience*. Now all indebtedness is grounded on dependence. . . .

§166 . . . we can see how true moral dependence differs from the merely overwhelming power of one over another, and thus what the difference is between a superior whose will has an obligating power and a more powerful being who can only compel to fulfillment of his will. For example, a highwayman can compel us to give him our money, but no obligation to do so follows from his will, which by contrast does take place with a true lawgiver. For we have to thank a lawgiver for certain goods, which come merely from his will because he has no superior over him. So not only does our benefit bid us obey him, in order not to lose the goods and also our perfection, because resistance would be in vain, which together make an obligation of prudence; but also because of the drive of conscience, we feel an indebtedness to obedience and naturally approve it, from which a legal obligation arises.

§168 . . . I presuppose here the existence and properties of God as demonstrated by natural theology. [I similarly assume that man depends wholly on God.]

§169 We can prove the certainty of divine natural laws first a posteriori from the drive of conscience, which also shows their content. Because all other basic drives have an existing object, likewise this drive must have one. Indeed, it must have an object; otherwise God has put it into the soul in vain, only to frighten men. . . .

§171 The necessity of divine laws and also their content can further be proved a priori. I assume that God wills the necessary perfections of things. . . . It follows from this that as soon as free beings are posited, God must necessarily will that their free actions and what follows from them be in accordance with the essential perfections of things. . . .

§172 . . . Now the natural relation in which we and all creatures stand to God is that we depend on him alone and necessarily for all things. That is the sole condition that is simply essential. All the rest are contingent. . . . Accordingly, God necessarily wills that all free actions by rational creatures, and what follows from them, be so directed that one can see from their direction that they recognize full and necessary dependence on God. . . .

§173 . . . it is not enough that we do what God wills, as his will, just out of love. . . . For from the fact that a soul tries to make itself pleasing to another out of love, it cannot be understood that the one recognizes his dependence on the other . . . we must do everything that God wills to be done . . . out of obedience to him as our creator, sustainer, and lawfully commanding superior and lawgiver. For only from such a direction of our deeds can it be understood that we recognize a dependence on God and have it in view. . . . Now, because God necessarily wills that we should act out of a sense of our dependence on him, there is also necessarily a divine natural law, whose content is here evident.

And just this necessary will of God is the ground of the morally good, from which we see that the morally good, like all other goods, has its ground in a will. Whether or not one could say that something might be in accordance with perfection without attention to the will of God, one can certainly not allow that without attention to it something could be morally good or bad. To say this would be to contradict oneself or to alter unnecessarily the ordinary notion of good and bad. Yet the morally good is not at all arbitrary, because the will of God, in which the highest laws of nature have their ground, is not a free but a necessary will.

§174 Here I have derived the highest natural law a priori, which previously, in §137, I obtained only from experience and which is this: do out of obedience toward the command of your creator as your natural and necessary superior everything that is in conformity with the perfection of God and the essential perfection of your own nature and of all other creatures and the relations of things to one another, and omit the opposite.

§176 The point is that obedience to God should be our unconditionally highest subjective end, God himself the highest objective end, and compliance with his will and command the highest formal end. . . . Then our happiness will follow of itself from virtue and in the condition of virtue; which we desire . . . but must not make the goal, because if we do, obedience will lose its essence. In order that it may be possible for us to make the desire to act in accordance with our dependence into our main end, the drive of conscience is implanted in us, by means of which the sense of our dependence leads us to obedience. . . . If the drive of conscience did not exist in us, then admittedly neither obedience nor virtue would be possible, for because of our other essential drives we would always make our own utility or pleasure our end or at least would act only out of love, which is not yet obedience.

§177 . . . What a rational being does in conformity with the essential perfection of things becomes virtue only when it is done out of obedience. Consequently, we can call the intention of being obedient to God the *form* of virtue. But an act or omission that taken in itself is in accordance with divine or human perfection and is distinguished from obedience constitutes the *matter* of virtue. . . .

§178 From what has been shown, we can now obtain the natural *principia cognoscendi*[2] of the divine law, that is, the way to determine exactly how we come to know it. The first is a posteriori, namely, the natural drive of con-science, when we attend to what – if our desires and feelings do not prevent – it teaches us about good or evil, honorable or shameful, approvable or disapprovable. From this source of knowledge not only the common people but also the learned obtain the greatest part of their knowledge of duty, but the latter look afterwards for clear proofs.

§179 There is indeed an erring and doubtful conscience. But the difficulties must not be thought to be so great that on their account it is not possible for the conscience to be able to be a sure source of a posteriori knowledge of duty. . . . It is the same with sensation. Who would say that this is an uncer-tain or unsuitable *principium* for obtaining truth, even though many alleged experiences deceive? . . .

§181 The second way to come to knowledge of divine natural laws through reason is the way of clear knowledge, in which one derives duties from the nature of divine and human essential perfection by clear and valid arguments, when one shows that something is in accordance with, or is opposed to, the concept of the perfection of God or a thing in general, or that the intention of God for the things of this world otherwise cannot be attained at all, or not surely attained, and especially that the essentially human basic desires cannot otherwise be satisfied. . . .

§184 A law is either a commanding law, saying that something is to happen, or a forbidding law, saying that something is to be omitted. For what conflicts with the essential perfection of things is forbidden, whereas what accords with it is commanded. A forbidding law thus must always be followed. A command-ing law, however, can speak of something that needs to happen only under certain circumstances.

§185 What is neither commanded nor forbidden is permitted. We know a posteriori that there are certain things that are merely permitted because when omitting certain things we feel no pangs of conscience. . . .

§194 We should guard against the mistaken belief that divine punishments and rewards are necessary so that the law may be obligatory, in that fear of the former and hope of the latter would drive man to obedience and must be the goal of obedience. For through this, all true legal obligation and also all true obedience would be destroyed. Divine perfection demands that observance of his laws be sustained in this way. Obligation under them, however, arises from our dependence on him. . . .

§203 The core idea of all duties, of virtue discoverable by reason taken together is called, in a broad sense, the law of nature. Now, because all duties of virtue have their obligation from God, and must be done out of obedience to divine command, the law of nature is in essence nothing but the practical part of natural theology.

§204 . . . natural moral theology deals with immediate duties to God; the law of nature, in the narrow sense, with the duties and authorizations of men toward other men; and ethics, with the duties that immediately concern the virtuous constitution of our own mind and condition, usually called duties to oneself. . . . There are indeed still other duties recognized by reason, namely, duties in relation to nonrational and lifeless creatures. Because they are easily understood from the universal basic law of virtue . . . they do not call for a special part of the law of nature.

§205 One of the ethical duties is, as will be shown, the obligation to prudence. Now, universal and useful rules of prudence can be given, which can be used with all other ends, even those to which one has no obligation. These must also be treated in moral theory. They do not, however, belong to the law of nature. . . .

Chapter II: Of the End of Human Life

§208 The end of the world, as far as it concerns humans, is this: through their common free efforts they increase the virtue in their souls, exercise it and strengthen it, and consequently have permission to use the goods of the world, with no detriment to virtue, for satisfaction and pleasure, whereupon they shall be translated into another life in which the virtuous will be completely happy but the disobedient will be punished and in which the punishments as well as the rewards will be in proportion to the virtue or vice. . . .

§210 We ask now about God's final objective ends. These must be made so that they can know the world and enjoy it, because otherwise many goods that could be enjoyed would exist in vain. Now only rational enjoyment counts as true enjoyment. Hence the world must be made for rational minds, among which humans belong. . . . A posteriori we find no others except humans on earth. . . . So humans are God's final objective ends, and at least the earth was created for their sake.

§211 . . . God's formal end for humans must be something served through their free acts. We understand this a posteriori because God made men with free will. The necessity thereof can be inferred a priori because otherwise the world would be pointless in God's view. For it would be as if God himself did everything. . . .

§212 We learn further a posteriori that God's end for humans must be something that should be reached through their common efforts. For God made men sociable, so that one always needs the help of another. . . .

§213 God's main goal in this life is virtue. . . . For in any world there must be free acts. Further, God necessarily wills that these be directed in accordance with virtue, upon which reward or punishment follows. Because of his goodness, however, God wants rational minds to be happy. These assertions fit together only if God first puts rational minds in the world in conditions in which they can exercise free virtue, and afterward distributes happiness in proportion to virtue. . . .

§216 . . . If virtue were not the end, it would have to be knowledge of truth, or happiness. But knowledge cannot be the main goal. For the understanding, in accordance with its nature, can only be for the sake of the will, that is, for an active being to be enabled through it to achieve certain ends.

Happiness in this life also cannot be God's goal. For the arrangement of the world is quite unsuited to this end. We are born with mere capacities. Nature brings us the things we need raw and not manufactured; she hides her treasures and mysteries from us. We can do nothing without sour toil and work. What can we conclude except that the creator's aim is that we should make ourselves toil and that humans should possess only as much readiness of wit and as much satisfaction in worldly goods as they acquire through their own strivings? And because God must desire that these strivings be directed in accordance with perfection, we see that virtue is the goal of human life. And anyone, in any walk of life, no matter what sort of work he does, can strive toward this and serve it. . . .

§218 The divine end for humans goes further than this present life, and the soul of man is immortal. [This is proved as follows:]

§220 We have shown, moreover, that God must reward all goodness in proportion to its amount and punish all wickedness in due proportion. Experience shows that this happens not at all or only rarely in the present life; so there must be another, which he has destined for the revelation of his rewarding and punishing justice. Because the rewards and punishments must be endless, the other life must be a condition of real immortality. . . .

§221 . . . Do not be surprised that I have derived [immortality] from purely moral grounds. These are the only ones fit for such a proof. Immortality cannot be derived from the essence of the soul. For because our soul once did not live, we see that life is contingent in it. . . .

Chapter III: On the Virtuous Direction of the Spirit

§239 We have the capacity to love God and . . . we owe him the highest possible love. . . .

§240 Accordingly, the love of God above all things is the main virtue from which all others must flow. Obedience considered in itself is still an indeterminate duty, merely the formal aspect of virtue. Where virtue is really to exist, there must also be a material aspect. The highest material virtue is thus the love of God, which belongs to obedience as its first determination and, taken with it, constitutes the determinate basic essence of virtue. The love of God makes obedience voluntary, as obedience makes the love of God into a true virtue. We can thus grasp the determinate concept of virtue as a disposition to love God as our highest ruler above all things and to recognize ourselves as bound to this.

THE LAW OF NATURE

Chapter I: Of the Law of Nature in General

§362 We speak now of the law of nature in the narrower sense, which is the core of natural duties of men toward other men. . . . The readiness to observe one's duties toward other men is called justice in the narrower sense.

§363 That there is a law of nature . . . is clear from this. God wills that we always should do what is in accordance with the perfection of God, our own being, and all other creatures, including also the connections he has made among them, and do it out of obedience to his will. Consequently, we have to follow this rule also in our acts and omissions concerning other humans.

§364 From this we see from what grounds we must derive the law of nature. . . . we must consider the connection God has made among humans. This consists first of sociability, that is, of that constitution of their condition because of which their ends must be reached by common effort. . . . The natural connection of men consists further in their having a natural love of mankind and in their being unable to live satisfactorily outside human society. There is finally another natural connection . . . by means of which humans must take their origin from other humans through birth.

§365 From this there comes immediately the following basic law: We are obligated [*schuldig*] (1) because of the love we owe to God, truly to love all men, because they are loved by God and are seen as the final end. For because we owe God the greatest possible love, we must also love those who are loved by him, simply because they are loved by him. Otherwise there would be no striving in love to make the ends of the beloved our own and to become as much as possible like the beloved, which would contradict love. To just this duty there is also an obligation [*Verbindlichkeit*] of prudence, because we make our own lives pleasant in this way and make others inclined to serve us. All men are (2) obligated to live socially. . . . From these two it follows (3) that men are obligated to provide comradely services to one another out of upright love, indeed, from a love grounded on love of, and obedience to, God, as all men are God's final end. Hence it comes with their perfection that we should not view their welfare merely as a means for us but that we should will it as a final end, and also that we should love them. . . . For if love is not the motive for comradely services, they become uncertain. . . . Finally, . . . we are (4) obligated to observe everything else that is in accordance with the connection of men and their physical dependence on one another, from which the duties of parents and children to one another will follow.

§366 If all men were virtuous and had the same earnestness in striving, all would be equally loved by God. Then we would have to love all equally. Because this is not so, even though the love of man that we owe is grounded on love to God, we must love each by so much more as each is loved by God for his virtue. Yet this much remains in addition, that we should see all as absolute ends of God and really love them, and we should accord natural rights to all equally; that is, we should conduct ourselves toward all as we – if we put ourselves in their places – would think we could demand with right. For these duties do not arise from the character of men but from their essence. And that is the meaning of the saying that one should love all humans as oneself. Love is taken, then, in a broader sense, as a mere inclination to serve the well-being of those we love, in which sense there is also a love of oneself. We are then in two senses bound to love all as ourselves. First, it should happen that – with just the same sort of inclination to serve their greatest good as we have to forward our own – we should view their welfare not as a mere means but as itself an end, because we want our own welfare in the same way. . . . Second, we should accord all men certain rights, those to which we would think ourselves justified if we were now in their position, under the condition that we judge this rightly and impartially. . . .

§368 We have up to now shown how the main duties of natural law can be derived from grounds through clear arguments. But because not all men have the acuteness for this and the disunity among scholars is itself very great . . . on this account the drive of conscience has been implanted in us as a ground of knowledge of natural law a posteriori. We have, as a result, a natural sensation of what is right and proper, which does us good service with its quickness in judging moral matters. But because the conscience, like other basic drives, can err, we must transform its feelings, as far as possible, into clear conclusions or at least beware lest self-love or other corrupt inclinations make us partial.

§372 I know well that some think that the law of nature need not rest on the will of God, but only on the social nature of man and his perfection and happiness. This would have the advantage that it would bind the atheist as well as the believer. But if one tries to do this, one must ground the obligatoriness of the rules of the law of nature on their being the sole or best means to our own welfare and the continuing increase of our perfection. Now this is indeed true. They are the sole means for the universal welfare of humankind, and they are also the surest means for the welfare of individuals separately. And to that extent an atheist must admit such rules as the nature of things themselves and his own essential ends make binding. But one must not on that account leave God and the obligatoriness of his will out of the law of nature. We may indeed always note the obligation to which mere prudence would put us under the rules of natural law. But if one were to give this out as the sole obligation to them, the rules would cease to be true laws. And as soon as they cease to be so, even the obligation of prudence will not block all the loopholes in particular cases. I noted earlier that one might allow that it would be for the best if all men observed the rules of natural law but that because few[3] do so, one must go with the times, and as the saying is, a single swallow does not make a summer. One can often bring this objection against the duties of justice and honesty to others, and through special individual circumstances it can often really seem as if by practicing certain injustices one would take the certain [good] instead of the uncertain. . . . Admittedly, things do not always go well for vicious people, but they are not always good for the virtuous either. And one would probably find more examples of people making good through falsehood and injustice than through strict virtue. At worst, one can only lose one's life, and if that is really the end of everything, one will not mind much. Loopholes like these cannot be blocked except through the certainty of divine command, and our obligation toward it, and through the unalterable justice of God, which will be revealed in due time. . . .

Editor's Notes

1. Crusius could not rely on an established vocabulary for the moral notions he is trying to elaborate. For example, Crusius's paragraph here would read more colloquially if the word "obligation" were substituted for "indebtedness," but I have tried to give the reader some sense of Crusius's own problems by carefully distinguishing "indebtedness" from "obligation."
2. Principle through which we can come to know.
3. *Die wenigsten*, literally "the fewest."

Further Reading

Crusius has not been studied much, and most of what has been written about him is in German. Lewis White Beck, *Early German Philosophy* (Cambridge, Mass.: Harvard University Press, 1969), chap. 16, discusses his epistemological and metaphysical views. Crusius's importance to the development of Kant's ethics is analyzed in Josef Schmucker, *Die Ursprünge der Ethik Kants* (Meisenheim am Glan, West Germany: Verlag Anton Hain KG, 1961). The only full study of Crusius's own ethics of which I know is Magdelene Benden, *Christian August Crusius: Wille und Verstand als Prinzipien des Handelns* (Bonn: Bouvier Verlag, 1972), which has a good bibliography.

Richard Price

Introduction

Richard Price was a Welsh Dissenting minister who, after writing a major work in moral philosophy, made important contributions to understanding of the statistics involved in life insurance, was active in the political and economic debates of his time, and returned to philosophy to carry on a debate with Joseph Priestley about free will. He was born in 1723, and he died in 1791. One of his last works was a defense of the French Revolution, which prompted Edmund Burke's impassioned attack on it, the *Reflections on the Revolution in France.* Price had earlier written in favor of the American colonies in the dispute between them and Great Britain. His political defense of the rights of individuals to determine the course of their own lives is of a piece with his philosophical defense of free will and individual agency and with his religious sense of the importance of each person's responsibility for his or her own actions.

Price's *Review of the Principal Questions in Morals,* first published in 1758 and revised for later editions in 1769 and 1787, is one of the most remarkable of British eighteenth-century treatises on ethics, bringing to some of the major controversies of the time a new degree of sophistication and insight. It opens with a long attack on Locke's claim that all ideas must come from sensation or reflection, contending that the mind can be the source of ideas not derived from experience. The epistemological involvement was forced on Price by the moral and religious positions he aimed to defend. He believed that if we grant Locke's epistemology, there may be no way to avoid the Lockean conclusion that morality is simply the result of God's arbitrary command. And this, Price held, destroys the possibility of considering that God has any comprehensible moral character, thereby ruling out any justification of God's ways of treating us.

An opposition to voluntarism by means of an appeal to a rationalist epistemology was not new. Price had read Cudworth and Clarke as well as the sentimentalist opposition to them. He added some new arguments in favor of the rationalist claim that morality derives from reason rather than from feeling, and he spelled out more fully than his predecessors did a way in which rationalists could understand the motivation to act as our moral knowledge tells us we should. Price did not deny feeling a role in morality. Like Shaftesbury he held that we all take right action to be morally beautiful, and he interpreted this response as emotional. But, he argued, moral feeling is based on cognitive awareness of the rightness of an action. It is a feeling that necessarily arises when we see that an act is one that ought to be done. It is not simply an arbitrary response due to our animal nature, which might have been otherwise. And although the feeling of the beauty of an action helps move us to do it, moral knowledge taken by itself is capable of giving us a sufficient motive for action. No additional motive, and certainly no appeal to sanctions, is required. Our intellectual nature is active, not simply contemplative. God gave us the capacity for moral feeling to assist reason, not to be a substitute for it.

The intellectualist is always in danger of making morality so independent of God that God's very existence becomes a matter of little moment to morality. Price's view of the relations between virtue and happiness enabled him to guard against that danger. Virtue, he insisted, cannot be reduced to following a single rule or principle. "How unreasonable," Price exclaimed in a Butlerian vein, "is that love of uniformity and simplicity which inclines men thus to seek them where it is so difficult to find them" (*Review*, chap. 7). According to Price, there are many intuitively evident principles that we are to obey. Benevolence is one of them, but so are truthfulness, piety, justice, and others. Hence "it is not to be conceived, that promoting the happiness of others should comprehend the whole of our duty." If virtue tends to produce happiness in general, it has other tendencies as well. And if virtue need not make others happy in every case, still less is it guaranteed to make its possessor happy in this life. But there is a God, and we know something of his character. He sees the very same moral truths that we see, and he has no temptation to act against them. Hence God is benevolent, and our happiness is the reason he created the world. But God is also just, and so we may infer that he rewards those who are deserving. Because he does not do so on earth, we can be assured that he will do so elsewhere. If this does not suffice to prove immortality, it at least opens the way to the revealed truth of the matter. And this enables us to reflect with joy, Price stated, "that as certainly as God exists, all is well."

Who, then, are the deserving? They are those who do as they ought simply because it is what they ought to do. Sensation and feeling are as incapable of explaining all of morality as they are of accounting for all of knowledge. Moral action must originate from us as free, self-determining rational agents. It must show that we see what is right and choose to do it because it is so. Action from feeling cannot have this character.

Price did not suppose that people are born ready to act virtuously. For him the moral life is a life of education and discipline, a painful process in which we may either develop virtue within ourselves or fail to do so. Our eternal happiness is at stake, but we can attain it only if we become devoted to duty. Price's philosophical version of Christian morality is as stern in its way as was the older Calvinist version of his forebears. Obedience to law because it is the law is what is required. The eternal law is an expression of God's nature, as God's will is, and so in doing our duty as such, we are obeying God, albeit not in the way that Locke and the Calvinists thought we could do so.

Price's views of the unanalyzability of obligation and of the psychology of dutiful action are thus as much an articulation of a fundamental moral and religious outlook as is his rejection of empiricist moral epistemology. They take Price further than his rationalist predecessors had gone in showing what is involved in a morality of duty that insists on the full responsibility of moral agents for their own character and actions. In effect, Price worked out a striking account of what a morality looks like that in itself has no need of a deity. His aim in doing so, however, was to show how we can be independent, self-governing agents while acknowledging our dependence on a just and loving God.

The following selections are from the edition of Price's *Review of the Principal Questions of Morals* edited by D. D. Raphael (Oxford: Oxford University Press,

1948), reprinted by permission of the Oxford University Press. The text is that of the third edition, 1787.

A Review of the Principal Questions in Morals

CHAPTER I: OF THE ORIGIN OF OUR IDEAS OF
RIGHT AND WRONG

Section I: The Question Stated Concerning the Foundation of Morals

Some actions we all feel ourselves irresistibly determined to approve, and others to disapprove. Some actions we cannot but think *right*, and others *wrong*, and of all actions we are led to form some opinion, as either *fit* to be performed or *unfit;* or neither fit nor unfit to be performed; that is, *indifferent*. What the power within us is, which thus determines, is the question to be considered.

A late very distinguished writer, Dr. *Hutcheson*,[1] deduces our moral ideas from a *moral sense;* meaning by this *sense*, a power within us, different from reason, which renders certain actions pleasing and others displeasing to us. As we are so made, that certain impressions on our bodily organs shall excite certain ideas in our minds, and that certain outward forms, when presented to us, shall be the necessary occasions of pleasure or pain. In like manner, according to Dr. *Hutcheson*, we are so made, that certain affections and actions of moral agents shall be the necessary occasions of agreeable or disagreeable sensations in us, and procure our love or dislike of them. He has indeed well shewn, that we have a faculty determining us *immediately* to approve or disapprove actions, abstracted from all views of private advantage; and that the highest pleasures of life depend upon this faculty. Had he proceeded no farther, and intended nothing more by the *moral sense*, than our *moral faculty* in general, little room would have been left for any objections: But then he would have meant by it nothing *new*, and he could not have been considered as the *discoverer* of it. From the term *sense*, which he applies to it, from his rejection of all the arguments that have been used to prove it to be an intellectual power, and from the whole of his language on this subject; it is evident, he considered it as the effect of a *positive constitution* of our minds, or as an *implanted* and *arbitrary* principle by which a *relish* is given us for certain moral objects and forms and aversion to others, similar to the relishes and aversions created by any of our other senses. In other words; our ideas of morality, if this account is right, have the same origin with our ideas of the sensible qualities of bodies, the harmony of sounds, or the beauties of painting or sculpture; that is, the mere good pleasure of our Maker adapting the mind and its organs in a particular manner to certain objects. Virtue (as those who embrace this scheme say) is an affair of taste. Moral right and wrong, signify nothing *in the objects themselves* to which they are applied, any more than agreeable and harsh; sweet and bitter; pleasant and painful; but only *certain effects in us.* Our perception of *right,* or moral good, in actions, is that agreeable *emotion,* or feeling, which certain actions produce in us; and of *wrong,* or moral evil, the contrary. They are particular modifications of our minds, or impressions which they are made to receive from the contemplation of certain actions, which the contrary actions *might* have occasioned, had the Author of nature so pleased; and which to suppose to belong to these actions themselves, is as absurd as to ascribe the pleasure or uneasiness, which the observation of a particular form gives us, to the form itself. 'Tis therefore, by this account, improper to say of an action, that it is *right,* in much the same sense that it is improper to say of an object of taste, that it is *sweet;* or of *pain,* that it is *in* fire.

The present enquiry therefore is: whether this be a true account of virtue or not; whether it *has* or has *not* a foundation in the *nature* of its object; whether *right* and *wrong* are real characters of *actions,* or only qualities of our *minds;* whether, in short, they denote what actions *are,* or only *sensations* derived from the particular frame and structure of our natures.

Section III: Of the Origin of Our Ideas of Moral Right and Wrong

Let us now return to our first enquiry, and apply the foregoing observations to our ideas of *right* and *wrong* in particular.

'Tis a very necessary previous observation, that our ideas of *right* and *wrong* are simple ideas,[2] and must therefore be ascribed to some power of *immediate* perception in the human mind. He that doubts this, need only try to give definitions of them, which shall amount to more than synonymous expressions. Most of the confusion in which the question concerning the foundation of morals has been involved has proceeded from inattention to this remark. There are, undoubtedly, some actions that are *ultimately* approved, and for justifying which no reason can be assigned; as there are some ends, which are *ultimately* desired, and for chusing which no reason can be given. Were not this true; there would be an infinite progression of reasons and ends, and therefore nothing could be at all approved or desired.

Supposing then, that we have a power *immediately* perceiving right and wrong: the point I am now to endeavour to prove, is, that this power is the *Understanding,* agreeably to the assertion at the end of the *first* section. I cannot but flatter myself, that the main obstacle to the acknowledgment of this, has been already removed, by the observations made in the preceding section, to shew that the understanding is a power of immediate perception, which gives rise to new original ideas; nor do I think it possible that there should have been many disputes on this subject had this been properly considered.

But, in order more explicitly and distinctly to evince what I have asserted (in the only way the nature of the question seems capable of) let me,

First, Observe, that it implies no absurdity, but evidently *may* be true. It is undeniable, that many of our ideas are derived from our INTUITION[3] of truth, or the discernment of the natures of things by the understanding. This therefore *may* be the source of our moral ideas. It is at least *possible*, that *right* and *wrong* may denote what we *understand* and *know* concerning certain objects, in like manner with proportion and disproportion, connexion and repugnancy, contingency and necessity, and the other ideas before-mentioned. – I will add, that nothing has been offered which has any tendency to prove the contrary. All that can appear, from the objections and reasonings of the Author of the *Enquiry into the Original of Our Ideas of Beauty and Virtue*,[4] is only, what has been already observed, and what does not in the least affect the point in debate: Namely, that the words *right* and *wrong*, *fit* and *unfit*, express simple and undeniable ideas. But that the power perceiving them is properly a *sense* and not *reason;* that these ideas denote nothing *true* of actions, nothing in the *nature* of actions; this, he has left entirely without proof. He appears, indeed, to have taken for granted, that if virtue and vice are *immediately* perceived, they must be perceptions of an *implanted* sense. But no conclusion could have been more hasty. For will any one take upon him to say, that all powers of immediate perception must be arbitrary and implanted; or that there can be no simple ideas denoting any thing besides the qualities and passions of the mind? – In short. Whatever some writers have said to the contrary, it is certainly a point not yet decided, that virtue is wholly factitious, and to be *felt* not *understood*.

As there are some propositions, which, when attended to, necessarily determine all minds to *believe* them: And as (which will be shewn hereafter) there are some ends, whose natures are such, that, when perceived, all beings immediately and necessarily *desire* them: So is it very credible, that, in like manner, there are some actions whose natures are such, that, when observed, all rational beings immediately and necessarily *approve* them.

I do not at all care what follows from Mr. *Hume*'s assertion, that all our ideas are either *impressions*, or *copies of impressions;* or from Mr. *Locke*'s assertion that they are all *deducible from* SENSATION *and* REFLEXION. [5] – The first of these assertions is, I think, destitute of all proof; supposes, when applied in this as well as many other cases, the point in question; and, when pursued to its consequences, ends in the destruction of all truth and the subversion of our intellectual faculties. – The other wants much explication to render it consistent with any tolerable account of the original of our moral ideas: Nor does there seem to be any thing necessary to convince a person, that all our ideas are not deducible from sensation and reflexion, except taken in a very large and comprehensive sense, besides considering how Mr. *Locke* derives from them our *moral ideas*. He places them among our ideas of relations, and represents *rectitude* as signifying the conformity of actions to some rules or laws; which rules or laws, he says, are either *the will of God, the decrees of the magistrate, or the fashion of the country:* From whence it follows, that it is an absurdity to apply *rectitude* to rules and laws themselves; to suppose the *divine* will to be directed by it; or to consider it as *itself* a rule and law. But, it is undoubted, that this great man would have detested these consequences; and, indeed, it is sufficiently evident, that he was strangely embarrassed in his notions on this, as well as some other subjects. But,

Secondly, I know of no better way of determining this point, than by referring those who doubt it to common sense, and putting them upon considering the nature of their own perceptions. – Could we suppose a person, who, when he perceived an external object, was at a loss to determine whether he perceived it by means of his organs of sight or touch; what better method could be taken to satisfy him? There is no possibility of doubting in any such cases. And it seems not more difficult to determine in the present case. . . .

It is true, some impressions of pleasure or pain, satisfaction or disgust, generally attend our perceptions of virtue and vice. But these are merely their effects and concomitants, and not the perceptions themselves, which ought no more to be confounded with them, than a particular truth (like that for which *Pythagoras* offered a Hecatomb)[6] ought to be confounded with the pleasure that may attend the discovery of it. Some emotion or other accompanies, perhaps, all our perceptions; but more remarkably our perceptions of right and wrong. And this, as will be again observed in the next chapter, is what has led to the mistake of making them to signify nothing but impressions, which error some have extended to all objects and knowledge; and thus have been led into an extravagant and monstrous scepticism.

. . . if right and wrong denote effects of sensation, it must imply the greatest absurdity to suppose them applicable to actions: That is; the ideas of *right* and *wrong* and of *action,* must in this case be incompatible; as much so, as the idea of pleasure and a regular form, or of pain and the collisions of bodies. – All sensations, as such, are modes of consciousness, or feelings of a sentient being, which must be of a nature totally different from the particular causes which produce them. A *coloured body,* if we speak accurately, is the same absurdity with a *square sound.* We need no experiments to prove that heat, cold, colours, tastes, &c. are not real qualities of bodies; because the ideas of matter and of these qualities, are imcompatible. – But is there indeed any such incompatibility between *actions* and *right?* Or any such absurdity in affirming the one of the other? – Are the ideas of them as different as the idea of a sensation, and its cause?

On the contrary; the more we enquire, the more indisputable, I imagine, it will appear to us, that we express necessary truth, when we say of some actions, they are right; and of others, they are wrong. . . . In the last place; let it be considered, that all actions, undoubtedly, have a *nature.* That is, *some character* certainly belongs to them, and somewhat there is to be *truly* affirmed of them. This may be, that some of them are right, others wrong. But if this is not allowed; if no actions are, *in themselves,* either right or wrong, or any thing of a moral and obligatory nature, which can be an object to the understanding; it follows, that, in themselves, they *are* all indifferent. This is what is essentially true of them, and this is what all understandings, that perceive right, must perceive them to be. But are we not conscious, that we perceive the contrary? And have we not as much reason to believe the contrary, as to believe or trust at all our own discernment? . . .

The following important corollary arises from these arguments:

That morality is *eternal and immutable.*

Right and wrong, it appears, denote what actions *are.* Now whatever any thing *is,* that it is, not by will, or decree, or power, but by *nature and necessity.* Whatever a triangle or circle is, that it is unchangeably and eternally. It depends upon no will or power, whether the three angles of a triangle and two right ones shall be *equal;* whether the periphery of a circle and its diameter shall be *incommensurable;* or whether matter shall be *divisible, moveable, passive,* and *inert.* Every object of the understanding has an indivisible and invariable essence; from whence arise its properties, and numberless truths concerning it. Omnipotence does not consist in a power to alter the nature of things, and to destroy necessary truth (for this is contradictory, and would infer the destruction of all wisdom, and knowledge) but in an absolute command over all *particular, external* existences, to create or destroy them, or produce any possible changes among them. – The natures of things then being immutable; whatever we suppose the natures of actions to be, they must be immutably. If they are indifferent, this indifference is itself immutable, and there neither is nor can be any one thing that, *in reality,* we *ought* to do rather than another. The same is to be said of right and wrong, of moral good and evil, as far as they express *real characters* of actions. They must immutably and necessarily belong to those actions of which they are *truly* affirmed.

No will, therefore, can render *any thing* good and obligatory, which was not so antecedently, and from eternity; or any action right, that is not so in itself; meaning by *action,* not the bare external effect produced, but the ultimate principle of conduct, or the determination of a reasonable being, considered as arising from the perception of some motives and reasons and intended for some end. According to this sense of the word *action,* whenever the principle from which we act is different, the action is different, though the external effects produced, may be the same. If we attend to this, the meaning and truth of what I have just observed, will be easily seen.

CHAPTER II: OF OUR IDEAS OF THE BEAUTY AND DEFORMITY OF ACTIONS

. . . Our intellectual faculties are in their infancy. The lowest degrees of reason are sufficient to discover *moral distinctions* in general; because these are self-evident, and included in the ideas of certain actions and characters. They must, therefore, appear to all who are capable of making actions the objects of their reflexion. But the extent to which they appear, and the accuracy and force with which they are discerned; and, consequently, their influence, must, so far as they are the objects of pure intelligence, be in proportion to the strength and improvement of the rational faculties of beings and their acquaintance with truth and the natures of things.

From hence, it must appear, that in men it is necessary that the *rational principle*, or the *intellectual discernment of right* and *wrong*, should be aided by *instinctive determinations*. – The dictates of mere reason, being slow, and deliberate, would be otherwise much too weak. The condition in which we are placed, renders many urgent passions necessary for us; and these cannot but often interfere with our sentiments of rectitude. Reason alone, (imperfect as it is in us) is by no means sufficient to defend us against the danger to which, in such circumstances, we are exposed. Our Maker has, therefore, wisely provided remedies for its imperfections; and established a due balance in our frame by annexing to our intellectual perceptions sensations and instincts, which give them greater weight and force.

In short. The truth seems to be that, "in contemplating the actions of moral agents, we have both a *perception of the understanding,* and a *feeling of the heart;* and that the latter, or the effects in us accompanying our moral perceptions, depend on two causes. Partly, on the positive constitution of our natures: But principally on the essential congruity or incongruity between moral ideas and our intellectual faculties."

It may be difficult to determine the precise limits between these two sources of our mental feelings; and to say, how far the effects of the one are blended with those of the other. It is undoubted, that we should have felt and acted otherwise than we now do, if the decisions of reason had been left entirely without support; nor is it easy to imagine how pernicious to us this would have proved. On this account it cannot be doubted, but that both the causes I have mentioned unite their influence: And the great question in morality is, not whether we owe *much* to implanted senses and determinations; but whether we owe *all* to them.

It was, probably, in consequence of not duly considering the difference I have now insisted on between the *honestum* and *pulchrum* (the δίκαιον and καλόν);[7] or of not carefully distinguishing between the discernment of the mind, and the sensations attending it in our moral perceptions; that the Author of the *Enquiry into the Original of Our Ideas of Beauty and Virtue,* was led to derive all our ideas of virtue from an implanted sense. Moral good and evil, he every where describes, by the effects accompanying the perception of them. The *rectitude* of an action is, with him, the same with its *gratefulness* to the observer; and wrong, the contrary. But what can be more evident, than that *right* and *pleasure, wrong* and *pain,* are as different as a cause and its effect; what is *understood,* and what is *felt;* absolute truth, and its *agreeableness* to the mind. – Let it be granted, as undoubtedly it must, that some degree of pleasure is inseparable from the observation of virtuous actions: It is just as unreasonable to infer from hence, that the discernment of virtue is nothing distinct from the reception of this pleasure; as it would be to infer, as some have done, that solidity, extension, and figure are only *particular modes of sensation;* because attended, whenever they are perceived, with some sensations of sight or touch, and impossible to be conceived by the imagination without them. . . .

Chapter III: Of the Origin of Our Desires and Affections

. . . Each of our affections has its particular end. Self-love leads us to desire and pursue *private,* and Benevolence, *public* happiness. Ambition is the love of fame, and distinction; and Curiosity is the love of what is new and uncommon. The objects of these and all our other affections, are desired for their own sakes; and constitute so many distinct principles of action. What is not at all desired *for itself,* but only as a means of something else, cannot, with any propriety, be called the object of an affection. If, for example, according to the opinion of some, we desire every thing merely as the means of our own good, and with an ultimate view to it, then in reality we desire nothing but our own good, and have only the one single affection of self-love.

As all moral approbation and disapprobation, and our ideas of beauty and deformity, have been ascribed to an internal sense; meaning by this, not "*any inward* power of perception," but "an *implanted power,* different from *reason*"; so, all our desires and affections have, in like manner, been ascribed to instinct, *meaning by instinct, not merely "the immediate desire of an object,"* but "the *reason* of this desire; or an *implanted propension.*" – The former opinion I have already at large examined. I am now to examine the latter.

"Is then all desire to be considered as *wholly instinctive?* Is it, in particular, owing to nothing but an original bias given our natures, which they might have either wanted or have received in a contrary direction; that we are at all concerned for our own good, or for the good of others?"

As far as this enquiry relates to *private* good, we may without hesitation answer in the negative. The desire of happiness for *ourselves,* certainly arises not from instinct. The full and adequate account of it, is, *the nature of happiness.* It is impossible, but that creatures capable of pleasant and painful sensations, should *love and chuse* the one, and *dislike and avoid* the other. No being, who knows what happiness and misery are, can be supposed indifferent to them, without a plain contradiction. Pain is not a *possible* object of *desire;* nor happiness, of *aversion.* No power whatsoever can cause a creature, in the agonies of torture and misery, to be pleased with his state, to like it for itself, or to wish to remain so. Nor can any power cause a creature rejoicing in bliss to *dislike* his state, or be *afraid* of its continuance. Then only can this happen, when pain can be *agreeable,* and pleasure *disagreeable;* that is, when pain can be pleasure; and pleasure, pain.

From hence I infer, that it is by no means, in general, an absurd method of explaining our affections, to derive them from the natures of things and of beings. For thus without doubt we are to account for one of the most important and active of all our affections. To the preference and desire of *private happiness* by all beings, nothing more is requisite than to *know* what it *is.* – "And may not this be true, likewise, of *public* happiness? May not benevolence be *essential* to *intelligent* beings, as well as self-love to *sensible beings?*"

But to enter a little more minutely into the discussion of this point. Let us, again, put the case of a being *purely* reasonable. It is evident, that (though by supposition void of *implanted* byasses) he would not want all principles of action, and all inclinations. It has been shown he would perceive Virtue, and possess affection to it, in proportion to the degree of his knowledge. The nature of *happiness* also would engage him to chuse and desire it for *himself.* And is it credible that, at the same time, he would be necessarily indifferent about it for *others?* Can it be supposed to have that in it, which would determine him to seek it for *himself;* and yet to have nothing in it, which could engage him to approve of it for *others?* Would the nature of things, upon this supposition, be consistent? Would he not be capable of seeing, that the happiness of others is to them as important as his is to him; and that it is in itself equally valuable and desirable, whoever possesses it?

Let us again enquire; would not this being assent to this proposition; "happiness is *better* than misery?" – A definition has been asked of the word *better* here. With equal reason might a definition be asked of the word *greater,* when the whole is affirmed to be *greater* than a part. Both denote simple ideas, and both *truth.* The one, what happiness is, compared with misery; and the other, what the whole is, compared with a part. And a mind that should think happiness not to be better than misery, would mistake as grossly, as a mind that should believe the whole not to be *greater* than a part. It cannot therefore be reasonably doubted, but that such a being, upon a comparison of happiness and misery, would as unavoidably as he perceives their difference, *prefer* the one to the other; and *chuse* the one rather than the other, for his fellow-beings. . . .

I cannot help, in this place, stepping aside a little to take notice of an opinion already referred to; I mean, the opinion of those who will allow of no *ultimate* object of desire besides *private* good. What has led to this opinion has been inattention to the difference between *desire,* and the *pleasure* implied in the gratification of it. The latter is subsequent to the former, and founded in it: That is, an object, such as *fame, knowledge,* or the *welfare of a friend,* is desired, not because we foresee that when obtained, it will give us pleasure; but, *vice versa;* obtaining it gives us pleasure, because we previously desired it or had an *affection* carrying us to it and resting in it. And, were there no such affections, the very foundations of happiness would be destroyed. It cannot be conceived, that obtaining what we do not desire, should be the cause of pleasure to us; or that what we are perfectly indifferent to, and is not the end of any affection, should, upon being possessed, be the means of any kind of gratification.

Besides; if every object of desire is considered – merely as the cause of pleasure; one would think, that, antecedently to experience, no one object could be desired more than another; and that the first time we contemplated fame, knowledge, or the happiness of others; or had any of the objects of our natural passions and desires proposed to us, we must have been absolutely indifferent to them, and remained so, till, by some means, we were convinced of the connexion between them and pleasure.

For farther satisfaction on this point, nothing can be more proper than to consider; whether, supposing we could enjoy the same pleasure *without* the object of our desire, we should be indifferent to it. Could we enjoy pleasures equivalent to those attending knowledge, or the approbation of others, without them, or with infamy and ignorance, would we no longer wish for the one or be averse to the other? Would a person lose all curiosity, and be indifferent whether he stirred a step to gratify it, were he assured he should receive equal sensations of pleasure by staying where he is? Did you believe, that the prosperity of your nearest kindred, your friends or your country, would be the means of no greater happiness to you, than their misery; would you lose all love to them, and all desires of their good? – Would you not chuse to enjoy the same quantity of pleasure *with* virtue, rather than *without* it? – An unbiassed mind must spurn at such enquiries; and any one, who would, in this manner, examine himself, might easily find, that all his affections and appetites (self-love itself excepted) are, in their nature, *disinterested;* and that, though the seat of them be *self,* and the effect of them the gratification of *self,* their direct tendency is always to some particular object different from private pleasure, beyond which they carry not our view. So far is it from being true, that, in following their impulses, we aim at nothing but our own interest; that we continually feel them drawing us astray from what we *know* to be our interest; and may observe men every day carried by them to actions and pursuits, which they acknowledge to be ruinous to them.

CHAPTER V: OF THE RELATION OF MORALITY TO THE DIVINE NATURE

. . . I shall conclude this chapter with a few observations on the general grounds of belief and assent. These may be all comprehended under the three following heads.

The first is immediate consciousness or FEELING. It is absurd to ask a reason for our believing what we *feel,* or are inwardly conscious of. A thinking being must necessarily have a capacity of discovering some things in this way. It is from hence particularly we acquire the knowledge of our own existence, and of the several operations, passions, and sensations of our minds. And it is also under this head I would comprehend the information we derive from our powers of recollection or memory.

The *second* ground of belief is INTUITION; by which I mean the mind's survey of its own ideas, and the relations between them, and the notice it takes of what is or is not true and false, consistent and inconsistent, possible and impossible in the natures of things. It is to this, as has been explained at large in the first chapter, we owe our belief of all self-evident truths; our ideas of the general, abstract affections and relations of things; our moral ideas, and whatsoever else we discover, without making use of any process of reasoning. – It is on this power of intuition, essential, in some degree or other, to all rational minds, that the whole possibility of all reasoning is founded. To it the last appeal is ever made. Many of its perceptions are capable, by attention, of being rendered more clear; and many of the truths discovered by it, may be illustrated by an advantageous representation of them, or by being viewed in particular lights; but seldom will admit of proper proof. – Some truths there must be, which can appear only by their own light, and which are incapable of proof; otherwise nothing could be proved, or known; in the same manner as, if there were no letters, there could be no words, or if there were no simple and undefinable ideas, there could be no complex ideas. – I might mention many instances of truths discernible no other way than *intuitively,* which learned men have strangely confounded and obscured, by supposing them subjects of *reasoning and deduction.* One of the most important instances, the subject of this treatise affords us; and another we have, in our notions of the necessity of a *cause* of whatever begins to exist, and our general ideas of *power and connexion:* And, sometimes, reason has been ridiculously employed to prove even our own existence.[8] . . .

Chapter VI: Of Fitness, and Moral Obligation, and the Various Forms of Expression, Which Have Been Used by Different Writers in Explaining Morality

After the account that has been given of the nature and origin of our ideas of morality; it will be easy to perceive the meaning of several terms and phrases, which are commonly used in speaking on this subject.

Fitness and *unfitness* most frequently denote the congruity or incongruity, aptitude or inaptitude of any means to accomplish an end. But when applied to actions, they generally signify the same with *right* and *wrong;* nor is it often hard to determine in which of these senses these words are to be understood. It is worth observing, that *fitness,* in the former sense, is equally undefinable with *fitness* in the latter; or, that it is as impossible to express, in any other than synonymous words, what we mean, when we say of certain objects, "that they have a *fitness* to one another; or are *fit* to answer certain purposes," as it is when we say, "reverencing the Deity is *fit,* or beneficence is *fit* to be practised." In the first of these instances, none can avoid owning the absurdity of making an arbitrary sense the source of the idea of *fitness,* and of concluding that it signifies nothing real in objects, and that no one thing can be properly the *means* of another. In both cases the term *fit,* signifies a simple perception of the understanding.

Morally good and *evil, reasonable* and *unreasonable,* are epithets also commonly applied to actions, evidently meaning the same with *right* and *wrong, fit* and *unfit.*

Approving an action is the same with discerning it to be *right;* as *assenting* to a proposition is the same with discerning it to be *true.*

But *Obligation* is the term most necessary to be here considered; and to the explication of it, the best part of this chapter shall be devoted.

Obligation to action, and *rightness* of action, are plainly coincident and identical; so far so, that we cannot form a notion of the one, without taking in the other. This may appear to any one upon considering, whether he can point out any difference between what is *right, meet* or *fit* to be done, and what *ought* to be done. It is not indeed plainer, that figure implies something figured, solidity resistance, or an effect a cause, than it is that *rightness* implies *oughtness* (if I may be allowed this word) or *obligatoriness*. And as easily can we conceive of figure without extension, or motion without a change of place, as that it can be *fit* for us to do an action, and yet that it may not be what we *should* do, what it is our *duty* to do, or what we are under an *obligation* to do. – *Right, fit, ought, should, duty, obligation*, convey, then, ideas necessarily including one another. From hence it follows,

First, That virtue, *as such,* has a real obligatory power antecedently to all positive laws, and independently of all will; for obligation, we see, is involved in the very nature of it. To affirm, that the performance of that, which, to omit, would be wrong, is not obligatory, unless conducive to private good or enjoined by a superior power, is a manifest contradiction. It is to say, that it is not true, that a thing is what it is; or that we are *obliged* to do what we *ought* to do; unless it be the object of a command, or, in some manner, privately useful. – If there are any actions fit to be done by an agent, besides such as tend to his own happiness, those actions, by the terms, are *obligatory*, independently of their influence on his happiness. – Whatever it is *wrong* to do, that it is our *duty* not to do, whether enjoined or not by any positive law. – I cannot conceive of any thing much more evident than this. – It appears, therefore, that those who maintain that all obligation is to be deduced from positive laws, the Divine will, or self-love, assert what (if they mean any thing contrary to what is here said) implies, that the words *right* and *just* stand for no real and distinct characters of actions; but signify merely what is *willed* and *commanded*, or conducive to private advantage, whatever that be; so that any thing may be both right and wrong, morally good and evil, at the same time and in any circumstances, as it may be commanded or forbidden by different laws and wills; and any the most pernicious effects will become just, and fit to be produced by any being, if but the smallest degree of clear advantage or pleasure may result to him from them.

Those who say, nothing can oblige but the will of God, generally resolve the power of this to oblige to the annexed rewards and punishments. And thus, in reality, they subvert entirely the independent natures of moral good and evil; and are forced to maintain, that nothing can *oblige*, but the prospect of pleasure to be obtained, or pain to be avoided. If this be true, it follows that *vice* is, properly, no more than *imprudence;* that nothing is right or wrong, just or unjust, any farther than it affects self-interest; and that a being, independently and completely happy, cannot have any moral perceptions. The justness of these inferences cannot be denied by one, who will attend to the coincidence here insisted on between obligation and virtue.

But to pursue this point farther; let me ask, would a person who either believes there is no God, or that he does not concern himself with human affairs, feel no *moral obligations*, and therefore not be at all *accountable?* Would one, who should happen not to be convinced, that virtue tends to his happiness here or hereafter, be released from every *bond* of duty and morality? Or, would he, if he believed no future state, and that, in any instance, virtue was against his *present* interest, be truly *obliged*, in these instances, to be wicked? – These consequences must follow, if obligation depends entirely on the knowledge of the will of a superior, or on the connexion between actions and private interest. –

Another observation worthy our notice in this place, is, that rewards and punishments suppose, in the very idea of them, moral obligation, and are founded upon it. They do not *make* it, but *enforce* it. They are the *sanctions* of virtue, and not its *efficients*. A reward supposes something done to *deserve* it, or a conformity to *obligation subsisting previously to it;* and punishment is always inflicted on account of some breach of *obligation*. Were we under no obligations, antecedently to the proposal of rewards and punishments, it would be a contradiction to suppose us subjects capable of them. – A person without any light besides that of nature, and supposed ignorant of a future state of rewards and punishments and the will of the Deity, might discover these by reasoning from his natural notions of morality and duty. But were the latter dependent on the former, and not *vice versa;* this could not be said, nor should we have any principles left, from which to learn the will of the Deity, and the conditions of his favour to us.

Secondly, From the account given of *obligation*, it follows that *rectitude* is a *law* as well as a *rule* to us; that it not only *directs*, but *binds* all, as far as it is perceived. – With respect to its being a *rule*, we may observe, that a rule of action signifying some measure or standard to which we are to conform our actions, or some information we possess concerning what we ought to do, there can, in this sense, be no *other* rule of action; all besides, to which this name can be properly given, implying it, or signifying only helps to the discovery of it. To perceive or to be informed how it is *right* to act, is the very notion of a *direction* to act. And it must be added, that it is such a direction as implies *authority*, and which we cannot disregard or neglect without remorse and pain. Reason is the guide, the *natural* and *authoritative* guide of a rational being. Where he has no discernment of right and wrong, there, and there only, is he (morally speaking) *free.* But where he has this discernment, where *moral good* appears to him, and he cannot avoid pronouncing concerning an action, that it is fit to be done, and evil to omit it; here he is tied in the most strict and absolute manner, in bonds that no power in nature can dissolve, and from which he can at no time, or in any single instance, break loose, without offering the most unnatural violence to himself; without making an inroad into his own soul, and immediately pronouncing his own sentence.

Thirdly, From the account given of obligation, it appears how absurd it is to enquire, what *obliges* us to practise virtue? as if obligation was no part of the idea of virtue, but something adventitious and foreign to it; that is, as if what was *due*, might not be our *duty*, or what was *wrong, unlawful;* or as if it might not be true, that what it is *fit* to do we *ought* to do, and that what we *ought* to do, we are *obliged* to do. – To ask, why are we *obliged* to practise virtue, to abstain from what is wicked, or perform what is just, is the very same as to ask, why we are *obliged* to do what we are *obliged* to do? – It is not possible to avoid wondering at those, who have so unaccountably embarrassed themselves, on a subject that one would think was attended with no difficulty; and who, because they cannot find any thing in *virtue and duty themselves*, which can induce us to pay a regard to them in our practice, fly to self-love, and maintain that from hence alone are derived all inducement and obligation.

Fourthly, From what has been observed, it may appear, in what sense obligation is ascribed to God. It is no more than ascribing to him the perception of rectitude, or saying, that there are certain ends, and certain measures in the administration of the world, which he approves, and which are *better* to be pursued than others. – Great care, however, should be taken, what language we here use. *Obligation* is a word to which many persons have affixed several ideas, which should by no means be retained when we speak of God. Our language and our conceptions, whenever he is the subject of them, are *always* extremely defective and inadequate, and *often* very erroneous. – There are many who think it absurd and shocking to attribute any thing of *obligation* or *law* to a being who is necessarily sufficient and independent, and to whom nothing can be prior or superior. How, I conceive, we are to frame our apprehensions on this subject, has already, in some measure, appeared. It should, methinks, be enough to satisfy such persons, that the obligations ascribed to the Deity arise entirely from and exist in his own nature; and that the eternal, unchangeable LAW, by which it has been said, he is directed in all his actions, is no other than HIMSELF; *his own infinite, eternal, all perfect understanding.*

Fifthly, What has been said also shews us, on what the obligations of religion and the Divine will are founded. They are plainly branches of universal rectitude. Our obligation to obey God's will means nothing, but that obedience is *due* to it, or that it is *right and fit* to comply with it. What an absurdity is it then, to make obligation *subsequent* to the Divine will, and the *creature* of it? For why, upon this supposition, does not *all* will oblige equally? If there be any thing which gives the preference to one will above another; that, by the terms, is *moral rectitude.*

CHAPTER VIII: OF THE PRINCIPLE OF ACTION IN A VIRTUOUS AGENT

In further explaining and proving what I have now in view, it will be proper to shew, "that the perception of right and wrong does *excite* to action, and is alone a sufficient *principle* of action"; after which we shall be better prepared for judging, "how far, without it, there can be *practical virtue.*"

Experience, and the reason of the thing, will, if we attentively consult them, soon satisfy us about the first of these points. All men continually feel, that the perception of right and wrong excites to action; and it is so much their natural and unavoidable sense that this is true, that there are few or none, who, upon having it at first proposed to them, would not wonder at its being questioned. There are many supposable cases and circumstances, in which it is impossible to assign any other reason of action. Why would we, all circumstances on both sides being the same, help a *benefactor* rather than a *stranger;* or one to whom we had given promises, and made professions of kindness, rather than one to whom we were under no engagements? Why would any good being chuse such methods to accomplish his end as were consistent with *faithfulness* and *veracity,* rather than such as implied *deceit* and *falsehood;* though he knew the latter to be equally safe, or, in a great degree, even more safe, more easy and expeditious? – Is it only for our own sakes, or out of a view to public utility, that we obey and honour the Deity? – How are we to account for a man's refraining from secret fraud, or his practising truth, sincerity, equity, justice, and honour, in many particular instances of their interfering, or seeming to interfere, with private and publick good, as well as with his strongest natural desires? – Let any one, for example, try what reasons he can find from benevolence or self-interest, why an honest man, though in want, though sure of being never suspected, would not secure a good estate, ease and plenty to himself, and relief and aid to his neighbours, by secreting or interpolating a will by which it of right devolved on a worthless person, already sufficiently provided for, and who, in all likelihood, would use it only to make himself and others miserable? What could influence, in such and many other like circumstances, besides a *sense of duty and honesty?* Or what other universal motive can there be to the practice of justice?

But further, it seems extremely evident, that excitement belongs to the very ideas of moral right and wrong, and is essentially inseparable from the apprehension of them. The account in a former chapter of *obligation,* is enough to shew this. – When we are conscious that an action is *fit* to be done, or that it *ought* to be done, it is not conceivable that we can remain *uninfluenced,* or want a *motive* to action. It would be to little purpose to argue much with a person, who would deny this; or who would maintain, that the *becomingness* or *reasonableness* of an action is no reason *for* doing it; and the *immorality* or *unreasonableness* of an action, no reason *against* doing it. An affection or inclination to rectitude cannot be separated from the view of it.* The knowl-

---

* Those who own, that an action may not be less right, though certain to produce no overbalance of private pleasure; and yet assert that nothing, but the prospect of this to be obtained, can influence the will, must also maintain, that the mere rightness of an action, or the consideration that it is fit to be done, apart from the consideration of the pleasure attending or following it, would leave us quite uninclined, and indifferent to the performance or omission of it. This is so inconceivable, that those whose principles oblige them to admit it, cannot, one would think, really mean by right and wrong the same with the rest of mankind. That, supposing virtue to denote any thing distinct from pleasure and independent of it, it is possible to *conceive,* that a virtuous action may not produce an overbalance of private pleasure; or, which answers the purpose as well, that an agent may *believe* this of an action to be done by him, which yet he does not the less consider as virtuous, it would be trifling to say any thing to prove: But this it is necessary those, whose opinion I have now in view, should deny.

edge of what is right, without any approbation of it, or concern to practise it, is not conceivable or possible. And this knowledge will certainly be attended with *correspondent, actual practice,* whenever there is nothing to oppose it. Why a *reasonable* being acts *reasonably;* why he has a disposition to follow reason, and is not without aversion to wrong; why he chuses to do what he knows he *should* do, and cannot be wholly indifferent, whether he abstains from that which he knows is evil and criminal, and *not to be done,* are questions which need not, and which deserve not to be answered.

Instincts, therefore, as before observed in other instances, are not necessary to the choice of ends. The intellectual nature is its own law. It has, within itself, a spring and guide of action which it cannot suppress or reject. Rectitude is itself an end, an ultimate end, an end superior to all other ends, governing, directing and limiting them, and whose existence and influence depend on nothing arbitrary. It presides over all. Every appetite and faculty, every instinct and will, and all nature are subjected to it. To act from affection to it, is to act with light, and conviction, and knowledge. But acting from instinct is so far acting in the dark, and following a blind guide. Instinct *drives* and *precipitates;* but reason *commands.* The impulses of *instinct* we may resist, without doing any violence to ourselves. Our highest merit and perfection often consist in this. The dictates of *reason* we can, *in no instance,* contradict, without a sense of shame, and giving our beings a wound in their most essential and sensible part. The experience we have of the operations of the former, is an argument of our imperfection, and meanness, and low rank. The other prevails most in the higher ranks of beings. It is the chief glory of God, that he is removed infinitely from the possibility of any other principle of action.

It being therefore apparent that the determination of our minds concerning the nature of actions as morally good or bad, suggests a motive to do or avoid them; it being also plain that this determination or judgment, though often not the prevailing, yet is always the first, the proper, and most natural and intimate spring and guide of the actions of reasonable beings: Let us now enquire, whether it be not further the *only* spring of action in a reasonable being, as far as he can be deemed morally good and worthy; whether it be not the *only* principle from which all actions flow which engage our esteem of the agents; or, in other words, whether virtue be not itself the end of a virtuous agent as such.

If we consider that alone as most properly *done* by an agent, which he *designs* to do, and that what was no way an object of his design is not strictly imputable to him, or at least cannot give him any claim to merit or praise, it will follow that he cannot be properly said to practise virtue who does not *design* to practise it, to whom it is no object of regard, or who has it not at all in his view. It seems indeed as evident as we can wish any thing to be, that an action which is under no influence or direction from a *moral judgment,* cannot be in the practical sense *moral;* that when virtue is not pursued or intended, there is no virtue in the agent. Morally good intention, without any idea of moral good, is a contradiction. To act virtuously is to obey or follow reason: But can this be done without knowing and designing it?

But it may be asked, "is not *Benevolence* a virtuous principle? And do we not approve all actions proceeding from it?" – I answer, Benevolence, it has been shewn, is of two kinds, *rational* and *instinctive*. *Rational benevolence* entirely coincides with rectitude, and the actions proceeding from it, with the actions proceeding from a regard to rectitude. And the same is to be said of all those affections and desires, which would arise in a nature as intelligent. It is not possible that endeavours to obtain an end which, as reasonable, we cannot but love and chuse, should not be by reason approved; or that what is *necessarily desirable* to all beings, should not be also *necessarily right to be pursued.*

But *instinctive benevolence* is no principle of virtue, nor are any actions flowing merely from it virtuous. As far as this influences, so far something else than reason and goodness influences, and so much I think is to be subtracted from the moral worth of any action or character. This observation agrees perfectly with the common sentiments and determinations of mankind. Wherever the influence of mere natural temper or inclination appears, and a particular conduct is known to proceed from hence, we may, it is true, love the person, as we commonly do the inferior creatures when they discover mildness and tractableness of disposition; but no regard to him as a *virtuous* agent will arise within us.

Editor's Notes

1. Much of Price's argument is directed against the moral philosophy of Francis Hutcheson, whose work is represented in selections earlier in this book.
2. Like Hutcheson, Price distinguished between simple and complex ideas, without arguing for or explaining the distinction.
3. Price explained what he meant by "intuition" in Chapter V.
4. Francis Hutcheson.
5. Hume, *A Treatise of Human Nature*, I.I.i.; Locke, *An Essay Concerning Human Understanding*, II.I.2.
6. A hecatomb is a sacrifice to the gods of a hundred cattle, or any similarly large offering of living animals. Pythagoras is traditionally said to have offered a hecatomb in thanks for his discovery that the square of the hypotenuse of a right triangle equals the sum of the squares of the two sides.
7. The just or decent and the beautiful or lovely. Price claimed that the Romans and Greeks made the distinction he is making in this chapter.
8. The third ground of belief is argument, which Price thought we use when intuition fails us, a very Cartesian view.

Further Reading

The only collected edition of Price's works is the one edited by William Morgan in 1815–16. Price's correspondence is now being edited by W. Bernard Peach and D. O. Thomas.

D. D. Raphael's "Introduction" to his edition of the *Review of the Principal Questions of Morals*, from which the selections here are taken, is a good survey of the main points of Price's ethics. Three books offer analytic studies of Price's moral philosophy: Lennart Aquist, *The Moral Philosophy of Richard Price* (Lund and Copenhagen: CWK Gleerup and Ejnar Munksgaard, 1960); A. S. Cua, *Reason and Virtue* (Athens: University of Ohio Press, 1966); and W. D. Hudson, *Reason and Right* (San Francisco: Freeman, 1970). Price is briefly discussed in the final chapter of Arthur Prior, *Logic and the Basis of Ethics* (Oxford: Oxford University Press, 1949); the entire volume is useful in providing some of the context of Price's work. D. O. Thomas, *The Honest Mind: The Thought and Work of Richard Price* (Oxford: Oxford University Press, 1977), provides a survey of the whole of Price's thought and contains a good bibliography. Carl B. Cone, *Torchbearer of Freedom: The Influence of Richard Price on the Eighteenth Century* (Lexington: University of Kentucky Press, 1952), discusses Price in relation to his times.

Jean-Jacques Rousseau

Introduction

In his later years Rousseau was proud of having been born a citizen of Geneva, but his childhood there was unhappy. His mother died almost immediately after his birth on June 28, 1712, and when he was sixteen he ran away from the home in which he had not been given much attention. He was befriended by an older woman, Mme. de Warens, through whose influence he converted to Roman Catholicism. While living with her he read a great deal and studied music, at which he hoped to earn a living. In 1742 Rousseau made his way to Paris, where he eventually obtained a post as secretary to the French ambassador to Venice. After losing his job because of a quarrel, he returned to Paris. There he established a liaison with an uneducated woman by whom he had five children, all of whom he sent to be raised in a home for foundlings.

In 1750 Rousseau won first prize in a contest with his *Discourse on the Arts and Sciences.* An opera he had written was performed with great success as well. He had been enlisted to write on music for the *Encyclopedia,* the repository of advanced thinking and up-to-date science that became one of the principal vehicles of enlightened throught, and he developed friendships with many of the other encyclopedists. In 1754 he rejoined his original Protestant church. The next years were a period of intense creative activity. In 1755 Rousseau published a second discourse, *On the Origin of Inequality;* in 1761 his novel, *Julie; or, The New Heloise,* was published, winning immense popular acclaim; and in 1762 there appeared both his book on education, *Emile,* and his main political work, *The Social Contract.*

Emile was condemned for the dangerous religious views it contained, and consequently Rousseau decided to flee Paris. For some years he led a restless life, haunted by fears of persecution. He went to England at David Hume's invitation, only to decide that Hume was part of a plot against him. He returned to France, finally settling in Paris again. Isolated from the encyclopedists by his anxieties as well as by his theories and protected by various wealthy patrons, Rousseau wrote an extraordinary autobiography, *Confessions* (published posthumously), as well as autobiographical and apologetic essays. After his death in 1778 he became a cult figure and popular hero, and his works inspired many of those who instigated the French Revolution.

Was Rousseau a philosopher? It hardly seems to matter. He had carefully studied the writers of modern natural law, and he knew much of the philosophy of his time. If his own theories did not always appear in the form of philosophical treatises, they nevertheless exerted a major influence on the philosophy that followed them, including that of Kant. Rousseau had metaphysical and epistemological views, but his interests in moral personality and in politics were at the center of his thinking. In his fiction as well as his more abstract writings, he presented a new vision of the self and its changing relations to other individuals and to society. It is this vision that makes him a significant figure for the history of moral thought.

Rousseau rejected the idea that the self exists and can be understood without taking into account its social relations. Grotius, Hobbes, and Pufendorf all assumed that the isolated individual in a state of nature has all the attributes needed to explain the fundamentals of morality. But Rousseau found this absurd. Individuals in a state of nature would be much more like animals than the natural lawyers supposed. Moved by a form of love of self, which Rousseau called *amour de soi,* a concern for one's own survival, such individuals would be mainly indifferent to the well-being of others and would live without more than animal dependence on one another. In society as it now is, people are, in addition, moved by another form of self-love, which Rousseau called *amour propre,* a concern for recognition and esteem by others. *Amour propre* requires moral relations, and until it develops, people are not ready for morality. Yet *amour propre* may also lead to destructive forms of reliance on, and subordination to, others. In the narrative Rousseau constructed of the passage from the state of nature to the civilized state, he portrayed a transition to the kind of society he thought he saw around him in France, in which the many are oppressed and miserable and the few are powerful and contemptible. The question he raised is whether it is possible for there to be any other kind of society.

The individual in the state of nature is good, Rousseau held; it is society that corrupts, and only in society can we be corrupt. Yet he was not recommending a return to the woods. The sexual relations through which the species is perpetuated are not the only acceptable relations. What is needed is a form of society without involuntary domination, a society that provides law and security and in which, therefore, authority exists, yet in which authority does not involve the denial that everyone equally needs and is entitled to recognition and esteem as a human being.

In the *Social Contract* Rousseau proposed his solution to this problem. He believed that there can be a society in which everyone is free because everyone is subjected only to laws that are self-imposed. The ruler would be someone we had ourselves willed to rule. In obeying, therefore, we would be obeying only ourselves. Rousseau admired the ancient classical republic and thought he saw its modern counterpart in his own Geneva. (See the section "The Classical Republic" in the Introduction to this anthology.) His moral psychology serves, among other things, the purpose of showing how this form of government answers our need for society without subservience.

Whether Rousseau meant the narrative of the transformation from animallike *amour de soi* to full-blown *amour propre* as a genuine historical report or as an analytical device is less important than is his claim that morality comes into human existence only when the material and social environment has brought human nature into a condition that needs and can sustain it. Rousseau was interested in, and perplexed by, the relation between the physical aspect of our existence and the moral aspect, and he did not profess to have a full account of their relations. Like Pufendorf, he saw that morality is not something that can be directly derived from our physical being or from anything else physical. Yet he did not think morality unnatural. On the contrary, he insisted, as in Book IV of *Emile,* with a slap at Pufendorf's "moral entities," that

the first voices of conscience arise out of the first movements of the heart . . . the first notions of good and bad are born of the sentiments of love and hate. . . . *justice* and *goodness* are not merely abstract words – pure moral beings formed by the understanding – but are true affections of the soul enlightened by reason, are hence only an ordered development of our primitive affections.

The famous speech in *Emile* that Rousseau put in the mouth of a vicar from the Swiss province of Savoy makes it clear that conscience is an essential part of our nature. But Rousseau was not content with reasserting that ancient view. He wanted to show as well how personal and social conditions must be structured in order that conscience may speak to us effectively. What is needed is not individual book learning; the simplest peasant can have a fully adequate conscience. What is needed is social transformation. Rousseau's assumption is that it is at least possible for us to replace our present corrupt society with one in which freedom and morality can be pervasive.

The following selections come from three different works: the first, from the *Discourse on the Origin of Inequality;* the second, from *The Social Contract;* and the third, which is part of the speech by the Savoyard vicar, from *Emile.* For the first I have used the translation in *Jean-Jacques Rousseau, the First and Second Discourses,* edited, translated, and annotated by Victor Gourevitch. Copyright © 1986 by Victor Gourevitch and reprinted by permission of Harper and Row, Publishers, Inc. The translation of the second selection comes from *Jean-Jacques Rousseau's On the Social Contract,* edited by Roger D. Masters and translated by Judith R. Masters (New York: St. Martin's Press, and London: Macmillan). Copyright © 1978 by St. Martin's Press and reprinted by permission of St. Martin's Press, Inc. The translation for the third selection is from *Emile, or On Education,* by Jean-Jacques Rousseau, introduction, translation, and notes by Allan Bloom. Foreword, introduction, English translation, and notes, copyright © 1979 by Basic Books, Inc. Reprinted by permission of Basic Books, Inc., Publishers.

Discourse on the Origin and the Foundations of Inequality Among Men

[2] I conceive of two sorts of inequality in the human Species: one, which I call natural or Physical, because it is established by Nature, and which consists in differences of age, health, strengths of Body, and qualities of Mind or of Soul; the other, which may be called moral, or political inequality because it depends on a sort of convention and is established, or at least authorized by Men's consent. It consists in the different Privileges which some enjoy to the prejudice of the others, such as to be more wealthy, more honored, more Powerful than they, or even to get themselves obeyed by them.

[4] What, precisely, then, is at issue in this Discourse? To mark, in the progress of things, the moment when, Right replacing Violence, Nature was subjected to Law; to explain by what succession of wonders the strong could resolve to serve the weak, and the People to purchase the idea of repose at the price of real felicity.

[5] The Philosophers who have examined the foundations of society have all felt the necessity of going back as far as the state of Nature, but none of them has reached it. Some have not hesitated to ascribe to Man in that state the notion of the Just and the Unjust, without bothering to show that he had to have that notion, or even that it would have been useful to him; Others have

spoken of everyone's Natural Right to keep what belongs to him, without explaining what they understood by belong; Others still, after first granting to the stronger authority over the weaker, had Government arise straightway, without giving thought to the time that must have elapsed before the language of authority and of government could have meaning among Men: Finally, all of them, continually speaking of need, greed, oppression, desires, and pride transferred to the state of Nature ideas they had taken from society; they spoke of Savage Man and depicted Civil man. It did not even enter the mind of most of our philosophers to doubt that the state of Nature had existed, whereas it is evident, from reading the Holy Scriptures, that the first Man, having received some lights and Precepts immediately from God, was not himself in that state, and that, if the Writings of Moses are granted the credence owed them by every Christian Philosopher, it has to be denied that, even before the Flood, Men were ever in the pure state of Nature, unless they by some extraordinary Occurrence relapsed into it: a Paradox most embarrassing to defend, and altogether impossible to prove.

PART I

[15] I see in any animal nothing but an ingenious machine to which nature has given senses in order to wind itself up and, to a point, protect itself against everything that tends to destroy or to disturb it. I perceive precisely the same thing in the human machine, with this difference that Nature alone does everything in the operations of the Beast, whereas man contributes to his operations in his capacity as a free agent. The one chooses or rejects by instinct, the other by an act of freedom; as a result the Beast cannot deviate from the Rule prescribed to it even when it would be to its advantage to do so, while man often deviates from it to his detriment. Thus a Pigeon would starve to death next to a Bowl filled with the choicest meats, and a Cat atop heaps of fruit or of grain, although each could very well have found nourishment in the food it disdains if it had occurred to it to try some; thus dissolute men abandon themselves to excesses which bring them fever and death; because the Mind depraves the senses, and the will continues to speak when Nature is silent.

[16] Every animal has ideas, since it has senses; up to a point it even combines its ideas, and in this respect man differs from the Beast only as more does from less: Some Philosophers have even suggested that there is a greater difference between one given man and another than there is between a given man and a given beast; it is, then, not so much the understanding that constitutes the specific difference between man and the other animals, as it is his property of being a free agent. Nature commands every animal, and the Beast obeys. Man experiences the same impression, but recognizes himself free to acquiesce or to resist; and it is mainly in the consciousness of this freedom that the spirituality of his soul exhibits itself: for Physics in a way explains the mechanism of the senses and the formation of ideas; but in the power of willing, or rather of

choosing, and in the sentiment of this power are found purely spiritual acts about which nothing is explained by the Laws of Mechanics.

[17] But even if the difficulties surrounding all these questions left some room for disagreement about this difference between man and animal, there is another very specific property that distinguishes between them and about which there can be no argument, namely the faculty of perfecting oneself; a faculty which, with the aid of circumstances, successively develops all the others, and resides in us in the species as well as in the individual, whereas an animal is at the end of several months what it will be for the rest of its life and its species is after a thousand years what it was in the first year of those thousand. Why is man alone liable to become an imbecile? Is it not that he thus returns to his primitive state and that, whereas the Beast, which has acquired nothing and also has nothing to lose, always keeps its instinct, man, losing through old age or other accidents all that his *perfectibility* had made him acquire, thus relapses lower than the Beast itself? It would be sad for us to be forced to agree that this distinctive and almost unlimited faculty is the source of all of man's miseries; that it is the faculty which, by dint of time, draws him out of that original condition in which he would spend calm and innocent days; that it is the faculty which, over the centuries, causes his enlightenment and his errors, his vices and his virtues to arise, and eventually makes him his own and Nature's tyrant. It would be frightful to be obliged to praise as a beneficent being him who first suggested to the inhabitant of the Banks of the Orinoco the use of the Slats he ties to his Children's temples, and which insure at least a measure of their imbecility and of their original happiness.

[35] Above all, let us not conclude with Hobbes[1] that because he has no idea of goodness, man is naturally wicked, that he is vicious because he does not know virtue, that he always refuses to those of his kind services which he does not believe he owes them, or that by virtue of the right which he with reason assigns himself to the things he needs, he insanely imagines himself to be the sole owner of the entire Universe. Hobbes very clearly saw the defect of all modern definitions of Natural right: but the conclusions he draws from his own definition show that he understands it in a sense that is no less false. By reasoning on the basis of the principles he established, this Author should have said that, since the state of Nature is the state in which the care for our own preservation is least prejudicial to the self-preservation of others, it follows that this state was the most conducive to Peace and the best suited to Mankind. He says precisely the contrary because he improperly included in Savage man's care for his preservation the need to satisfy a multitude of passions that are the product of Society and have made Laws necessary. A wicked man is, he says a sturdy Child; it remains to be seen whether Savage Man is a sturdy Child. Even if it were granted him that it is, what would he conclude? That if this man were as dependent on others when he is sturdy as he is dependent on them when weak, he would not stop at any kind of excess, that he would strike his Mother if she were slow to give him the breast, that he would strangle one of his young brothers if he inconvenienced him, that he

would bite another brother's leg if he hurt or bothered him; but being sturdy and being dependent are two contradictory assumptions in the state of Nature; Man in weak when he is dependent, and he is emancipated before he is sturdy. Hobbes did not see that the same cause that prevents the Savages from using their reason, as our Jurists claim they do, at the same time prevents them from abusing their faculties, as he himself claims they do; so that one might say that Savages are not wicked precisely because they do not know what it is to be good; for it is neither the growth of enlightenment nor the curb of the Law, but the calm of the passions and the ignorance of vice that keep them from evil-doing; *so much more does the ignorance of vice profit these than the knowledge of virtue profits those.* There is, besides, another Principle which Hobbes did not notice and which, having been given to man in order under certain circumstances to soften the ferociousness of his vanity or of the desire for self-preservation prior to the birth of vanity, tempers his ardor for well-being with an innate repugnance to see his kind suffer. I do not believe I need fear any contradiction in granting to man the only Natural virtue which the most extreme Detractor of human virtues was forced to acknowledge. I speak of Pity, a disposition suited to beings as weak and as subject to so many ills as we are; a virtue all the more universal and useful to man as it precedes the exercise of all reflection in him, and so Natural that the Beasts themselves sometimes show evident signs of it. . . .

[37] Mandeville² sensed clearly that for all their morality, men would never have been anything but monsters if Nature had not given them pity in support of reason: but he did not see that from this single attribute flow all the social virtues he wants to deny men. Indeed, what are generosity, Clemency, Humanity, if not Pity applied to the weak, the guilty, or the species in general? Even Benevolence and friendship, properly understood, are the products of a steady pity focused on a particular object; for what else is it to wish that someone not suffer, than to wish that he be happy? Even if it were true that commiseration is nothing but a sentiment that puts us in the place of him who suffers, a sentiment that is obscure and lively in Savage man, developed but weak in Civil man, what difference could this idea make to the truth of what I say, except to give it additional force? Indeed commiseration will be all the more energetic in proportion as the Onlooking animal identifies more intimately with the suffering animal: Now this identification must, clearly, have been infinitely closer in the state of Nature than in the state of reasoning. It is reason that engenders vanity, and reflection that reinforces it; It is what turns man back upon himself; it is what separates him from everything that troubles and afflicts him: It is Philosophy that isolates him; it is by means of Philosophy that he secretly says at the sight of a suffering man, perish if you wish, I am safe. Only dangers that threaten the entire society still disturb the Philosopher's tranquil slumber, and rouse him from his bed. One of his kind can with impunity be murdered beneath his window; he only has to put his hands over his ears and to argue with himself a little in order to prevent Nature, which rebels within him, from letting him identify with the man being assassinated.

Savage man has not this admirable talent; and for want of wisdom and of reason he is always seen to yield impetuously to the first sentiment of Humanity. In Riots, in Street-brawls, the Populace gathers, the prudent man withdraws; it is the rabble, it is the Marketwomen who separate the combatants and keep honest folk from murdering each other.

[38] It is therefore quite certain that pity is a natural sentiment which, by moderating in every individual the activity of self-love, contributes to the mutual preservation of the entire species. It is pity which carries us without reflection to the assistance of those we see suffer; it is pity which, in the state of Nature, takes the place of Laws, morals, and virtue, with the advantage that no one is tempted to disobey its gentle voice; it is pity which will keep any sturdy Savage from robbing a weak child or an infirm old man of his hard-won subsistence if he hopes he can find his own elsewhere: It is pity which instead of the sublime maxim of reasoned justice *Do unto others as you would have them do unto you* inspires all Men with this other maxim of natural goodness, much less perfect but perhaps more useful than the first: *Do your good with the least possible harm to others.* It is, in a word, in this Natural sentiment rather than in subtle arguments that one has to seek the cause of the repugnance to evil-doing which every human being would feel even independently of the maxims of education. Although Socrates and Minds of his stamp may be capable of acquiring virtue through reason, Mankind would long ago have ceased to be if its preservation had depended solely on the reasonings of those who make it up.

[39] With such sluggish passions and such a salutary curb, fierce rather than wicked, and more intent on protecting themselves from the harm they might suffer than tempted to do any to others, men were not prone to very dangerous quarrels: since they had no dealings of any kind with one another; since they therefore knew neither vanity, nor consideration, nor esteem, nor contempt; since they had not the slightest notion of thine and mine, or any genuine idea of justice; since they looked on any violence they might suffer as an easily repaired harm rather than as a punishable injury, and since they did not even dream of vengeance except perhaps mechanically and on the spot like the dog that bites the stone thrown at him; their disputes would seldom have led to bloodshed if they had had no more urgent object than Food: but I see one that is more dangerous, which it remains for me to discuss.[3] . . .

[46] Let us conclude that, wandering in the forests without industry, without speech, without settled abode, without war, and without ties, without any need of others of his kind and without any desire to harm them, perhaps even without ever recognizing any one of them individually, subject to few passions and self-sufficient, Savage man had only the sentiments and the enlightenment suited to this state, that he sensed only his true needs, looked only at what he believed it to be in his interest to see, and that his intelligence made no more progress than his vanity. If he by chance made some discovery, he was all the less in a position to communicate it as he did not recognize even his Children. The art perished with the inventor; there was neither education nor

progress, generations multiplied uselessly; and as each one of them always started at the same point, Centuries went by in all the crudeness of the first ages, the species had already grown old, and man remained ever a child.

PART II

[1] The first man who, having enclosed a piece of ground, to whom it occurred to say *this is mine* and found people sufficiently simple to believe him, was the true founder of civil society. How many crimes, wars, murders, how many miseries and horrors Mankind would have been spared by him who, pulling up the stakes or filling in the ditch, had cried out to his kind: Beware of listening to this impostor; you are lost if you forget that the fruits are everyone's and the Earth no one's: But in all likelihood things had by then reached a point where they could not continue as they were; for this idea of property, depending as it does on many prior ideas which could only arise successively, did not take shape all at once in man's mind: Much progress had to have been made, industry and enlightenment acquired, transmitted, and increased from one age to the next, before this last stage of the state of Nature was reached. Let us therefore take up the thread earlier, and try to fit this slow succession of events and of knowledge together from a single point of view, and in their most natural order.

[18] But it must be noted that beginning Society and the already established relations among men, required in them qualities different from those they derived from their primitive constitution; that, since morality was beginning to enter into human Actions and since, before there were Laws, everyone was sole judge and avenger of the offenses he had received, the goodness suited to the pure state of Nature was no longer the goodness suited to nascent Society; that punishments had to become more severe in proportion as the opportunities to offend became more frequent, and that the terror of vengeance had to take the place of the Laws' restraint. Thus, although men now had less endurance, and natural pity had already undergone some modification, this period in the development of human faculties, occupying a just mean between the indolence of the primitive state and the petulant activity of our vanity, must have been the happiest and the longest-lasting epoch. The more one reflects on it, the more one finds that this state was the least subject to revolutions, the best for man, and that he must have left it only by some fatal accident which, for the sake of the common utility, should never have occurred. The example of the Savages, almost all of whom have been found at this point, seems to confirm that Mankind was made always to remain in it, that this state is the genuine youth of the World, and that all subsequent progress has been so many steps in appearance toward the perfection of the individual, and in effect toward the decrepitude of the species.

[24] From the cultivation of land, its division necessarily followed; and from property, once recognized, the first rules of justice necessarily followed: for in order to render to each his own, it has to be possible for each to have some-

thing; moreover, as men began to extend their views to the future and all saw that they had some goods to lose, there was no one who did not have to fear reprisals against himself for wrongs he might do to another. This origin is all the more natural as it is impossible to conceive the idea of nascent property in any other way than in terms of manual labor: for it is not clear what more than his labor man can put into things he has not made, in order to appropriate them. It is labor alone which, by giving the Cultivator the right to the product of the land he has tilled, therefore also gives him a right to the land, at least until the harvest, and so from one year to the next, which, as it makes for continuous possession, is easily transformed into property. . . .

[27] Here, then, are all our faculties developed, memory and imagination brought into play, vanity interested, reason become active, and the mind almost at the limit of the perfection of which it is capable. Here are all natural qualities set in action, each man's rank and fate set, not only in terms of the quantity of goods and the power to benefit or harm, but also in terms of mind, beauty, strength or skill, in terms of merit or talents, and, since these are the only qualities that could attract regard, one soon had to have them or to affect them; for one's own advantage one had to seem other than one in fact was. To be and to appear became two entirely different things, and from this distinction arose ostentatious display, deceitful cunning, and all the vices that follow in their train. Looked at in another way, man, who had previously been free and independent, is now so to speak subjugated by a multitude of new needs to the whole of Nature, and especially to those of his kind, whose slave he in a sense becomes even by becoming their master; rich, he needs their services; poor, he needs their help, and moderate means do not enable him to do without them. He therefore constantly has to try to interest them in his fate and to make them find their own profit, in deed or in appearance, in working for his: which makes him knavish and artful with some, imperious and harsh with the rest, and places him under the necessity of abusing all those he needs if he cannot get them to fear him and does not find it in his interest to serve them usefully. Finally, consuming ambition, the ardent desire to raise one's relative fortune less out of genuine need than in order to place oneself above others, instills in all men a black inclination to harm one another, a secret jealousy which is all the more dangerous as it often assumes the mask of benevolence in order to strike its blow in greater safety: in a word, competition and rivalry on the one hand, conflict of interests on the other, and always the hidden desire to profit at another's expense; all these evils are the first effect of property, and the inseparable train of nascent inequality.

[29] Thus, as the most powerful or the most miserable claimed, on the basis of their strength or of their needs, a kind of right to another's goods, equivalent, according to them, to the right of property, the breakdown of equality was followed by the most frightful disorder: thus the usurpations of the rich, the Banditry of the Poor, the unbridled passions of all, stifling natural pity and the still-weak voice of justice, made men greedy, ambitious, and wicked. A perpetual conflict arose between the right of the stronger and the right of the

first occupant, which ended only in fights and murders. Nascent Society gave way to the most horrible state of war: Mankind, debased and devastated, no longer able to turn back or to renounce its wretched acquisitions, and working only to its shame by the abuse of the faculties that do it honor, brought itself to the brink of ruin.

> Shocked by the novelty of the evil,
> at once rich and miserable,
> He seeks to escape his wealth, and
> hates what he had just prayed for.[4]

[30] It is not possible that men should not at last have reflected on such a miserable situation and the calamities besetting them. The rich, above all, must soon have sensed how disadvantageous to them was a perpetual war of which they alone bore the full cost, and in which everyone risked his life while only some also risked goods. Besides, regardless of the color they might lend to their usurpations, they realized well enough that they were only based on a precarious and abusive right, and that since they had been acquired solely by force, force could deprive them of them without their having any reason for complaint. Even those whom industriousness alone had enriched could scarcely base their property on better titles. No matter if they said: It is I who built this wall; I earned this plot by my labor. Who set its boundaries for you, they could be answered; and by virtue of what do you lay claim to being paid at our expense for labor we did not impose on you? Do you not know that a great many of your brothers perish or suffer from need for what you have in excess, and that you required the express and unanimous consent of Mankind to appropriate for yourself anything from the common subsistence above and beyond your own? Lacking valid reasons to justify and sufficient strength to defend himself; easily crushing an individual, but himself crushed by troops of bandits; alone against all, and unable, because of their mutual jealousies, to unite with his equals against enemies united by the common hope of plunder, the rich, under the pressure of necessity, at last conceived the most well-considered project ever to enter man's mind; to use even his attackers' forces in his favor, to make his adversaries his defenders, to instill in them other maxims and to give them different institutions, as favorable to himself as natural Right was contrary to him.

[31] To this end, after exhibiting to his neighbors the horror of a situation which armed all of them against one another, made their possessions as burdensome to them as their needs, and in which no one found safety in either poverty or wealth, he easily invented specious reasons to bring them over to his purpose: "Let us unite," he told them, "to protect the weak from oppression, restrain the ambitious, and secure for everyone the possession of what belongs to him: Let us institute regulations of Justice and of peace to which all are obliged to conform, which favor no one, and which in a way make up for the vagaries of fortune by subjecting the powerful and the weak alike to mutual duties. In a word, instead of turning our forces against ourselves, let us

gather them into a supreme power that might govern us according to wise Laws, protect and defend all the members of the association, repulse common enemies, and keep us in eternal concord."

[32] Much less than the equivalent of this Discourse was needed to sway crude, easily seduced men who, in any event, had too much business to sort out among themselves to be able to do without arbiters, and too much greed and ambition to be able to do for long without Masters. All ran toward their chains in the belief that they were securing their freedom; for while they had enough reason to sense the advantages of a political establishment, they had not enough experience to foresee its dangers; those most capable of anticipating the abuses were precisely those who counted on profiting from them, and even the wise saw that they had to make up their mind to sacrifice one part of their freedom to preserve the other, as a wounded man has his arm cut off to save the rest of his Body.

[33] Such was, or must have been, the origin of Society and of Laws, which gave the weak new fetters and the rich new forces, irreversibly destroyed natural freedom, forever fixed the Law of property and inequality, transformed a skillful usurpation into an irrevocable right, and for the profit of a few ambitious men henceforth subjugated the whole of Mankind to labor, servitude and misery. . . .

On the Social Contract

CHAPTER I: SUBJECT OF THIS FIRST BOOK

Man was/is born free, and everywhere he is in chains.[5] One who believes himself the master of others is nonetheless a greater slave than they. How did this change occur? I do not know. What can make it legitimate? I believe I can answer this question.

If I were to consider only force and the effect it produces, I would say that as long as a people is constrained to obey and does so, it does well; as soon as it can shake off the yoke and does so, it does even better. For in recovering its freedom by means of the same right used to steal it, either the people is justified in taking it back, or those who took it away were not justified in doing so. But the social order is a sacred right that serves as a basis for all the others. However, this right does not come from nature; it is therefore based on conventions. The problem is to know what these conventions are. Before coming to that, I should establish what I have just asserted.

CHAPTER II: ON THE FIRST SOCIETIES

The most ancient of all societies, and the only natural one, is that of the family. Yet children remain bound to the father only as long as they need him for self-preservation. As soon as this need ceases, the natural bond dissolves. The children, exempt from the obedience they owed the father, and the father, exempt from the care he owed the children, all return equally to independence. If they continue to remain united, it is no longer naturally but voluntarily, and the family itself is maintained only by convention.

This common freedom is a consequence of man's nature. His first law is to attend to his own preservation, his first cares are those he owes himself; and as soon as he has reached the age of reason, as he alone is the judge of the proper means of preserving himself, he thus becomes his own master.

The family is therefore, so to speak, the prototype of political societies. The leader is like the father, the people are like the children; and since all are born equal and free, they only alienate their freedom for their utility. The entire difference is that in the family, the father's love for his children rewards him for the care he provides; whereas in the State, the pleasure of commanding substitutes for this love, which the leader does not have for his people.

Grotius[6] denies that all human power is established for the benefit of those who are governed. He cites slavery as an example. His most persistent mode of reasoning is always to establish right by fact. One could use a more rational method, but not one more favorable to tyrants.

It is therefore doubtful, according to Grotius, whether the human race belongs to a hundred men, or whether these hundred men belong to the human race; and throughout his book he appears to lean toward the former view. This is Hobbes's sentiment as well. Thus the human species is divided into herds of livestock, each with its leader, who tends it in order to devour it.

. . . Before any of them, Aristotle too had said that men are not naturally equal, but that some are born for slavery and others for domination.[7]

Aristotle was right, but he mistook the effect for the cause. Every man born in slavery is born for slavery; nothing could be more certain. Slaves lose everything in their chains, even the desire to be rid of them. They love their servitude as the companions of Ulysses loved their brutishness.[8] If there are slaves by nature, therefore, it is because there have been slaves contrary to nature. Force made the first slaves; their cowardice perpetuated them. . . .

Chapter III: On the Right of the Strongest

The strongest is never strong enough to be the master forever unless he transforms his force into right and obedience into duty. This leads to the right of the strongest, a right that is in appearance taken ironically and in principle really established. But won't anyone ever explain this word to us? Force is a physical power. I do not see what morality can result from its effects. Yielding to force is an act of necessity, not of will. At most, it is an act of prudence. In what sense could it be a duty?

Let us suppose this alleged right for a moment. I say that what comes of it is nothing but inexplicable confusion. For as soon as force makes right, the effect changes along with the cause. Any force that overcomes the first one succeeds to its right. As soon as one can disobey without punishment, one can do so legitimately, and since the strongest is always right, the only thing to do is to make oneself the strongest. But what is a right that perishes when force ceases? If it is necessary to obey by force, one need not obey by duty, and if one is no longer forced to obey, one is no longer obligated to do so. It is apparent, then, that this word right adds nothing to force. It is meaningless here.

Obey those in power. If that means yield to force, the precept is good, but superfluous; I reply that it will never be violated. All power comes from God, I admit, but so does all illness. Does this mean it is forbidden to call the doctor? If a brigand takes me by surprise at the edge of a woods, must I not only give up my purse by force; am I obligated by conscience to give it even if I could keep it away? After all, the pistol he holds is also a power.

Let us agree, therefore, that might does not make right, and that one is only obligated to obey legitimate powers. Thus my original question still remains.

Chapter IV: On Slavery

Since no man has any natural authority over his fellow man, and since force produces no right, there remain only conventions as the basis of all legitimate authority among men.

If a private individual, says Grotius, can alienate his freedom and enslave himself to a master, why can't a whole people alienate its freedom and subject itself to a king? There are many equivocal words in this that need explaining, but let us limit ourselves to the word *alienate*. To alienate is to give or to sell. Now a man who makes himself another's slave does not give himself, he sells himself, at the least for his subsistence. But why does a people sell itself? Far from furnishing the subsistence of his subjects, a king derives his own only from them, and according to Rabelais a king does not live cheaply. Do the subjects give their persons, then, on condition that their goods will be taken too? I do not see what remains for them to preserve.

It will be said that the despot guarantees civil tranquillity to his subjects. Perhaps so, but what have they gained if the wars that his ambition brings on them, if his insatiable greed, if the harassment of his ministers are a greater torment than their dissensions would be? What have they gained, if this tranquillity is one of their miseries? Life is tranquil in jail cells, too. Is that reason enough to like them? The Greeks lived tranquilly shut up in the Cyclops' cave as they awaited their turn to be devoured.

To say that a man gives himself gratuitously is to say something absurd and inconceivable. Such an act is illegitimate and null, if only because he who does so is not in his right mind. To say the same thing about an entire people is to suppose a people of madmen. Madness does not make right.

Even if everyone could alienate himself, he could not alienate his children. They are born men and free. Their freedom belongs to them; no one but themselves has a right to dispose of it. Before they have reached the age of reason, their father can, in their name, stipulate conditions for their preservation, for their well-being; but he cannot give them irrevocably and unconditionally, because such a gift is contrary to the ends of nature and exceeds the rights of paternity. For an arbitrary government to be legitimate, it would therefore be necessary for the people in each generation to be master of its acceptance or rejection. But then this government would no longer be arbitrary.

To renounce one's freedom is to renounce one's status as a man, the rights of humanity and even its duties. There is no possible compensation for anyone who renounces everything. Such a renunciation is incompatible with the nature of man, and taking away all his freedom of will is taking away all morality from his actions. Finally, it is a vain and contradictory convention to stipulate absolute authority on one side and on the other unlimited obedience. Isn't it clear that one is in no way engaged toward a person from whom one has the right to demand everything, and doesn't this condition alone – without equivalent and without exchange – entail the nullification of the act? For what right would my slave have against me, since all he has belongs to me, and his right being mine, my right against myself is a meaningless word?

With regard to the right of conquest, it has no basis other than the law of the strongest. If war does not give the victor the right to massacre the vanquished peoples, this right he does not have cannot establish the right to enslave them. One only has the right to kill the enemy when he cannot be made a slave. The right to make him a slave does not come, then, from the right to kill him. It is therefore an iniquitous exchange to make him buy his life, over which one has no right, at the cost of his freedom. By establishing the right of life and death on the right of slavery, and the right of slavery on the right of life and death, isn't it clear that one falls into a vicious circle?

Even assuming this terrible right to kill everyone, I say that a man enslaved in war or a conquered people is in no way obligated toward his master, except to obey for as long as he is forced to do so. In taking the equivalent of his life, the victor has not spared it; rather than to kill him purposelessly, he has killed him usefully. Therefore, far from the victor having acquired any authority over him in addition to force, the state of war subsists between them as before; their relation itself is its effect, and the customs of the right of war suppose that there has not been a peace treaty. They made a convention, true; but that convention, far from destroying the state of war, assumes its continuation.

Thus, from every vantage point, the right of slavery is null, not merely because it is illegitimate, but because it is absurd and meaningless. These words *slavery* and *right* are contradictory; they are mutually exclusive. Whether it is said by one man to another or by a man to a people, the following speech will always be equally senseless: *I make a convention with you that is entirely at your expense and entirely for my benefit; that I shall observe for as long as I want, and that you shall observe for as long as I want.*

Chapter V: That It Is Always Necessary to Go Back to a First Convention

Even if I were to grant everything I have thus far refuted, the proponents of despotism would be no better off. There will always be a great difference between subjugating a multitude and governing a society. If scattered men, however many there may be, are successively enslaved by one individual, I see only a master and slaves; I do not see a people and its leader. It is an aggregation, if you wish, but not an association. It has neither public good nor body politic. That man, even if he had enslaved half the world, is nothing but a private individual. His interest, separate from that of the others, is still nothing but a private interest. If this same man dies, thereafter his empire is left scattered and without bonds, just as an oak tree disintegrates and falls into a heap of ashes after fire has consumed it.

A people, says Grotius, can give itself to a king. According to Grotius, a people is therefore a people before it gives itself to a king. This gift itself is a civil act; it presupposes a public deliberation. Therefore, before examining the act by which a people elects a king, it would be well to examine the act by which a people becomes a people. For this act, being necessarily prior to the other, is the true basis of society.

Indeed, if there were no prior convention, what would become of the obligation for the minority to submit to the choice of the majority, unless the election were unanimous; and where do one hundred who want a master get the right to vote for ten who do not? The law of majority rule is itself an established convention, and presupposes unanimity at least once.

CHAPTER VI: ON THE SOCIAL COMPACT

I assume that men have reached the point where obstacles to their self-preservation in the state of nature prevail by their resistance over the forces each individual can use to maintain himself in that state. Then that primitive state can no longer subsist and the human race would perish if it did not change its way of life.

Now since men cannot engender new forces, but merely unite and direct existing ones, they have no other means of self-preservation except to form, by aggregation, a sum of forces that can prevail over the resistance; set them to work by a single motivation; and make them act in concert.

This sum of forces can arise only from the cooperation of many. But since each man's force and freedom are the primary instruments of his self-preservation, how is he to engage them without harming himself and without neglecting the cares he owes to himself? In the context of my subject, this difficulty can be stated in these terms:

"Find a form of association that defends and protects the person and goods of each associate with all the common force, and by means of which each one, uniting with all, nevertheless obeys only himself and remains as free as before." This is the fundamental problem which is solved by the social contract.

The clauses of this contract are so completely determined by the nature of the act that the slightest modification would render them null and void. So that although they may never have been formally pronounced, they are every-where the same, everywhere tacitly accepted and recognized, until the social compact is violated, at which point each man recovers his original rights and resumes his natural freedom, thereby losing the conventional freedom for which he renounced it.

Properly understood, all of these clauses come down to a single one, namely the total alienation of each associate, with all his rights, to the whole community. For first of all, since each one gives his entire self, the condition is equal for everyone, and since the condition is equal for everyone, no one has an interest in making it burdensome for the others.

Furthermore, as the alienation is made without reservation, the union is as perfect as it can be, and no associate has anything further to claim. For if some rights were left to private individuals, there would be no common superior who could judge between them and the public. Each man being his own judge on some point would soon claim to be so on all; the state of nature would subsist and the association would necessarily become tyrannical or ineffectual.

Finally, as each gives himself to all, he gives himself to no one; and since there is no associate over whom one does not acquire the same right one grants him over oneself, one gains the equivalent of everything one loses, and more force to preserve what one has.

If, then, everything that is not of the essence of the social compact is set aside, one will find that it can be reduced to the following terms. *Each of us puts his person and all his power in common under the supreme direction of the general will; and in a body we receive each member as an indivisible part of the whole.*

Instantly, in place of the private person of each contracting party, this act of association produces a moral and collective body, composed of as many members as there are voices in the assembly, which receives from this same act its unity, its common *self*, its life, and its will. This public person, formed thus by the union of all the others, formerly took the name *City,* and now takes that of *Republic* or *body politic,* which its members call *State* when it is passive, *Sovereign* when active, *Power* when comparing it to similar bodies. As for the associates, they collectively take the name *people;* and individually are called *Citizens* as participants in the sovereign authority, and *Subjects* as subject to the laws of the State. But these terms are often mixed up and mistaken for one another. It is enough to know how to distinguish them when they are used with complete precision.

CHAPTER VII: ON THE SOVEREIGN

This formula shows that the act of association includes a reciprocal engagement between the public and private individuals, and that each individual, contracting with himself so to speak, finds that he is doubly engaged, namely toward private individuals as a member of the sovereign and toward the sovereign as a member of the State. But the maxim of civil right that no one can be held responsible for engagements toward himself cannot be applied here, because there is a great difference between being obligated to oneself, or to a whole of which one is a part.

It must further be noted that the public deliberation that can obligate all of the subjects to the sovereign – due to the two different relationships in which each of them is considered – cannot for the opposite reason obligate the sovereign toward itself; and that consequently it is contrary to the nature of the body politic for the sovereign to impose on itself a law it cannot break. Since the sovereign can only be considered in a single relationship, it is then in the situation of a private individual contracting with himself. It is apparent from this that there is not, nor can there be, any kind of fundamental law that is obligatory for the body of the people, not even the social contract. This does not mean that this body cannot perfectly well enter an engagement toward another with respect to things that do not violate this contract. For with reference to the foreigner, it becomes a simple being or individual.

But the body politic or the sovereign, deriving its being solely from the sanctity of the contract, can never obligate itself, even toward another, to do anything that violates that original act, such as to alienate some part of itself or to subject itself to another sovereign. To violate the act by which it exists would be to destroy itself, and whatever is nothing, produces nothing.

As soon as this multitude is thus united in a body, one cannot harm one of the members without attacking the body, and it is even less possible to harm the body without the members feeling the effects. Thus duty and interest equally obligate the two contracting parties to mutual assistance, and the same men should seek to combine in this double relationship all the advantages that are dependent on it.

Now the sovereign, formed solely by the private individuals composing it, does not and cannot have any interest contrary to theirs. Consequently, the sovereign power has no need of a guarantee toward the subjects, because it is impossible for the body ever to want to harm all its members, and we shall see later that it cannot harm any one of them as an individual. The sovereign, by the sole fact of being, is always what it ought to be.

But the same is not true of the subjects in relation to the sovereign, which, despite the common interest, would have no guarantee of the subjects' engagements if it did not find ways to be assured of their fidelity.

Indeed, each individual can, as a man, have a private will contrary to or differing from the general will he has as a citizen. His private interest can speak to him quite differently from the common interest. His absolute and naturally independent existence can bring him to view what he owes the common cause as a free contribution, the loss of which will harm others less than its payment burdens him. And considering the moral person of the State as an imaginary being because it is not a man, he might wish to enjoy the rights of the citizen without wanting to fulfill the duties of a subject, an injustice whose spread would cause the ruin of the body politic.

Therefore, in order for the social compact not to be an ineffectual formula, it tacitly includes the following engagement, which alone can give force to the others: that whoever refuses to obey the general will shall be constrained to do so by the entire body; which means only that he will be forced to be free. For this is the condition that, by giving each citizen to the homeland, guarantees him against all personal dependence; a condition that creates the ingenuity and functioning of the political machine, and alone gives legitimacy to civil engagements which without it would be absurd, tyrannical, and subject to the most enormous abuses.

Chapter VIII: On the Civil State

This passage from the state of nature to the civil state produces a remarkable change in man, by substituting justice for instinct in his behavior and giving his actions the morality they previously lacked. Only then, when the voice of duty replaces physical impulse and right replaces appetite, does man, who until that time only considered himself, find himself forced to act upon other principles and to consult his reason before heeding his inclinations. Although in this state he deprives himself of several advantages given him by nature, he gains such great ones, his faculties are exercised and developed, his ideas broadened, his feelings ennobled, and his whole soul elevated to such a point that if the abuses of this new condition did not often degrade him beneath the condition he left, he ought ceaselessly to bless the happy moment that tore him away from it forever, and that changed him from a stupid, limited animal into an intelligent being and a man.

Let us reduce the pros and cons to easily compared terms. What man loses by the social contract is his natural freedom and an unlimited right to everything that tempts him and that he can get; what he gains is civil freedom and the proprietorship of everything he possesses. In order not to be mistaken about these compensations, one must distinguish carefully between natural freedom, which is limited only by the force of the individual, and civil freedom, which is limited by the general will; and between possession, which is only the effect of force or the right of the first occupant, and property, which can only be based on a positive title.

To the foregoing acquisitions of the civil state could be added moral freedom, which alone makes man truly the master of himself. For the impulse of appetite alone is slavery, and obedience to the law one has prescribed for oneself is freedom. But I have already said too much about this topic, and the philosophic meaning of the word *freedom* is not my subject here.

Chapter IX: On Real Estate

. . . I shall end this chapter and this book with a comment that ought to serve as the basis of the whole social system. It is that rather than destroying natural equality, the fundamental compact on the contrary substitutes a moral and legitimate equality for whatever physical inequality nature may have placed between men, and that although they may be unequal in force or in genius, they all become equal through convention and by right.

Emile

After having thus deduced the principal truths that it mattered for me to know from the impression of sensible objects and from the inner sentiment that leads me to judge of causes according to my natural lights, I still must investigate what manner of conduct I ought to draw from these truths and what rules I ought to prescribe for myself in order to fulfill my destiny on earth according to the intention of Him who put me there. In continuing to follow my method, I do not draw these rules from the principles of a high philosophy, but find them written by nature with ineffaceable characters in the depth of my heart. I have only to consult myself about what I want to do. Everything I sense to be good is good; everything I sense to be bad is bad. The best of all casuists is the conscience; and it is only when one haggles with it that one has recourse to the subtleties of reasoning. The first of all cares is the care for oneself. Nevertheless how many times does the inner voice tell us that, in doing our good at another's expense, we do wrong! We believe we are following the impulse of nature, but we are resisting it. In listening to what it says to our senses, we despise what it says to our hearts; the active being obeys, the passive being commands. Conscience is the voice of the soul; the passions are the voice of the body. Is it surprising that these two languages often are contradictory? And then which should be listened to? Too often reason deceives us. We have acquired only too much right to challenge it. But conscience never deceives; it is man's true guide. It is to the soul what instinct is to the body; he who follows conscience obeys nature and does not fear being led astray. This point is important [continued my benefactor, seeing that I was going to interrupt him]. Allow me to tarry a bit to clarify it.

All the morality of our actions is in the judgment we ourselves make of them. If it is true that the good is good, it must be so in the depths of our hearts as it is in our works, and the primary reward for justice is to sense that one practices it. If moral goodness is in conformity with our nature, man could be healthy of spirit or well constituted only to the extent that he is good. If it is not and man is naturally wicked, he cannot cease to be so without being corrupted, and goodness in him is only a vice contrary to nature. If he were made to do harm to his kind, as a wolf is made to slaughter his prey, a humane man would be an animal as depraved as a pitying wolf, and only virtue would leave us with remorse.

Let us return to ourselves, my young friend! Let us examine, all personal interest aside, where our inclinations lead us. Which spectacle gratifies us more – that of others' torments or that of their happiness? Which is sweeter to do and leaves us with a more agreeable impression after having done it – a beneficent act or a wicked act? In whom do you take an interest in your theaters? Is it in heinous crimes that you take pleasure? Is it to their authors when they are punished that you give your tears? It is said that we are indifferent to everything outside of our interest; but, all to the contrary, the sweetness of friendship and of humanity consoles us in our suffering; even in our pleasures we would be too alone, too miserable, if we had no one with whom to share them. If there is nothing moral in the heart of man, what is the source of these transports of admiration for heroic actions, these raptures of love for great souls? What relation does this enthusiasm for virtue have to our private interest? Why would I want to be Cato,[9] who disembowels himself, rather than Caesar triumphant? Take this love of the beautiful from our hearts, and you take all the charm from life. He whose vile passions have stifled these delicious sentiments in his narrow soul, and who, by dint of self-centeredness, succeeds in loving only himself, has no more transports. His icy heart no longer palpitates with joy; a sweet tenderness never moistens his eyes; he has no more joy in anything. This unfortunate man no longer feels, no longer lives. He is already dead.

But however numerous the wicked are on the earth, there are few of these cadaverous souls who have become insensitive, except where their own interest is at stake, to everything which is just and good. Iniquity pleases only to the extent one profits from it; in all the rest one wants the innocent to be protected. One sees some act of violence and injustice in the street or on the road. Instantly an emotion of anger and indignation is aroused in the depths of the heart, and it leads us to take up the defense of the oppressed; but a more powerful duty restrains us, and the laws take from us the right of protecting innocence. On the other hand, if some act of clemency or generosity strikes our eyes, what admiration, what love it inspires in us! Who does not say to himself, "I would like to have done the same"? It is surely of very little importance to us that a man was wicked or just two thousand years ago; nevertheless, we take an interest in ancient history just as if it all had taken place in our day. What do Catiline's crimes[10] do to me? Am I afraid of being his victim? Why, then, am I as horrified by him as if he were my contemporary? We do not hate the wicked only because they do us harm, but because they are wicked. Not only do we want to be happy; we also wish for the happiness of others. And when this happiness does not come at the expense of our own, it increases it. Finally, in spite of oneself, one pities the unfortunate; when we are witness to their ills, we suffer from them. The most perverse are unable to lose this inclination entirely. Often it puts them in contradiction with themselves. The robber who plunders passers-by still covers the nakedness of the poor, and the most ferocious killer supports a fainting man.

We speak of the cry of remorse which in secret punishes hidden crimes and so often brings them to light. Alas, who of us has never heard this importunate voice? We speak from experience, and we would like to stifle this tyrannical sentiment that gives us so much torment. Let us obey nature. We shall know with what gentleness it reigns, and what charm one finds, after having hearkened to it, in giving favorable testimony on our own behalf. The wicked man fears and flees himself. He cheers himself up by rushing outside of himself. His restless eyes rove around him and seek an object that is entertaining to him. Without bitter satire, without insulting banter, he would always be sad. The mocking laugh is his only pleasure. By contrast, the serenity of the just man is internal. His is not a malignant laugh but a joyous one; he bears its source in himself. He is as gay alone as in the midst of a circle. He does not draw his contentment from those who come near him; he communicates it to them.

Cast your eyes on all the nations of the world, go through all the histories. Among so many inhuman and bizarre cults, among this prodigious diversity of morals and characters, you will find everywhere the same ideas of justice and decency, everywhere the same notions of good and bad. Ancient paganism gave birth to abominable gods who would have been punished on earth as villains and who presented a picture of supreme happiness consisting only of heinous crimes to commit and passions to satisfy. But vice, armed with a sacred authority, descended in vain from the eternal abode; moral instinct repulsed it from the heart of human beings. While celebrating Jupiter's debauches, they admired Xenocrates' continence.[11] The chaste Lucretia[12] worshiped the lewd Venus. The intrepid Roman sacrificed to fear. He invoked the god who mutilated his father, and he himself died without a murmur at his own father's hand. The most contemptible divinities were served by the greatest men. The holy voice of nature, stronger than that of the gods, made itself respected on earth and seemed to relegate crime, along with the guilty, to heaven.

There is in the depths of souls, then, an innate principle of justice and virtue according to which, in spite of our own maxims, we judge our actions and those of others as good or bad. It is to this principle that I give the name *conscience.*

But at this word I hear the clamor of those who are allegedly wise rising on all sides: errors of childhood, prejudices of education, they all cry in a chorus. Nothing exists in the human mind other than what is introduced by experience, and we judge a thing on no ground other than that of acquired ideas. They go farther. They dare to reject this evident and universal accord of all nations. And in the face of this striking uniformity in men's judgment, they go and look in the shadows for some obscure example known to them alone – as if all the inclinations of nature were annihilated by the depravity of a single people, and the species were no longer anything as soon as there are monsters. But what is the use of the torments to which the skeptic Montaigne[13] subjects himself in order to unearth in some corner of the world a custom opposed to the notions of justice? Of what use is it to him to give to the most suspect travelers the authority he refuses to give to the most celebrated writers? Will some uncertain and bizarre practices, based on local causes unknown to us, destroy the general induction drawn from the concurrence of all peoples, who disagree about everything else and agree on this point alone? O Montaigne, you who pride yourself on frankness and truth, be sincere and true, if a philosopher can be, and tell me whether there is some country on earth where it is a crime to keep one's faith, to be clement, beneficent, and generous, where the good man is contemptible and the perfidious one honored?

It is said that everyone contributes to the public good for his own interest. But what then is the source of the just man's contributing to it to his prejudice? What is going to one's death for one's interest? No doubt, no one acts for anything other than for his good; but if there is not a moral good which must be taken into account, one will never explain by private interest anything but the action of the wicked. It is not even likely that anyone will attempt to go farther. This would be too abominable a philosophy – one which is embarrassed by virtuous actions, which could get around the difficulty only by fabricating base intentions and motives without virtue, which would be forced to vilify Socrates and calumniate Regulus.[14] If ever such doctrines could spring up among us, the voice of nature as well as that of reason would immediately be raised against them and would never leave a single one of their partisans the excuse that he is of good faith.

It is not my design here to enter into metaphysical discussions which are out of my reach and yours, and which, at bottom, lead to nothing. I have already told you that I wanted not to philosophize with you but to help you consult your heart. Were all the philosophers to prove that I am wrong, if you sense that I am right, I do not wish for more.

For that purpose I need only to make you distinguish our acquired ideas from our natural sentiments; for we sense before knowing, and since we do not learn to want what is good for us and to flee what is bad for us but rather get this will from nature, by that very fact love of the good and hatred of the bad are as natural as the love of ourselves. The acts of the conscience are not judgments but sentiments. Although all our ideas come to us from outside, the sentiments evaluating them are within us, and it is by them alone that we know the compatibility or incompatibility between us and the things we ought to seek or flee.

To exist, for us, is to sense; our sensibility is incontestably anterior to our intelligence, and we had sentiments before ideas. Whatever the cause of our being, it has provided for our preservation by giving us sentiments suitable to our nature, and it could not be denied that these, at least, are innate. These sentiments, as far as the individual is concerned, are the love of self, the fear of pain, the horror of death, the desire of well-being. But if, as cannot be doubted, man is by his nature sociable, or at least made to become so, he can be so only by means of other innate sentiments relative to his species; for if we consider only physical need, it ought certainly to disperse men instead of bringing them together. It is from the moral system formed by this double relation to oneself and to one's fellows that the impulse of conscience is born. To know the good is not to love it; man does not have innate knowledge of it, but as soon as his reason makes him know it, his conscience leads him to love it. It is this sentiment which is innate.

Thus I do not believe, my friend, that it is impossible to explain, by the consequences of our nature, the immediate principle of the conscience independently of reason itself. And were that impossible, it would moreover not be necessary; for, those who deny this principle, admitted and recognized by all mankind, do not prove that it does not exist but are satisfied by affirming that it does not; so when we affirm that it does exist, we are just as well founded as they are, and we have in addition the inner witness and the voice of conscience, which testifies on its own behalf. If the first glimmers of judgment dazzle us and at first make a blur of objects in our sight, let us wait for our weak eyes to open up again and steady themselves, and soon we shall see these same objects again in the light of reason as nature first showed them to us. Or, rather, let us be more simple and less vain. Let us limit ourselves to the first sentiments that we find in ourselves, since study always leads us back to them when it has not led us astray.

Conscience, conscience! Divine instinct, immortal and celestial voice, certain guide of a being that is ignorant and limited but intelligent and free; infallible judge of good and bad which makes man like unto God; it is you who make the excellence of his nature and the morality of his actions. Without you I sense nothing in me that raises me above the beasts, other than the sad privilege of leading myself astray from error to error with the aid of an understanding without rule and a reason without principle.

Thank heaven, we are delivered from all that terrifying apparatus of philosophy. We can be men without being scholars. Dispensed from consuming our life in the study of morality, we have at less expense a more certain guide in this immense maze of human opinions. But it is not enough that this guide exists; one must know how to recognize it and to follow it. If it speaks to all hearts, then why are there so few of them who hear it? Well, this is because it speaks to us in nature's language, which everything has made us forget. Conscience is timid; it likes refuge and peace. The world and noise scare it; the prejudices from which they claim it is born are its cruelest enemies. It flees or keeps quiet before them. Their noisy voices stifle its voice and prevent it from making itself heard. Fanaticism dares to counterfeit it and to dictate crime in its name. It finally gives up as a result of being dismissed. It no longer speaks to us. It no longer responds to us. And after such long contempt for it, to recall it costs as much as banishing it did.

How many times in my researches have I grown weary as a result of the coldness I felt within me! How many times have sadness and boredom, spreading their poison over my first meditations, made them unbearable for me! My arid heart provided only a languid and lukewarm zeal to the love of truth. I said to myself, "Why torment myself in seeking what is not? Moral good is only a chimera. There is nothing good but the pleasures of the senses." O, when one has once lost the taste for the pleasures of the soul, how difficult it is to regain it! How much more difficult gaining it is when one has never had it! If there existed a man miserable enough to be unable to recall anything he had done in all his life which made him satisfied with himself and glad to have lived, that man would be incapable of ever knowing himself; and for want of feeling the goodness suitable to his nature, he would necessarily remain wicked and be eternally unhappy. But do you believe there is a single man on the whole earth depraved enough never to have yielded in his heart to the temptation of doing good? This temptation is so natural and so sweet that it is impossible always to resist it, and the memory of the pleasure that it once produced suffices to recall it constantly. Unfortunately it is at first hard to satisfy. One has countless reasons to reject the inclination of one's heart. False prudence confines it within the limits of the human *I*; countless efforts of courage are needed to dare to cross those limits. To enjoy doing good is the reward for having done good, and this reward is obtained only after having deserved it. Nothing is more lovable than virtue, but one must possess it to find it so. Virtue is similar to Proteus in the fable: when one wants to embrace it, it at first takes on countless terrifying forms and finally reveals itself in its own form only to those who did not let go. . . .

I shall never be able to conceive that what every man is obliged to know is confined to books, and that someone who does not have access to these books, or to those who understand them, is punished for an ignorance which is involuntary. Always books! What a mania. Because Europe is full of books, Europeans regard them as indispensable, without thinking that in three-quarters of the earth they have never been seen. Were not all books written by men? Why, then, would man need them to know his duties, and what means had he of knowing them before these books were written? Either he will learn these duties by himself, or he is excused from knowing them.

Editor's Notes

1. For Hobbes, see Part I of this anthology. Hobbes did not draw the conclusion that Rousseau here attributes to him.
2. For Mandeville, see Part III of this anthology.
3. Rousseau here turned to a discussion of sexuality, distinguishing the physical from the moral in the feeling of love. Physical desire is common to us all; the moral aspect of love is a cultural artifact that functions to focus physical desire on one person. It uses notions of beauty that the savage does not have; hence imagination does not stir him, and his passions are much cooler than those of civilized men. It is only in society that love or sexual desire leads men to fight. The fact that male animals fight over females is due to biological facts about their breeding cycles that do not apply to humans. Hence sexuality does not disprove Rousseau's thesis concerning the state of nature.
4. Ovid, *Metamorphoses*, XI, pp. 127ff.
5. The original French can be translated as either "Man *is* born free" or "Man *was* born free," and the translator signals this important ambiguity in the translation.
6. For Grotius, see Part I of this anthology. Grotius did not think that slavery is prohibited by the laws of nature.
7. Aristotle, *Politics*, I.ii, 1252a; I.v–vi, 1254a–1255b.
8. Rousseau was referring to a dialogue by Plutarch, in which one of Ulysses' companions, turned into an animal by Circe, argues that animals' souls are more disposed to virtue than human souls are.
9. Cato of Utica (95–46 B.C.E.), often held up as a model of how the Stoic sage should live, committed suicide when faced with political defeat.

10. Catiline, in the first century B.C.E., tried to start a revolution in order to save his own fortunes.
11. Xenocrates was a philosopher, a late leader of the Platonic Academy in Athens.
12. Lucretia, wife of a Roman leader, was raped, told her husband, and then committed suicide.
13. For Montaigne, see the Prolegomena to this anthology.
14. Captured by Rome's enemies, Regulus was allowed to go to Rome to seek the city's surrender. He went, advised the Romans to continue to fight, returned to his captors, and was put to death.

Further Reading

Rousseau's works are readily available in many translations. The best edition in French is that edited by Bernard Gagnebin and Marcel Reymond, *Oeuvres Complètes* (Paris: Bibliothèque de la Pléiade), four volumes of which have been published.

Several good biographical studies of Rousseau are available, among them F. C. Green, *J. J. Rousseau* (Cambridge, England: Cambridge University Press, 1955); and James Miller, *Rousseau, Dreamer of Democracy* (New Haven, Conn.: Yale University Press, 1984).

There is much difference of opinion about the proper interpretation of Rousseau's thought. A good place to begin is N. J. H. Dent, *Rousseau* (Oxford: Blackwell Publisher, 1988), which concentrates on making philosophical sense of the texts from which excerpts are given in this book. David Gauthier, "The Politics of Redemption," in J. MacAdam, M. Neumann, and G. Lafrance, *Trent Rousseau Papers, Revue de l'Université de Ottawa* 49 (1980), also gives a convincing systematic reconstruction of Rousseau's philosophy, which the reader may wish to compare with Dent's. Ronald Grimsley, *The Philosophy of Rousseau* (Oxford: Oxford University Press, 1973), is a good introduction. Judith Shklar, *Men and Citizens: A Study of Rousseau's Social Theory* (Cambridge, England: Cambridge University Press, 1969), is a fine study with a chapter on Rousseau's moral psychology. John Charvet, *The Social Problem in the Philosophy of Rousseau* (Cambridge, England: Cambridge University Press, 1974), is brief and rather critical of Rousseau. Roger D. Masters, *The Political Philosophy of Rousseau* (Princeton, N.J.: Princeton University Press, 1968), is a comprehensive review of its subject, and C. W. Hendel, *Jean-Jacques Rousseau: Moralist*, 2nd ed. (Indianapolis: Bobbs-Merrill, 1962), a study of Rousseau's development, covers all of his work concerning the individual and society.

Patrick Riley, *The General Will Before Rousseau* (Princeton, N.J.: Princeton University Press, 1986), discusses the prehistory of one of Rousseau's central ideas. Rousseau figures largely in two volumes by Lester Crocker: *An Age of Crisis, Man and World in Eighteenth Century French Thought* (Baltimore: Johns Hopkins University Press, 1959), and *Nature and Culture, Ethical Thought in the French Enlightenment* (Baltimore: Johns Hopkins University Press, 1963). The reader will need to consult the index in each volume to find the specific places where Rousseau is discussed.

Thomas Reid

Introduction

Reid was one of the creators of the Scottish Enlightenment. Born in 1710, he was a younger contemporary of Hutcheson's, a year older than Hume and a dozen years older than Adam Smith, but he outlived them all. We are apt to forget his close intellectual and personal connections with many of these figures, because he published his major works very late in his life. Reid studied in Aberdeen, was ordained in the Presbyterian church in 1731, and from 1737 until 1751 served as parish minister in the small town of New Machar. Thereafter he was a university professor, first at King's College, Aberdeen, and from 1764 on at Glasgow. His *Inquiry into the Human Mind on the Principles of Common Sense* (1764) is an epistemological study, directed against Hume, of the nature of sensation and its role in our perception of the external world. Throughout his career Reid was actively involved in various societies of intellectuals and literary men trying to cope with Scotland's economic and social problems. An effective and conscientious teacher, he published after his retirement in 1780 much of the material from one course that he regularly gave as *Essays on the Intellectual Powers of Man* in 1785 and material from another as *Essays on the Active Powers of the Human Mind* in 1788. He died in 1796.

Unlike any of the other philosophers of the Scottish Enlightenment, Reid became the founder of a school. A number of Scottish thinkers from the end of the eighteenth until the middle of the nineteenth century carried forward Reid's views in Britain. For several decades after his death, he had enthusiastic disciples in France. And in the United States his philosophy of common sense became almost an orthodoxy in eastern universities, holding sway for half a century or more.

It was as a critic of Hume (admired by Hume himself) that Reid made his first major appearance in print, and it was as a critic of Hume that he was chiefly remembered for a long time. Hume's fatal misstep in epistemology, Reid held, was one he was not alone in taking. It had been taken by Descartes and by just about every other philosopher since then. The error lay in believing that in perception we are immediately aware only of something – sensations, impressions, or, as Reid usually said, ideas – in our own mind. Ideas are supposed to "represent" external objects, but that thesis cannot be defended, for we cannot get outside or beyond the ideas to compare them with what they are supposed to represent. Consequently, we cannot support any claim to knowledge of what is past, future, or even present, beyond the content of our immediate awareness. Hume, Reid thought, was the first to see the full consequences of this theory of perception, though Berkeley had drawn some of the drastic conclusions it entails. In his *Intellectual Powers,* accordingly, Reid went to great lengths to attack the representative theory of perception and to replace it with a view according to which, although sensation does indeed play a role in giving us knowledge of the external world, so does a rational faculty of judgment.

The judgments involved are themselves direct and untaught. Sensations serve as natural signs. Our ability to understand them reflects our possession of principles that enable us to know what the signs mean and thereby to acquire knowledge of the external world. These are the principles of common sense concerning matters of fact. They can be stated with more or less precision, but the only defense they need or can be given is to show that attacks on them, such as Hume's, rest on untenable presuppositions. Because they are first or ultimate principles, all reasoned argument rests on them, and no positive proof is to be expected.

One of Hume's errors regarding morals, Reid believed, was akin to his basic error regarding knowledge: He reduced moral judgments to feelings within the agent, thus denying them any objective standing. In reply, Reid produced the earliest version of some now well-known arguments against the "subjectivist" interpretation of the meaning of moral language. He also went beyond criticizing Hume on the meaning of moral terms. Avowedly an admirer of Bishop Butler's, Reid gave a far fuller exposition of the kind of position Butler sketched, filling in details about the standing and the content of moral principles as well as about the moral psychology needed to sustain the position.

Butler had not made a decisive response to the question of whether or not morality lies within the domain of knowledge, but Reid, like Price, clearly opted for a positive answer. The first principles of morals, he claimed, are self-evident, as are the first principles of theoretical knowledge. Ordinary people know them and are able to apply them. Like Butler, Reid did not think they could be reduced to any single principle. He offered a list of them, not because his readers need the list as moral agents but because spelling out what everyone will find obvious is part of the defense of the claim that the principles really are self-evident.

Butler had said little about free will and moral motivation; in Essay IV of his *Essays on the Active Powers,* Reid gave a defense (which there is insufficient space to include here) of the commonsense belief in free will and sketched a psychology according to which we can be moved to act simply by recognizing the validity of moral principles. Reid abandoned the age-old view that if we are not moved to pursue what seems to us to be good, we are either perverse or irrational. He held that we can be moved to act as moral principles require, simply because we see them to be binding on us as rational agents and not because we see the good that complying with them will bring about or because we fear punishment if we fail to comply.

Reid thus believed that it is consonant with common sense to portray us as fully capable of self-direction and self-motivation in morality. He did not think this was in any way incompatible with the teachings of Christianity. (Reid was a devout Christian.) Although the point is not stressed in his writings, the belief that we were made by the Christian God lies behind Reid's general reliance on human cognitive capacities. His confidence that there can be no conflict between the principle that one ought to be concerned for one's own good on the whole and the principles requiring us to be concerned for justice and the good of others rests in the end on the belief that God made the moral world as harmonious as he made the physical world. And Reid's belief in our competence as moral agents was also in keeping with his understanding of his faith. God will hold us each accountable for acting as morality requires. Reid observed that God must therefore have made it possible for us each to know, without any theory, what those requirements are and to act accordingly. In his view we are being responsive to God's highest demand on us when we choose freely to do what we see for ourselves to be right. Reid worked out one of the clearest and most influential portrayals of moral autonomy to emerge in the eighteenth century, in order to show how it is that we can be what God wishes us to be.

The following excerpts are from the *Essays on the Active Powers of the Human Mind*. I have eliminated some of the italicization of the early editions.

Essays on the Active Powers of the Human Mind

Essay II: Of the Will

Chapter II: Of the Influence of Incitements and Motives upon the Will

Thus, I think, it appears, that the common sense of men, which, in matters of common life, ought to have great authority, has led them to distinguish two parts in the human constitution, which have influence upon our voluntary determinations. There is an irrational part, common to us with brute animals, consisting of appetites, affections, and passions; and there is a cool and rational part. The first, in many cases, gives a strong impulse, but without judgment, and without authority. The second is always accompanied with authority. All wisdom and virtue consist in following its dictates; all vice and folly in disobeying them. We may resist the impulses of appetite and passion, not only without regret, but with self-applause and triumph; but the calls of reason and duty can never be resisted, without remorse and self-condemnation. . . .

The reason of explaining this distinction here is, that these two principles influence the will in different ways. Their influence differs, not in degree only, but in kind. This difference we feel, though it may be difficult to find words to express it. We may perhaps more easily form a notion of it by a similitude.

It is one thing to push a man from one part of the room to another; it is a thing of a very different nature to use arguments to persuade him to leave his place, and go to another. He may yield to the force which pushes him, without any exercise of his rational faculties; nay, he must yield to it, if he do not oppose an equal or a greater force. His liberty is impaired in some degree; and, if he has not power sufficient to oppose, his liberty is quite taken away, and the motion cannot be imputed to him at all. The influence of appetite or passion seems to me to be very like to this. If the passion be supposed irresistible, we impute the action to it solely, and not to the man. If he had power to resist, but yields after a struggle, we impute the action, partly to the man, and partly to the passion.

If we attend to the other case, when the man is only urged by arguments to leave his place, this resembles the operation of the cool or rational principle. It is evident, that, whether he yields to the arguments or not, the determination is wholly his own act, and is entirely to be imputed to him. Arguments, whatever be the degree of their strength, diminish not a man's liberty; they may produce a cool conviction of what we ought to do, and they can do no more. But appetite and passion give an impulse to act and impair liberty, in proportion to their strength.

With most men, the impulse of passion is more effectual than bare conviction; and, on this account, orators, who would persuade, find it necessary to address the passions, as well as to convince the understanding; and, in all systems of rhetoric, these two have been considered as different intentions of the orator, and to be accomplished by different means.

ESSAY III: OF THE PRINCIPLES OF ACTION

Part III: Of the Rational Principles of Action

Chapter I: There are rational principles of action in man

. . . Whatever we believe, we think agreeable to reason, and, on that account, yield our assent to it. Whatever we disbelieve, we think contrary to reason, and, on that account, dissent from it. Reason therefore is allowed to be the principle by which our belief and opinions ought to be regulated.

But reason has been no less universally conceived to be a principle, by which our actions ought to be regulated.

To act reasonably, is a phrase no less common in all languages, than to judge reasonably. We immediately approve of a man's conduct, when it appears that he had good reason for what he did. And every action we disapprove, we think unreasonable, or contrary to reason.

A way of speaking so universal among men, common to the learned and the unlearned in all nations, and in all languages, must have a meaning. To suppose it to be words without meaning, is to treat, with undue contempt, the common sense of mankind.

Suppose this phrase to have a meaning, we may consider in what way reason may serve to regulate human conduct, so that some actions of men are to be denominated reasonable, and others unreasonable.

I take it for granted, that there can be no exercise of reason without judgment, nor, on the other hand, any judgment of things abstract and general, without some degree of reason.

If, therefore, there be any principles of action in the human constitution, which, in their nature, necessarily imply such judgment, they are the principles which we may call rational, to distinguish them from animal principles, which imply desire, and will, but not judgment.

Every deliberate human action must be done either as the means, or as an end; as the means to some end, to which it is subservient, or as an end, for its own sake, and without regard to any thing beyond it.

That it is a part of the office of reason to determine, what are the proper means to any end which we desire, no man ever denied. But some philosophers, particularly Mr. Hume, think that it is no part of the office of reason to determine the ends we ought to pursue, or the preference due to one end above another. This, he thinks, is not the office of reason, but of taste or feeling.

If this be so, reason cannot, with any propriety, be called a principle of action. Its office can only be to minister to the principles of action, by discovering the means of their gratification. Accordingly, Mr. Hume maintains, that reason is no principle of action; but that it is, and ought to be, the servant of the passions.[1]

I shall endeavour to show, that, among the various ends of human actions, there are some, of which, without reason, we could not even form a conception; and that, as soon as they are conceived, a regard to them is, by our constitution, not only a principle of action, but a leading and governing principle, to which all our animal principles are subordinate, and to which they ought to be subject.

These I shall call *rational* principles; because they can exist only in beings endowed with reason, and because, to act from these principles, is what has always been meant by acting according to reason.

The ends of human actions I have in view, are two, to wit, what is good for us upon the whole, and what appears to be our duty. They are very strictly connected, lead to the same course of conduct, and co-operate with each other; and, on that account, have commonly been comprehended under one name, that of *reason*. But as they may be disjoined, and are really distinct principles of action, I shall consider them separately.

Chapter II: Of regard to our good on the whole

It will not be denied, that man, when he comes to years of understanding, is led by his rational nature, to form the conception of what is good for him upon the whole.

How early in life this general notion of good enters into the mind, I cannot pretend to determine. It is one of the most general and abstract notions we form.

Whatever makes a man more happy, or more perfect, is good, and is an object of desire as soon as we are capable of forming the conception of it. The contrary is ill, and is an object of aversion. . . .

That which, taken with all its discoverable connections and consequences, brings more good than ill, I call *good upon the whole.*

That brute animals have any conception of this good, I see no reason to believe. And it is evident, that man cannot have the conception of it, till reason be so far advanced, that he can seriously reflect upon the past, and take a prospect of the future part of his existence.

It appears therefore, that the very conception of what is good or ill for us upon the whole, is the offspring of reason, and can be only in beings endowed with reason. And if this conception give rise to any principle of action in man, which he had not before, that principle may very properly be called a rational principle of action. . . .

I observe, in the *next* place, that as soon as we have the conception of what is good or ill for us upon the whole, we are led, by our constitution, to seek the good and avoid the ill; and this becomes, not only a principle of action, but a leading or governing principle, to which all our animal principles ought to be subordinate. . . .

To prefer a greater good, though distant, to a less that is present; to choose a present evil, in order to avoid a greater evil, or to obtain a greater good, is, in the judgment of all men, wise and reasonable conduct; and, when a man acts the contrary part, all men will acknowledge, that he acts foolishly and unreasonably. . . .

Thus, I think, it appears, that to pursue what is good upon the whole, and to avoid what is ill upon the whole, is a rational principle of action, grounded upon our constitution as reasonable creatures. . . .

Chapter V: Of the notion of duty, rectitude, moral obligation

A being endowed with the animal principles of action only, may be capable of being trained to certain purposes by discipline, as we see many brute animals are, but would be altogether incapable of being governed by law.

The subject of law must have the conception of a general rule of conduct, which, without some degree of reason, he cannot have. He must likewise have a sufficient inducement to obey the law, even when his strongest animal desires draw him the contrary way.

This inducement may be a sense of interest, or a sense of duty, or both concurring.

These are the only principles I am able to conceive which can reasonably induce a man to regulate all his actions according to a certain general rule, or law. They may therefore be justly called the *rational* principles of action, since they can have no place but in a being endowed with reason, and since it is by them only, that man is capable either of political or of moral government.

. . . there is a nobler principle[2] in the constitution of man, which, in many cases, gives a clearer and more certain rule of conduct, than a regard merely to interest would give, and a principle, without which man would not be a moral agent.

A man is prudent when he consults his real interest, but he cannot be virtuous, if he has no regard to duty.

I proceed now to consider this regard to duty as a rational principle of action in man, and as that principle alone by which he is capable either of virtue or vice.

I shall first offer some observations with regard to the general notion of duty, and its contrary, or of right and wrong in human conduct; and then consider how we come to judge and determine certain things in human conduct to be right, and others to be wrong.

With regard to the notion or conception of duty, I take it to be too simple to admit of a logical definition.

We can define it only by synonymous words or phrases, or by its properties and necessary concomitants; as when we say that it is what we ought to do, what is fair and honest, what is approvable, what every man professes to be the rule of his conduct, what all men praise, and what is in itself laudable, though no man should praise it.

I observe, in the *next* place, that the notion of duty cannot be resolved into that of interest, or what is most for our happiness.

Every man may be satisfied of this who attends to his own conceptions, and the language of all mankind shows it. When I say this is my interest, I mean one thing; when I say it is my duty, I mean another thing. And though the same course of action, when rightly understood, may be both my duty and my interest, the conceptions are very different. Both are reasonable motives to action, but quite distinct in their nature.

I presume it will be granted, that in every man of real worth, there is a principle of honor, a regard to what is honorable or dishonorable, very distinct from a regard to his interest. It is folly in a man to disregard his interest, but to do what is dishonorable is baseness. The first may move our pity, or, in some cases, our contempt, but the last provokes our indignation.

As these two principles are different in their nature, and not resolvable into one, so the principle of honor is evidently superior in dignity to that of interest.

No man would allow him to be a man of honor, who should plead his interest to justify what he acknowledged to be dishonorable; but to sacrifice interest to honor never costs a blush.

It likewise will be allowed by every man of honor, that this principle is not to be resolved into a regard to our reputation among men, otherwise the man of honor would not deserve to be trusted in the dark. He would have no aversion to lie, or cheat, or play the coward, when he had no dread of being discovered.

I take it for granted, therefore, that every man of real honor feels an abhorrence of certain actions, because they are in themselves base, and feels an obligation to certain other actions, because they are in themselves what honor requires, and this, independently of any consideration of interest or reputation.

This is an immediate moral obligation. This principle of honor, which is acknowledged by all men who pretend to character, is only another name for what we call a regard to duty, to rectitude, to propriety of conduct.[3] It is a moral obligation which obliges a man to do certain things because they are right, and not to do other things because they are wrong.

Ask the man of honor, why he thinks himself obliged to pay a debt of honor? The very question shocks him. To suppose that he needs any other inducement to do it but the principle of honor, is to suppose that he has no honor, no worth, and deserves no esteem.

There is therefore a principle in man, which, when he acts according to it, gives him a consciousness of worth, and when he acts contrary to it, a sense of demerit.

From the varieties of education, of fashion, of prejudices, and of habits, men may differ much in opinion with regard to the extent of this principle, and of what it commands and forbids; but the notion of it, as far as it is carried, is the same in all. It is that which gives a man real worth, and is the object of moral approbation. . . .

All the ancient sects, except the Epicureans, distinguished the *honestum* from the *utile*,[4] as we distinguish what is a man's duty from what is his interest. . . .

This division of our active principles can hardly indeed be accounted a discovery of philosophy, because it has been common to the unlearned in all ages of the world, and seems to be dictated by the common sense of mankind.

What I would now observe concerning this common division of our active powers, is, that the leading principle, which is called *reason*, comprehends both a regard to what is right and honorable, and a regard to our happiness upon the whole.

Although these be really two distinct principles of action, it is very natural to comprehend them under one name, because both are leading principles, both suppose the use of reason, and, when rightly understood, both lead to the same course of life. They are like two fountains whose streams unite and run in the same channel.

When a man, on one occasion, consults his real happiness in things not inconsistent with his duty, though in opposition to the solicitation of appetite or passion; and when, on another occasion, without any selfish consideration, he does what is right and honorable, because it is so; in both these cases he acts reasonably; every man approves of his conduct, and calls it reasonable, or according to reason.

So that, when we speak of reason as a principle of action in man, it includes a regard both to the *honestum* and to the *utile*. . . .

If we examine the abstract notion of duty, or moral obligation, it appears to be neither any real quality of the action considered by itself, nor of the agent considered without respect to the action, but a certain relation between the one and the other.

When we say a man ought to do such a thing, the *ought,* which expresses the moral obligation, has a respect, on the one hand, to the person who ought, and, on the other, to the action which he ought to do. Those two correlates are essential to every moral obligation; take away either, and it has no existence. So that, if we seek the place of moral obligation among the categories, it belongs to the category of *relation*.

There are many relations of things, of which we have the most distinct conception, without being able to define them logically. Equality and proportion are relations between quantities, which every man understands, but no man can define.

Moral obligation is a relation of its own kind, which every man understands, but is perhaps too simple to admit of logical definition. Like all other relations, it may be changed or annihilated by a change in any of the two related things, I mean the agent or the action. . . .

Chapter VI: Of the sense of duty

We are next to consider, how we learn to judge and determine, that this is right, and that is wrong.

The abstract notion of moral good and ill would be of no use to direct our life, if we had not the power of applying it to particular actions, and determining what is morally good, and what is morally ill.

Some philosophers, with whom I agree, ascribe this to an original power or faculty in man, which they call the moral *sense,* the moral *faculty, conscience.* Others think, that our moral sentiments may be accounted for without supposing any original sense or faculty appropriated to that purpose, and go into very different systems to account for them.

I am not, at present, to take any notice of those systems, because the opinion first mentioned seems to me to be the truth, to wit, that, by an original power of the mind, when we come to years of understanding and reflection, we not only have the notions of right and wrong in conduct, but perceive certain things to be right, and others to be wrong.

The name of the *moral sense,* though more frequently given to conscience since lord Shaftesbury and Dr. Hutcheson wrote, is not new. The *sensus recti et honesti* is a phrase not unfrequent among the ancients, neither is the *sense of duty* among us.

It has got this name of *sense,* no doubt, from some analogy which it is conceived to bear to the external senses. And if we have just notions of the office of the external senses, the analogy is very evident, and I see no reason to take offence, as some have done, at the name of the *moral sense.*

The offence taken at this name seems to be owing to this, that philosophers have degraded the senses too much, and deprived them of the most important part of their office.

We are taught, that by the senses, we have only certain ideas which we could not have otherwise. They are represented as powers by which we have sensations and ideas, not as powers by which we judge.

This notion of the senses I take to be very lame, and to contradict what nature and accurate reflection teach concerning them.[5]

A man who has totally lost the sense of seeing, may retain very distinct notions of the various colours; but he cannot judge of colours, because he has lost the sense by which alone he could judge. By my eyes I not only have the ideas of a square and a circle, but I perceive this surface to be a square, that to be a circle.

By my ear, I not only have the idea of sounds, loud and soft, acute and grave, but I immediately perceive and judge this sound to be loud, that to be soft, this to be acute, that to be grave. Two or more synchronous sounds I perceive to be concordant, others to be discordant.

These are judgments of the senses. They have always been called and accounted such, by those whose minds are not tinctured by philosophical theories. They are the immediate testimony of nature by our senses; and we are so constituted by nature, that we must receive their testimony, for no other reason but because it is given by our senses.

In vain do skeptics endeavour to overturn this evidence by metaphysical reasoning. Though we should not be able to answer their arguments, we believe our senses still, and rest our most important concerns upon their testimony.

If this be a just notion of our external senses, as I conceive it is, our moral faculty may, I think, without impropriety, be called the *moral sense.*

In its dignity it is, without doubt, far superior to every other power of the mind; but there is this analogy between it and the external senses, that, as by them we have not only the original conceptions of the various qualities of bodies, but the original judgments that this body has such a quality, that such another; so by our moral faculty, we have both the original conceptions of right and wrong in conduct, of merit and demerit, and the original judgments that this conduct is right, that is wrong; that this character has worth, that, demerit.

The testimony of our moral faculty, like that of the external senses, is the testimony of nature, and we have the same reason to rely upon it.

The truths immediately testified by the external senses are the first principles from which we reason, with regard to the material world, and from which all our knowledge of it is deduced.

The truths immediately testified by our moral faculty, are the first principles of all moral reasoning, from which all our knowledge of our duty must be deduced. . . .

All reasoning must be grounded on first principles. This holds in moral reasoning, as in all other kinds. There must therefore be in morals, as in all other sciences, first or self-evident principles, on which all moral reasoning is grounded, and on which it ultimately rests. From such self-evident principles, conclusions may be drawn synthetically with regard to the moral conduct of life; and particular duties or virtues may be traced back to such principles, analytically. But, without such principles, we can no more establish any conclusions in morals, than we can build a castle in the air, without any foundation.

An example or two will serve to illustrate this.

It is a first principle in morals, that we ought not to do to another, what we should think wrong to be done to us in like circumstances. If a man is not capable of perceiving this in his cool moments, when he reflects seriously, he is not a moral agent, nor is he capable of being convinced of it by reasoning.

From what topic can you reason with such a man? You may possibly convince him by reasoning, that it is his interest to observe this rule; but this is not to convince him that it is his duty. To reason about justice with a man who sees nothing to be just or unjust; or about benevolence with a man who sees nothing in benevolence preferable to malice, is like reasoning with a blind man about colour, or with a deaf man about sound. . . .

Thus we shall find that all moral reasonings rest upon one or more first principles of morals, whose truth is immediately perceived without reasoning, by all men come to years of understanding.

And this indeed is common to every branch of human knowledge that deserves the name of science. There must be first principles proper to that science, by which the whole superstructure is supported.

The first principles of all the sciences, must be the immediate dictates of our natural faculties; nor is it possible that we should have any other evidence of their truth. And in different sciences the faculties which dictate their first principles are very different. . . .

The faculties which nature has given us, are the only engines we can use to find out the truth. We cannot indeed prove that those faculties are not fallacious, unless God should give us new faculties to sit in judgment upon the old. But we are born under a necessity of trusting them.

Every man in his senses believes his eyes, his ears, and his other senses. He believes his consciousness, with respect to his own thoughts and purposes, his memory, with regard to what is past, his understanding, with regard to abstract relations of things, and his taste, with regard to what is elegant and beautiful. And he has the same reason, and, indeed, is under the same necessity of believing the clear and unbiassed dictates of his conscience, with regard to what is honorable and what is base. . . .

Chapter VII: Of moral approbation and disapprobation

Our moral judgments are not, like those we form in speculative matters, dry and unaffecting, but from their nature, are necessarily accompanied with affections and feelings; which we are now to consider.

It was before observed, that every human action, considered in a moral view, appears to us good, or bad, or indifferent. When we judge the action to be indifferent, neither good nor bad, though this be a moral judgment, it produces no affection nor feeling, any more than our judgments in speculative matters.

But we approve of good actions, and disapprove of bad; and this approbation and disapprobation, when we analyze it, appears to include, not only a moral judgment of the action, but some affection, favourable or unfavourable, toward the agent, and some feeling in ourselves.

Nothing is more evident than this, that moral worth, even in a stranger, with whom we have not the least connection, never fails to produce some degree of esteem mixed with good will.

The esteem which we have for a man on account of his moral worth, is different from that which is grounded upon his intellectual accomplishments, his birth, fortune, and connection with us.

Moral worth, when it is not set off by eminent abilities, and external advantages, is like a diamond in the mine, which is rough and unpolished, and perhaps crusted over with some baser material that takes away its lustre.

But, when it is attended with these advantages, it is like a diamond cut, polished, and set. Then its lustre attracts every eye. Yet these things which add so much to its appearance, add but little to its real value.

We must further observe, that esteem and benevolent regard, not only accompany real worth by the constitution of our nature, but are perceived to be really and properly due to it; and that, on the contrary, unworthy conduct really merits dislike and indignation.

There is no judgment of the heart of man more clear, or more irresistible, than this, that esteem and regard are really due to good conduct, and the contrary to base and unworthy conduct. Nor can we conceive a greater depravity in the heart of man, than it would be to see and acknowledge worth without feeling any respect to it; or to see and acknowledge the highest worthlessness without any degree of dislike and indignation.

ESSAY IV: OF THE LIBERTY OF MORAL AGENTS

Chapter XI: Of the Permission of Evil

The defenders of necessity,[6] to reconcile it to the principles of theism, find themselves obliged to give up all the moral attributes of God, excepting that of goodness, or a desire to produce happiness. This they hold to be the sole motive of his making and governing the universe. Justice, veracity, faithfulness, are only modifications of goodness, the means of promoting its purposes, and are exercised only so far as they serve that end. Virtue is acceptable to him, and vice displeasing, only as the first tends to produce happiness and the last misery. He is the proper cause and agent of all moral evil as well as good; but it is for a good end, to produce the greater happiness to his creatures. He does evil that good may come; and this end sanctifies the worst actions that contribute to it. All the wickedness of men being the work of God, he must, when he surveys it, pronounce it, as well as all his other works, to be very good. . . .

If we form our notions of the moral attributes of the Deity from what we see of his government of the world, from the dictates of reason and conscience, or from the doctrine of revelation; justice, veracity, faithfulness, the love of virtue and dislike of vice, appear to be no less essential attributes of his nature than goodness.

In man, who is made after the image of God, goodness, or benevolence, is indeed an essential part of virtue, but it is not the whole.

I am at a loss what arguments can be brought to prove goodness to be essential to the Deity, which will not, with equal force, prove other moral attributes to be so; or what objections can be brought against the latter, which have not equal strength against the former, unless it be admitted to be an objection against other moral attributes, that they do not accord with the doctrine of necessity.

ESSAY V: OF MORALS

Chapter I: Of the first principles of morals

Morals, like all other sciences, must have first principles, on which all moral reasoning is grounded. . . .

I propose, therefore, in this chapter, to point out some of the first principles of morals, without pretending to a complete enumeration.

The principles I am to mention, relate either to virtue in general, or to the different particular branches of virtue, or to the comparison of virtues where they seem to interfere.

1st, There are some things in human conduct, that merit approbation and praise, others that merit blame and punishment; and different degrees either of approbation or of blame, are due to different actions.

2ndly, What is in no degree voluntary, can neither deserve moral approbation nor blame.

3dly, What is done from unavoidable necessity may be agreeable or disagreeable, useful or hurtful, but cannot be the object either of blame or of moral approbation.

4thly, Men may be highly culpable in omitting what they ought to have done, as well as in doing what they ought not.

5thly, We ought to use the best means we can to be well informed of our duty, by serious attention to moral instruction; by observing what we approve, and what we disapprove, in other men, whether our acquaintance, or those whose actions are recorded in history; by reflecting often, in a calm and dispassionate hour, on our own past conduct, that we may discern what was wrong, what was right, and what might have been better; by deliberating cooly and impartially upon our future conduct, as far as we can foresee the opportunities we may have of doing good, or the temptations to do wrong; and by having this principle deeply fixed in our minds, that as moral excellence is the true worth and glory of a man, so that knowledge of our duty is to every man, in every station of life, the most important of all knowledge.

6thly, It ought to be our most serious concern to do our duty as far as we know it, and to fortify our minds against every temptation to deviate from it; by maintaining a lively sense of the beauty of right conduct, and of its present and future reward, of the turpitude of vice, and of its bad consequences here and hereafter; by having always in our eye the noblest examples; by the habit of subjecting our passions to the government of reason; by firm purposes and resolutions with regard to our conduct; by avoiding occasions of temptation when we can; and by imploring the aid of him who made us, in every hour of temptation.

These principles concerning virtue and vice in general, must appear self-evident to every man who has a conscience, and who has taken pains to exercise this natural power of his mind. I proceed to others that are more particular.

1st, We ought to prefer a greater good, though more distant, to a less; and a less evil to a greater. . . .

2dly, As far as the intention of nature appears in the constitution of man, we ought to comply with that intention, and to act agreeably to it.

The Author of our being has given us not only the power of acting within a limited sphere, but various principles or springs of action, of different nature and dignity, to direct us in the exercise of our active power.

From the constitution of every species of the inferior animals, and especially from the active principles which nature has given them, we easily perceive the manner of life for which nature intended them; and they uniformly act the part to which they are led by their constitution, without any reflection upon it, or intention of obeying its dictates. Man only, of the inhabitants of this world, is made capable of observing his own constitution, what kind of life it is made for, and of acting according to that intention, or contrary to it. He only is capable of yielding an intentional obedience to the dictates of his nature, or of rebelling against them. . . .

The intention of nature, in the various active principles of man, in the desires of power, of knowledge, and of esteem, in the affection to children, to near relations, and to the communities to which we belong, in gratitude, in compassion, and even in resentment and emulation, is very obvious, and has been pointed out in treating of those principles. Nor is it less evident, that reason and conscience are given us to regulate the inferior principles, so that they may conspire, in a regular and consistent plan of life, in pursuit of some worthy end.

3dly, No man is born for himself only. Every man, therefore, ought to consider himself as a member of the common society of mankind, and of those subordinate societies to which he belongs, such as family, friends, neighbourhood, country, and to do as much good as he can, and as little hurt to the societies of which he is a part.

This axiom leads directly to the practice of every social virtue, and indirectly to the virtues of self-government, by which only we can be qualified for discharging the duty we owe to society.

4thly, In every case, we ought to act that part toward another, which we would judge to be right in him to act toward us, if we were in his circumstances and he in ours; or, more generally, what we approve in others, that we ought to practise in like circumstances, and what we condemn in others we ought not to do.

If there be any such thing as right and wrong in the conduct of moral agents, it must be the same to all in the same circumstances.

We stand all in the same relation to Him who made us, and will call us to account for our conduct: for with him there is no respect of persons. We stand in the same relation to one another as members of the great community of mankind. The duties consequent upon the different ranks, and offices, and relations of men, are the same to all in the same circumstances. . . .

As the equity and obligation of this rule of conduct is self-evident to every man who has a conscience; so it is, of all the rules of morality, the most comprehensive, and truly deserves the encomium given it by the highest authority, that *it is the law and the prophets.*

It comprehends every rule of justice without exception. It comprehends all the relative duties, arising either from the more permanent relations of parent and child, of master and servant, of magistrate and subject, of husband and wife; or from the more transient relations of rich and poor, of buyer and seller, of debtor and creditor, of benefactor and beneficiary, of friend and enemy. It comprehends every duty of charity and humanity, and even of courtesy and good manners.

Nay, I think, that, without any force or straining, it extends even to the duties of self-government. For, as every man approves in others the virtues of prudence, temperance, self-command and fortitude, he must perceive, that what is right in others must be right in himself in like circumstances. . . .

It may be observed, that this axiom supposes a faculty in man by which he can distinguish right conduct from wrong. It supposes also, that, by this faculty, we easily perceive the right and the wrong in other men that are indifferent to us; but are very apt to be blinded by the partiality of selfish passions when the case concerns ourselves. Every claim we have against others is apt to be magnified by self-love, when viewed directly. A change of persons removes this prejudice, and brings the claim to appear in its just magnitude.

5thly, To every man who believes the existence, the perfections, and the providence of God, the veneration and submission we owe to him is self-evident. Right sentiments of the Deity and of his works, not only make the duty we owe to him obvious to every intelligent being, but likewise add the authority of a divine law to every rule of right conduct.

There is another class of axioms in morals, by which, when there seems to be an opposition between the actions that different virtues lead to, we determine to which the preference is due.

Between the several virtues, as they are dispositions of mind, or determinations of will to act according to a certain general rule, there can be no opposition. They dwell together most amicably, and give mutual aid and ornament, without the possibility of hostility or opposition, and, taken altogether, make one uniform and consistent rule of conduct. But, between particular external actions, which different virtues would lead to, there may be an opposition. Thus, the same man may be in his heart, generous, grateful, and just. These dispositions strengthen, but never can weaken one another. Yet it may happen, that an external action which generosity or gratitude solicits, justice may forbid.

That in all such cases, unmerited generosity should yield to gratitude, and both to justice, is self-evident. Nor is it less so, that unmerited beneficence to those who are at ease should yield to compassion to the miserable, and external acts of piety to works of mercy, because God loves mercy more than sacrifice.

At the same time, we perceive, that those acts of virtue which ought to yield in the case of a competition, have most intrinsic worth when there is no competition. Thus, it is evident that there is more worth in pure and unmerited benevolence than in compassion, more in compassion than in gratitude, and more in gratitude than in justice.

I call these *first principles,* because they appear to me to have in themselves an intuitive evidence which I cannot resist. I find I can express them in other words. I can illustrate them by examples and authorities, and perhaps can deduce one of them from another; but I am not able to deduce them from other principles that are more evident. And I find the best moral reasonings of authors I am acquainted with, ancient and modern, heathen and christian, to be grounded upon one or more of them.

The evidence of mathematical axioms is not discerned till men come to a certain degree of maturity of understanding. A boy must have formed the general conception of *quantity,* and of *more,* and *less,* and *equal;* of *sum,* and *difference;* and he must have been accustomed to judge of these relations in matters of common life, before he can perceive the evidence of the mathematical axiom, that equal quantities, added to equal quantities, make equal sums.

In like manner, our moral judgment, or conscience, grows to maturity from an imperceptible seed, planted by our Creator. When we are capable of contemplating the actions of other men, or of reflecting upon our own calmly and dispassionately, we begin to perceive in them the qualities of honest and dishonest, of honorable and base, of right and wrong, and to feel the sentiments of moral approbation and disapprobation. . . .

From the principles above mentioned, the whole system of moral conduct follows so easily, and with so little aid of reasoning, that every man of common understanding, who wishes to know his duty, may know it. The path of duty is a plain path, which the upright in heart can rarely mistake. Such it must be, since every man is bound to walk in it. There are some intricate cases in morals which admit of disputation; but these seldom occur in practice; and, when they do, the learned disputant has no great advantage: for the unlearned man, who uses the best means in his power to know his duty, and acts according to his knowledge, is inculpable in the sight of God and man. He may err, but he is not guilty of immorality.

Chapter IV: Whether an action deserving moral approbation, must be done with the belief of its being morally good

There is no part of philosophy more subtile and intricate than that which is called the *Theory of Morals.* Nor is there any more plain and level to the apprehension of man than the practical part of morals.

In the former, the Epicurean, the Peripatetic and the Stoic, had each his different system of old; and almost every modern author of reputation has a system of his own. At the same time, there is no branch of human knowledge in which there is so general an agreement among ancients and moderns, learned and unlearned, as in the practical rules of morals.

From this discord in the theory, and harmony in the practical part, we may judge, that the rules of morality stand upon another and a firmer foundation than the theory. And of this it is easy to perceive the reason.

For in order to know what is right and what is wrong in human conduct, we need only listen to the dictates of our conscience, when the mind is calm and unruffled, or attend to the judgment we form of others in like circumstances.

But, to judge of the various theories of morals, we must be able to analyze and dissect, as it were, the active powers of the human mind, and especially to analyze accurately that conscience or moral power, by which we discern right from wrong. . . .

From this remarkable disparity between our decisions in the theory of morals and in the rules of morality, we may, I think, draw this conclusion, that where-ever we find any disagreement between the practical rules of morality, which have been received in all ages, and the principles of any of the theories advanced upon this subject, the practical rules ought to be the standard by which the theory is to be corrected; and that it is both unsafe and unphilosophical to warp the practical rules, in order to make them tally with a favourite theory.

Chapter VII: That moral approbation implies a real judgment

The approbation of good actions, and disapprobation of bad, are so familiar to every man come to years of understanding, that it seems strange there should be any dispute about their nature.[7]

Whether we reflect upon our own conduct, or attend to the conduct of others with whom we live, or of whom we hear or read, we cannot help approving of some things, disapproving of others, and regarding many with perfect indifference.

These operations of our minds we are conscious of every day, and almost every hour we live. Men of ripe understanding are capable of reflecting upon them, and of attending to what passes in their own thoughts on such occasions; yet, for half a century, it has been a serious dispute among philosophers, what this approbation and disapprobation is, whether there be a real judgment included in it, which, like all other judgments, must be true or false; or, whether it include no more but some agreeable or uneasy feeling, in the person who approves or disapproves. . . .

When I exercise my moral faculty about my own actions or those of other men, I am conscious that I judge as well as feel. I accuse and excuse, I acquit and condemn, I assent and dissent, I believe, and disbelieve, and doubt. These are acts of judgment, and not feelings.

Every determination of the understanding, with regard to what is true or false, is judgment. That I ought not to steal, or to kill, or to bear false witness, are propositions, of the truth of which I am as well convinced as of any proposition in Euclid. I am conscious that I judge them to be true propositions; and my consciousness makes all other arguments unnecessary, with regard to the operations of my own mind.

That other men judge, as well as feel, in such cases, I am convinced, because they understand me when I express my moral judgment, and express theirs by the same terms and phrases.

Suppose that, in a case well known to both, my friend says, *Such a man did well and worthily; his conduct is highly approvable.* This speech according to all rules of interpretation, expresses my friend's judgment of the man's conduct. This judgment may be true or false, and I may agree in opinion with him, or I may dissent from him without offence, as we may differ in other matters of judgment.

Suppose, again, that in relation to the same case, my friend says, *The man's conduct gave me a very agreeable feeling.*

This speech, if approbation be nothing but an agreeable feeling, must have the very same meaning with the first, and express neither more nor less. But this cannot be, for two reasons.

1st, Because there is no rule in grammar or rhetoric, nor any usage in language, by which these two speeches can be construed, so as to have the same meaning. The *first* expresses plainly an opinion or judgment of the conduct of the man, but says nothing of the speaker. The *second* only testifies a fact concerning the speaker; to wit, that he had such a feeling.

Another reason why these two speeches cannot mean the same thing is, that the first may be contradicted without any ground of offence, such contradiction being only a difference of opinion, which, to a reasonable man, gives no offence. But the second speech cannot be contradicted without an affront; for, as every man must know his own feelings, to deny that a man had a feeling which he affirms he had, is to charge him with falsehood.

If moral approbation be a real judgment, which produces an agreeable feeling in the mind of him who judges, both speeches are perfectly intelligible, in the most obvious and literal sense. Their meaning is different, but they are related, so that the one may be inferred from the other, as we infer the effect from the cause, or the cause from the effect. I know, that what a man judges to be a very worthy action, he contemplates with pleasure; and what he contemplates with pleasure, must, in his judgment, have worth. But the judgment and the feeling are different acts of his mind, though connected as cause and effect. He can express either the one or the other with perfect propriety; but the speech which expresses his feeling is altogether improper and inept to express his judgment, for this evident reason, that judgment and feeling, though in some cases connected, are things in their nature different.

If we suppose, on the other hand, that moral approbation is nothing more than an agreeable feeling, occasioned by the contemplation of an action, the second speech above mentioned has a distinct meaning, and expresses all that is meant by moral approbation. But the first speech either means the very same thing, which cannot be, for the reasons already mentioned, or it has no meaning.

Now, we may appeal to the reader, whether, in conversation upon human characters, such speeches as the first are not as frequent, as familiar, and as well understood, as any thing in language; and whether they have not been common in all ages that we can trace, and in all languages?

This doctrine, therefore, that moral approbation is merely a feeling without judgment, necessarily carries along with it this consequence, that a form of speech, upon one of the most common topics of discourse, which either has no meaning, or a meaning irreconcileable to all rules of grammar or rhetoric, is found to be common and familiar in all languages, and in all ages of the world, while every man knows how to express the meaning, if it have any, in plain and proper language.

Such a consequence I think sufficient to sink any philosophical opinion on which it hangs. . . .

All the words most commonly used, both by philosophers and by the vulgar, to express the operations of our moral faculty, such as *decision, determination, sentence, approbation, disapprobation, applause, censure, praise, blame,* necessarily imply judgment in their meaning. When, therefore, they are used by Mr. Hume, and others who hold his opinion, to signify feelings only, this is an abuse of words. If these philosophers wish to speak plainly and properly, they must, in discoursing of morals, discard these words altogether, because their established signification in the language, is contrary to what they would express by them.

They must likewise discard from morals the words *ought* and *ought not,* which very properly express judgment, but cannot be applied to mere feelings. Upon these words Mr. Hume has made a particular observation in the conclusion of his first section above mentioned. I shall give it in his own words, and make some remarks upon it.

"I cannot forbear adding to these reasonings, an observation which may, perhaps, be found of some importance. In every system of morality which I have hitherto met with, I have always remarked, that the author proceeds for some time in the ordinary way of reasoning, and establishes the being of a God, or makes observations concerning human affairs; when, of a sudden, I am surprised to find, that, instead of the usual copulations of propositions, *is,* and *is not,* I meet with no proposition that is not connected with an *ought,* or an *ought not.* This change is imperceptible, but is, however, of the last consequence. For as this *ought* or *ought not* expresses some new relation or affirmation, it is necessary that it should be observed and explained; and, at the same time, that a reason should be given for what seems altogether inconceivable; how this new relation can be a deduction from others which are entirely different from it. But as authors do not commonly use this precaution, I shall presume to recommend it to the readers; and I am persuaded that this small attention would subvert all the vulgar systems of morality, and let us see, that the distinction of vice and virtue, is not founded merely on the relations of objects, nor is perceived by reason."[8]

We may here observe, that it is acknowledged, that the words *ought* and *ought not* express some relation or affirmation; but a relation or affirmation which Mr. Hume thought inexplicable, or, at least, inconsistent with his system of morals. He must, therefore, have thought, that they ought not to be used in treating of that subject.

He likewise makes two demands, and, taking it for granted that they cannot be satisfied, is persuaded, that an attention to this is sufficient to subvert all the vulgar systems of morals.

The *first* demand is, that *ought* and *ought not* be explained.

To a man that understands English, there are surely no words that require explanation less. Are not all men taught, from their early years, that they ought not to lie, nor steal, nor swear falsely? But Mr. Hume thinks, that men never understood what these precepts mean, or rather that they are unintelligible. If this be so, I think indeed it will follow, that all the vulgar systems of morals are subverted.

Dr. Johnson, in his Dictionary, explains the word *ought* to signify, being obliged by duty; and I know no better explication that can be given of it. The reader will see what I thought necessary to say concerning the moral relation expressed by this word, in Essay III. part 3. chap. 5.

The *second* demand is, that a reason should be given why this relation should be a deduction from others, which are entirely different from it.

This is to demand a reason for what does not exist. The first principles of morals are not deductions. They are self-evident; and their truth, like that of other axioms, is perceived without reasoning or deduction. And moral truths, that are not self-evident, are deduced not from relations quite different from them, but from the first principles of morals.

In a matter so interesting to mankind, and so frequently the subject of conversation among the learned and the unlearned as morals is, it may surely be expected that men will express both their judgments and their feelings with propriety, and consistently with the rules of language. An opinion, therefore, which makes the language of all ages and nations, upon this subject, to be improper, contrary to all rules of language, and fit to be discarded, needs no other refutation.

Editor's Notes

1. Hume's most striking presentation of his position occurs in the *Treatise of Human Nature,* bk. II, part III, sec. III, where he says, "Reason is, and ought only to be, the slave of the passions, and can never pretend to any other office than to serve and obey them."
2. Than the principle of self-interest.
3. Reid seems here to take the term "honor" as having the broad meaning of the Latin *honestum.*
4. The decent or honorable or proper, as contrasted with the useful or profitable.
5. In his *Essays on the Intellectual Powers of Man,* Reid argued at length for the epistemological position sketched here.
6. Reid was discussing here the problem of evil, in particular the question of why God permits evil in the world.
7. Reid was attacking here Hume's theory that morality "is more properly felt than judged of," for which Hume argued in the *Treatise,* bk. III, sec. I–II. The version of this doctrine that Hume presented in the later *Essay Concerning the Principles of Morals* (excerpts from which are given earlier in this section of the anthology) is stated in a more conciliatory fashion, without giving up the main point of the earlier version.
8. This is the final paragraph of Hume's *Treatise,* bk. III, part I, sec. I.

Further Reading

The only complete edition of Reid's works is that edited in the nineteenth century by Sir William Hamilton, in two volumes.

For general background, see Nicholas Phillipson, "The Scottish Enlightenment," in Roy Porter and Mikulas Teich, eds., *The Enlightenment in National Context* (Cambridge, England: Cambridge University Press, 1981). The volume of essays, R. H. Campbell and Andrew S. Skinner, eds., *The Origins and Nature of the Scottish Enlightenment* (Edinburgh: John Donald, 1982), provides valuable insights into the context of Reid's work, although Reid himself is not extensively discussed.

For a careful analytic study, see Keith Lehrer, *Thomas Reid* (London: Routledge & Kegan Paul, 1989). The literature on Reid's ethics is scanty. S. A. Grave, *The Scottish Philosophy of Common Sense* (Oxford: Oxford University Press, 1960), discusses the epistemology of commonsense philosophy, paying a great deal of attention to Reid, but only Chapter 7 concerns morality. J. B. Schneewind, *Sidgwick's Ethics and Victorian Moral Philosophy* (Oxford: Oxford University Press, 1977), examines Reid's ethics and the theories of the nineteenth-century Scottish commonsense philosophers who followed him. Knud Haakonssen, *Thomas Reid: Practical Ethics* (Princeton, N.J.: Princeton University Press, 1990), includes important manuscripts drawn from courses that Reid taught, giving us much insight into the importance of natural law thinking for Reid's own views. Haakonssen also wrote a valuable introduction covering Reid's life and philosophy.

The following essays also will be helpful:

Ardal, Páll S. "Hume and Reid on Promise, Intention, and Obligation." In V. Hope, ed., *Philosophers of the Scottish Enlightenment*. Edinburgh: Edinburgh University Press, 1984.

Dalgarno, Melvin T. "Reid's Natural Jurisprudence: The Language of Rights and Duties." In V. Hope, ed., *Philosophers of the Scottish Enlightenment*. Edinburgh: Edinburgh University Press, 1984.

Duggan, Timothy. "Active Power and the Liberty of Moral Agents." In Stephen F. Barker and Tom L. Beauchamp, eds., *Thomas Reid: Critical Interpretations*. Philadelphia: University City Science Center, 1976.

Haakonssen, Knud. "Reid's Politics: A Natural Law Theory." *Reid Studies* 1 (1986–7).

Jensen, Henning. "Common Sense and Common Language in Thomas Reid's Ethical Theory." *The Monist* 61 (1978):299–310.

Pritchard, Michael. "Reason and Passion: Reid's Reply to Hume." *The Monist* 61 (1978):283–98.

Weinstock, Jerome. "Reid's Definition of Freedom." In Stephen F. Barker and Tom L. Beauchamp, eds., *Thomas Reid: Critical Interpretations*. Philadelphia: University City Science Center, 1976.

Immanuel Kant

Introduction

Immanuel Kant was born in 1724 in Königsberg (now called Kaliningrad) in the eastern part of Prussia. A child of poor parents, he received scholarships that enabled him to go to school and to the small university in his hometown. After graduation he served as a tutor for wealthy local families and then obtained a position at the university. There he taught until almost the end of his life, never traveling and never marrying. He lectured on a wide variety of subjects (including the art of fortification, which he taught to Russian officers when Königsberg was occupied by Catherine the Great's troops during the 1750s), generally attracting a large number of students. Kant kept up with developments in science, literature, and world affairs; was one of the founders of the discipline of physical geography; introduced a course on anthropology; and made contributions to our understanding of the movement of the weather. His main work, however, was in philosophy, and there, it is generally agreed, what he wrote was epoch making.

Though Kant published several books and essays while he was young, his major writings began to appear only when he was in his middle years. In 1781 he published the *Critique of Pure Reason,* announcing a radical break with the epistemology and metaphysics of the entire philosophical past. He then proceeded to elaborate the implications of his new outlook for history, ethics, aesthetics, religion, and politics in a series of books and articles that he continued to write until a year or two before his death in 1804. His work was quickly seen to be of the utmost importance. It was widely discussed during his lifetime, winning followers and arousing criticism, and has been indispensable to philosophy ever since.

Kant's ethical theory was the most original contribution to moral philosophy to be made during the seventeenth and eighteenth centuries. The topics on which he wrote were standard topics of the time, and some of the views he developed had been anticipated by earlier writers, but no one had proposed a systematic ethic as fully and radically at odds with all previous views as Kant did. He claimed that the central principle of morality is one that makes the rightness or wrongness of actions altogether independent of the goodness or badness of their consequences. He held that everyone equally can apply this principle and that everyone can be motivated by knowledge of its requirements. We can therefore be moved by a concern that is not a concern for good or bad but is still rational. Only by accepting these points, he held, can we understand how all human beings can be fully self-governing, or autonomous, subjected to the rule of no one other than themselves in the most important choices we

651

need to make and yet still bound by strict obligations. And he believed that only this view of humanity was commensurate with our intrinsic dignity.

Morality and metaphysics are complexly blended in Kant's ethics. He considered the categorical imperative – the basic principle of morality as we understand it – capable of providing better moral guidance than any other principle ever proposed, and he gave examples designed to show that its guidance accords more closely with moral convictions that we all already have than does any alternative view. His principle also requires, so Kant believed, that we think of ourselves as possessing free will in a very strong sense of the term and that we regard our actions as wholly undetermined by antecedent events. In order to defend this view, Kant appealed to the elaborate theory about the limits of knowledge that he presented first in the *Critique of Pure Reason*.

Many people have thought that the categorical imperative or something like it must be at the heart of morality but have resisted the metaphysical entanglements that it entails in Kant's presentations. Critical questions must therefore be asked not only about the moral adequacy of Kant's principle, which to many readers from his own time to ours has seemed deeply misguided, but also about the extent to which the principle can be detached from the rest of his philosophical system and used simply as a test of the morality of our behavior.

Kant presented the classic exposition of the basic principle of his ethics in the *Groundwork of the Metaphysics of Morals* (1785). He elaborated the metaphysical bearings of the principle in the *Critique of Practical Reason* (1788); in *Religion Within the Limits of Reason Alone* (1794), he discussed the ways in which the principle leads us to reasonable religious beliefs and practices; and in the *Metaphysics of Morals* (1797) he spelled out some of its more detailed practical implications for politics and for personal life.

From 1756 until 1794, Kant lectured on ethics quite regularly. Several sets of student notes on these lectures have survived and been published, and it is generally agreed that they give us a reasonably accurate account of what Kant said in class. What he taught before the publication of the *Groundwork* was in many respects different from what he said in the book, although he did expound some of the book's leading ideas. We have one set of notes from lectures Kant gave after the *Groundwork* appeared that contains an account of its ideas. But the fullest classroom exposition of his mature moral philosophy was given the last time he taught the subject. The following selections are from the notes on these late lectures, delivered in 1793–4, on the subject of metaphysics of morals. The notes were taken not by an undergraduate but by an older man, a lawyer named Vigilantius who knew Kant personally. Kant spent most of his time during this course on the applications of the categorical imperative, introducing this subject by reviewing the main points contained in the *Groundwork* and in the second *Critique*. These parts of the lectures, therefore, provide an adequate if sketchy overview of the distinctive features of Kant's positions on the central topics of moral philosophy.

The reader will find the lectures difficult to understand. But none of Kant's work is easy. The *Groundwork* is one of the most difficult books ever written, and in the excerpts presented here Kant is covering everything it covers and more besides. Only by studying the published works on moral philosophy and by using the commentators will the reader be able to grasp Kant's ethics fully, but I hope that these excerpts will help by providing a first glimpse of his remarkable theory.

The text I have translated here is the *Metaphysik der Sitten Vigilantius*, in Kant's *Gesammelte Schriften*, vol. XXVII.2.1 (Berlin: Walter de Gruyter, 1975). I give in square brackets the page numbers of this edition, the so-called Akademie edition, as they are the page numbers used in scholarly works on Kant.

Lectures of Mr. Kant on the Metaphysics of Morals (1793–4)

[479] DETERMINATION OF THE OBJECT

§1. Philosophical, and indeed systematic, knowledge coming from rational concepts either concerns the form of thought (or logic) as the formal part of philosophy or it relates to the objects [of thought] themselves and the laws under which they stand. The latter constitutes the material part of philosophy, whose objects must be reduced simply to
    nature and freedom, and their laws and which divides thus into
    a. the philosophy of laws of nature, or physics
    b. the philosophy of laws of morality. . . .
The latter really concerns itself with developing the idea of freedom. . . . Both [parts of philosophy] are grounded on pure or rational concepts.[1] Moreover, the natural as well as the moral laws that are basic here are built on a priori principles and thus make up the two objects of the part of philosophy called metaphysics, as this judges objects according to pure (independent of all experience) basic propositions, in contrast with historical disciplines judged according to empirical, conditioned, basic propositions given in experience. . . .
    [481] §2(c). The laws of freedom are now either
    1. simply necessary or objective. . . . These occur only in God
or
    2. necessitating. These occur in humans and are objectively necessary but subjectively contingent. For man has a drive to transgress these laws, even when he recognizes them, and so the legality and morality[2] of his actions are merely contingent. The necessitation through the moral law to act in accordance with it is obligation. The action itself in accord with the moral law is duty, and moral philosophy or theory of ethics is grounded on the theory of duty. . . .
    [485] §5. Morality has the rules of duty as its object. These rules are never theoretical [rules] that contain only the conditions under which something is but are always just practical [rules] that give only the conditions under which something ought to occur, that is, those laws of reason that contain the sufficient grounds determining to action and would move action to conform to the laws of reason if reason had sufficient free strength to be effective.
    The distinction in the rules is that some are laws of nature[3] and others [are laws] of morality. The former never show that something ought to occur and what [ought to occur] but show only the conditions under which something does occur. Moral laws, by contrast, are always concerned with the will and its freedom. Essentially these laws are presented by reason in such a way that if it alone had influence and it alone contained the ground of the reality of action,

there would never be a deviation from these laws. For instance, everyone would, without admonition, pay his debts. Now man is obstructed from giving the laws of reason free and unobstructed obedience, insofar as inclinations opposed to them, sensuous drives, and ends aroused in connection with his actions incline him toward transgression. Therefore, it is necessary that practical rules always be imperatives for humans – that is, rules to which their will must be subordinated in order to determine what ought to happen. Consequently, because men are indeed subordinated to the laws of reason but man does not unconditionally follow reason, the moral actions of men are said to be *objectively necessary* and *subjectively contingent*. It is therefore necessary that man be *necessitated* to take morally free action. This necessitation is the determination of the human will, by means of which the action becomes necessary, and it is a *moral* necessitation because it comes about through moral rules. This moral necessitation, which [486] is always expressed through an imperative, is thus what is called "obligation." . . .

Now all imperatives are either

1. conditioned; and these are
    a. problematic, that is, imperatives of skill;
    b. pragmatic, that is, imperatives of prudence[4]

or

2. unconditioned or categorical, that is, imperatives of morality, of duty.

Categorical imperatives are distinguished from problematic and pragmatic [imperatives] essentially by the fact that the ground for determination of action lies only in the law of moral freedom; but in the latter, by contrast, the ends connected with them bring the action into being and are therefore the condition of action.

Problematic [imperatives] are further distinguished from the pragmatic in that the ends in the former are possible and contingent whereas in the latter they are determinate.

Problematic imperatives are [imperatives yielding the solution of] all mathematical problems, in which the laws for solving the problem constitute the imperatives, as they prescribe what you must do if you want to solve the problem, for example, to divide a straight line into two parts. . . .

[487] Pragmatic imperatives, by contrast, have only the universal happiness of all humans as their object and indicate the means to help other men in the service of their happiness. The goal is thus universally determined, namely, to bring about the greatest sum of well-being, and the rules of skill necessary for this are the pragmatic imperatives. But they are conditional, because one needs these imperatives only if one wants to achieve this well-being in human life, and so they will drop out if one abstracts from it.[5]

In contrast, there are, finally, human actions that are necessary without any end and to whose existence no goal or end is the motive [*Triebfeder*]. These are the moral actions, whose imperative thus attends to neither skill, wisdom, happiness, nor any other end that could set the activity into motion; rather, the necessitation to the action lies simply in the imperative alone. These are the categorically unconditioned imperatives, for example, to keep your promise, to speak the truth. A witness who in giving his testimony is counseled on the one side by the duty of friendship and on the other by fear of punishment and of revenge, decides on his deposition in a way contrary to duty. For instead of determining himself through the imperative of duty, he merely directs himself according to the consequence that his future condition will have for his happiness, which certainly should have no influence on the categorical imperative. Therefore, those philosophers who thought that in order to bring about moral action, the happiness of mankind is the necessary goal and driving force have false views.

The rule of my will must, all by itself, also be the determining ground [*Bestimmungsgrund*] of the will. The action must rest only on this unconditional imperative, without [488] any end tied to it – whether profit or loss, gain or sacrifice. Material grounds for a will of that sort simply do not belong to the (so-named) formal determining grounds of moral actions. . . .

[489] Every "ought" expresses an objective necessity that nonetheless is at the same time subjectively contingent. . . . These conflicting qualities of the action contain together, under the expression "ought," the necessitation to action. . . . Now, if this necessitation occurs through the moral law, that is, if the action that would not be done from one's own desires is made necessary by the moral law and the subject is necessitated to follow the law, it is obligation or being duty bound, and the action to which the subject is necessitated through the moral law is duty. Necessitation is thus thinkable only when contravention of the moral law is possible. Therefore, something can be morally necessary without being a duty. This is the case if the subject, without necessitation, would always act according to the moral law. Then there would be no duty or obligation to do it. So these do not hold for a morally perfect being. . . . If there is no necessitation, there also is no moral imperative, no obligation, duty, virtue, or ought. Because the moral laws presuppose a subject subordinated to natural impulses, they are called laws of duty. We can think of God, in contrast, as a being who alone is *holy*, that is, who has the property that the moral laws are followed by him without necessitation and whose will is already conformed to the moral law; as alone *blessed*, that is, who finds himself in complete possession and satisfied enjoyment of all goods; as alone *wise*, that is, who not only sees the relation of his acts to the final goal but also makes the goal the determining ground for his actions. . . .

[491] It would be good if men were so perfect that they did their duty out of free drives, without force and laws, but this is beyond the horizon of human nature.[6]

All conditioned or hypothetical imperatives are technical–practical imperatives. . . . they say only what I should do *if* I want this or that. They are distinguished only according to the kind of end connected with them. . . . To the technical–pragmatic imperatives are opposed the moral–practical or the imperatives of morality, which determine simply what one must do, without reference to the ends. . . .

[493] §10. The determining ground of the power of choice is the *causa impulsiva* of action, the cause of movements. . . .

The cause of movement is called either motive or stimulus, a distinction that is noteworthy because of the dual nature of man: man has a natural being and a free being.

1. A motive [*motivum*] is always a moral *causa impulsiva* or determining ground, which determines his will according to the laws of freedom and so addresses man as a free being. In contrast, the stimulus is the cause that determines the will of men according to laws of nature and of the sensuous drive. Natural cause, inclination, exists when, for example, someone is brought to obedience to his parents or to industriousness through hunger or physical suffering. Even with animals, these determining causes leading to possible ends – to taming – can occur, and man in this is like them. . . .

[494] 2. As a natural being, man can be affected by stimuli. In contrast, as a free being, this means is quite fruitless. Insofar as sensuous drives affect man, he is only passive: he must suffer these drives, as he cannot elude them. Motives, by contrast, occur only when man is thought of as a free being. They contain his activity and are therefore totally opposed to the condition that depends on inclinations. They are grounded in the spontaneity of the human will, which is led by representations of reason and thus merely by the moral law, quite independently of all determining causes of nature.

3. Through stimuli, man can only be affected but never determined to action. It is possible for him as a free being to omit all actions to which natural drives tempt him and that he as a natural being would undertake.

4. So we can name the stimuli the "animal will" and the motives the "free will." This distinction leads now

§11. to the concept of freedom, which consists *negatively* of the independence of the power of choice from all determination by stimuli . . . *positively* in spontaneity or the power to determine itself through reason, without needing motives from nature.

The proof that the actions of man should occur only according to the law of freedom will be given farther on.

§12. Now, because understanding and reason should determine the imperative of moral action, we ask,

What is the determining ground of action, insofar as it [495] lies in reason, from which arises a moral necessitation as the ground of obligation?

The basic categorical imperative is a morally practical [imperative], that is, a law of freedom, and the determining cause, *causa moralis*. The latter therefore cannot lead man passively to action, as the laws of nature can; rather, he must determine himself and his power of choice through his reason. Now if in his action he took account of ends or means to reach them and were the imperative to prescribe these, then the material of the law that the imperative expresses, and the object of the law that is given for action, would be the determining ground of action. For the end or the means in the action constitute the material of the action. . . .

This is impossible because the categorical imperative carries with it an unconditioned moral necessitation, without having the end and goal of the action as ground. There remains therefore only the form, which is the determining ground of free action. That is, moral actions must be carried out according to the form of lawfulness, to which condition they are subordinated in this way: their maxim[7] must accord with lawfulness. The *maxim* of action differs from an objective principle in that the latter occurs only when the possibility of the action according to certain grounds of reason is thought; the former, however, in general includes all subjective grounds for action in itself insofar as these are considered real. . . .

The formula of the universal imperative would thus be:

> You ought to act according to the maxim that is qualified for universal lawgiving; that is, you ought to act so that [496] the maxim of your action may become a *universal law,*

would have to be universally recognized as a universal law, or act so that you can present yourself through the maxim of your action as universally lawgiving, that is, so that the maxim of your action is fit for universal lawgiving. In this form of moral action lies the determining ground of being bound by duty, through which it attains lawful force.

The qualification of the maxim for universal legislation rests, however, on the agreement of the action with the imperative of reason. For example: "You should always tell the truth" is an imperative of reason and, in application, a maxim that reason makes into a universal law. Suppose that someone followed the maxim that he might tell a lie if thereby he could acquire a big profit. Then ask whether this maxim could exist as a universal law. It is then to be assumed that no one would tell the truth to his own loss, and in that case no one would trust [anyone] anymore. The liar in that case could not come to be in a position to deceive through his lie. The law would thus defeat itself by itself.

That is how it is with all perfect duties.[8] If the opposite [maxims] existed, they would so determine action that it would contradict itself, which could never be a universal law. This lies in the nature of the unconditioned necessitation of the law, which – without end, goal, and [thought of] profit and loss – commands fulfillment of duty. Thus *every action is forbidden* whose maxim is not qualified for universal legislation.

It is quite different with the so-called imperfect duties. Here the action does not immediately defeat itself through its contradictory law by itself. . . . But it can never be the will of a person that the action become a universal law. For example, [consider] the duty of love of mankind through beneficence toward the suffering. If one wanted to act on a maxim that had indifference to the necessities and needs of other humans as its basis, one could not say that such a law would contradict the moral freedom of men. A human could attain all his goals; only he could not make claims to the assistance of others. But this latter – because every subject can come to be in a [497] similarly needy situation – is the reason no one will be able to make this maxim into a universal law.

If, then, the determining ground of moral action lies not in the *material part of the law,* namely, the end of the law, but in its form of universal lawfulness, then it is quite wrong to put the ground in the following:

a. in the individual happiness of men; for then

1. the categorical imperative would be conditioned and hypothetical, for it would have to pay attention to the end of universal happiness and to the means to attain it. But then it would be an imperative of prudence and artfulness. But then it would not say that something ought to occur, entirely unconditionally and simply, without attending to an end. And this is what the categorical imperative should [say] if it is to convey to it duty and obligation and necessitation. It cannot therefore be enunciated in the conditioned way.

2. Under this principle is really meant the principle of self-love, which regards acquired skills as the means to make oneself – as the end connected with them – happy through them. The condition of happiness consists of the consciousness of satisfaction and of the possession of means to acquire any ends, even merely possible ones, and through this to satisfy all [one's] wishes. It is natural that because the ends may be different, the practical rules may be different as well, that is, as inclination, sensibility, and personal bent require. A universality of principle cannot, as such, be even thought of – but that is what is sought.

3. To be happy is the universal will of man. But the decision whether someone will be pleased or happy depends first of all on merely his resolution and will. The ground of duty – moral necessitation – is lacking here, as is an unconditioned imperative. Here the constraint that commands immediate obligation is not thinkable. The imperative itself can relate only to the means to bring oneself happiness.

b. The relation of our will to our *moral feeling* can just as little be the ground of duty. Rather, the feeling presupposes this ground. Man is supposed to be drawn to a certain material of the law, namely, complacency,[9] which [498] is not happiness and not duty but is nonetheless moral. Now, the will is affected by the feeling of pleasure and pain, and especially here, where the act is to be moral, [it is affected] by the moral law. It should therefore feel pleasure or pain after the law is satisfied or transgressed by it. This effect cannot be conceived without assuming an idea of the concept of duty as its ground. It must therefore have knowledge of the law and its obligation before it can be filled with pleasure or pain because of following or transgressing it and before it connects its action with self-satisfaction or dissatisfaction (for the latter is the feeling of pleasure or pain). The *moral* feeling or the consciousness that one has acquired self-satisfaction through following the moral law is thus the end but not the ground of duty. . . .

c. Finally, not even the *divine* will can be considered the highest principle of morality. Rather, it presupposes knowledge of our duty. . . .

N.B., and this would remain the case if it [the principle] were not the principle of happiness or of moral feeling and also not the form of lawfulness of action.

One cannot think the will of God otherwise than as one that binds us. If it is to make us duty bound, the *idea of duty must already be available,* so that we can *recognize* that something is in accord with the will of God.

N.B., and we can really only conclude that something is in accord with the will of God by recognizing it as a duty. . . .

[499] §13. Now if moral actions ought to be grounded in the form of lawfulness, then the moral laws must have their basic determination in a lawgiving force that [said Kant] constitutes the legislation. Moral lawgiving is the lawgiving of human reason, which is the lawgiver for all laws and is so simply through itself. This is the autonomy of reason, according to which it determines the laws of the free power of choice through its own independent legislation, independent of all influence. The principle of autonomy is thus the self-possessed legislation of the power of choice through reason. The opposite would be heteronomy, that is, legislation resting on grounds other than the freedom of reason.

If, for example, the principle of universal happiness were at the basis of the determination of moral laws, then what would matter would be how far, by following the laws, the entire sum of our needs would be satisfied. But the laws of nature are involved in this, and the moral laws would have to be subordinated to them. Moreover, reason would have to be obedient – and necessarily so (for, according to our physical constitution, reason is so anyhow) – to the laws of nature and sensibility. But this would plainly be an abandonment of the autonomy of reason, and therefore heteronomy.

But that the determining grounds of the laws of duty cannot be built on natural laws is already shown in the quality of these laws [of duty], that they must be necessarily and universally valid. Now [500] natural laws as bases would carry necessary consequences and effects with them, but they would never be universally valid and thus not objectively necessary and unconditioned. For the determination of the means that will bring us happiness and the satisfaction of our needs is plainly grounded in experience. The principle derived from it would therefore be empirical. And because no empirical basic proposition can yield more than the natural quality of things – though not the basic determinations under which they are possible – they would never become universal laws of moral duty. Experience itself contradicts this. For example, the means to happiness are too different to allow us to determine them before we have agreed on the way in which someone wants to be happy. So different methods would be needed, for example, for the greedy, restless businessman and for the peaceful, phlegmatic person. Still less is the moral feeling or the principle of divine will qualified for the universal lawgiving of morality, but this principle is grounded only in reason. It is the autonomy of reason.

All autonomy of reason must therefore be independent of (a) all empirical principles, that is, the principle of one's own happiness . . . (b) the aesthetic principle or that of moral feeling, (c) all external will (theological [principle]).

§14. How, then, is a categorical necessitation to duty possible, and how can it be demonstrated? Not as easily as the conditioned imperatives and their principles. For whether these are problematic or pragmatic, the necessitation always rests on the end to be achieved, to which the imperative prescribes means. Then, as soon as it is determined that I want this or that bit of culture or that I seek my happiness in this or that manner, it follows of itself that I must use the means leading to it. But the categorical imperative is unconditioned. . . . It can in no way be proved or illustrated,[10] but it must be thought by every being that is aware of his freedom that he necessitates himself to duty through the autonomy of his reason. Where this comes from and how it occurs [501] cannot be determined, but that it is so can be exemplified in the following manner:

1. If we suppose that a being has freedom of will or a free power of choice, then this power of choice must be able to be determined by the mere form of the lawfulness of its actions. From what has been said, one cannot assume that the principle of the power of choice that is to be determined lies in an object of purposive activity, sensibility, or an external will, without incurring heteronomy. It [the principle] should be independent of all objects of the will; it must therefore lie in the autonomy of the will. This, however, determines itself categorically. Therefore, the principle of duty is connected with this freedom through a categorical principle, and the necessitation to duty follows *entirely* and unconditionally through the autonomy of reason. But freedom must also be determined through existing grounds. These, however, cannot be natural laws, as they contain the material of the laws, to which the free power of choice pays no attention. They must be determined without an object and thus through themselves, and this determination must rest on form alone.

2. Conversely, if man is under moral law, that is, if the mere form of lawfulness is the determining ground of his actions and his will, he must be entirely free, for the moral law involves a categorical imperative. It is thus not like any material law, which would be a natural law; it is therefore independent of natural laws in its relation to the determination of its morality. Its determinations of duty follow, therefore, through reason, and thus through itself, and so freely.

§15. Man, however, is simultaneously a natural being and subordinated to the determining grounds of nature. In his actions he is thus entwined with the grounds of nature, which, as a natural man, he must follow. For example, his needs demand ends and actions in accordance with them. . . .

This relation in which man is tied to the means, effects, and causes of nature is mechanism, natural necessity. In this connection his actions are directed through natural determining grounds; his actions emerge from him as natural man in a necessary way because each action [502] here follows only as an effect that, like everything in nature, must have its causes . . . finally, all actions that he undertakes as natural man are predetermined; that is, they are to be viewed as effects of past causes. . . .

[504] §16. All actions fall under the principle of determinism; one can call them predetermined only if the grounds of an action are to be found in

preceding time. One must assume the opposite if the grounds of the action are not predetermined but the agent is the source and complete cause of his act. In the former case, the action is not in his power; in the latter case, the agent determines himself to action all alone, without the addition of external causes. Now, in the actions of man, both [sorts of] determining grounds are to be found. Hence, in order for man to be thought of as free,[11] he must be considered either

a. as a being of sense. Here he does not notice himself as he is but as he appears. We call this side "phenomenon." He is taken into account here insofar as he is aware of his existence and actions through his outer senses as well as through his inner sense. The conditions of his sensibility [505] and the constitution of his inner sense here provide the measure of his action.

b. as an intelligible being, that is, as a being who is made independent of all influence of sensibility and who must be considered in this way. We call this side "noumenal." In this quality the determining grounds of his action are independent of all time and space, and the causality of his actions is given simply through reason. In this quality alone man can be free, for then and only then he has absolute spontaneity; his actions are grounded on the autonomy of reason, and their determination is categorical. . . .

There seems to be a clear contradiction in saying that a man determines himself through himself and yet is already predetermined. This could not be resolved if we were not compelled to consider man from two sides, namely [506], as phenomenon, that is, as an appearance through his inner sense, and as noumenon, that is, insofar as he is aware of himself through the moral law itself. The question is whether we can be taught that we are free through empirical psychology or only through morally practical principles and our consciousness [of them]. From principles of the first [empirical] sort, we would know ourselves only in the world of sense. Moreover, if we had no moral laws, if there were in us no categorical imperative of duty, if instead our actions fell only under natural conditions and our grounds of determination were only hypothetical, then there would be no obligation, and all actions would rest on technical, practical laws. Morality is therefore the sole means for becoming aware of our freedom.

. . . You ought to act in such-and-such a way: this presupposes that I recognize the duty and obligation according to which I must act. The duty is, by its nature, absolute, unconditional, and necessary. But what is necessary must also be possible. The consciousness of the dutiful execution of an action must therefore not be immediate but be inferred from a moral imperative of freedom. . . . To become conscious of freedom without being aware of duty would be impossible. One would hold freedom to be absurd . . . for example, consider a case in which I should tell the truth. Consider also, on the other side, the loss to my friend, bodily pains, profits I could make. Regardless of all evil [and] of all physical force, there is a necessitation to truthful testimony, even though all the physical motives draw me to the opposite. I determine myself now through my reason. This is freedom. But my reason determines itself according to a [507] moral law – precisely the one that necessitates me to overcome the drives of nature. If what I say follows accordingly, then I act freely, not out of immediate consciousness but because I have concluded from the categorical imperative how I ought to act. There is therefore in me a power to resist all sensuous motives as soon as a categorical imperative speaks. Here we have freedom known through an inference (from the moral law) and not immediately felt. . . . For no man is in a position to say ahead of time that in a given case he would simply tell the truth, ignoring all physical evil. He knows only that he ought to obey the categorical imperative. Therefore he must be able to do so, and for this, a ground must be present, not an immediate consciousness. Therefore, it is not possible to know freedom in a psychological way; it is possible [to know it] only through the moral law. So it is not worth the trouble to reply to all the objections to freedom. With this determination of the consciousness of freedom, that is, through the categorical imperative, the already noted main question is, How is such a categorical imperative possible? This is the most difficult [point], as it can be neither proved nor made conceivable.[12] The possibility rests only on the presupposition of freedom.

If man is free, he is not dependent on nature. Nonetheless, there must be a ground for determining his moral actions. This must be a law of reason that immediately commands and is therefore categorical. For if outside freedom or the power of reason another end or the sum of all ends were to be the ground, then the imperative would lie in an object of sensibility and so be sensuously conditioned. But that is the opposite of the moral imperative. The latter is the only thing that can have the possibility of freedom as its consequence. So the latter must be a categorical imperative that necessitates man to action. And this follows necessarily from it, that if in action one assumes a categorical imperative, then man must be free.

[512] §20 Viewed as free actions, the actions of men stand under moral laws. . . . [513] It follows that actions must be specially compared with the moral laws but not that they must also be moral actions. For the laws do not determine something about all human actions, and it would be, moreover, a horrible limitation if for every act a command or prohibition were basic in determining what I ought to do. For example, it is morally indifferent what I eat, if it simply suits me. I might not even know whether it will harm me. . . .

Editor's Notes

1. The distinction between "pure" concepts and "empirical" concepts is central to Kant's philosophical enterprises. Whereas most ordinary concepts are, he believes, derived from experience, some concepts are imposed by the mind on experience. They are "prior" to it and give it its form. Philosophy does not concern itself with empirical concepts, which are the business of the sciences and of history. Instead, philosophy must explore the a priori concepts, explaining how it is possible for such concepts to be valid and showing their connections with one another. Thus philosophy does not deal with the specific details of physics, but it

must explain how there can be laws of physics showing necessary connections between events. And philosophy does not provide the empirical information needed to apply the moral law in particular cases. But it does have to show how there can be a moral law, a law imposing necessity on our free actions. Kant's examples are intended to help one grasp this law, but strictly speaking, they are not part of philosophy.

2. The "legality" of action is its behavioral conformity to what the moral law requires. Its "morality" lies in its motivation. If it is motivated by respect for the law, then it possesses morality as well as legality.

3. Here Kant was using this phrase in its contemporary sense; he did not mean by it the kind of directive command that the natural law theorists had used it to mean.

4. Kant called both these kinds of imperative "hypothetical imperatives" because they command only on the hypothesis that the agent desires the end to which they indicate the means. Categorical imperatives, by contrast, command regardless of the agent's ends.

5. Everyone, in fact, wants happiness, Kant held; hence pragmatic imperatives do in fact hold for everyone. But not everyone wants to solve mathematical problems, and so rules showing how to solve them do not hold for everyone.

6. Humans have obligations simply because by nature we are not only rational but also needy beings, dependent, as God is not, on things outside ourselves for our lives, and consequently driven by desire. Because everyone has needs and desires, everyone can be tempted to transgress the moral law, and therefore morality comes in the form of obligation for everyone.

7. There is disagreement over exactly what Kant meant by this term, but he did mean at least this much: My maxim contains the reasons I have for acting as I am about to (or did), so far as I am honestly aware of them. Of course, my reasons relate to the actual circumstances in which I find myself, as well as to my needs and desires and to my beliefs about the consequences of my action. Thus the categorical imperative brings the form of law to the material contained in my maxim.

8. Kant here took up the distinction between perfect and imperfect duties that the natural lawyers, especially Grotius and Pufendorf, had introduced and shows how he can account for it.

9. That is, self-satisfaction because one is pleased with one's moral performance.

10. Kant cannot mean that the application of the categorical imperative cannot be illustrated, as he has given some examples of its application. He did, however, think that we can never be certain that we have acted solely for the sake of the lawful form of our maxim, or solely out of respect for the law; nor can we ever be certain that anyone else has done so. Our reasons for action are obscure to us, Kant believed, and we like to deceive ourselves into thinking we are better than we perhaps are. It is because we cannot point to a clear historical example of pure moral motivation that the determination of action by the form of law cannot be illustrated.

11. Here Kant is drawing on the distinction he elaborated in the *Critique of Pure Reason* between the "phenomenal" world, or the world as we perceive it through our senses in space and time, and the "noumenal" world, or the world as it is in itself, regardless of anyone's perceiving or thinking about it. Because Kant held that space and time are themselves modes in which human beings perceive the world, the noumenal world is the world considered as not being in time or space.

12. We cannot, Kant believed, explain how freedom is possible for beings who, in addition to having a rational nature, are also part of a determined physical world. Because the categorical imperative is binding only for free beings, and is binding just because they are free, we cannot explain how the categorical imperative is possible. In general, however, Kant argued, we can understand why it is impossi-

ble to have knowledge of any aspect of the noumenal world. Briefly, knowledge requires empirical perception as well as categories to organize the perceptions, and the noumenal world is the world as it is, independent of perception. Because there can be no knowledge of noumena, and freedom belongs to us as noumena, we can understand why we cannot have knowledge of freedom and therefore why we cannot demonstrate exactly how the categorical imperative is possible. But this is the limit beyond which we cannot go.

Further Reading

There are good translations of all of Kant's major works and many of his essays. H. J. Paton translated the *Groundwork of the Metaphysics of Morals* in *The Moral Law* (London: Hutchinson, 1948), with a brief commentary. Lewis White Beck's translation of the *Critique of Practical Reason* (Indianapolis: Bobbs-Merrill, 1958), and the translation of *Religion Within the Limits of Reason Alone* by Theodore M. Greene and Hoyt H. Hudson (New York: Harper Bros., 1960), are widely used. Translations of the *Metaphysics of Morals* by John Ladd, by James Ellington, and by Mary Gregor also are available.

The reader should consult Kant's other works as well as the writings directly concerned with morality. Several general introductions are helpful guides. Ralph C. S. Walker, *Kant* (London: Routledge & Kegan Paul, 1978), is brisk and analytic, with a good bibliography. Two less demanding introductions, which, like Walker's, treat the ethics only briefly, are S. Körner, *Kant* (London: Penguin, 1955), and John Kemp, *The Philosophy of Kant* (Oxford: Oxford University Press, 1968). A brief introduction to the ethical theory is provided in H. B. Acton, *Kant's Moral Philosophy* (London: Macmillan, 1970).

For more detailed discussion of Kant's moral philosophy, the reader may wish to consult some of the following books: For an extensive commentary on Kant's *Groundwork*, see H. J. Paton, *The Categorical Imperative* (London: Hutchinson, 1946). Lewis White Beck has written a most helpful *Commentary on Kant's Critique of Practical Reason* (Chicago: University of Chicago Press, 1960). Mary Gregor, *Laws of Freedom* (Oxford: Blackwell, 1963), is a study of Kant's late *Doctrine of Virtue*. Onora Nell, *Acting on Principle* (New York: Columbia University Press, 1975), is the best study of the problems involved in applying the categorical imperative to cases. T. C. Williams studies Kant's principle generally in *The Concept of the Categorical Imperative* (Oxford: Oxford University Press, 1968). Robert Paul Wolf, *The Autonomy of Reason* (New York, Harper & Row, 1973), is a critical study of the *Groundwork*. Bruce Aune, *Kant's Theory of Morals* (Princeton, N.J.: Princeton University Press, 1979), covers a wide range of topics and offers a number of criticisms. Roger J. Sullivan, *Immanuel Kant's Moral Theory* (Cambridge, England: Cambridge University Press, 1989), is a systematic presentation summarizing every aspect of Kant's moral thought. In Eckhart Förster, ed., *Kant's Transcendental Deductions* (Stanford, Calif.: Stanford University Press, 1988), are three valuable discussions of Kant's ethics, by John Rawls, Henry E. Allison, and Barbara Herman.

The periodical literature on Kant is enormous and constantly growing. A special journal, *Kant-Studien*, is devoted to Kant, publishing articles in English as well as other languages and frequently giving extensive bibliographic reviews.

7762-10
5-17

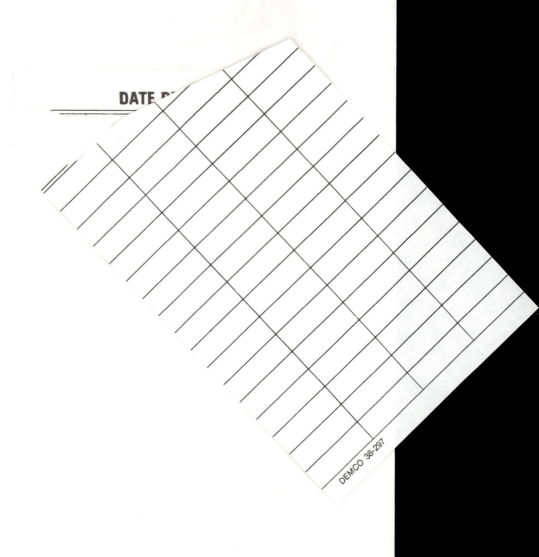

DATE D

DEMCO 38-297